Two blades of grass

Two blades of grass

Rural cooperatives in agricultural modernization

edited by Peter Worsley
with the assistance of Ann Allen

Manchester University Press

Published by the University of Manchester at

THE UNIVERSITY PRESS

316-324 Oxford Road, Manchester M13 9NR

ISBN 0 7190 0444 6

Made and printed in Great Britain by
William Clowes & Sons, Limited, London, Beccles and Colchester

Contents

Preface

This book arose out of a conference held at the University of
Sussex at Easter 1969. The conference was sponsored by Professor
Ronald Dore, Professor Leonard Joy, Dr P. S. Cohen and myself.
The presence of a good number of distinguished academics from
overseas was made possible by the generosity of the Agricultural
Development Council Inc, of New York and the Nuffield Foun-
dation. We thank them, and the University of Sussex, for financial
support of the conference.

Those who attended either contributed a paper or acted as dis-
cussants. They included:

Mr Raymond Apthorpe *	Mr A. D. Jones
Dr A. F. Braid	Professor Henry A. Landsberger *
Mr E. A. Brett	Professor Perry F. Philipp *
Dr T. F. Carroll *	Dr Vicente V. Quintana *
Dr R. G. Crocombe *	Dr Teodor Shanin *
Dr Martin Doornbos	Dr Geoffrey Shillinglaw *
Mr David Feldman *	Professor Daniel Thorner *
Mrs Rayah Feldman *	Dr John Saul *
Professor B. Galeski *	Dr Dov Weintraub *
	Dr K. Kanungo

Papers were contributed by those asterisked. In addition, Professor Jan Tauber and M J. M. Texier contributed papers, though
they were not present. Some of these papers have subsequently
been published elsewhere. Mr Feldman's paper on 'The economics of ideology: some problems of achieving rural socialism in
Tanzania' has been published in *Politics and change in developing
countries* (ed. Colin Leys, Cambridge University Press, 1969).
Professor Baviskar's paper, included in this volume, has previously
appeared in the *Sociological Bulletin*, Delhi, vol. xviii, No. 2, of
September 1969. Dr Weintraub's paper is part of his book *Immigration and social change* (Manchester University Press and Israel
Universities Press, 1971). A fuller version of Dr Carroll's paper in
this volume is to be published also by the United Nations Re-

search Institute for Social Development at Geneva, and the same
body is publishing a study by Raymond Apthorpe of which the
paper in this volume is a section. We wish to thank these bodies
for allowing us to publish the papers, as well as the Inter-American Committee for Agrarian Development (CIDA) and Cornell
University's School of Industrial and Labor Relations for permission to publish the paper by Professor Landsberger and Mrs
Hewitt de Alcantara. We also thank Professors Prodipto Roy,
Joseph Kivlin, Frederick Fliegel and Lalit Sen, and George Jacob,
Dean of the National Institute of Community Development,
Hyderabad, for agreeing to let us use a title—*Two blades of grass*
—that the editor had long thought of using but which they in fact
used first in their publication of 1968.

The theme of the conference was the extent to which patterns
of relationship in traditional communities can be used as a basis
for modern cooperative development. This theme is discussed in
the papers included in Part I of this volume, firstly by Dore (who
incorporates some of Cohen's contributions), a theme further
explored from an economist's point of view by Joy. Apthorpe
draws upon wide and deep knowledge of a variety of East African
settlement schemes where these issues have been serious concerns of everyday political life, whilst Weintraub and Carroll
discuss the equally wide-ranging and significant experience of
Israel and Latin America respectively. Shillinglaw shows how
existing rural markets persist vigorously and shape community life
in the Chinese countryside, despite strong attempts to alter the
agrarian economy and society. Crocombe, like Carroll, undertakes
a panoptic survey of a whole vast region, in this case the Pacific
islands.
   Carroll's paper marks the transition to Part II of the book, in
which we look at rural cooperatives in their wider setting—their
place in the economic, social and political life of the country,
their relationship to parties, governments, movements, markets
and other 'constituencies' in the environing society.
   We begin this part of the book with Galeski's discussion of
Polish developments since world war II. Here cooperatives are set
against the background of peasant farming and pre-war large
estates, followed by the post-war experience of collectivization.
Shanin discusses the Soviet experience and, like Galeski, suggests
that the State farm may have a brighter future than the cooperative. Baviskar also shows us a cooperative in close interdepen-

dence with a processing factory and closely involved, too, in party and trade union politics, and in national and regional alignments as well as those of caste. Landsberger's *ejidos*, even more, emerged out of wholesale revolution in Mexico. Finally, Saul examines the interplay between government, party, class, and cooperative in a newly independent and radical country, Tanzania.

Taken together, the papers cover a great deal of the entire globe. Some are surveys of continents, regions or countries; others smaller case studies. All of them raise general theoretical issues about development which are, we hope, relevant also for sociology generally. A sociology which has no place for the life of most of contemporary humanity, we feel, is bound to be a singularly distorted science.

Rural sociology has classically flourished in the West hitherto in the shape of studies of farming communities in the USA. In Eastern Europe it has a lengthy and impressive pedigree reaching back to the beginnings of modern social science in the second half of the nineteenth century. Here, too, the debate about the countryside was only part of a wider debate embracing the great issues of development, of revolution, of national identity, of social class and of modernization. But these sociological traditions occurred independently of each other; we now need to bring them together, to extract, distil and synthesize the thinking and knowledge generated in these and many other previously-separated cultural provinces, so that the problems of the fate of three-quarters of the world can be discussed more fruitfully—and, hopefully, some better practice arrived at.

Jonathan Swift's irony, in the quotation from which this book draws its title, implies that politicians were pretty poor types of creature as compared to the producer. Elsewhere he implies the same about academics, too. It is healthy for both politicians and academics to be reminded that all of us depend upon the lowly-valued farmer—or, more widely, that culture, civilization, 'superstructures' of government, law, etc., depend, in the end, on the mundane but vital activity of those who produce 'material values'.

Yet the image of 'basis' and 'superstructure' breaks down, for the farmer today is increasingly a skilled worker, using the latest technology, dependent upon science and industry. Nor is even peasant farming 'mindless' traditional activity, as classic studies have long insisted.[1] An elaborate knowledge of the land, the crops and the seasons is part of the very fibre of African husbandry, to name no other. Today, Lévi-Strauss insists on the same theme.[2]

Secondly, the politicians Swift despised are absolutely central to developments in the rural world of today; they may initiate, control or repress—but they certainly actively intervene. This reflects the growing importance of the peasant as a major political force in the twentieth century world scene.

While we all hope that more and more blades of grass will be grown to feed those who at present starve, the scientist and the politician cannot be dismissed in any analysis of how these improvements might be brought about. 'Green revolutions' alone, even if they were successful, still do not solve (and may even intensify) social problems of distribution and inequality. Hence social scientists too may be able to contribute something of value by analysing developments in a field traditionally left to economists and agriculturists, but where a sociological understanding is urgently needed. The main literatures relating to the issue of the relevance of traditional social arrangements for modern cooperativism is given in the bibliography contributed by Mrs Montanari. We hope, in producing this book, that the virtual absence of any serious sociological study of agricultural development in poor countries will henceforth begin to be corrected.

Peter Worsley

Department of Sociology
University of Manchester
July 1970

[1] See, for example, A. I. Richards, *Land, labour and diet in Northern Rhodesia*, Oxford University Press, 1939, and W. Allan, *Studies in African land usage in Northern Rhodesia*, Rhodes-Livingstone Paper No. 15, Livingstone, 1949 (reprinted for the Institute for Social Research, University of Zambia, by Manchester University Press, 1969).

[2] C. Lévi-Strauss, *The savage mind*, Weidenfeld & Nicolson, 1962, pp. 1–33.

[The King of Brobdingnag] gave it for his opinion that whoever could make two ears of corn or two blades of grass to grow upon a spot of ground where only one grew before would deserve better of mankind, and do more essential service to his country, than the whole race of politicians put together.

Jonathan Swift, *Gulliver's travels*

Peter Worsley **Introduction**

To say that cooperation is a phenomenon of modern times might immediately raise the objection that cooperation is surely co-extensive with human society, with 'social organization' itself. Some degree of specialization of functions—whether on the basis of ascribed characteristics (age, sex, ethnicity, etc.) or achieved ones (e.g. specialization on the basis of appropriate training), 'sponsored' or 'contest' selection of talent, or on the basis of proved practical superiority 'on the job' or a 'natural talent' for doing certain things well (and the converse restriction of talent which forces yet others into dead-end and inferior occupations)— some such division of labour is to be found in every culture, no matter how simple its technology. The term 'cooperation' in this sense is simply a one-word synonym for the division of labour in the sense of specialization of function. But specialization of function also implies coordination and complementarity as between these separate specialisms—the mutual 'social' adaptation that results from or is consonant with 'functional' specialization. There may even be wider, moral overtones of limitation of self-interest, of what Dore below calls 'sacrifice', even in this general type of cooperation. There may even be, more positively, some notion of social *redistribution* of resources by the collectivity from the more to the less fortunate.

But both the functional and the redistributive senses of the term relate to 'cooperation' in the sense of the general social division of labour, rather than to that special kind of social organism which we describe in common parlance as a 'cooperative'. This latter has features of the ideal types both of the organization and of the association, in sociological terms, with variations of emphasis upon one or the other in different concrete cases. Thus State-instituted and bureaucratized settlement schemes are much more 'organizations' than the cooperative 'associations' established by small producers or consumers who come together in their mutual interest. 'Organization' and 'association', being ideal types, clearly cannot be expected to be found in pure form in reality, and most cooperatives contain features of each.

Because the modern cooperative, and modern cooperation, are quite distinct from cooperation in the first, diffuse, sense, we shall occasionally use the term *cooperativism* for the modern phenomenon where ambiguity threatens. This kind of cooperation, the theory and practice of cooperativism, then, is no 'element' or Simmelian form of sociation to be found in all behaviour, it is a special type of social organization, and one which, further, is usually located within a wider social *movement*—normally the Cooperative and/or Labour movements. Being part of a social movement, it has goals which transcend the purely technical or economic, embodied in a social philosophy that usually stresses the moral themes we saw to be part of the penumbra of the term 'cooperation' even in the diffuse sense; the ethical ideals of sharing with and helping one's fellows. Cooperativism, then, is not just a technical *division of labour*; it is *mutual aid*, to use Kropotkin's term, a positive orientation towards others in society, and a particular identification with the ordinary, the humble and the least privileged, together with a collectivistic orientation which implies the limitation of self-interest and the institutionalization of altruism. At the same time, as we shall see, cooperativism also always promises the participant an individual payoff, and this element can easily come to override altruism. The cooperative is, in fact, in uneasy, eternal tension between both principles, individualism and altruism. What it does exclude, ideally, is exploitation—both the internal exploitation of some members by others, and external exploitation of society by the cooperative as an organization. Of course, both kinds of exploitation do occur, because ideals are deviated from: Saul gives ample evidence of 'internal' exploitation below, and the British movement's ownership of Ceylonese tea estates constitutes an example of a cooperative which became a colonial (later neocolonial) employer.

Both cooperation in the diffuse sense, then, and the modern institutional practice of cooperativism, contain ethical ideals. They embody attitudes not only towards sharing and helping, but also towards work itself. The technical phrase 'the division of labour' is, in comparison, ethically neutral: it implies a purely rational distribution of effort and reward. Yet we know that 'labour' is often hard work, drudgery, and that the 'division' is one that sentences the majority to mystification, stupefaction, exploitation, and the fragmentation of the personality. Modern cooperation, typically, has usually tried to counter these tendencies. Crucially, it has tried to find alternatives to unbridled competition and to replace market rationality by social control, even while operating (and competing) perforce on the market.

Most sociological studies of cooperation have been concerned with cooperation in the diffuse sense, e.g. Margaret Mead's *Cooperation and competition among primitive peoples*,[1] treating cooperation and competition as analytical elements to be found in differential combination from culture to culture, structure to structure, or situation to situation.

But however clinically research has been conducted, there has usually been a realization that the issues being researched are not simply of a technical kind, lacking in moral significance. Rather, they have been seen to touch upon our deepest moral concerns, and therefore to give off powerful emotional vibrations, for it is not simply the dispassionate analysis of who does what to whom or with whom in a given situation that we are engaged in: our observations have meaning and relevance for the fundamental images of man which we hold. People, that is, study cooperation and conflict because they hope that some light may be shed on human nature—to see whether man is 'naturally' competitive or cooperative, whether evidences of proclivities towards behaviour of either kind are culture-bound or universal, whether one tendency or the other is more efficient or productive, or might be fostered or repressed according to our ideological bent.

At its *most* diffuse, cooperation can simply mean opposition, response or 'adaptation to the existence of the Other', or—slightly more positively—coordination or coaptation. If we adopt the first of these usages any relationship becomes cooperative: the term becomes so broad as to include even relationships of hostility, conflict or competition, even violence and warfare. Thus armies locked in battle are intimately adapted to each other. Every move each makes, or might make, produces responses[2]—retaliation, strategic or tactical plans, 'intelligence' operations, pre-emptive strikes, etc.

It is therefore confusing, not to say mystifying, to use 'cooperation' virtually as a synonym for interaction or coaptation. The confusion generated is similar to that created by Malinowski and

[1] McGraw-Hill, New York, 1937.
[2] Anatol Rapaport, *Clausewitz on War* (ed. Anatol Rapaport), Penguin Books, Harmondsworth, 1968.

others who have used the term 'reciprocity' to describe both equal and unequal relationships.[3]

There may be mutual expectations, in the sense of *anticipations* or even predictions, and even mutually accepted *normative ideals* as to what is right and proper, even in the relationship between slave and slave-owner. To expect that your master will work you to death may be a reasonably accurate anticipation; that he will work you hard may even be accepted and internalized as legitimate death is rarely likely to be accepted, though it does happen, as with royal slaves who go to the sacrificial grave on their master's death. But the very basis of the relationship is one of inequality of power and status; hence to use 'reciprocity' to include both unequal and equal relationships (though, of course, no relationship is ever *fully* 'equal') leads to a blurring of the crucial distinction between equality and inequality, a defect not only of analysis but of fundamental human and moral vision.

To most people 'reciprocity' implies some balance of advantages, not inequality. 'Cooperation', similarly, is a term redolent with meanings fundamentally opposed to inequality and to competitive and possessive individualism. Indeed, it describes producer and consumer not as 'possessors', or as individuals or role occupants, but as social beings consciously pooling their resources in mutually beneficial ways, in the name of a common ideal and in common opposition, too, to those people and institutions seeking to exploit them.

True, there is ambiguity, as we shall see, about equality and equity. The modern cooperative does not insist on total equality of *holding*. It contains people who own different amounts of land, or who purchase more than their fellows in a consumer cooperative and thus receive greater dividends. The cooperative does not depend upon total equalization (such as can be brought about only via total social control—by the State, or as a result of accepting ideological values enjoying complete equality). Hence the cooperative does not end inequality, even though it treats its members, in other key respects, as equal. Of particular importance is the principle that all members are of similar political status within the enterprise—one man, one vote. This principle of equity does not mean full equality. It is a principle which restricts the otherwise unbridled power of the stronger rather than actively reduces it. To this extent it is restraining rather than

[3] See Alvin Gouldner, 'The norm of reciprocity', *American Sociological Review*, 25, 1960, pp. 161–78.

reforming. But to the extent that cooperatives cut into the profits of the private sector by competing with middlemen or with multiple chains of retail stores and private shops it creates inroads on market mechanisms which institutionalize inequality, e.g. capitalism.

The cooperative, in so far as it is a coming together of individual private producers or consumers, is thus not especially either collectivistic or equalizing. It does not imply the elimination of private property, nor even of the profit-oriented mode of economy.

In this respect it is authentically part of a major stream of socialist thought that goes back at least to Saint-Simon, for whom a society based on those directly involved in production—*les producteurs*—would include both workers *and* owners—if the latter were 'working' owners engaged on the day-to-day managing of the enterprise and not mere *rentiers*, shareholders and coupon-clippers, parasitic on the work of *les producteurs*—owners and managers and workers. A parallel mode of thought is to be found in the later writings of Thorstein Veblen on the other side of the Atlantic in his *The theory of the leisure class*[4] and other works which celebrated the technician, the engineer, the worker, the creator of value, the source of creativity and innovation, the contributors of manual and mental *input*, as contrasted with those who toil not, nor spin, but simply collect, milk and batten on other men's labour.

Such a critique of capitalist society is a functional rather than a *class* critique. It sees the dysfunctions of capitalism as the consequence of the dominance of non-creators and exploiters. They are non-creative and exploitative because they do not contribute actively to the production process. To a certain extent this critique thus overlaps with Marxist socialism. But the capitalist who is the managing director of the enterprise he owns is spared from criticism. *He is, in fact, a worker* in this theoretical model. Hence the institutions of private property and private profit, the existence of capitalists as a class, the destruction and replacement of capitalism, the creation of a classless society which would know only differences of function, not class differences and class distinctions, are not part of the technicist–functional critique. It would not be a very fruitful exercise to debate to what extent these latter views were 'socialist' or not. Socialist emphases and

[4] Mentor Books, 1953 (see introduction by C. Wright Mills), and Veblen's *The theory of business enterprise*, Mentor Books, New York, 1958.
2—T.B.O.G.

themes are certainly there, but contained within an acceptance
of capitalism, albeit often a reformed capitalism master-minded
by engineers, *samurai*, technocrats and workers in varying permutations and combinations.

In the nineteenth century the dominant image of man in industrial capitalist society was of man as an individual competing
on the market against his fellow. True, the growth of large-scale
industry was at the same time bringing about ever-increasing
concentrations of people, all highly interdependent, highly
specialized contributors to a detailed and complementary division
of labour. In this sense 'cooperation' was becoming more and more
the dominant feature of advanced economies. But the interdependence was a technical–production interdependence, not a
moral one. Except to the extent that both workers and owners
had some parallel (rather than 'common') interest in the continued operation of the plant (providing profits for one and wages
for the other), the 'social' nature of production arrangements was
cut across, vitiated by a rival and more decisive principle, that of
the primacy of private ownership. This was exactly the significance of the term 'social-ism': that the time had come to bring
social distribution into line with social production via the establishment of social ownership. Private appropriation was an
anachronism under the modern conditions of the large-scale
industrial plant—a 'social' enterprise if there ever was one—and
of modern corporations which were even supranational in scope.

Where the private appropriators have been expropriated—in
Russia, China, Eastern Europe, Cuba, North Vietnam and North
Korea—the State has become the principal embodiment of
society, and has therefore also come to be regarded and used as
the appropriate agency for the operation of socialized industrial
enterprise. In non-socialist countries State or 'parastatal' organizations (local and national, central and regional) have also been
the normal mode of instituting public control over banks, railways, mines and social service 'industries' (health, education, etc.).

But 'social ownership' does not necessarily mean State or parastatal forms of ownership and control; even less, centralized
ones. The principle of indirectness, of mediation between the
central State apparatuses and the places and milieux in which
people lead their lives, has often been used because men have
feared the negative social effects of over-centralization and regula-
tion on society and on the economy at large, and the negative
implications for the autonomy of the citizen if he finds himself

up against, and cannot insulate himself from, the same authority controlling him in all spheres of life—controlling the enterprise he works in, the school his children attend, the shops he buys in, and so on. So, in capitalist Britain, we find a great deal of public enterprise which is characteristically 'mediated' in form; the 'public corporation'—responsible to Parliament but not a direct organ of the State—controls the BBC, the mines and the railways. We also find the devolution of central power to local authorities (in education, housing, etc.) and a whole variety of forms of State participation in different kinds of industrial, cultural and other activities (via share-holding, the provision of finance, representation on governing bodies, and so forth).

In other countries, too, mediated forms of social ownership or social operation are being increasingly experimented with. They are 'intermediate' in another sense, too, in that they are neither *étatiste* nor private, and similar experiments occur both in capitalist and communist societies. Most of the latter, which went through drastic transformation on the lines of Soviet centralized 'command' planning of the 1930s type, are now devolving more and more power to the level of the individual enterprise, to regions, to management rather than to the central political directorate, to control by the market rather than physical control by the planning authority. In Yugoslavia (and to a lesser extent in Poland) devolution and decentralization have been accompanied by a complementary deliberate fostering of grass-roots participation and decision-making at the 'point of production', with the direct election of and control over management at the level of the factory. The extent to which this has been effective in encouraging self-movement, in eliminating alienation and in inhibiting bureaucratic rigidity and inhumanity are matters we cannot go into here. Suffice to say that the attempt is being made, and that whilst the overall authority of Party and State remains decisive the general thrust is in the direction of encouraging individual and collective creativity, autonomy and criticality, in some spheres at least, and of building defences against 'over-socialized' institutional arrangements that have proved neither efficient nor humane—and hence not socialist. Perhaps the most dramatic movement of all has been the 'cultural revolution' in China, where bureaucracy, hierarchy, inequality, status and cultural divisions (e.g. between mental and manual work, between town and country, between senior generations and junior ones) have all been subjected to the most withering reappraisals.

Most of these instances of de-institutionalization, devolution and mediation between State and citizen have occurred as a late reaction to processes of the centralization of control which have grown up either within 'late' *étatiste* capitalism, in which State ownership and other forms of intervention in or control over the economy have become important, or within socialist societies whose initial organization was even more heavily *étatiste* and in which the industrial sector was the heart of the economy.

Production relations within industrial societies, that is to say, have been highly 'socialized' and large-scale, both under capitalism and under socialism, and 'reform' movements have centred on the search for less centralized modes both of social ownership and of the organization of production. The 'cooperative' organization of the factory, though, is no new notion; it has always been a classic socialist recipe, long eclipsed in the *étatiste* era but now revived, in some measure, in 'workers' control' and similar movements. But what was once only an ideal utopian experiment has become reality, even if, apart from Yugoslavia and, to a minor extent, Poland, actual institutions with this kind of producer control built into them are few.

In capitalist industrial societies, where ideas and ideals about cooperation were first elaborated, the cooperative notion of the participation of all members (workers in production cooperatives, consumers in consumer cooperatives, borrower/contributors in credit cooperatives, etc., etc.) in the governing and day-to-day running of the enterprise were most dramatically translated into institutional reality, not in the sphere of production but in consumer cooperatives. In England, the home of modern cooperation, 'the Co-op' means the retail shop (only later underpinned by large-scale cooperatively owned production and wholesaling facilities). But 'cooperation', in Britain, has never been simply a movement for the more efficient performance of economic operations, or an 'economizing' way of reducing costs to the consumer. It has been also a social movement with its own ideology: a social and moral critique of the existing society and the existing economy. For it was this overall society and economy that produced the poverty which made 'economizing' a practical necessity for the poor; it was the ever-increasing centralization of production and distribution which rendered the continued independence of the petty trader increasingly ineffective and obsolete, and which led to ever-diminishing freedom of choice as to product, and to increasing monopolization, effectively diminishing the consumer's 'sovereign' capacity to exercise choice or sanctions by moving to a rival shop. Increasing tendencies to domination of the mass-market, of course, often meant that the results of inefficiency, as well as deliberately high profit margins, could be passed on to the consumer in the form of high prices.

But the latter was by no means the unique or inevitable feature of large-scale mass-consumption, only of capitalist mass-marketing. Rather, the lesson to be learned, the knowledge to be harnessed for the benefit of the mass of consumers rather than in the interests of higher profits for private owners, was the lesson of the advantages accruing from economies of scale in production and distribution—of *mass-ness* in economic organization. Co-operation, here, involved not so much the coordination of numerous privately owned small retail outlets, benefiting from combining to finance production which would permit economies of scale to be passed on to the retailer (and, to some degree, the consumer), on the pattern of the contemporary international Spar organization, as the creation *ab initio* of a network of *jointly owned* shops, linked to cooperative production facilities and wholesaling.

The result is the elimination of private profit both in production and at retail outlet. At neither end is any element of private profit taken. The resulting economy of scale, and economies resulting from the removal of private profit-taking, can thus be passed on to the consumer in the form of lower prices or, more indirectly, by being ploughed back into the enterprise so as to provide improved services, or in other ways.

These economic arrangements, however, were only part of, and were always suffused by, wider social aspirations which looked to the enrichment of the consumer's life not only in the form of higher material welfare through cheaper and better quality goods but also by virtue of a new sense of identification and sharing with one's fellows, a sense of joint-ness and brotherhood rooted not just in utopian dreams but in the unromantic yet fertilizing soil of consumer cooperation. This enrichment was therefore to be an expansion of educational horizons as well as of trade, and an improvement in the quality of life generally, not simply an improvement in the quality of soap and matches. Cooperation, that is, was social and not simply economic, both as ideal and as practice.

The loss of impetus, and the shrinkage of imagination and practice, has been well documented for British consumer cooperation.[5] The reasons for this, again, we cannot go into here, except to note the general diminution of the participatory element and the concomitant growth of professional bureaucracies. Though there is plainly a tendency for these things to happen in large-scale organizations of *any* kind (and Michels deliberately selected the German Social Democratic Party for study because of its nominal commitment to an internal socialist democracy, even 'higher' than 'bourgeois' democracy),[6] we need not assume that the historical exhaustion of this particular surge and of these particular forms of organization is the end of the matter. For the impulse to speak and act, to have a say in the running of one's life, is inexhaustible. It is the populist dimension of 'democracy'[7] that so much structural political sociology ignores, concentrating as it does on the formal constitutional elements in democracy—the institutionalization of opposition and the machinery through which opposition can legitimately become government. The 'iron law of democracy', Gouldner has pointed out, is as real as the 'iron law of oligarchy'.[8]

The challenge the ossification of British cooperativism presents, of course, is the challenge to perform that supremely difficult human operation—to invent new social arrangements. For it is recognized on all sides that man's ingenuity in inventing *things*—artefacts—is much superior to this ability to dream up new *ideas*—ideofacts—and particularly ideas about how social life might be better organized (sociofacts). (Of course, to be exact, ideas are needed even to produce artefacts.) It would be wild nonsense to say that the creation of lunar vehicles is easy—no innovation of that order of complexity is—but it certainly appears to be a problem of much greater magnitude and complexity even to *think up* improved social institutions that would help human emancipation. (Of course, all sorts of social innovations are developed for anti-human purposes—from brainwashing to riot control systems). And it is the institutionalization of such ideas that proves to be most difficult of all. (To solve *world* problems, particularly, in a world society of nation States and blocs, seems

[5] G. N. Ostergaard and A. H. Halsey, *Power in co-operatives*, Blackwell, Oxford, 1965, and the *Report of the Cooperative Independent Commission*, Cooperative Union Ltd, Manchester, 1958—the 'Gaitskell–Crosland' Report.

[6] Roberto Michels, *Political Parties*, Constable, London, 1959.

[7] See my 'The concept of populism' in *Populism*, ed. G. Ionescu and E. Gellner, Weidenfeld & Nicolson, London, 1969, pp. 212–50.

[8] Alvin W. Gouldner, 'Metaphysical pathos and the theory of bureaucracy', *American Political Service Review*, 49, 1955, pp. 496–507.

to defeat us, as we head inexorably towards famine and nuclear extinction.)

However, new ideas do emerge and are tried out. The proven shortcomings of cooperativism as we have known it, the limitations of rigid State planning, the absorption of trade unionism and of revolutionary and social-democratic parties within both capitalist and communist society, the horrors of total Party control, have all led to renewed exercise of the human imagination and to a resurgence of human creativity in action via a search for forms of economic and social life which meet the requirements of modern life, in that they transcend individualistic competition and permit the pooling of collective wisdom and effort for the common good, whilst avoiding the establishment of social machines that grow beyond the control of the ordinary citizen.

Cooperation, too, has been part of a very particular kind of social movement—the Labour movement. Thus in Britain the trade unions, the specialized 'political' organizations of the constituency parties, and the cooperatives came together to make up a tripartite Labour Party. They still do. Cooperation has been a part, that is, of the *socialist* tradition. But only a part, for the solidary collectivism of trade unionism has been a significantly different—however parallel—part, too: much more collectivistic, more centralized and 'machine'-like. Cooperativism to a greater extent embodies the decentralizing, participatory, communitarian, sometimes utopian and pacifist, elements in socialist democracy. This is not to say that face-to-face participation is not present in the trade union branch, or centralized organization in the Co-operative movement—nor that the consumer cooperatives have not become sterile and soulless machines with only vestigial, microscopic 'grass-roots' involvement, much of it by the ambitious, the 'busy' or, merely, the old.

As big business, consumer cooperation is still very much alive in Britain. As a social movement it is virtually dead. Where it does flourish today as social movement is not in developed countries at all, but in the newly or re-developing States of the Third World.

Cooperatives in under-developed countries

In under-developed countries, consumer retail cooperativism has had its place. The really significant movements and organizations, however, have not been in this sphere but, inevitably—since the overwhelming majority of the population are peasant producers—in the fields of the production and marketing of the peasant farmers' primary products. Cooperativism in the Third World has been a rural phenomenon, deriving from the fragmented powerlessness of the petty farming enterprise (the peasants being in *parallel* circumstances, but having no corporate identity or self-awareness—as Marx so splendidly put it, like 'potatoes in a sock'); from their common subjection to exploitative landowners, money-lenders, middlemen, police, armies, central governments and local manifestations of government or misgovernment; from their 'abstract' exploitation by the impersonal market (via prices and terms of trade); and from their common interests in cheaper and easier credit, seed and implements. Technical–functional, political, class and economic pressures all interweave to generate a consciousness (gradually or suddenly) that goes beyond parochial boundaries and can even expand into a nationwide or even internationalist outlook.

But it would be wrong to represent the process of modern cooperativism as only one of the 'parallel' growing-together of autonomous entities (peasant farms). They commonly grow together because they have *common* oppressors (whether money-lenders, middlemen or gendarmes): such common life-situations therefore generate a higher level of intersubjectivity and of identification than that which arises where multiple units have their own separate, discrete and private enemies. It is a truism of conflict theory that the presence of a common enemy counterbalances, and may even overide, other divisions of interest—depending, of course, on the seriousness of the threat.[9] Peasant solidarity, then, often contains elements of collectivism which are commonly missed by those who contrast them with the 'commonness' of life situation which is so much more striking in, say, the assembly plant. To categorize them as 'particularistic' or 'ascriptive' in orientation, rather than 'achievement-oriented', is equally to subscribe to stereotypes of a privatized economic actor encapsulated within primary group structures of family, kinship group, village and self-sufficient local economy.[10]

There is much debate today about the extent of 'subsistence',

[9] See Georg Simmel on the triad in *The sociology of Georg Simmel*, ed. Kurt H. Wolff, Free Press, New York, 1950, pp. 145–69. See also Lewis A. Coser, *The functions of social conflict*, Routledge, London, 1956.

[10] For a devastating critique of naive 'pattern-variable' analysis, see A. Gunder Frank, 'Sociology of development and under-development of sociology' in *Latin America: under-development or revolution?* Monthly Review Press, New York, 1969.

'non-market', 'self-sufficient' peasant or 'tribal' agriculture. The terms are not precise or interchangeable and can be subjected to much greater and lengthier specification. No society, for example, is 'purely' subsistence-oriented in that some surplus always exists, and anything above the nutritional requirements of basal metabolism in any case involves a satisfaction of socio-cultural *wants* rather than biological *needs*, which have to be satisfied, in any case, via social economic activity. Markets of some kind for some products at some times always exist, though they may be less institutionalized, regular, specialized, and localized to one degree or another, with non-universal measures of value, media of exchange, etc. (In the widest sense, of course, all social interaction —not merely economic—can be treated as 'exchange'.[11]) 'Pure' self-sufficiency, equally, is only a limiting category or ideal type.

The introduction of book-keeping controls into small-scale farming, and the organization of production in response to the market, represent a mode of farming very different—even if the technology remains unchanged, and even the scale of operation —from the peasant household, which does not 'rationally' economize its time, labour and capital but allows 'social' needs of the family to cut across pure 'market rationality'.

Plainly, specialized production for a world market, involving universal measures for converting particular commodity values into the common language of money, constitutes a very special institutional form of exchange. The difference is similar to that between 'capitalism' in ancient Rome, or in the form of profit-taking transactions in the interstices of a non-market (e.g. feudal) economy, or as only one of a number of (usually more dominant) modes of economic activity, and 'capitalism' as a specialized, developed and dominant economic mode, based on machinofacture and on differentiation into 'capitalists' and other social classes.[12]

The typification of under-developed countries, and particularly the agrarian sectors of those societies, as 'non-market', 'feudal' and the like has been blisteringly excoriated by Andrew Gunder Frank, who has argued that hardly any visible part of the capitalist world can be said to be unaffected by the world

[11] See Peter Blau, *Exchange and power in social life*, Wiley, New York, 1967.
[12] See also the debate between 'formalists' and 'substantivists' in *Economic anthropology*, ed. E. E. LeClair and H. K. Schneider, Holt Rinehart, New York, 1968.

economy—all have become integrated into the market, as producers, or both, to one degree or another.[13]

Others argue that, empirically, the extent of such involvement is not very considerable, or intermittent, for this or that area. Without going into the minutiae of this debate and the regional variants of the overall pattern, the general trend is obvious—that the direction of change is clearly that which Frank indicates, with whatever qualifications as to extent, rate, local incidence and variation, etc., and that the least successful in agriculture are, in any case, entering the world economy by another gate—emigrating to the city (where they wait for, as often as obtain, urban employment).

The peasant today, then, is not normally an isolate, though he may be still confined to the village as far as most of his social relationships are concerned. He is likely to be affected, as a producer, by changes in world prices for primary goods, and as a citizen by the intrusion and demands of a whole series of representatives of the State. The 'little community', the postulated closed world of the peasant, has long been shown to be an illusion or half-truth, even in the very area where this famous concept was generated, for Oscar Lewis's re-study of Tepoztlan showed that Redfield's descriptions of that village as a self-contained world omitted to draw the reader's attention to the existence there of political and other schisms so serve as to culminate in 'open violence bordering on civil war', a situation which finally resulted in Redfield leaving the village.[14]

Dore points out below, too, that the existence of the small-scale community is compatible with various forms of authority, which may be far from egalitarian in terms of the distribution of power, as in the case of domination of the village by privileged kin groups, richer peasants, by chiefs, aristocrats and the like. Nor do the kinds of experience entailed in older village relationships necessarily equip its members for the forms of living together or the authority structure—committees, functional divisions of responsibility, etc.—required by modern cooperation, especially coping with the external market and coping with new kinds of superordinate authority: district levels of local government, cooperative federations, Ministries of Agriculture, etc. Apthorpe,

[13] See Andrew Gunder Frank, *Capitalism and Development in Latin America*, Monthly Review Press, New York, 1967.

[14] Oscar Lewis, *Life in a Mexican village: Tepoztlan restudied*, University of Illinois Press, Urbana, Ill., 1951, p. 430.

again, points to the common phenomenon of the modern cooperative's dependence upon the labour of seasonal or hired workers and upon the services of specialists who form no part of the community of cooperative members, and who are often either more powerful than the members themselves, or, alternatively, virtually exploited by them. In either case the autonomy and equality of the cooperative is severely qualified. It may exploit weaker members, or non-members.

Though there are still areas where annual cash income is very small indeed, the interrelationship between town and country has developed so far that labour migration, cash-crop production and the 'revolution of rising expectations' on the part of rural consumers are more typical than subsistence farming. Moreover, new man-made substitutes for primary commodities threaten the knife-edge economic viability of areas which have already become dependent upon the national and international markets both for the marketing of their produce and for the consumer goods which are now part of the everyday wants of even the poorest. And petty entrepreneurship has become a significant feature of the economy even within the village.

Colonialism has been the major factor which has brought this about. The imposition of taxes which had to be paid in cash was often the initial stimulus; today market stimuli perpetuate involvement in the world outside the village. But the post-colonial State has continued the process, for modernizing States have set out to encourage cash-crop production, and the local processing of raw materials, as well as general 'social' modernization in the shape of schools and village-level medical services, however limited these may be.

Many of the new States have intervened to stimulate commercial agriculture more directly. They have not left peasant agriculture to develop spontaneously or by mere exhortation, education, or demonstration effect; they have sought to assist such development directly, by regulating prices through floor-price arrangements, technical aid to the producer, extension services, credit provision, improvement of communications and the like. For most of them, whatever their dominant ideological orientation, too, development policy has been influenced by the examples of countries which have made the most rapid strides towards modernization through some form of State or parastatal action—notably through cooperative or, more rarely, collectivist forms of agricultural organization.

Examples of strictly collectivized agriculture have rarely been attractive, mainly because of the negative lessons of the dysfunctions of forced-draught collectivization in the Soviet Union and Eastern Europe. Moreover, radical transformation of agriculture of this kind would require a machinery of social control which is lacking in societies where single parties may control government but where village-level autonomy is still very strong. And to enforce such radical change would call forth resistances that few post-colonial governments are prepared to risk unleashing. They have preferred to attempt to stimulate agriculture by encouraging the smallholder to maximize his production. But they have provided infrastructural and 'superstructural' forms of 'vertical' integration of the kind envisaged by Chayanov and his school in the 'twenties and 'thirties in the USSR (see Shanin's article in this symposium, and the practical experience of Poland outlined by Galeski). The kinds of massive transformation attempted in the USSR or China have, of course, run into serious blockages in the former country, where the private plots of the peasantry still yield a disproportionately large share of total national agricultural output (about one-third from three per cent of the total agricultural land), and where *kolkhoz* collective farms absorb an uneconomically large share of the available labour force. In China, as Shillinglaw shows, following G. W. Skinner, the initial drive to create large-scale communes ('horizontal' integration) has similarly slowed down, and even been reversed, as the 'natural' (or rather, institutionalized and entrenched) market zones at the successive levels of 'standard', 'intermediate' and 'central' markets have reasserted themselves.

But typologies which only emphasise the single dichotomy of 'socialized' *v.* 'private' agriculture—however important this is— neglect a whole series of intermediate forms and levels of organization of agriculture which transcend smallholder production, even though agriculture remains an economic activity of independent petty producers. Even in advanced capitalist countries both horizontal and vertical integration has proceeded apace as small farmers have been driven under, as the unit of production becomes ever larger in scale, and as mechanization and rationalization depend increasingly on imports of capital unavailable to the small man.[15] The processing of food and of raw materials, too, involves an ever closer coordination of the producer's farming activity with the requirements of the processing industries, to

[15] S. H. Franklin, *The European peasantry*, Methuen, London, 1969.

such an extent that may leave the small farmer legally still an 'independent' owner and entrepreneur but *de facto* ever more controlled by the firms which purchase his crop, specify what strains he will grow, when and how he will grow them, and set standards of quality control, delivery conditions and price which leave him as little more than a small subsidiary supplier. The same process occurs in the industrial sphere, where small factories produce consumer goods which are sold by supermarkets and retail chain stores, or components which are utilized by large-scale corporate industry producing complex industrial machinery.

By this stage the distinctions between agriculture and industry become mainly those of differences in the kind of product, but the modalities of the organization of production converge. Moreover, the growth of small-scale industry within the village, not even necessarily industry processing agricultural products, becomes more pronounced. It is encouraged as the initial stages of an industrialization that is not highly capital-intensive and which can take up the labour force displaced from agricultural production. The convergence of town and country, too, proceeds not just on the economic plane but in growing convergence of wider life styles under the unifying influence of common educational institutions and the standardizing influence of the mass media and common consumption patterns. The 'worker-peasant' of Eastern Europe, the village 'housing estate' where most employed persons work locally in industry and commerce, the satellite commuter community, may retain a 'rural' residential form but the content is unmistakably urban in terms of employment and general mode of life.[16] The 'rural–urban' dichotomy breaks down with seasonal agriculture, or seasonal non-agricultural duality of employment, and with the transformation of even the farming community into rural townships as places of residence.[17]

The tendency, then, is for the town to think it knows how to run the countryside, and to try and apply the modes of organization that have proved successful in the town. They are usually disastrous, because—despite convergences—agriculture still retains certain crucial characteristics, noted long ago by Chayanov. It is not the case (as Shanin points out later in this volume) that

[16] See S. H. Franklin, 'Gosheim, Baden-Württemberg: a Mercedes *Dorf*', *Pacific Viewpoint*, Vol. 5, No. 2, pp. 127–8.
[17] See R. Frankenberg, *Village on the border*, Cohen & West, London, 1957.

increases in scale lead to increased efficiency and productivity; the utilization of machinery is not always the optimal procedure in cultivation; the skills required of the worker on the land tend to be generalized and multiple rather than specialized in one given activity, and require local, not universalistic, knowledge; etc., etc.

The modernization of the countryside thus takes place under the increasing influence and hegemony of the town and the penetration into the physical countryside of urban patterns of employment and life styles, and central government control. Weingrod, following Geertz,* has pointed out that such modernization does little to *develop* the countryside, now inhabited by an indeterminate 'post-peasantry'.

The search for forms of modern agriculture which are compatible with private ownership, and particularly with small-scale agriculture, makes the rural cooperative singularly attractive to the modernizing State. Rejecting collectivized agriculture, the cooperative offers economies of scale, infrastructural support to innovating farmers and socialization via vertical integration. The State intervenes not only via technical and extension assistance but also by providing credit, by organizing cooperative marketing in a way that replaces the private middleman by State marketing boards or marketing cooperative monopolies, by subsidizing transport and storage facilities. The State also underwrites subsidies and price stabilization arrangements, and by forward trade agreements seeks to ensure a guaranteed market so as to protect the small producer from the vagaries of fluctuating demand and the uncertainties of Nature that still constitute the principal hazard confronting the farmer (however integrated into the market system), and from which his urban counterpart does not suffer.

These varying forms and levels of 'social' intervention not only reflect the growing presence of the State even within the private sector but also cut across, to some degree, the gross distinction between 'private' and 'public' enterprise. Moreover, there can be many different areas and permutations of public and private activity. Large-scale, mechanized, capital-intensive farming, on estates and plantations, can co-exist with smallholder-based cooperative organization of marketing and credit provision. Further, all kinds of combinations are to be found, so that the same enter-

---

* Clifford Geertz, 'Studies in peasant life: community and society', *Biennial Review of Anthropology* (ed. Bernard J. Siegel), Stanford University, 1962, pp. 5 and 6.

prise may be involved in several different sets of relationships. Thus cooperatives commonly leave the individual farmer (more accurately, the farming family) to get on with his own production, whilst retaining certain more strictly collective interests, in the shape of common pastures, communally owned orchards or forest, cooperative-owned processing plants, cooperative purchasing of agricultural supplies and consumer goods. The cooperative may also act on behalf of its members in contracting for the sale of produce, the provision of machinery or crop spraying services, in dealing with agricultural experimental stations, research institutions, and so forth.

Agricultural cooperation between small farmers and State aid to agriculture are by no means as novel or recent as is often assumed, even for the heartlands of capitalism. The settlement of Canada's western frontier, for instance, involved extensive public infrastructural support, e.g. in the shape of land-grant colleges, which experimented with crop strains, rotations, soil testing, etc., as well as the training of future and present prairie farmers. Thus the University of Saskatchewan was founded as early as 1907, with precisely such an agricultural focus, simultaneously with the very first major waves of immigration into the province, between the turn of the century and world war I. And the State, too, removed those other competitors for rights over the soil, the Indians. Cheap land was then made available, and railroads were constructed with strong State support and even direct development by the State. The grain exchanges, the agricultural machinery industry and the credit-providing instrumentalities (the banks) were, however, left to the private sector. In the face of the great power of these financial and industrial institutions the farmers themselves created their own counter-organizations of cooperatives, farmers' lobbies, and the like.

Various 'mixes' of collectivism, cooperation and private enterprise have thus been characteristic of agriculture even in advanced capitalist countries, and even large-scale farmers have used their economic and political power to pressurize the State into public support of private agriculture, through tariff and price policies, subsidies, international trade agreements, stabilization devices, credit provision, research and technical institutions, education and extension services, transport facilities, insurance, tax relief and many other devices.

In contemporary under-developed societies the State has been even more active, because capital accumulation will be inade-

quate if left to the free play of the market. The classical capital
accumulation and capital formation mechanisms which powered
much of the modernized capitalist development of British agriculture are precluded, because the world within which the
would-be capitalist producer now has to make his way is already
dominated and 'taken-up' by established interests. The spoliation
of the Indies, the destruction of Indian industry, the ransacking
of the Aztec and Inca empires, the appropriation of foreign lands
are no longer serious options. Nor can the micro-farmer hope to
accumulate capital on the required scale unaided. Moreover, the
State needs to stimulate petty agriculture as the basic source of
capital for its entire modernization programme, including its
plans for industrialization. Hence the renewed interest in the
kinds of modernization via the 'milking' of agriculture canvassed
by Preobazhensky in the USSR of the 1920s.[18]

The dilemma is that in the process class polarization may run
rampant, giving rise to a small class of more successful and
wealthy land-owners, a class of middling entrepreneurial farmers,
a larger mass always vulnerable to extinction, and an ever-grow-
ing rural or ex-rural population which has lost its land and become an agricultural proletariate working on estates or plantations
or swelling the *bidonvilles* of the Third World, where they are
not absorbed into industrial employment, and hence constitute
an impoverished and alienated mass threatening the stability of
the established order. Land reform in the shape of land redistribution has been one classic response, albeit one which meets with
the resistance of the land-owning class. But land reform which
merely consists in redistribution, if it does not result in greatly
increased production, is only a palliative, above all in an era of
population explosion. No serious student of agricultural modernization today advocates distributional land reform if it is not
coupled with the raising of productivity. Here again the State has
to provide the means of enabling the smallholder to improve his
output, either directly or by helping farmers to pool their resources. Otherwise, they merely pool their separate poverties. The
technical requirements of modern agriculture, too, are beyond the
private initiative of the smallholder, who needs the agricultural
experimental stations, training centres, extension services, etc.,
which can be provided only by some kind of supra-individual
agency.

[18] E. Preobazhensky, *The new economics* (English translation by B.
Pearce), Oxford University Press, London, 1965.

The spectre of 'internal' class war in the countryside (which never actually matured in tsarist Russia or in the USSR) has led some governments to attempt to inhibit class polarization by imposing limits upon land holding (e.g. in the Sudan Gezira cotton growing scheme, or in Tanzanian settlement schemes). This in turn can arouse resentment on the part of the ambitious yeoman who finds a ceiling set on his expansive proclivities, with a danger, too, of lowered aspiration and innovation. Great ingenuity is used to circumvent such restrictions—relatives and dependants become nominal 'tenants' whose holdings are in fact operated as a single economic entity; the larger farmers dominate cooperatives in a variety of subtle ways that require microscopic analysis of the kind presented by John Saul below, for the kinds of skills which are effective in farming are also effective in facilitating control of organisations in which all nominally have an equal share. What Saul calls 'crypto' class distinctions emerge that soon harden into more serious differentiation—rich farmers, middling smallholders and pocket-handkerchief horticulturists. Straight corruption is a more direct way of monopolizing opportunities, and the cooperative becomes a major resource worth controlling. Cooperatives, then, very often fall into the hands of the rich, being the most interested and powerful, and thereby entirely negate any redistributive ideals.

One form of check upon such tendencies is to introduce external controls or official managers who guide or control policy on settlement and other kinds of development schemes. Here there are many problems: flexible, agriculturally competent and skilled administrators who can combine leadership with the ability to work with farmers' committees are extremely rare birds. They are often expatriates, a factor which reinforces social distance and imperious styles of administration. They easily become 'brokers' who manipulate or dominate the organization they are supposed to serve.[19] They develop career interests that make for low levels of commitment to the farms in their charge, and tend to put the interests of the Ministry before those of the farmers. They bureaucratically force the rich variety of agricultural activity into Procrustean moulds which lead to disasters of under-production, over-production, bottlenecks, over-dependence on single crops, and ludicrously standardized forms of organization and agricultural production that take quite inadequate account of diversities

[19] See Eric R. Wolf, 'Aspects of group relations in a complex society: Mexico', *American Anthropologist*, vol. 58, pp. 1066–78.

of soil, seasons, rainfall, carrying capacity, variations of scale
required by the different crops, inadequacies of labour and capital
provision (especially seasonal) or of equipment.
One of the commonest problems is shortage of labour. Paradoxically, a country which is modernizing successfully often
draws upon existing supplies of unemployed and under-employed
labour—which thereafter are no longer available for agriculture.
Then even successful crops have to be rescued by mobilization
at harvesting time, at planting, or at periodic weedings which the
local farmers cannot manage on their own. Prison or military
labour has saved more than one settlement scheme from disaster
at harvest time. (In Cuban socialized agriculture the whole available population has had to be mobilized.) Machinery-intensive
cultivation often involves a low utilization of labour on the part
of cooperative members who own parcels of land worked extensively as a single unit by operators of planting machinery and
combine harvesters.

Joy's paper is sceptical, indeed, as to whether analysis of pre-
existing socio-cultural attributes can be very rewarding at all,
either because we lack the power to control such factors or because they are so complex that no simple criteria emerge to guide
the policy-maker. Instead, he suggests, we should concentrate on
specifying the organizational forms appropriate to the requirements of the kind of agriculture being practised.

Often entirely inadequate attention is given to the utterly
different requirements of different crops—the intensive care
needed in tea growing, which imposes strict limits on the acreage
that can be handled by a peasant family, the 'extensive' requirements of wheat, which lends itself to mechanization and to managerial rather than smallholder farming. And the variations in sheer
size of the various cooperative enterprises described in this volume
carry quite different implications. The extent of participation varies
in the studies presented from 0·7 per cent in one community to
75 per cent in another. Cooperative associations like the KNCU in
Tanzania become major power blocs in national politics as well
as in the national economy. Such organizations, like trade unions
in industrial countries, provide channels of mobility and opportunities for the acquisition of skills for the ambitious, as well as
jobs in the organization rather than on the land itself. The interests of specialists, officials and managers, inevitably differ from
those of the small producers whom they are controlling or helping. At worst, the manager lives away from the scheme altogether

(sometimes the farmers do, too), and the cooperative ceases to represent its members' interests. It may even exploit them, via deliberate swindling, inefficiency passed on in the form of lower prices due to the high cost of running the cooperative, poor marketing, etc. The large organization, too, may be under government pressure to do what *it* says, and to provide capital for State projects rather than expand services which are directly in the members' interests.

The contradictory demands of absorbing surplus, landless labour, of settling people of different backgrounds on new land, of inducing them to work under quite novel conditions of cooperative life, of fostering democratic participation whilst ensuring adequate standards of agricultural practice, of establishing schools, roads, water supplies and building houses whilst struggling to grow unfamiliar crops with unaccustomed partners on unfamiliar soils, and often with inadequate motivation, make the cooperative settlement in many ways one of the most difficult operations one can conceive of.

Cooperative organization also involves cultural changes which may often be more difficult and slower in emerging than structural changes. New levels of relevant skills, and inadequate facilities for overcoming these shortcomings, constitute one such drawback. Landsberger has pointed out that the internationalization of the necessary time perspectives, habituation to adhering to unfamiliar divisions of labour, and the notion and practice of selection according to competence rather than on the basis of ascriptive or particularistic criteria, all constitute facets of 'rationality' required of the modern cooperator. Dore, again, notes the difficulty of inducing members to accept 'institutionalized suspicion'—accounting and wider kinds of accountability, inspection, and so forth—and the problems he draws attention to, notably that of corruption, are shown by Saul to have been major obstacles to the efficient operation of cooperatives in Tanzania, not only in terms of pocket-lining by officials, but because the influential have used cooperatives to maximize their own economic advantage at the expense of the poorer members. The resources contributed by the State thus go to assist those already advantageously placed, and instead of promoting equality or redistribution foster new and increasing class differentiation in the countryside. Traditional ties of kinship and neighbourhood, caste and ethnicity, too, often work against the requirements of strict economic rationality. Established solidarities, that is, may be dysfunctional for the cooperative rather than a social foundation on which modern cooperation can be based.

Physical controls on class differentiation—limits on land holding, the provision of land for failed farmers, or for those fleeing from agriculture (even to the extent of transporting the urban unemployed back to the villages)—tend to create inadequately or even negatively motivated cooperative populations. The landless, would-be farmer may well be motivated; he may also be a bad farmer. And the pragmatic peasant, aware of the difficulties and the known past failures, tends not to try too hard. He has seen groundnut schemes in the colonial era, and fears repetitions under independence. He keeps his own holding, or some alternative source of income, outside the 'scheme' and often invests more energy in these, like the Soviet peasant on his private plot. It is wrong to label such prudence 'conservatism': it is simply rational, calculative instrumentalism.

To list the problems is much easier than to find the answers. But the answers are even harder to find when ideology is substituted for analysis, as in so many of those African and Asian settlement and rural development schemes that have been founded upon assumptions about the 'natural' communalism of peasant or tribal society, notably by populists and socialists.

Populist ideas flourish vigorously today in the Third World. But the nature of this postulated 'communalism' or 'collectivism' and its relationship to 'individualism' (i.e. family/kinship rights) is rarely spelt out, except by anthropologists, who find gross terms like 'collectivistic', 'cooperative' or 'individualistic' inadequate conceptual tools. They prefer to use these labels not as descriptions of whole social systems but as *ideal-type* elements which will be more or less present in any given situation. Thus 'cooperation' in the 'division of labour' sense is a necessity even in organizations devoted to competition or aggression. As we saw, 'cooperation' can, however, refer to an ideological commitment, and in this sense we rightly think of a cooperative as a special kind of *institution* because its policies and arrangements are conditioned (negatively) by limitations on individualism and competition and (positively) by stress upon mutual aid, the common good—at the extreme, socialist ideals of social production and/or social appropriation, of equality and participatory democracy. At one end of this spectrum of ideological emphases we find mere rationalizing 'economies of scale' or banding together for mutual economic advantage; at the other, thoroughgoing insertion into a movement of Labour.

There are elements of mutual aid in peasant and tribal society, of course: at harvest time, weeding, planting, sowing, etc., in house building, hunting, etc. There are 'communal' rights over land, pasture, woodlot, etc. But these are not strictly 'collective', because individual or, more importantly, kinship-group rights are firmly established, and not just some general, overriding 'communal' rights of the collectivity as a whole or of its component units.

Yet the existence of cross-cutting ties, webs of kinship and village membership, however qualified and whatever the counteracting mechanisms, does mean that the 'market' model of the coming together of autonomous economic units or actors via recognition of their parallel (like) interests in cooperating with each other is inadequate if applied to many situations of both spontaneous and planned cooperativism in the contemporary Third World. For the units involved are often *not* autonomous economic entities, like the consumer in the British Cooperative, or the American homesteaders who banded together. *These* economic entities are *already* linked via a complex network of ties of kinship, marriage, religion, culture etc., etc. The separate units, then, are already parts of a wider whole, not atoms combining after a purely autonomous existence. It is this cultural commonness, plus the practice of mutual aid, even, at rare times, highly collectivistic, as in communal turn-outs (usually of the sexes separately) for hunting or rotational work on neighbours' farms, that the populist emphasizes.

Yet, as Gluckman has pointed out, the ties that unite us with some divide us from others. Tensions and rivalries, competitiveness, witchcraft accusations, intense face-to-face rivalries for status and privilege, are equally the everyday stuff of village life, and no quarrel is so bitter as a family quarrel. Village life, in fact, is no populist idyll. To the outsider, the visiting politician or the 'expert' visiting hurriedly in his Land-Rover, they are all poor peasants stamped with the uniformity of poverty. Some anthropologists, even, have given currency to notions about the uniformity of the culture of poverty.[20] But this has been challenged increasingly by other anthropologists and sociologists as a crude generalization which neglects the rich variety of types of people

[20] Oscar Lewis, *La Vida*, Random House, New York, 1966; see introduction on the 'culture of poverty'.

and the variety of their responses to poverty[21] and of their perceptions and definitions of their own situation. Certainly they are poor, and they know it, but there are many adaptations to that situation and many identities other than 'poor person' that people work out for themselves.[22]

In peasant society, differences in social status which are invisible to the airport sociologist loom very large under the anthropologist's microscope, not simply because his analysis is close-textured but because it incorporates more adequately the subjectivity of the people he observes. But he is also more microscopic, and he observes, too, over time, or has events over time described and interpreted for him in depth by his informants. Thus Barth among the Swat Pathans found competition for land to be so intense that 'a stronger landlord generally attempts to encroach on the land of his weaker neighbours by the slow but steady technique of ploughing the borderpath between the fields ... The amount that can be gained by twice yearly adding one furrow along the whole length may be spectacular in the course of a generation'.[23]

Not only land, but also political prestige and power, Barth shows, were the fuel which fed the ever-flickering, now blazing flames of intra- and inter-village rivalries. Yet countervailing this was the 'integrative' institution of the men's house, which is 'at one and the same time club house, dormitory, guest house and place for ritual and feasting' (p. 52).

'Cellular' or segmental divisions of interest, which threaten fissiparity, may thus be counteracted by mechanisms engendering 'communal' solidarity such as the men's house. And horizontal divisions—stratification—are commonly countervailed by cross-cutting, vertical affiliations. Thus Dutch sociologists, highly conscious that their society, so patently a horizontally stratified *class* society, is also vertically divided into 'pillars' of *religious* persuasion and non-persuasion—since Roman Catholics, Protestants and humanists have separate schools, separate political parties, separate radio stations and separate newspapers—have, consciously or otherwise, projected the notion of *verzuiling* ('piling'; *zuil*, a pillar or pile) onto Indonesian society (an interesting case, per-

[21] Charles A. Valentine, *Culture and poverty*, University of Chicago Press, 1968.

[22] E. V. Walter, of Harvard Medical School, in various unpublished papers, has perhaps explored this line of analysis most effectively, both on the basis of historical materials and in field research.

[23] Fredrik Barth, *Political leadership among Swat Pathans*, LSE Monographs on Social Anthropology, No. 19, 1959, p. 75.

haps, of the common phenomenon of imperialist transference to
or imposition of categories of thought and institutional forms
reigning in the metropolis to the colonies and ex-colonies). They
see Indonesian society as divided into *aliran*, vertical divisions
of society on the basis of differences in ideological orientation,
expressed in organizational affiliations. Thus the Javanese *prijaji*
aristocracy are associated with the Indonesian Nationalist Party
(PNI), the *abangan* village commoners with the Indonesian Communist Party (PKI), the religious *santri* into the 'orthodox' (supporting the Nahdatal Ulama Party) and the 'modernists' supporting
Masjumi. These divisions, however, are not simply party divisions,
but penetrate women's associations, youth organizations, boy
scouts, sports clubs, charitable societies, labour and peasant
unions, and art groups also. The major division is between the
pious *santri* and the syncretistic, nominally Moslem *prijaji* and
abangan.[24]

The notion, then, that peasants are natural, 'available' com-
munalists, and therefore ready-made potential modern cooperators or collectivists, is so much illusion. Paradoxically, as Apthorpe
notes, it is a notion subscribed to, in part, both by exponents of
'African socialism' and by Ian Smith. The model nevertheless does
contain grains of truth, as we have seen, in that there is mutual
aid, there are parallel, communal, even collective rights and
activities. And there are traditional cultural identities sustained
at higher levels than the village—the level of the tribe or
peasant stratum—and sustained, too, often by dialectical reaction
to oppression, by the sharing of discriminations practised upon
them as a collectivity or category: disprivileges, exactions—
whether legal, political, economic, or other—imposed on tribes
and peasants, *qua* peasant 'estate', or against this or that tribe or
category of tribes as against town-dwellers. The identities, that is,
do not just grow outwards from roots in village culture, but are
products of interaction: between town and country, State and
society, centre and periphery, industry and agriculture, national
or dominant culture *v.* regional or local, or ethnic minority, etc.;
in which sets of oppositions the first term is always the more
powerful.

Populist notions about the natural equality and *Gemeinschaft*
of the village are thus 'mythological charters' for social change, as

---

[24] See Clifford Geertz, *The social history of an Indonesian town*, Cambridge, Mass., 1965, and W. F. Wertheim, 'From aliran towards class struggle
in the countryside of Java', *Pacific Viewpoint*, Vol. 10, No. 2, 1969, pp. 1–17.

Crocombe points out below, rather than historical accounts of
'customary' land tenure and land usage. Many contemporary beliefs about 'customary' land tenure are simply retrospective fic-
tions, buttressing the rival claims of competing groups who appeal
to 'history' and 'custom'. But ideologies mislead as well as moti-
vate, and many of the practical and very expensive mistakes made
in modern development projects occur because of illusions about
natural proclivities towards cooperation in peasant society.

Crocombe points out below that in the south Pacific in pre-
European times villagers never had equal rights in land, nor was
their social status (and hence their access to land) simply a function of economic criteria; it was always conditioned by wider
social considerations, such as commoner or chiefly status. Dore
further points out that much joint activity within the community
was competitive, enhancing the status of rival groupings, rather
than expressive of communal solidarity or benefiting everybody.

The terms 'tradition' and 'modernity', so commonly used as
basic categories in development studies, are themselves highly
suspect. Writers like Frank have demonstrated that the penetration of the capitalist economy into much of the contemporary
Third World is no recent phenomenon. Others have insisted that
neither markets nor money, capitalist or otherwise, are new, and
that beliefs about 'natural' pre-colonial economies are simply bad
history or imperialist arrogance. This has forced those who retain
the terms to invest them with a much more diffuse and less time-
bound content: thus at the conference where these papers were
presented, Cohen used the term 'traditional' in a very general
sense, to describe social systems resistant to change; Weintraub
spoke of 'modernity' as meaning a receptivity to new ideas, a capacity to initiate and adjust to changes beyond the existing value system. There can thus be 'modernity' in historically remote societies.

It is also important to emphasize, following the lead of East
European rural sociologists, as well as anthropologists generally,
the centrality of the independent *family-household* as the basic
unit of production, not the village, the sub-lineage, the lineage,
the clan or any other higher level entity—and certainly not the
'individual'. Such dichotomies as 'individualistic' *v.* 'communal' or
—Parsonian language—'self' *v.* 'other' orientations in any case
need 'decomposing' or specification according to the activity that
is being so labelled. In one respect, though, the Parsonian approach is more helpful than such dichotomies as 'traditional' *v.*
'modern', for Parsons pattern variables are (or can be used as)

merely ideal-type, polar concepts. We can, therefore, think of 'mixes' or points along a continuum from 'self-orientation' to 'collectivity-orientation' rather than typifying whole societies, social groups or even social situations as, crudely dichotomously 'self'-oriented or 'collectively'-oriented. (I am not interested here in exegis upon Parsons' own varying uses of the 'pattern variable' concept, simply in picking it up and trying to develop what is positive in it—and in this particular pattern-variable especially —a little further.)

'Individualism', 'cooperation', 'competition', 'collectivism', 'self-orientation', 'collectivity-orientation', then, constitute emphases, dimensions, aspects, elements of social activities; they are not exhaustive typifications of wholes. Thus whilst many cooperatives are empirically articulated to socialist or nationalist movements, or infused with socialist or nationalist ideology—such as the *moshavim* described by Weintraub—others are very hard-headed business associations of individual producers, and little more. (To say that they are organizational descendants of the socialist cooperative tradition is to adopt the limited perspective of the positivistic historian of ideas, for although present-day practice in Mexican *ejidos* or Indian cooperatives may be traced, in some measure, from Robert Owen or from Fourier, via a lengthy chain of events, this is an objectivist explanation in terms of historical genesis or the transmission of culture. As such, though phenomenologists wrongly exclude this kind of explanation, it is *part* of an explanation both of particular cooperatives and of the cooperative movement more generally. It is, however, a mode of explanation that takes *no* account of what phenomenologists rightly take account of: the meaning of the cooperative to the actor who has never heard of Robert Owen or Fourier.)

In this book we are concerned with *agricultural* cooperatives, principally those set up for marketing produce, though credit and consumer activities sometimes enter in, whether under the umbrella of the production/marketing coop or as separate organizations, in which case the peasant is often a member of more than one cooperative. Normally, however, they tend to be connected organizations, either because they are wings of an overall co-operative movement, or because they are affiliated to the same political party or backed by the same government. We exclude from our discussions fully-fledged, capitalist, large-scale agriculture, e.g. estates or plantations. Collectivized agriculture, co-operative working within a capitalist market, and small-scale peasant or tribal agriculture (or 'horticulture'), whether 'subsistence', commercial cash-crop or some combination of the two, are what concern us here. For all these represent, in different ways, agricultural modes which are alternatives to large-scale capitalist organization; true, alternatives very different in kind, but analytically to be categorized together because of a common distinctiveness, even opposition of interest, *vis-à-vis* their large capitalist-farmer competitors. State and collective farms, *moshavim* and marketing cooperatives are all 'statal' socialist or semi-socialist alternatives to pure capitalist agriculture. And small-scale peasant farming, albeit fiercely competitive and often striving towards increase of its size as a private capitalist enterprise, is usually doomed to failure, wretched in terms of the life it provides, and hostile to large-scale capitalist farming (as well as to the even larger-scale State).

Of course, the end of capitalism does not mean the end of conflict between the peasant household and the environing society, or between town and country more generally. The solution adopted in the USSR—to eliminate peasant farming—proved so economically ineffectual, not to say disastrous in its first years, and the human agonies and social consequences so severe, that few countries, even in the communist world, have risked a repetition. They have usually left the peasant household in possession of its land and the fruits of its labour, and encouraged higher productivity via various forms of State or parastatal assistance, whilst clamping ceilings on land-holding, restricting the hiring of labour, or taking other steps to inhibit the differentiation of classes in the countryside. It is best to think, then, of a continuum between two poles of 'collectivism' and 'individualism', as far as these various forms of agriculture are concerned. The State farm would come at the collective end of the continuum, in so far as those who work on it have no title to nor share in the enterprise as individuals—their income does not depend, as does that of the worker on the *kolkhoz* collective farms of the USSR, upon the profits made by the enterprise, profits in which each individual shares according to the work he has contributed. The State farm, *per contra*, is even more collective, in that ownership is vested in the *State*, not in the community that works on the farm. The situation of the worker *vis-à-vis* the means of production is closely analogous to that of the factory worker; each, similarly, is rewarded 'abstractly' in the form of a wage paid by the State. The State farm worker is an agricultural proletarian who sells his labour power and owns no means of production, like the factory worker. The collective farmer retains an individual 'share' in the enterprise, which gives his status an element of residual fractionalized and highly attenuated entrepreneurship and proprietorship (always subject of course to the over-riding control of Party and government). A much more real possessive individualism is represented by the famous private plots which yield so much despite their severely limited size.

The *kolkhoz*, though far less rationalized than the State farm proper, is fairly collectivistic in character, as compared to the normal type of cooperative in the under-developed countries. Here the Israeli *moshav* can be used as the ideal type. The accent is on cooperation not so much in *production* but in *marketing*. The production unit is the family-household form. There is often common access to and ownership of such resources as orchards, etc., which are worked on behalf of the collectivity in varying ways, and there are various arrangements for the pooling of agricultural machinery. Here the State plays a critical role, for many services—e.g. agricultural 'extension' services—are provided to the collectivity by the State, or to the individual farmers by virtue of their membership of the *moshav*. (In concentrating on the *moshav* here as an ideal type, I have in mind the *moshav ovdim* and ignore deliberately the variety of forms to be found in actuality, in particular the much more collectivistic *moshavim shitufiyim*.)[25]

The other end of the continuum is represented by the archetypal peasant farm engaged in a hermetic subsistence economy, with minimal interchange with its neighbours. In some ways, cash-cropping is *more* individualistic, and 'subsistence' more 'cooperative'. But in reality pure subsistence farming is rare and peasants, as we have noted, are normally involved in the market as sellers of agricultural produce, as consumers and sometimes as sellers of their labour-power. They also practise various kinds and degrees of mutual aid with neighbours. The continuum can be schematically represented thus:

Collectivism	State farm
↑	*Kolkhoz* (collective)
↓	*Moshav*
Possessive	⎰ Peasant cash-cropping and ⎱
Individualism	⎱ subsistence farming ⎰

[25] See *Agriculture Planning and Village Community in Israel*, Arid Zone Research Paper No. xxiii, UNESCO, 1964.

We have deliberately used Macpherson's term 'possessive' individualism because it denotes both the *general* character of the pattern of ownership, and mode of working the farm. Strictly, peasant farming is never 'individual': it is *household* farming, as East European rural sociologists have insisted from the time of the *'zemtsvo* statisticians' of the last century, through to Chayanov and such contemporary students as Galeski. The pattern of ownership and the mode of working the land, naturally, to go hand in hand.

Yet ownership may vary independently of other aspects of farming: 'individual' *title* is quite compatible with the most highly mechanized *cultivation* of wheat on blocks made up of small parcels of land which are ploughed, planted, sprayed, harvested on one single stretch of land as unitary agricultural operations. The owners thus participate in the farming of all these combined plots of land taken together either in some specialized role such as tractor driver, or as unskilled labour, or in non-agricultural roles (book-keeper, teacher, etc.), or—sometimes—are underemployed.[26]

The degree of collectivism or individualism thus varies for different areas of social activity: here we find highly collective cultivation combined with individual tenure. But we can also have ownership of resources *other* than land—machinery, draught animals, water resources, trucks, woodlots, pasture, etc., etc., which can take many diverse forms: pure private ownership, shared rights, common ownership, leasing, renting, etc., and at different levels and between different sets of actors: village level, between groups of kin, neighbours, partnerships, based sometimes on a purely economic association, at others on traditional rights, sometimes on legal title (sometimes formally granted or recognized by the State), and so on and so forth. This rich diversity of forms of ownership of different *resources* means that the dichotomy between 'collectivistic' and 'individualistic' is not very illuminating. As we have seen, there are sets and hierarchies of rights which have to be spelled out carefully for each type of resources. Modern producer cooperatives, too—particularly settlement schemes—usually have an overarching level of State rights in the land—at least in the early phases—which are absent in traditional

[26] See Simon Charlsley, 'The group farm scheme in Uganda: a case study from Bunyoro' in *Land settlement and rural development in Eastern Africa,* ed. Raymond Apthorpe, Nkanga editions, Transition Books, Kampala, 1968, pp. 57–64.

farming. The cooperative, too, usually involves some intrusion of State control or influence (e.g. by providing credit, initial capital, etc., or via quality control) that diminishes the strict autonomy of the peasant as producer and seller, whatever his title to the land. Furthermore, most of the types of farming we are concerned with, and which governments are increasingly trying to foster in developing countries, fall into the 'cooperative' area *between* the 'collectivistic' and 'individualistic' poles. Most of these swans are neither black nor white, but grey.

If 'ownership' itself is differentiable, then, according to what it is that is owned—and resource A may be 'communally' (collectively) owned whilst resource B is family–household property, so too the many activities of farming can vary enormously in the degree to which they involve different kinds, ranges and levels of social cooperation with varying sets of people, in many different areas of life. Production and marketing are usually the fundamental areas. But modern cooperativism involves much more, very often, than strictly economic, legal and technical matters such as ownership or cultivation, however vital these are. Education, health, housing, access to 'urban values'—all these are central concerns of many kinds of cooperative, which provide a sponsor or act as brokers in the procurement of such services for their members, in varying degrees. The most collectivistic units of all are the *kibbutzim*, where the principle of collectivism is extended to the rearing of children, the minimization of residential individualism, and—crucially—the minimization of personal property and the hiring of labour. Cooperatives proper do not even begin to approach this degree of socialization of common life, but they nowadays usually do handle very much more than agricultural activities alone; the State or the Party also propagates ideologies among the cooperative's members. In the extreme type of collective, the *kibbutz*, ideological orthodoxy is a *sine qua non* of membership. In a *moshav* or settlement scheme, ideological proselytization is a much more diffuse and permissive, a propagation of general national and social ideals rather than a rigid set of requirements for personal behaviour in all dimensions of everyday life.

Where ideological commitment is lacking the major incentives are primarily instrumental, and everything tends to turn on the pay-off to the producer. In many planned production cooperatives such rewards are often unimpressive in the early years, and ideological commitment is too weak to sustain the required degree of dedication to the enterprise. Where both instrumental and moral sanctions are weak there is the danger of resort to the third of Etzioni's sanctions[27]—using force of various kinds to induce conformity on the part of the peasant. If, for any of these reasons, the cooperative fails to work effectively, its 'demonstration' effect for the surrounding countryside is negative rather than positive.

As Professor Baviskar's paper eminently shows, however, ideological and other attachments often divide rather than unify. National and regional politics, and ethnic and religious divisions, manifest themselves within the cooperative community, though he also shows that a pluralistic system is not necessarily ineffective, any more than competition between rival political parties is in a polity where the 'rules of the game' are accepted. Institutionalized conflict, too, can lead to the healthy competition of policies, and not simply to stalemate or collapse into warring factions. In the Israeli case the role of the State is even more crucial, since the whole operation is part of a policy of nation-building. The State, and even international influences, are equally central in settlement schemes such as those described by Saul for Tanzania, by Shillinglaw for China's communes, by Landsberger for the Mexican *ejidos*, and by Galeski and Shanin for Eastern Europe, to name no others.

Cooperation or 'cooperativism' today, then, is not simply the coming together of autonomous producers or consumers on the market to pool their resources, to achieve economies of scale, or to defend themselves against common enemies, as in the nineteenth century *laissez-faire* model. As Carroll's paper, and Crocombe's, show, this does still occur. But the typical development, increasingly, is the utilization, sponsorship or incorporation of cooperatives with organizational structures and within policy frameworks that are set by those who control government.

Modern cooperativism thus reflects the general increase of scale and the increasing intrusion of the State which have characterized all forms of activity in modern society, capitalist or communist, and which both Marx and Weber drew attention to, and not solely in the economic sphere either.

The cooperative represents a form intermediate between the pure collective and the traditional peasant family-form. It has its attractions to the peasant in so far as it pays off and protects him. It is attractive to the State because it avoids a head-on clash with

[27] Amitai Etzioni, *A comparative analysis of complex organizations*, Free Press, New York, 1961.

the peasantry such as collectivization would involve; in any case, this latter is not considered an economically viable answer to the problem of stepping up agricultural productivity. It also seems to provide the means of attaining a number of different ends. It promises to accumulate the capital (particularly foreign earnings) needed by the State for the modernization not only of agriculture but of the whole society, via the development of industry. At the same time, ideological influence can be more easily exerted via the network of communication and control represented by the cooperatives (as well as through other novel channels under State control or influence).

The State also hopes to solve the problem of absorbing surplus labour, mainly by more intensive farming and the opening up of new land, and to raise living standards in the countryside as a result. It goes without saying that these several ends are often incompatible. 'Milking' the peasantry and raising rural income simultaneously may either be impossible or involve knife-edge balancing acts. 'Modernizing' and educating the peasant may make him a more efficient exponent of his own interests, and collectively so. Far from generating 'self-development', the peasant tries to 'exploit' the State, benefiting from health, education and welfare facilities, but refraining from total commitment to the development scheme. (As Dore points out, whatever its advantages, the cooperative, too, does impose some limitation upon the freedom of its members to act independently.) The new social machinery usually works badly, certainly initially, and gives the grower a poor return. And since modern agriculture responds to ever-degenerating world terms of trade by trying to increase productivity, this often means capital-intensive, not labour-intensive, agriculture, extensive rather than intensive. The State, far from 'milking' agriculture to subsidize industry, finds itself investing ever more heavily in a vulnerable, often degenerating, rural economy. Further, agricultural modernization normally increases the flow of labour from the villages to the cities rather than absorbing surplus population. In this vicious circle the failure of the cities to become centres of *industry* is the crucial weakness.

Finally the cooperative *movement* at secondary and higher levels becomes a key resource in the political power game. Its financial resources constantly beckon the central government, which tries to harness the capital reserves and income of the cooperative movement for a variety of projects, ranging from the establishment of processing plants, e.g. cotton ginneries, in the rural areas themselves to investment in urban factories or in a variety of other enterprises and projects.

The likelihood of success for the cooperatives thus depends upon an extremely complex set of factors, amongst which the nature of existing 'traditional' social bonds is merely one—and a highly ambiguous—set. Nor are modern cooperatives by any means necessarily built out of existing on-going communities. Weintraub's cases show how *hamoula* and ethnic divisions are built into the new Israeli *moshavim* and constitute barriers that are difficult to overcome. The nature of motivation is a second crucial set, as Galeski points out: whether the farmers are appropriately skilled or not (and few contain ex-musicologists and ex-bankers, as in cases cited for Israel!), whether they are culturally and structurally homogeneous or heterogeneous, whether they are responding to instrumental or ideological inducements, or are merely subject to the pressure of authority, or some combination of all of these. There is a particularly important difference between the 'spontaneous' cooperative and those which are planned. Planned cooperatives are likely to be supported by other institutions (political parties, central and local governmental organizations, credit and marketing agencies); often, though not always, 'spontaneous' ones are more or less vigorously opposed by these interests, as well as by land-owners, private middlemen, etc. Carroll's survey of Latin America, for example, shows that hostility is only too common. Obviously, the chances of success are likely to be higher where support rather than opposition is the order of the day. And though the existence of a common enemy can be a factor promoting solidarity (hostility to the Rochdale grocer, or hostility to the Indian in West Africa), the enemy must not be *too* strong, as the fate of so many of the *ejidos* described by Landsberger shows (he concentrates, in fact, on one or two of the 'success stories'). Weintraub clearly demonstrates how crucial central sponsorship and assistance has been for Israeli *moshavim*. Favourable legislation is especially helpful—but governments can change, and the laws with them. The other side of the coin is the ultimate ineffectiveness of cooperation where the 'push from below', consciousness and commitment on the part of the cooperative's members, is too feeble, as Saul shows to be often the case.

The social characteristics of the membership of the cooperative are thus one crucial set of factors: they may be immigrants, resettled populations, refugees, squatters, existing populations *in situ*: each such population will have different predispositions towards the cooperative. Selection may be careful, but is usually hurried and indiscriminatory. The land they are given and its suitability for the crops they decide to grow—or, more often, are told to grow—also crucially affect the chances of success. Variability in the quality of the land within the cooperative area affects the individual's chances and makes for dissension. The other term in the equation is the nature of the cooperative organization and its position in national life. Here governmental sponsorship, the hostility of established interests, the characteristics of those who manage the cooperative are every bit as crucial to success or failure as recruitment, motivation or agricultural skill.

When we begin to list the factors which make for or inhibit success we begin to realize that to concentrate simply on the question of the nature of pre-existing social bonds is wrongly to isolate only one aspect of the problem. Nor, if we do isolate it, can any unequivocal or universal answer be given, for we cannot force the variety of human circumstance into such crude categories as 'traditional', 'collectivistic', 'communal', 'individualistic' and so forth.

In the various contributions to this volume the reader will find many differences of viewpoint on many of these questions. Some contributors, for instance, regard ideological mobilization as a generative force needed even for economic success. Others regard the infusion of political ideals into cooperatives as divisions or as distractions, as 'leakage of efficiency' from what should be the central aim of improved productivity, or as the 'overloading' of usually embryonic and weak economic organizations with other tasks they are unfitted to cope with, such as political development, welfare functions, etc.

Finally, there is dispute as to what constitutes 'success' and about the time scale over which it can be adjudged. Some point to the 'spontaneous' cooperatives, most of which fail, but where the fittest may survive, so that massive investment may pay off because it is the selective experience of the *successful*—even if only a minority—that counts as a model for future agricultural transformation. Most deny that success should be measured in economic terms alone, and that the other contributions are of crucial social value—a view that seldom attracts either economists or poverty-stricken governments anxious to generate capital in the agricultural sector so as to finance general national development. *They* feel that agriculture must be the main source, not the absorbent, of capital.

4—T.B.O.G.

Taken overall, the promise of the cooperatives described in these papers is extremely varied. In Poland, where the 'Agricultural Circles' are supported by the State, they produce over 70 per cent of gross agricultural production, and totally eclipse collectives (1·1 per cent). In Latin America, they are weak and thinly-represented generally. Even in Mexico and Chile, where they have achieved sizeable success, they have not broken the power of the big land-owner or achieved any significant increase in productivity.

Weintraub, like many contemporary East European rural sociologists, argues on the basis of Israeli experience that the best policy is to pluralize, to experiment with a variety of types, with flexibility of policy and constant evaluation. And in view of the limited success, so far, of the cooperative, except under such favourably supportive conditions as those in Israel, it is worth noting the suggestions of Shanin, Crocombe and Galeski that in Eastern Europe collective and cooperative farming has proved less popular and effective than *either* peasant farming *or* the State farm, and that the latter may well be 'the wave of the future' for that part of the world—a view which will seem heresy to those who have become accustomed to 'writing off' collectivized agriculture because of their awareness of its ineffectiveness three decades ago. State farms, they suggest, are more attractive both to the technocrat *and* to those who work them, since they provide the latter with social services and cultural facilities analogous to those the industrial worker enjoys, and provide greater opportunities for social mobility than do collective farms, as well as a security of income that is more independent of the fluctuations of the market.

Certainly haste in agricultural innovation invites disaster. In the nature of things, it is an industry with very peculiar characteristics in that it is regulated by the cyclical movement of Nature's seasons. Experiments take years, not months or weeks. Large-scale innovation, reliance on a single policy, can mean starvation for a nation or region. But the pressure to fill the mouths of the hungry and earn the wherewithal for advancing into an era of universal, or at least national, modern prosperity is such that caution is often condemned as conservatism. The history of planned development is full of disasters. The history of private agriculture is equally impressive, notably in the USA and Canada and in Western Europe. But this has been achieved where the growth of industry has supported technological innovation in agriculture and absorbed the surplus population freed—often agonizingly 'freed'—from the countryside. It has also created a class-divided society, and particularly in the rural areas has thrown up the most serious threats—until the 1960s—to the stability of the social order. As Lipset has remarked:

Agrarian radicalism, although it is rarely socialist, has directed its attacks against big-business domination. In certain economic areas farmers have openly challenged private ownership and control of industry, either through governmental or cooperative ownership, to eliminate private control of banking, insurance, transport, natural resources, public utilities, manufacture of farm implements, wholesale and retail distribution of consumers' goods, and food commodity exchanges. The large measure of socialism without doctrines that can be found in the programs of agrarian political and economic organizations is in many respects more socialistic than the nationalization policies of some explicitly socialist parties.[28]

As a model for societies which are going to be predominantly agrarian for the visible future, the USA is, therefore, unattractive and in any case inimitable. Such conditions are entirely lacking in the non-communist Third World. The USSR, still hampered by shoots of pain in its Achilles heel, is no more attractive as a model and its example in the field of industrialization is qualified in that it was achieved only at the—very dangerous—expense of risking class warfare in the countryside. The indications from Shillinglaw's paper, and from general information, seem to be that China's progress is one of secular improvement, following a disastrous attempt to impose ideology upon agriculture in the heyday of the communes. It cannot be urged too strongly that there is no *general* optimal way of growing crops—there are only *differential* optima for different crops in different regions, as Chayanov insisted. All in all, agriculture is the area least amenable to radical transformation but most in need of it. At present, experiment, experiment and experiment, without total commitment to any one formula, is required, and no unitary solution should be looked for, since history and culture have produced very different agricultures in communist and capitalist, developed and underdeveloped, societies. Failures, of course, must be expected in plenty, and the history of capitalist development in particular is the history of the failure of countless smaller enterprises and the converse

[28] S. M. Lipset, *Agrarian socialism: the Cooperative Commonwealth Federation in Saskatchewan, a study in political sociology*, University of California Press, Berkeley, 1950, p. 18.

success of even fewer and even larger corporations. Probably a great deal of risky investment has to occur before answers begin to emerge. The history of Soviet experience seems to suggest that answers can be found, even at the price of large setbacks, and that the views of orthodox economists who regularly predicted economic collapse rather than development, and who (often rightly) ridiculed utopian, ill-considered innovations, seem to have been belied by history.

We cannot here open up the major questions of planned development *v.* peasant/market economy. The latter has achieved striking success in countries like the Ivory Coast or Kenya.[29] In other cases there has been 'involution': the ever greater refinement of a given set of techniques of production in a way that allows a constantly, often dramatically, increasing population to be supported, but with no fundamental transformation of the economy: growth without development.[30] There have also been significant social costs, dysfunctions and conflicts, even in the relatively 'successful' countries, and very major problems, some new, still persist in those countries, whilst others are becoming ever more serious. Certainly, planning in some form, and a large role for the State, seem to arise from necessity in many countries, and from ideological commitments in others. It is important, therefore, that we begin to assess the experience of novel forms of agriculture in the Third World, and in countries which have already modernized their agriculture. The papers which follow are contributions to such a discussion.

[29] See, for example, Hans Ruthenberg, *African agricultural development policy in Kenya, 1952–65*, Springer-Verlag, Berlin, 1966.

[30] See Clifford Geertz, *Agricultural involution*, University of California Press, Berkeley, 1968.

Part I

Ronald F. Dore **Modern cooperatives in traditional communities**

There are parts of Africa, Oceania, Latin America and some of the fringe areas of Asia where the tenure of land remains in some sense communal. Either all or some of the land available to a group of people is seen as belonging to them collectively, or to a chief acting as in some sense the group's trustee.

Most colonial governments in such societies made it possible for individuals, or individual families, to get, either from their own or from some other land-owning group, secure, legally protected and heritable rights to particular parcels of land. In fact they generally tried to promote such a change. By and large, post-independence governments have not altered that policy.

There is, however, a common, not unplausible and indeed attractive argument in favour of holding back the process of individualizing communal tenures. It runs as follows. The communal tenure of land provides a material basis for a take-off into cooperative or collective farming. The limitations of individual family smallholdings are everywhere increasingly apparent. Wherever agriculture is progressive and go-ahead, farmers are forming ever closer cooperative links. The bonds of community solidarity should not be destroyed but preserved, and gradually rationalized into modern cooperative forms. People who already *are* a group will take more easily to group farming than a collection of individualistic farmers.

The argument is not new. It was propounded by the Russian populists of the nineteenth century, who saw the traditional Russian village community, the *mir*, as a basis for modern cooperatives. The late developer, they argued, could skip all the intermediate stages of development. History is like a grandmother who scoops the marrow out of the bone for her youngest grandchild, letting the older grandchildren cut their fingers on splintered bones trying to get at theirs.[1]

[1] See the view of N. G. Chernyshevsky, quoted in F. Venturi, *The roots of rebellion*, 1962, pp. 150–2.

Equally, the contrary view has a long history. Modern cooperative forms, it is urged, are the result of a long and painful transition from a communal to an individualistic and thence to a new collective stage: the process of development cannot so easily be short-circuited. This view was never put with more vigour and clarity than by Frederik Engels.

All civilised peoples begin with the common ownership of the land. With all peoples who have passed a certain primitive stage in the course of the development of agriculture, this common ownership becomes a fetter on production. It is abolished, negated, and after a longer or shorter series of intermediate stages is transformed into private property. But as a higher stage of agricultural development, brought about by private property in land itself, private property in land becomes in its turn a fetter on production, as is the case today with both small and large ownership. The demand that it also be negated, that it should once again be transformed into common property, necessarily arises. But this demand does not mean the restoration of the old original common ownership, but the institution of a far higher and more developed form of possession in common which, far from being a hindrance to production, on the contrary for the first time frees production from all fetters and gives it the possibility of making full use of modern chemical discoveries and mechanical inventions.[2]

Though not everyone would agree with this particular evolutionary scheme of human history, many would accept the view that there is a sharp distinction to be made between traditional community forms and modern types of cooperation. Clauson, for instance, speaks of modern collective agriculture (in his terminology, based on 'tertiary' communal tenure) as 'fundamentally different in character' from the more primitive forms of communal tenures he describes, being 'based on conscious planning, . . . the product . . . of an advanced stage of human thought'.[3]

However, the fact that many countries *have* moved from early communal forms to modern collectivist forms through a stage of private property does not necessarily imply that all societies must. And if we have now to unlearn many of the things which our fathers taught us about the errors of the social evolutionists, most of us at least remain suspicious of glib characterizations about 'advanced' and 'less advanced' processes of thought. Without accepting every demonstration of the essential rationality of men in the simplest societies, without going all the way from the smug-

---

[2] Quoted from *Anti-Dühring* by D. Mitrany, *Marx against the peasant*, 1951, p. 30.

[3] Sir Gerald Clauson, *Communal land tenure*, FAO, Rome, 1953, p. 23.

ness of 'Your peasant, of course, takes a simple view of life' to the new-style bourgeois-baiting 'The bloody peasants are every bit as smart as you are, chum', one still asks for plausible criteria, plausible indices and plausible evidence before one is prepared to accept sweeping assertions about 'fundamental differences' between patterns of social relations in preliterate societies and those in our own.

It is the burden of this paper that such differences can indeed be discerned but that, although these differences are very great, certain features of traditional relations of solidarity are not only not inhibitive of, but perhaps even essential to, modern forms of cooperation.

Definitions

Perhaps the terms of the argument should first be clarified. By agricultural cooperation is meant any sacrifice of the managerial sovereignty of individual farm households in their farming operations in favour of a group of such households or householders, or their representatives, the sacrifice being justified (by the sovereignty-sacrificing individuals themselves if the cooperative is voluntary; by the government if it is forced) as promoting their common well-being.

The whole spectrum of cooperatives is therefore included, from a simple single-crop marketing cooperative to a full production collective—and without reference to the spontaneity or otherwise of the process of their formation.

For 'modern' a simple definition will suffice. An organization is modern if it is new; if the sacrifice of sovereignty referred to is, or was within living memory, a conscious act of commitment or submission, rather than part of a set of social relations inherited from time unremembered. Most of the forms of cooperative organization which are modern in this sense do have other characteristics in common too—thanks to the similarity in the purposes for which these organizations are created in different societies, and to the processes of cultural diffusion which ensure that certain organizational inventions which seem most conducive to these purposes are widely adopted. Some of these organizational devices will be discussed later. It will suffice here to point out that the word 'modern' should not be taken to refer to some elusive, but desirable, 'quality of modernity'.

A brief definition is also required, perhaps, of what one means by the 'success' of a cooperative. It would be equally absurd to adopt either on the one hand a rigid absolute standard like 'achieving strict adherence to Rochdale principles' or, on the other hand, a completely relativistic standard like 'achieving whatever were the declared purposes of the cooperative in the first place'. Consider, on the one hand, a group of farmers who achieve their purposes of greatly reducing their marketing costs, and on the other hand a group of farmers who manage by cooperating to qualify for 7 per cent cooperative credit, which they then re-lend to less astute farmers at 15 per cent. Both achieve their purposes, but are we to consider them equally and indiscriminately 'successful'? Consider two governments, one of which successfully uses cooperatives to diffuse new agricultural practices, or even, perhaps, democratic committee-man skills, and the other which is successful only in using cooperatives to distribute patronage in such a way as to perpetuate the dominance of a particular political faction. Clearly, for a generalizing argument of the kind attempted here one needs a more discriminating criterion of 'success' than that.

And if one is not prepared to be entirely relativistic in this way, one has to make moral judgments if one wishes to use the word 'success' at all. I assume that my moral judgments will coincide with those of most of my readers if I define success primarily in terms of achieving for its members benefits derived from economic activity of the kind intended when the cooperative was created, in so far as the economic and natural environment makes this possible—'failure' being, at the other end of the scale, an inability to obtain these benefits due to lack of efficiency or honesty in the organization. (Clearly, a change in market situations or a crop failure can cause a cooperative to collapse without it necessarily being a 'failure' in this sense.) I would add further that the intended benefits to members should also, when achieved, be distributed as intended among members—that is to say, that the cooperative should function, if not exactly according to the rules, at least in a way which does not do violence to the principles on which the rules were based, in particular that it should not be corrupt in the sense that some persons are able to receive disproportionately large benefits at the expense of other members without the knowledge or against the will of the latter.

Confining one's perspectives on cooperatives to these aspects is not, of course, by any means to deplore the conscious use of cooperative organizations by governments as a means of agricultural or political education, as training in associational behaviour, as a means of tying subsidies to certain improvements in practice, and so on. Often these aims are (in my view) highly laudable, and they may be even more important than the securing of economic benefits for members. But since these aims are subject to so much greater variation from society to society than is the aim of material advancement, it will simplify matters if we limit the criteria for the success–failure continuum in the manner suggested here.

Isolating the social structural factors

The discussion which follows takes for granted that there are many other factors besides the degree of traditional solidarity among a group of farmers which will determine whether they will, or will not, take to modern forms of cooperation. A cotton grower on the shores of Lake Victoria with only a cooperative ginnery nearby to take his cotton to is not relinquishing much when he sacrifices his right to market his own cotton, his right to set his own selling grades, even his right to choose the strains of cotton he will grow. But a farmer near a big city who grows miscellaneous vegetables would be relinquishing a wide degree of autonomy if he bound himself to a marketing cooperative; an Israeli immigrant who enters a *moshav* relinquishes much more, and a family which enters a full production collective very much more.

Similarly, the rewards prospectively to be gained by the sacrificing individual will vary. The cotton grower may gain a reduction in ginning costs, access to otherwise inaccessible markets, secure prices; the suburban vegetable grower only a marginal reduction in his marketing costs. Sometimes the gain will be cheap access to common facilities; often (all too often, perhaps) it will be privileged access to cheap government credit.

The balance of real advantage which the situation offers, the balance of sacrifice and reward for the individual cooperator, is very clearly one of the factors affecting the willingness of the individual to cooperate and hence the chances of the cooperative organization's success. Even this vastly over-simplifies, of course. The 'economic factors' cannot be so neatly isolated. It is not the balance of 'real' advantage as it would be drawn up by an FAO expert economist, but people's *perception* of the balance, which affects their decisions, and these perceptions are determined by the conception of welfare which the people concerned hold either individually or in common with other members of their society.

Even if one restricts oneself to apparently quantifiable material costs and benefits the rate of time discount remains a crucial cultural variable. In fact, one could make out a good case for the argument that a lowering of the rate of time discount, a changed evaluation of long-term as against short-term gains, is *the* single most important factor likely to predispose a hitherto reluctant community towards agricultural cooperation.

However that may be, there remain other cultural and social structural variables. The question to be discussed in this paper may be rephrased as follows: for any given economic opportunity situation, and the given balance of perceived rewards over perceived sacrifices which a particular form of cooperation would offer in that situation, experience suggests that some groups of people will take more readily to cooperation and operate more viable cooperatives than others. Is it true that groups which still have the kind of 'primordial' solidarity which goes along with communal land tenure are, other things being equal, likely because of that solidarity to be among the more successful? Or is there such a 'fundamental difference' between that kind of traditional solidarity and the solidarity of a cooperative that there is no correlation at all? Or, indeed, is the correlation a negative one, traditional solidarity being a positive *dis*advantage for would-be organizers of cooperatives?

How solidary is the traditional solidary community?

The first thought that occurs to one when reading of a good many societies is that there is indeed a fundamental difference; the difference being that the so-called traditional solidary societies, for all their communal tenures, simply are not very solidary. 'Primitive communism' is a myth, or at least by no means the universal accompaniment of a communal form of tenure.

Descriptions of African societies, for example, suggest that, communal 'ownership' of land is often accompanied by highly individualistic exploitation of it. If individuals often work in common with friends, 'it is communal help given to an individual, not community work, still less sharing of a community product'.[4] And where, in a situation of balance between communal ownership and individual use, the density of the population increases,

[4] A. Gaitskell, *Report on land tenure and land use problems in the Trust Territories of Tanganyika and Ruanda–Urundi*, FAO, Rome, 1959, pp. 12–13.

'it is the individual usufruct feature rather than the communal one which predominates'.[5]

Again, even if communal labour is an important feature of these societies, the communal work groups do not always necessarily define a community, since the composition of the groups may shift according to the task. For some agricultural purposes, and especially for the purpose of organizing land use, a single compound may work as a unit. For building a school or clearing a market-place it may be a wider segment of a lineage, or perhaps an age-set within a lineage. For clearing paths to new field areas or building a bridge across a stream it may be a group of neighbours from several segments of the lineage, grouped for this purpose by geographical rather than by kinship criteria—and so on.[5]

Then again, the purpose of the cooperation is not always mutual assistance. Sometimes an essential subsidiary purpose is competitive display. It is reported of the Tiv that the big 'hoeing parties' are called by senior women, and that 'if a woman calls a big hoeing party, supplying generous amounts of food and beer to all those who worked for her, she will be called "important woman" by them, the men of her compound and all her other neighbours for months afterwards'.[6] Similarly, in one district of Ethiopia, a clear distinction is made between strictly 'bread and butter' work exchanges, and the kind of 'potlatch' occasion when work is exchanged for lavish entertainment, and different words are used for the two kinds of occasion.[7]

In Latin America it appears that whatever the nature of the pre-colonial community (and the Incas, at least, had a well developed system of communal land holding and exploitation which Clauson counts, along with the Russian *mir*, as a prototype of advanced 'tertiary' forms),[8] in the post-colonial period the Indian peasant communities have proved anything but cohesive. Thus in Bolivia an authoritative witness warned a land reform commission soon after the revolution that 'the indigenous communities of our days, contrary to what is generally believed, are based neither on common property in the land nor on the collective organization of labour. . . . Actual control over the land has an individual character . . . community of ownership remains only

[5] See P. Bohannan, *Tiv farm and settlement*, London, HMSO, 1954, p. 23.
[6] Ibid., p. 25.
[7] H. S. Mann, *Pilot field study in systems of land tenure: landlord–tenant relations in Chore Mikitil Woreda*, 1964, pp. 49–50 (mimeograph).
[8] Op. cit., p. 23.

vestigially in the right which community members have to use
pastures and *sierras* in certain areas and, as far as labour cooperation is concerned, it is rather exceptional.[9] Ten years later a survey
of developments in Bolivia remarked that it was thought that 'the
ayllu, the traditional Indian community with its shared obligations, would provide the basis for a collectivist agrarian structure.
But paradoxically it is precisely those communities which have
shown most resistance to collective property'.[10] In Mexico, when
collective *ejidos* were created in the 1930s, there was little sense
of returning to or reinforcing tradition. Instead the new measures
were looked on as real innovations, urged by their proponents as
necessary to 'create a collective conscience and drive away selfish
individualism' and denounced by their opponents as essentially
unrealistic because 'the Mexican peasant is essentially an individualist, and individual utilization of the land by him, without
any control or discipline, is the method best suited to his psychological conditions and mentality'.[11]

Authority patterns

All the above may be granted. It is still true that in a good many
parts of the world—particularly where, for instance, irrigation
facilities are used in common—there are small village communities which maintain some kind of community control over land
use, cooperate regularly in all matters of daily life and agricultural production and have the kind of cohesive group spirit—a
sense of intimacy with each other and sharp differentiation from
the world outside—of the kind which sociologists call variously
community-like, affective and particularistic, family-like, *gemein-
schaftlich*, primary, etc. In these cases, at least, there should be
social bonds capable of being mobilized for modern forms of
cooperation.

Not necessarily, however. There is another dimension which
has to be considered besides that of cohesive solidarity, and that
is the question of the type of traditional authority. Small traditional communities may be patriarchal or fraternal, despotic or

[9] Dr Arturo Urguidi Moralis, quoted in Casto Ferragut, *Informe al
gobierno de Bolivia sobre reforma agraria*, EPTA report No. 1856, Rome,
1964, p. 61.

[10] C. A. M. Hennessy, 'Shifting forces in the Bolivian revolution', *The
World Today*, May 1964, p. 203.

[11] Solomon Eckstein, 'Collective farming in Mexico', Ph.D. thesis, Harvard,
May 1961, p. 113.

egalitarian; status may be ascribed by birth or it may be achieved by skill or magic; differences in status may be marked by minimal forms of defence and command, or by the most elaborated and exaggerated of such forms. Communities of both types may show equal solidarity. Effective cooperation of a modern type, however, is rarely, if ever, successful under ascribed authoritarian leadership. One of the features of the European transition from feudal village communitarianism, through private-property individualism to modern quasi-collectivism, is that the *individualizing* phase was also an *equalizing* phase—the period which saw the end of aristocracy as a form of government, and of legal discrimination between serfs and freemen: the period in which emerged the concepts of citizenship and equality before the law, and in which 'masters' and 'servants' became employers and employees. Without this equalizing trend—and the gradual evolution of democratic constitutional forms which enable groups of equals to secure for themselves effective and respected leadership—modern forms of cooperation would be impossible.

Where, therefore, the traditional community is authoritarian in form one cannot expect any easy transition to modern systems of cooperation. Indeed, one often cannot expect any effective development at all. In the Gash delta of the Sudan, where cotton is grown by flash irrigation, and land is allotted every season on a tribal basis (because the extent of the floods varies from year to year), the chiefs of local tribes usually take larger and more fertile plots than the average tenant, and they also claim a levy from their 'subjects'—a system confirmed and institutionalized by the colonial government. Such chiefs, according to one report, have no interest in development which might raise the living levels of their tribesmen and so make them less available for working on their own fields. Least of all are they interested in the development of a cooperative, which would provide a new structure of leadership rivalling their own, inevitably at the expense of their power and prestige.[12]

In Bolivia, too, the testimony quoted earlier went on to point out that the traditional communities were not only individualistic; they were also highly stratified, with *originarios* holding more privileges and owning twice as much land on average as the next stratum of *agregados*, and a large part of the population being

---

[12] Ali El Tom, *Land reform and associated rural institutions in the Republic of the Sudan*, Khartoum, 1961, p. 94 (mimeograph).

utaguaguas or dependent hangers-on with no privileges and no land whatever.[13]

It is not only that such stratification inhibits development. Where communities do have an authoritarian structure and are at the same time cohesive, development might take place if the authoritarian leaders can be captured for the development ideal —and it might even take place faster than in more egalitarian communities.[14] But the transition to modern *cooperative* forms will still be immensely difficult, for the cohesiveness and the authoritarianism are inextricably combined in the traditional structures, and the destruction of the authority patterns is likely to lead immediately to a breakdown in solidarity too, and the loss of what is supposed to be the initial advantage of traditional communities.

Institutionalized suspicion

The field is being narrowed. Some traditional settlements are ruled out of the discussion because they lack cohesive solidarity; others which are cohesive are authoritarian. But there are some traditional communities which are both cohesive *and* egalitarian. It is to these, then, that one might look for promise of a 'leap' across the individualistic private-property phase into modern forms of cooperation.

One difficulty arises when the cohesion is concentrated within excessively small groups—when factional divisions within a larger community prevent community-wide cooperation. Percy Cohen, after reviewing a number of Israeli studies which make this point, concludes:

diffuse sentiments and ideas of solidarity, which have a traditional basis, may well be advantageous, if not entirely necessary, for the establishment of modern co-operatives; while specific systems of rights, obligations and powers which inhere in traditional forms of cohesion and solidarity may well obstruct the formation of contractual relationships.[15]

[13] Ferragut, op. cit. p. 61.

[14] Compare the Vicos experiment in Peru, an example of change induced by the changers' purchase of the *hacienda* owners' authority: A. Holmberg, 'Changing community attitudes and values in Peru' in R. N. Adams, *Social change in Latin America today*, 1960; and R. P. Dore, 'Agricultural development in Japan, 1870–1900', *Economic development and cultural change*, 9, iii, part 2, October 1960, p. 86.

[15] P. S. Cohen, 'Tradition and co-operation', a paper originally written for

What is perhaps more serious is that the diffuse sentiments of solidarity may themselves, even when widely diffused over the community, provide obstacles to the long-term development of cooperatives. One might cite in illustration what seems, *prima facie*, a particularly fine example of a cooperative in New Guinea.[16] Here the traditional social structure was clearly egalitarian. There was no institutionalization of factional rivalry. There was no institution of strong chieftainship. Leaders were chosen, not born—chosen for age, wisdom, experience or military prowess. In this context a new type of organization was developed. On the initiative of an illiterate ex-policeman with no knowledge of cost accounting and no position of inherited power, but only a shrewd business sense, considerable energy and an ability to communicate his enthusiasm and his vision of future prosperity, a group of five villages were persuaded to pool their savings to buy first one and then a second tractor. In time they developed a successful sweet-potato farm of nearly two thousand acres, producing crops to the value of £6,000 a year and considerably increasing the income of the five hundred people who were, from time to time, engaged in working on it.

Already at the time it was studied, however, there were obvious questions to be asked concerning the viability of this venture in the long run. Several of its features are worth examining closely.

1. The venture undoubtedly depended for its success at the time it was studied on the fact that it utilized traditional community sentiments. Without the bonds of mutual trust which bound the members to each other, it would have collapsed. For instance, all the marketing transactions were handled by the energetic leader of the project, the ex-policeman, who made up for his illiteracy by a considerable shrewdness as well as initiative and persuasive power. Neither he nor his literate cousin, who acted as treasurer, kept proper accounts, nor did he make any clear distinction between the cooperative's funds and his own private spending money. Nevertheless, he appeared to live modestly and was not, apparently, the object of suspicion or resentment.

---

the Sixth World Congress of Sociology. The present paper has generally benefited a good deal from Cohen's paper, which, but for the author's modesty, would have appeared in this volume.

[16] Described in R. G. Crocombe and G. R. Hogbin, 'The Erap mechanical farming project', *New Guinea Research Institute Bulletin No. 1*, 1963.

Similarly, a sense of obligation to one's fellows seemed to be an effective driving force in the work organization. Absenteeism was not common, and once the morning meeting had been held and the work tasks allocated (the discussion might last for an hour) one overseer and two foremen were enough for a work force of eighty people.

2. One implication of what has just been said is that there was no differentiation between the social community as an all-embracing group and the project as a functional organization. This is clearly illustrated in the wage system. There were slight variations in the wages paid, not just according to function in the project (the tractor drivers and foremen, of course, received more) but also according to status within the community—an extra bonus was given to the village officials even though they did the same work in the gardens as others.

3. The project was not, in other words, organized on a basis of exact reciprocity, guaranteeing to each a return exactly proportionate to his contribution. Thus, for instance, members of the village contributed various amounts to the collection when the tractor was bought, but they did not receive strictly proportionate repayments. Instead they recognized a vaguer claim to call on project money for emergency needs. Economic transactions within the project, in other words, were assimilated to the traditional patterns of gift exchange, with their much looser and longer-term criteria of reciprocity.

This, quite clearly, is not the particular form of rationality of modern economic man. An attempt to get the project to adopt a formal constitution, with carefully defined powers of general assemblies, elections of officers, formalized audit, etc., rapidly foundered on the people's illiteracy.

Nevertheless, such systems will eventually be needed. Modern forms of cooperative organization are based on institutionalized suspicion. They are predicated on a belief in original sin. Man, the assumption is, has an inevitable tendency to corruption. Therefore organizations must build in checks and balances such as the audit and the periodic re-election of officers. The modern cooperative does deserve, in fact, to be called a 'higher form' because it requires a rather sophisticated appreciation of the idea that this institutionalized suspicion in the long run benefits all, including those against whom it is directed. Thus the treasurer welcomes the audit—even though the audit makes sense only on the assumption that the treasurer might have been dishonest—

because it clears him of suspicion. That justice should be done may be in the interest of the members; that it should be seen to be done is in the interest of the elected officials.

It can be predicted with fair certainty that the Erap mechanical farming project of New Guinea will sooner or later need these institutional checks, certainly if the organization is to grow. If an organization is held together by bonds of personal affect rather than of an impersonal sense of responsibility to play by the rules, corruption, or at least nepotism, is bound to occur as the organization grows. The manager is not tied to *all* the members by equal bonds of personal affect; since he is fonder of his brothers or of his nephews than he is of unrelated fellow members, as long as personal ties are the guiding principle he will make use of his power to favour them. The other kind of corruption—purely individualistic abuse of position for personal gain—is also likely to occur sooner or later (if no institutional checks are created) simply by the law of averages, and a single instance is enough to shatter the bonds of mutual trust and destroy the organization.

And if the checks of institutionalized suspicion are necessary, they will also be immensely difficult to create. Where personal bonds predominate the action of the auditor in calling for every document and scrutinizing every signature is not looked on simply as a following of the rules, fully legitimate and in the best interest of everyone, including the treasurer; it is seen as John X the auditor personally demonstrating, by the fact that he takes his duties seriously, his suspicions regarding the personal probity of James Y, the treasurer. And James Y is likely to be resentful. To be sure, such reactions are not unknown in the sophisticated cooperatives of modern Western societies—so much so that as soon as a cooperative can afford it, it impersonalizes the process by calling in an outside firm of accountants as auditors. Most governments which seek to promote agricultural cooperatives in developing societies provide a similar external auditing service and require that cooperatives use it. But the situation remains fraught with possibilities of friction and resentment. 'I intend it, Mr Chairman, as no reflection whatever on the officers of our cooperative when I suggest that in principle the auditors' report should be made available to every member of the cooperative' is not the kind of formulation which members of peasant societies are likely to be skilled in; nor is the disclaimer, insisting on the separation of institutionalized role relationships from total interpersonal relationships, likely to be easily believed. The necessary effort of imagination and of control of affect is not one which people in small rural communities anywhere get enough practice to acquire the habit of.

The same difficulties—of accepting behaviour conforming to the universalistic principles required by the role of cooperative member or official from a person with whom one has a wide-ranging, diffuse relationship—recur in other situations. The cooperative's grant of credit to individuals is usually supposed to be determined by fairly clear, universalistic criteria of eligibility and priority. But to James Y, the non-eligible member, that John Y, the cooperative secretary, should have strictly applied these rules, treating him just like any other member even though they are second cousins, may seem incomprehensible, unkind or even downright immoral. That, in a marketing cooperative, Richard X, the cooperative grader, should insist for all comers that every sack of cotton a grower turns in should be sampled (at random from the bottom, middle and top, on the institutionally suspicious assumption that if growers could cheat the grader they would), and that he should reject as under-grade half of the cotton of his age-mate William Z, may seem similarly outrageous. And the possibility of such personal friction is, of course, the greater the more the criteria to be applied do, like cotton grades or apple or tobacco qualities—anything where grading is not simply a function of size or weight—require subjective interpretation.This increases the possibility that William Z could believe that Richard X was not simply refusing properly to bend the rules in his favour but in fact bending them against him and letting through equally poor cotton from some other age-mate.

And the plain fact is that he is reasonably likely to be right. Precisely *because* the difficulty members have in separating specific institutionalized roles from general personal relations exposes a scrupulously rule-observing secretary or grader to so much likely animosity, it is rare in such societies to find secretaries or graders who really *are* prepared to be so scrupulous.

This, then, is the dilemma in which cooperatives are caught. Either the objective rules, with their suspicious assumptions of original sinfulness, are scrupulously applied—with the likelihood, given the diffusely personal nature of social relations in such societies and the principle that no quarrels are as fierce as family quarrels, of arousing such animosity between those who apply rules and those to whom they are applied that the organization is burst asunder—or else the rules are not scrupulously observed and the non-observance eventually becomes so flagrant that the losers in the game of influence withdraw from the cooperative or it founders in the factional struggle for advantage.

Valuable elements of tradition

The transition to modern, rationalized forms is an immensely difficult one; but, of course, it is not a complete transition, from all to nothing or from black to white. Modern cooperatives rest on a delicate balance between mutual trust and mutual suspicion, between disinterested sentiments of loyalty and self-interested calculation. The institutional checks on the honesty of officials must be confined to broad general checks: if there is not *some* trust the system becomes unworkable. In one region of Africa where cooperatives have suffered from official dishonesty, systems of minute checks have been planned. Cooperative officials had been known to steal half the content of a bag of fertilizer and substitute flour. A suggested solution was a system of seals on the fertilizer bags, plus a rule that cooperative officials should not open bags except in the presence of appointed delegates of the members. But are the delegates always going to insist on their rights to be present, even if the business of finding them when- ever a bag has to be opened leads to a frequent waste of time and even if their insistence will inevitably be interpreted as a vote of non-confidence in the manager? It is unlikely. The only workable kinds of check, the only tolerable forms of institutional- ized suspicion, are those which serve as periodic reminders of the sanctions against dishonesty and so help marginally to reinforce internalized sanctions, and marginally to reassure members who have a good deal of trust in their officials' honesty anyway. If there are *no* internalized sanctions inhibiting dishonesty, so that the chance of being caught out is the only deterrent, and if there is little or no trust on the part of members, little or no expecta- tion that officials ever *will* be honest,[17] then one can only say that the conditions for successful cooperation do not exist.

[17] There may also, of course, be no strong feeling that they *ought* to be honest. There are many societies where 'the strong should not take advan- tage of their weaker neighbours' would seem as a rather fatuous injunction. In such societies, if the economic pay-offs of cooperation are big enough to yield substantial benefits to a cooperative's members as well as to its officials—even though on a radically different scale—a cooperative can still manage to flourish without too much overt dissension, though not by the moralistic criteria used in this paper 'successful'. See, for example, the old

There is another aspect of the traditional community which still plays its part in the modern cooperative—the sense of group solidarity breeding the kind of loyalty that makes members willing to make some immediate personal sacrifices in the interests of the ultimate common good. The workers of Rochdale would never have formed their organization on the basis solely of a perceived coincidence of individual self-interest. The sense of class solidarity, of being fellow workers embattled in a hostile environment, was an essential element in their motives. Similarly, in the village cooperatives of Japan one frequently finds a high degree of loyalty to the village cooperative, members being willing, for instance, to give a day or two of voluntary labour to repair the cooperative buildings. But this is often divorced from any adherence to cooperative principles or any sense of common interest; it is an expression of village solidarity; it is 'their' cooperative and it should not be allowed to decline; 'their' cooperative should put up as good a show as their neighbours, on exactly the same level as they hope that 'their' baseball team will do as well as the next village's.[18]

The possibilities

These, then, are two elements of the traditional solidary community which need, in some measure, to be carried over into the modern cooperative—the sense of mutual trust between members, and the sense of loyalty to the group. The trick lies in retaining these elements while at the same time introducing the rationalized accounting methods which replace the loose reciprocity of gift exchanges by a strict apportionment of benefits to contributions, and (even more difficult) the devices of institutionalized suspicion which prevent the abuse of leadership powers. The trick is an immensely difficult one for the reasons noted. Not many marriages

---

Victoria Cooperative Federation described in John Saul's paper in the companion volume. Some writers would find in such cases further evidence for the view of the 'functionality' of corruption in developing countries. While this seems to me misguided as a general thesis, one can agree that there are societies where norms of public probity are so little developed that the only choice lies between having a corrupt cooperative or having none at all. And it may well be that the former is the better choice if one is concerned to promote economic development. But this is not to say that economic development would not be *more* rapidly promoted if norms of public probity *were* strongly institutionalized and internalized.

[18] R. P. Dore, *Land reform in Japan*, London, 1959, p. 291.

survive long after the wife starts insisting, for instance, that the husband should never break the seal of his wage packet except in her presence.

But this is not to say that the trick is impossible. Some marriages do survive the accepted institutionalization of suspicion, however contrary that may seem to the canons of affective personal relations, most particularly when both partners realize that their prospects outside their present marriage are grim. It is perhaps the same kind of circumstances which account for the fact that the trick has been managed in Japan. There cooperatives of a modern type have been built—and built successfully—on the basis of what, a hundred years ago, were traditional communities. The new accounting systems and auditing systems and systems of electing officers have been introduced according to models set by the central government, and by and large they work as intended. They were not introduced without friction, occasional charges of favouritism and corruption, factional and personal quarrels. But these were kept within bounds, largely perhaps because divorce was impossible. In the tight structure of Japanese agriculture, there was nowhere else to go; farming which depended on irrigation depended, *ipso facto*, on cooperation. If cooperation ceased, the water ceased to flow, the rice ceased to grow and people starved.[19]

If there were, thus, strong negative sanctions on disruption, there have also, in recent years, been strong positive sanctions on unity; agricultural cooperatives have been the only source of certain material advantages, since they were the channel of a good deal of government aid—credits, cheap supplies and preferential marketing arrangements.

And so we come back to our 'economic factors'. The transition from a traditional community to a modern associational cooperative is a difficult one, but it might be managed if the balance of material advantage derived from cooperation is favourable enough—if the losses to be expected if people stopped cooperating, or the gains to be anticipated if they cooperated more, are great enough. Sensibly, Clauson suggests that the best prospects

[19] It must also be said that Japanese rural communities did not start, a hundred years ago, from quite the same level of unsophisticated family-like community bonds as are common in many parts of the modern world. The organization of irrigation, for instance, was highly rationalized on a basis of fairly strict equation of contribution and benefits, and even literacy was fairly common.

for agricultural development in Africa lie in those areas where the existing communal tenures can be utilized to introduce immediate and effective mechanized farming.[20] It needs to be stressed, however, that the material advantages of these new departures need to be quick and obvious, and this has not always been the case in the group farming schemes of Africa.

We may sum up the foregoing arguments as follows. There are several reasons for doubting the likelihood that the solidary nature of traditional communities, united by family-like bonds and often holding land in common, can help to create new cooperative or collective farms of a modern type. In the first place, many of the traditional communities are not so solidary. Second, they often have a highly authoritarian structure which militates against any kind of development, and the solidarity and authoritarianism are inextricably linked and cannot be separated. Third, even if traditional communities are solidary and egalitarian it is difficult for them to take on the formal institutions of modern cooperatives, such as rational auditing and control over managers, without destroying the very bonds of solidarity and mutual trust which are supposed to be their advantage.

This still does not answer the question with which we started, however. Is the traditional, solidary, perhaps communally land-owning community *better* placed to develop cooperatives than more atomized collections of individuals? The answer is that it may face worse difficulties. But if the balance of material advantage from cooperation is sufficiently great, and if the other norms and values of the society (time discounts, evaluation of truthfulness, etc.) are sufficiently favourable to enable it to survive the difficult transitional period, it may emerge with a stronger and more efficient organization than a cooperative which did not start from a similar traditional base line.

[20] Op. cit., p. 56.

J. Leonard Joy The analysis of existing social factors favourable to successful modern cooperatives

It has been suggested that it would be valuable to explore generalizations about social factors which would tend to promote the
success of modern cooperatives. Were we able to state that, in
general, such and such an existing social pattern or characteristic
was conducive to success in cooperation, then, it is argued, those
responsible for promoting cooperatives would be guided as to
where to direct their efforts. I think there is some merit in this
argument and I would support attempts to explore such generalizations but I would not encourage researchers to spend much
time on the matter for two reasons: as a scientific activity I would
regard it as incidental to and deriving from much more fundamental and profitable analysis; as an aid to policy-makers it is
likely to produce results of very limited value.

Let us consider first the value of possible generalizations on this
subject to those responsible either for policy regarding the promotion of modern cooperatives or for the design and oversight of
cooperative projects. On questions of policy, let us ask how the
sorts of generalizations under discussion would offer guidance.
Would they help guide the attention of government cooperative
departments towards, for example, societies that were traditionally strongly solidary? Or only those that were also egalitarian?
Or, alternatively, authoritarian? Would administrators be warned
to avoid (or perhaps to seek out), say, situations where potential
cooperators would be drawn from diverse societies? Presumably
the generalizations that are being sought are broadly of this
nature. It is conceivable that such generalizations could be found
which so clearly predicted success for some situations or failure
for others that policy-makers would at least be able to avoid
inevitably abortive schemes. This would indeed be a great gain,
for there is no doubt that the cost of failed schemes has been
high. It is to be questioned, however, how far past failures have
been due to promoting cooperation in inappropriate social en-

vironments and how far they have been due rather to a failure to understand how to design and manage cooperative enterprises in ways which recognize the significance of social—and for that matter technical and economic—factors in particular situations. Be that as it may, if generalizations are to be useful they must relate to clearly identifiable situations. It is necessary that policy-makers can be guided to identify solidary, authoritarian, egalitarian or whatever characteristics so that they can say unambiguously, and as a matter of policy, that cooperatives will not be promoted in such situations.

But is it possible to set down criteria by which the relevant characteristics can be identified? There are two questions here: first, whether or not there are clear diagnostic tests which will locate a social situation under the relevant heading of a typology (does it matter how solidary and in what way? how egalitarian and in what way?); second, whether or not the significance of social characteristics is dependent on the type of cooperative in question (marketing or processing or production? perennial crops or annual crops or beef cattle or dairy cattle or fish? etc. etc.). As a hunch, it is suggested that the number of dimensions by which situations need to be defined is so large that, even if a typology were to be elaborated, the degree of sophistication required to apply it might make it of little practical value—or to be such as to require for its application the services of at least a professional sociologist.

I would argue, however, that we should discourage policy-makers from asking where they can best promote cooperatives and encourage them to ask instead what form of organization is—for particular schemes of banana marketing, irrigation, settlement, grazing control or tobacco growing—most likely to achieve policy objectives. It is true, of course, that cooperation is frequently advocated for its own sake. In Tanzania, for example, cooperatives are seen as alternatives to private capitalist enterprise, to be promoted because they are thought to encourage desired attitudes by individuals to one another. However, the objective of changing (or reinforcing) inter-personal attitudes imposes extra, rather than different, criteria of success, for business efficiency criteria will still need to be met. If cooperatives cannot succeed, or if they can succeed only for a period, or only in the business sense and without securing the attitudes desired, then other forms of business might be required and new approaches to the encouragement of desired inter-personal attitudes must be sought.

What is required, therefore, is not so much guides to policy as to where to promote cooperative enterprise, but, rather, guides to those attempting to promote economic activity as to how to analyse the organizational alternatives and to select, design or promote the patterns desired. Thus in appraising, for example, the possibilities of irrigation development it will be necessary to have a view of the structure of socioeconomic organization envisaged: what pattern of ownership and control of land, water and other resources; how costs and returns are to be allocated and so on. In designing an organizational structure the answers to such questions need to be given not simply in relation to policy objectives but also in relation to the outcome to be expected from adopting alternative solutions. Thus designers will need to know not only the choice of organizational structures open to them but also how the effectiveness of their operation will relate to technological, economic and social factors. It would normally prove to be relatively straightforward to calculate the costs of different capital works appropriate to different types of irrigation scheme—independent smallholders, 'disciplined' smallholders (receiving water only when it is supplied to them and having to plant prescribed crops on prescribed dates), 'group farms', or a 'State farm'; it may be relatively easy to forecast management practices, crop patterns and water requirements for such different organizational patterns; what we need to know is how these organizational patterns should relate to the social characteristics of the people involved. Is it possible, for example, to envisage smallholders organized in groups sharing sprinkler equipment? Could they, must they, be left to design their own system for controlling its use and, say, the transfer of individuals' property rights in the communally owned equipment? Should marketing be envisaged on a small-group basis or should it be organized centrally for the whole irrigation settlement? One could go on listing such questions that scheme designs would need to face. What is clear is that the issue is less one of whether or not there is a social predisposition to cooperation and more one of what structure of organization, even what structure of cooperative organization, is the one to aim for.

If this is the issue, then what is required is guidance to those trying to raise incomes by promoting improved marketing and production in how to identify alternative patterns of organizational structure relevant for consideration in particular situations. Guidance is also required in the sequence of questions that needs to be asked by them in designing structures and procedures for the control of resources and the allocation of costs and returns to suit both the product and technology and the people—their culture and their skills. What we need is an improved understanding of social organization and processes and the way in which these relate to economy and technology. The challenge to the social sciences is enormous. My own view is that, while one should properly search for generalizations, these are most likely to be found by seeking improved understanding of particular case studies. What we must seek is a capacity to predict, and as we improve our capacity to predict for particular situations so we shall improve our understanding of the factors which govern the range of situations for which we can predict and of the characteristics which define these situations. We should then proceed to analyse adjacent sets of situations analytically, to determine how to allow for those differences which significantly distinguish the sets for which we cannot predict from those for which we can.

It seems worth asking under what conditions an attempt to construct, at this stage, a typology of situations from which to derive generalizations might be successful. An analysis of the cases studied (of attempted cooperation) in order to define such a typology would need to compromise between being too simple and being too sophisticated. One might attempt to find simple criteria for identifying postulated key factors predisposing to success (solidary–non solidary; authoritarian–egalitarian) and defining these so as to ease classification, and crudely testing whether or not success or failure could be strongly associated with one or more categories thus simply defined. This might give results— though Dore's paper suggests that we should expect them to need considerable qualification, and, taken with the above arguments, also suggests that a much more elaborate classification would be necessary. Ultimately, this could be very elaborate. One might need to identify the initial (pre-cooperative) state in social, technological and economic terms; key features of the economics of the business on which the cooperative was to be centred including the product/operation (e.g. tobacco growing) and the technology involved; the size and composition of the cooperating group in relation to the society from which it was drawn; who initiated proposals for cooperation; the nature of the relation of the cooperative to government; the structure of cooperative authority in relation to traditional authority; the attempted pattern of decision-making and asset control; the nature of conflicts of interests between individuals in the cooperative with regard to alternative policies of the cooperative; differences in the gains accruing to different people from cooperative membership and so on. An attempt to build a typology on these lines would be enormously complex. The simplest possible version using the above headings would produce tens of thousands of categories. There would be many 'empty boxes'—in part because some combinations are unlikely (though some pretty unlikely things have been tried), and in part because many more cases would need to be studied for the boxes to be filled. Because of this I am sceptical about the value of studying cooperatives by classifying them in order to derive thereby generalizations about conditions predisposing to cooperative success.

In the last resort what we want to know is *why* certain results are to be expected, given an initial state and a sequence of actions and what is significant about the initial state and the sequence of actions for the prediction of outcomes. An attempt to build a typology would have the merit of making explicit those assumptions that are made about what is significant and lead us to asking why. I should like to see sociologists working with economists on the *design* of cooperative projects. I believe that a sustained attempt to cumulate knowledge by this means would be very productive. It would, of course, lead those concerned every now and again to see whether, on the problem that concerned them, generalizations were possible from previous experience. It would also, I believe, lead to a healthy appreciation of the limitations of such generalizations for prescription and an increased concern to use them to suggest hypotheses for an understanding of how social systems work.

Raymond Apthorpe[1] **Some evaluation problems for cooperative studies, with special reference to primary cooperatives in highland Kenya**

The discussion that follows aims to convey something of the enormity of the problem of any 'evaluation', in the sense of 'project evaluation', of only one aspect of just the economic performance of a rural development scheme with implications for social structural or institutional change. The case for study comes from the Million Acres scheme in highland Kenya.[2] This scheme as a whole has unusually vast fiscal, administrative, economic, infrastructural, political and social dimensions, not even to mention its primary agricultural and technological objectives. It was from the beginning, however, both officially and popularly predicted in Kenya (by everyone except the plot-holders) that the economic output as well as other aspects of the Million Acres would succeed or fail according to whether the primary cooperatives that were to be responsible for much of the day to day business would succeed or fail.

The development philosophies or general theories which government policies or assessments of policies in Eastern Africa commonly invoke to evaluate different or the same aspects of the performance of agricultural (and other) cooperatives vary in different circumstances. But two themes recur and recur. One, the

[1] Currently Project Director at UNRISD, Geneva, of a series of studies of rural institutions and planned social change in North, Western and Eastern Africa. The present essay comprises some reflections on the writer's own work in Eastern Africa in 1964–8. He is indebted for many discussions on the problems of the Kenya 'Million Acres' scheme in particular to Brian van Arkadie, John MacArthur and William Omamo, with whom he carried out a joint enquiry into the problem in 1966 for the governments of Kenya and the United Kingdom. The present essay is part of a study extending to Tunisia, Senegal, Ghana, Cameroun and Gambia as well as the countries of Eastern Africa.

[2] No attempt will be made here to review or cite the extensive bibliography on this scheme. The most comprehensive selection of references is in Robert Chambers, *Settlement schemes in tropical Africa*, Routledge & Kegan Paul, London, 1969.

'social values theory of development', as I have called it else-where,[3] puts the blame when things go wrong on socially and culturally-based obstructive, destructive or indifferent motivations or attitudes. The spate of government enquiries into cooperatives as well as other studies very often invoke this theory, now as in the colonial period, to argue that the overall record thus far has not been a very successful one. Another point of view attributes what success there has been to the technical qualities of the officials or committee members, etc., who planned, managed or administered it. This is the well known development adminis-tration theory. Certainly these are not the only two points of view adopted by economic development planners or the informed pub-lic generally, where such public opinion can be said to exist or to express itself in a low-income country. Moreover, I have put them here only in crude terms reduced to bare essentials. None-theless, they are two very pervasive themes and, with the proviso that they manifest themselves in subtle as well as simple formu-lations, they provide us with a rudimentary framework for one aspect to be explored in the following case study as this is socially current and acted upon in the country concerned.

The pyrethrum problem

Soon after the introduction of marketing cooperatives as part of the Million Acres land settlement programme, evaluation was called for. It seemed that in several respects the programme and its cooperatives were not achieving the performance their plan-ners had anticipated of them. Unfortunately, it is rare for evalua-tions to be sought at less pessimistic moments. This gloomy starting point itself goes some way to explain why so many development studies focus on supposed failures and not recognized successes. Furthermore, it is usually only economic problems that are singled out even for social analysis in development studies, and even when someone has in advance defined the nature of solution to them as something to be sought in, say, some form of social plan-ning. Most studies of cooperatives are no exception to this general rule. Despite the various kinds of social, political, ideological or even spiritual purpose for which they may originally have been set up in addition to the economic considerations of production

[3] Cf. the writer's 'Two planning theories of economic development' in *Public policy and agricultural development in East Africa*, ed. E. A. Brett, Frank Cass, London, and East Africa Publishing House, Nairobi, 1970.

and sometimes of distribution as well, it is specifically their economic performance, when it is on the downward curve, that tends
to come up for 'evaluation'. In effect, this gives an economicist slant
to development studies whether they are carried out by economists or not. It is a bias that is given in the terms of reference.
This in itself leads to curiosities of analysis that, in the context of
one or another single social science discipline, not consciously
given to 'interdisciplinary' development studies (yet concerned
with development and planning all the same), would give rise to
doubts and frowns if not sheer gaping disbelief.[4]

It is a fall in the output of pyrethrum that I wish to discuss
here. I have somewhat dramatized this case for the expository
purposes it is to serve here, though it is factual in its essentials
even if the statistical dimensions of these have not been established and the material is incomplete in other ways. In a wider
view, however, even the pyrethrum story itself in the land settlement schemes, as it continued after the survey on which this note
is based, is more of a success than a failure however measured
and for whatever reason. This appears to be true of the entire
Million Acres project. The particular aspect of it isolated for discussion here should not lead the opposite to be assumed. The
drop in production followed *uhuru* and the decolonization of the
Kenya highlands, which had been reserved for white settlement
only for nearly two generations. Kenya being among the largest
world producers of this raw material for insecticides, central economic planners were quick to find that this shortfall posed a
serious problem. As in many other cases a 'problem', albeit an
economic one, was identified not so much because of its implications for the immediate casualties, namely the people who actually
derived their livelihood from the production of the crop in question. Overriding this was concern with that abstraction, 'the
national economy'. In this particular instance, world as well as
national economy was threatened, given the Kenya share in the
world volume of pyrethrum (but within the lesser global constraints due to artificial insecticide raw material substitutes). This
was interpreted as making the matter all the more urgent and
critical, again according to the abstract conceptualization preferred by the development planning concerned.

---

[4] Cf. the writer's 'Development studies and social planning' in Raymond
Apthorpe, Nicholas Bennett *et al.*, *People, planning and development
studies*, Frank Cass, London, 1970.

To account for this, several 'general theories' were fashionable in Kenya in the mid-1960s—among several planners, that is, not the farmers themselves. The status of these 'theories' was, for the greater part, not that of assessments of scientific information derived from an analytical study of the particular circumstances and situations involved. These 'theories' were more like those factors in the culture and social structure that planners and others find among farmers or peasants. As such, certainly they must be included within the scope of any analysis which aims to take 'the human factor' into account. There is no reason to confine this latter, however inaptly characterized it may be and often is, only to the receiving end of central planning.[5] Any evaluation of a rural (or, for that matter, an urban) development project must concern itself *both* with the circumstances themselves locally judged to be problematic *and* with the assumptions and theories which put them into this category.

First of all, in Kenya in the later middle 1960s this economic problem of pyrethrum production, or rather the lack of it, was put down in general terms to the political situation. Formerly under the regime of European settlerdom, there had recently been a transfer of power in Kenya following independence. It was widely believed at and shortly after that time, among both African and European planners[6]—and no doubt with an understandable measure of realism, given the circumstances especially of Mau Mau and the recent history of the country, which was understood then more in political than in agrarian terms—that a wide range of disasters were bound to follow independence. Of these the fall in pyrethrum output was but merely one instance. Indeed, according to one account the very inception of the Million Acres scheme was as a device to minimize the risk of possibly grave security problems given the political sensitivity to the highlands' white settlement. If this is so, then a care-and-maintenance or a containment approach was more important in the beginning than development goals as such and early planning (which in any case was done very hurriedly) must not be judged too harshly or on wrong grounds.

Specifically, in the highlands the colonial regime was a European settlerdom characterized by large-scale land holdings and

[5] Cf. the writer's 'Rural development planning and "the human factor" in Africa' in *People, planning and development studies,* op. cit.

[6] 'Planners' here as elsewhere in this note refers to a professional category of 'manpower', unqualified ethnically.

extensive farming operations. Independence had led to the re-placement of this pattern with one based on intensive land utilization by African smallholdings. The scatter of primary mar-keting societies was instituted for the benefit of these small farms. It was widely believed, if for the wrong reasons, that inevitably the problems of Kenyan agriculture would be particularly acute in this time of political transition and that, given the importance of the highland region in the overall agricultural and political scene, this would be the part of the country most affected.

Second, it was also *à la mode* at the time to take it for granted that, in any event, the solution for the country's development problems lay not in the rural sector at all, but in any prospects for industrialization and urbanization. No less suddenly than it had appeared and had become fashionable three or four years earlier, this particular belief had disappeared in Eastern Africa almost altogether by 1967. But it dominated many points of view in planning in 1965 particularly. It was a general assumption about African economic development that was applied to labour and labour considerations as follows. For agricultural productivity it was held that much hard work, skill and self-discipline were required, qualities that planistrators[7] tend to believe are not readily found among peasants. Indeed, very largely the former self-defined themselves in opposition to the latter precisely on the basis of grounds such as these. In the setting of industrial enter-prise it was planned that 'discipline' should and could be effec-tively enforced corporately from above, and that unskilled and part-time labour would do. Thus the social obstacles that 'eco-nomic development' would allegedly encounter in 'tradition' could be controlled adequately—again according to the extremist interpretation of the theory of the centrally planned economy fashionable at that time. Irrigation schemes in the rural areas were believed to form a class of development projects apart from others in so far as both the social and technical problems they posed were seen to be amenable to direction and control from above.[8] The reasons why cooperatives are *not* integral to irrigation schemes as planned in Kenya is a subject for discussion in itself.

---

[7] Planners-cum-administrators, administrators-cum-planners. Cf. the writer's 'Peasants and planistrators in Eastern Africa', *The Bulletin of the Institute of Development Studies*, vol. 1, No. 3, February 1969.

[8] See, for example, E. G. Giglioli, 'Mechanical cultivation of rice on the Murea irrigation settlement', *East African Agricultural and Forestry Journal*, January 1965. I am indebted to R. J. Chambers for this reference.

They show how one must be wary of generalizations about 'rural development' unqualified on the basis of technological (as well as other) aspects. But this will be taken for granted here.

It was added as a kind of modification of this general labour theory that while perhaps there was some evidence to the effect that African women in the fields (and, according to the stereotype, especially Kikuyu women) might work harder than African men, this was true only for subsistence or domestic purposes and not in the context of the money economy. This particular line of argument, however, was also peculiarly inapposite when applied to the pyrethrum problem, as will also be pointed out in a moment.

Third, there was a more subtle and technocratic explanation.[9] It was reckoned that social as well as economic and all other kinds of progress necessarily 'went with' progressive economies of scale. Large-scale organization was supposed to be somehow inherently less counter-productive than smaller-scale organization, especially for production but for marketing as well. The Kenya highlands had seen a reversal of this trend that was believed to go against the grain of economic progress. It was only 'inevitable', therefore, the explanation went, that output would fall. Not only were the land resettlement schemes and cooperatives but a political expedient and running headlong into socio-cultural obstacles but 'evolution' was against them too.

On investigation the matter appeared very differently indeed. Really none of the accounts given above could be found to explain very much. What proved to have happened was, essentially, that organizational change in the form of the introduction of a cooperative had severely and adversely affected the marketing and pricing of the crop. In particular, the labour input in pyrethrum production had, so to put it, been alienated from the customary commensurate return. Before this change the growers, who were predominantly women,[10] had taken the dried flowers direct to the Board. They had been paid immediately, accordingly and directly, without deductions or delays. Under the new system of marketing through the cooperative, payouts were made only

[9] That even found expression in the first of a two-volume work on planning and development in Kenya, Uganda and Tanzania in a passage on the Kenya land decolonization schemes. A. Meister, *L'Afrique peut-elle partir? Changement social et développement en Afrique orientale*, Editions du Seuil, Paris, 1966.

[10] On this point, which is certainly in need of statistical verification, at present no data are available.

to the members of the cooperative society—the plot-holders—who were men in most cases. Only the plot-holder members were entitled to an account at the society. And in any event, when finally the pay-out was made, this was only after a period of delay and with deductions for the running of the cooperative and other expenses. The cultivation in the fields, and the drying of the pyrethrum flowers, continued as before to be very largely carried out by women, the wives. But now it was their husbands who received the returns—deductions—on their labour, not themselves. It was reported that in their own estimation what the wives received from their husbands was too little to make it materially sufficiently worth their while to continue to labour for long hours. So, rationally and realistically in the circumstances, their output fell.

Some wider implications

Several points arise for any rural development project evaluation from this particular case, which has now been described sufficiently for present purposes.

First, the change in productive performance was not due to any qualitative change in the labour force. Indeed, no change occurred on the labour front at all in the sense that for the most part the same people worked in the fields as before (but there are no reliable statistics on the population changes brought about by the settlement programme). Too many theories about productivity and cooperatives in relation to this focus exclusively on labour and its qualities virtually to the exclusion of other factors and always in the broadest of terms. Too few take account in any systematic way of either the special circumstances of the product or those of its market and marketing facilities as understood by (*a*) the peasants and (*b*) the planistrators or analyse the various differences and any similarities there may be between these two viewpoints. Very few, if any, recognize anything like the full plurality of causes—and functions. The older social science studies on Africa that sought to relate labour productivity to single-factor causes such as its residential stability are examples of a very narrow approach. Certainly it would have no practical meaning to plan even for the very limited objective of labour productivity without reference to particular forms and bases of leadership, given and possible communications methods and organizational skills, and stated marketing conditions. Similarly, it is completely unrealistic to appeal to 'cooperation' as a kind of social magic regardless of everything else, to bring about economic or social change.

Marketing considerations are overlooked so regularly in development projects that are laid down in the context of a highly centrally planned economy that this cannot be just written off as just an error in planning, due to chance. Partly, no doubt, this systematic omission relates to the innocence of most planistrators in Africa of commercial experience of their own—other than with reference to their own wage careers in another sector altogether. But more important may be the posing of a policy dilemma at the outset as necessarily involving a crucial choice between the market economy and the planned economy. In going completely for the latter, according to socialist principles in various interpretations of these, the former seems to get left out of the picture altogether.

Specifically, with regard to marketing cooperatives there are instances (though they are not discussed in this brief analysis) which cannot bear any other interpretation but the view that the cooperative principle appealed to (*a*) is virtually a substitute for even thinking about marketing facilities, for a contribution to the expensive provision of which central planning ought not to evade responsibility, (*b*) is more directed to a management or human relations theory of production in which the market and marketing in any case is given little, if any, place altogether. Marketing was left to the same magic that was to produce the instant harmony and consensus of interests and leadership that cooperation itself, it was hoped, was to represent.

Second, the assumption recurs—and recurs in development planning for rural areas especially—that there is, necessarily, some peculiar and inherent relationship between land, and thence land reform, and agricultural and rural change. Oddly, perhaps not so oddly if the matter is not seen in isolation from rural planning as just described, urban land and land values may be left out of account altogether in urban development planning.[11] Certainly, land questions *may* and sometimes do figure very prominently in problems of rural society and its reorganization. This has led to generalizations about land as a factor of productivity being not less vague than those about labour which were referred to above. Usually they too blandly ignore situational exigencies such as

[11] I owe this observation on urban planning to Jean-Michel Collette.

local scarcities or specialized use. There was a strong tendency, especially among the social anthropological African studies in the 1950s, which are still very prominent, to regard land in 'traditional' or 'tribal' society as subject to control simply by the political body corporate.[12] Yet the social facts are different (although they will not be discussed here). Depending on circumstances and intentions, land may be treated diplomatically, religiously, economically or domestically as well as politically, regardless of however traditional or traditionalist the obtaining social system may be by one standard or another. The social structures and organizations of authority involved in these different contexts simply cannot all be reduced one to another as if they were all the same or always dominated by a single one of them.

While it would of course be absurd to deny the relevance of certain soil and ecological circumstances for the cultivation of tender plants with special requirements, it is neither logically nor empirically the case, excluding gravitational theory, that because a farm or a cooperative is on the land it necessarily depends on it very characteristically in a peculiarly significant way contrasted with all other kinds of human organization. Organizational and marketing factors might far outweigh any questions pertaining to land use, land ownership, or land exchange in certain regards. This is the case in the material under discussion here. Most enterprises on the ground, and even an aeroplane in flight, require some sort of ground contact. Clearly, a farm or any other social organization in a rural area is no exception to this. But it is not necessarily a special case either.

Third, a problem for that abstraction a 'national economy' is also a problem for a number of individuals and groups. As such its solution is not to be found in isolation from the groups and individuals who are immediately affected. The pyrethrum case, sketchily presented above though it has been, illustrates price/reward/return responsiveness on the part of, here, especially women farmers. Such price responsiveness on the part of the intended beneficiaries of plans tends so often to be systematically under-estimated by the central planners. What they, the planners, assume the more significant factors to be in social behaviour in

[12] Instances of this in the East African studies by the authorities in those years, such as Max Gluckman and Thomas Fallers, contrast strikingly with the work that in fact derives from approximately the same period by, for example, Charles White.

what they term 'peasantries' are socio-cultural factors. In Eastern
Africa the outstanding example of such a line of reasoning is
comprised in 'the cattle complex', a complex about cattle that
belongs as much if not more to the society and culture of the
planistrators as it does to the peasants. As many of the cooperatives in the Million Acres project are dairying concerns, it will be
of particular as well as general interest to discuss this for a
moment.

The cattle complex was a phenomenon in the colonial period as
familiar to social science as to administration and planning. It
amounted to a theory that people would not sell their cattle because they loved them too dearly, because their religious, symbolic or aesthetic value was greater by far than any price that
could be put on them. Economic under-development in the region
concerned was quite categorically put down to 'the cattle complex', which was explained as some kind of alternative to, or
substitute for, 'market behaviour'. It is to be noted that seldom
was the economic importance of husbandry given its due in the
plethora of cultural affirmations made about it. Also, the economic
under-development that it was supposed to account for was
seldom described in any detail. If it had been it would have
become perfectly clear that in many contexts, and for many
people, cattle spelled wealth rather than poverty. Owing to the
system of intersecting rights of ownership, few cattle were owned
(or used or disposable) by individuals and individuals alone. Many
people enjoyed rights of various kinds in the same animal.

Now, it was and continues to be perfectly true that in societies
in Eastern Africa where animal husbandry affords the principal
mode of livelihood, cattle represent social as well as many other
kinds of value. So does land in societies based on cultivation and
sedentary residence. Why were animal husbandry and the nomadic
or migratory way of life that went with it in East Africa vested
with so much cultural peculiarity as seen by planners, administrators and others? I think the answer must be that the Masai, the
Gogo, the Turkana, the Suk and many others followed a way of life
so apparently alien to the experience of those who observed it
superficially from a distance that the latter believed they had no
alternative but to put it into the realm of mystery and exoticism.
The parallel with land in land-based societies that it would have
been more apposite to make with cattle and cattle-based was,
simply, overlooked. It was too familiar.

Land has for long entered into various kinds of transaction in

Eastern Africa (cf. C. M. N. White) and cattle have too. The factors which influence the buying and selling in the market for cash of both land and cattle in their respective contexts, as described above, depend on a number of circumstances. One of these, in the case of cattle especially, is simply how near or far in terms of local communications the market is physically. What has been extremely well documented indeed—for example for Masai cattle sales (by Alan Jacobs)—is that, when the price is right, sales of cattle have increased steadily as the market facilities for selling them have increased, with buying points being extended deeper and deeper into Masai country. Where there is evidence of the existence of a 'cattle complex' of beliefs, certainly this may have some implications for 'market' behaviour. But primarily it relates more to other aspects of social structures which are concerned with often quite separate matters.

All this is not to say either that behaviour *like* optimizing behaviour is necessarily the same *as* optimizing behaviour,[13] or that peasants either do or should 'respond to the market' any more than anyone else does or should. Also—and the importance of this cannot be over-estimated, because it is so neglected in current development studies—'the market' is anything but a given. Its prices vary enormously, especially for agricultural products, given especially that the economic value of land and cattle outside the market is consistently high when a mode of life that is also outside the market (and inside subsistence, in the conventionally misleading terminology) heavily depends on them. Moreover— and it is another vital point—here again it is not production that is under-developed (although of course there is room always for new breeds, as for new seeds) so much as the distribution, marketing and advertising facilities to promote this. Perhaps it is a consequence of the administrative approach to economic development in the rural sector in much of Africa that the benefits of specialization, and advertising especially, from which industrial development gains so much, are seldom extended to agriculture to anything nearly like the same extent.

Fourth, our case shows that it is an interrelation between on the one hand 'traditional' social and cultural factors, husband–wife relationships, and on the other an 'organizational' policy decision, the introduction of cooperatives, that accounts for the

[13] Cf. Michael Lipton, 'The theory of the optimizing peasant', *Journal of Development Studies*, April 1968.

decline in output.[14] But while both are to be taken into account overall, more crucial was the policy decision from above that (a) introduced cooperatives and (b) limited membership in them to the plot-holders, who in most cases were men. The sex-based division of work and control over its proceeds was crucial here. A different organizational policy decision need not necessarily have broken the chain between labour and its reward that thus far had worked in the interests of output, not against them.

Again it is to be stressed that only a much more comprehensive analysis than is possible here could put all of the blame on to the introduction of cooperatives. And, clearly, it would be absurd to judge the whole idea and organization of a cooperative by only one detail, the limitation of membership in it to the plot-holders, although this and the delay in payments and deductions that was also mentioned above also have been very widely reported in cooperative studies from all parts of Africa. On the other hand, it is a general aim of 'the cooperative movement' to promote socialism and to inhibit social class formation, especially social class with a basis in landed property. It is to be specially recognized, therefore, that the effects of introducing a cooperative organization can be precisely to the contrary, when the functions of the cooperative are intended to be communal in orientation and to be based on maximum social participation, but when membership in the organization excludes, for instance, all hired labour and other people in the area whose occupations are not mainly agricultural. This may mean, as in this Kenyan case, that a large majority of the people in the areas concerned are excluded, while a new exclusive social authority is created and conferred on a small minority who may and probably do have outside interests in any case. Whether, even in a limited economic sense, the small or the smallest farmer does not gain from having to sell his crops to the cooperative compared with the prices the private buyer can or could offer is very much a matter open to doubt on the basis of the available evidence. But important though this is, it is not possible to enter the debate here. It is,

[14] Here, as elsewhere in this study, the contrast expressed in terms of 'traditional' v. 'organizational' is open to misunderstanding in that it relies not on technical terms but on words which have so many uses. It is *not* implied that the husband–wife relationship is *only* a traditional one in the sense that nothing has changed in it since time immemorial. And, to turn now to central policy decisions, in Africa it has indeed become traditional or customary for administrations to look to cooperatives for a solution to their problems, as is discussed elsewhere in this study.

in any event, not susceptible to an answer in general terms. Much will depend on the nature of the crop, e.g. whether it is easily stored or not, whether it is for home or overseas domestic consumption in its produced state or only after manufacture or processing, etc., etc.

Some further issues

In discussing briefly a single case study to bring into relief some aspects of the problem to 'evaluate' even the economic performance of cooperatives limited to questions of output, I have attempted to touch on several issues. Each of these would deserve further examination in itself. And there are several case studies we could draw upon in addition. Development studies as well as development planning are very familiar with the experience that the results even of research officially commissioned may not be acted upon by the authorities concerned. Sometimes this is because the case studies themselves are at fault, or have interpreted their terms of reference badly (e.g. too narrowly). Sometimes it is because the obstacles that policy aims to overcome lie more in the formulation of that policy itself than in 'the human factor' in the rural area concerned. There is another 'human factor' to be taken into account—in the staffing of the central planning office, and in the currents of popular or public opinion, which are very changeable, about what precisely *is* the problem to be worried about. Furthermore, in attempting to go as far beyond the details of the particular case that formed our starting point as possible for expository purposes, these have nevertheless been confined to the very narrow—if basic—criterion of one local economic aspect. Like many similar organizations for rural development in a broad sense, a cooperative may or may not act, in addition to its function as an economic organization, as: an agent of local government; a source and a disseminator of social services; a means—however limited—of social and perhaps limited political expression; or as a far-flung presence of the centre at the periphery of a country—as a link, that is to say, between the local and national levels, where it is possible to separate them.[15] These are only a few, if perhaps the most prevalent, of the possibilities along one dimension of the subject.

[15] Cf. the writer's 'Planned social change and land settlement' in *Land settlement and rural development in Eastern Africa*, Nkanga Editions 3, Kampala, 1968.

One of the many others would pertain to the context of the wider political economy of which cooperatives form only part. Are cooperatives—as was, for example, argued for Tunisia a few years ago (how much matters have changed there since!)— potentially so important that they could and perhaps should transform the whole state *vers une république coopérative*?[16] Or are the primary societies, if that is what are under review (secondary societies and higher unions of course present different problems again), merely atoms within but one sector of national affairs which may be confined to agriculture (or some of it) alone, and where the expansion of 'cooperative principles' to other sectors is not, perhaps certainly not, anticipated? Then again, many other aspects of the structure and organization of cooperatives as such must be taken into account in any relatively more complete evaluation, as well as the question of membership alone. Distinctions would have to be drawn, for example, as between production *v.* marketing cooperatives, compulsory *v.* voluntary membership, food crops *v.* manufacturing materials, cooperatives in new schemes rather than in long settled communities, etc., etc., etc.

Finally, reference must be made even in this brief account not to cooperatives but to the aims of 'the cooperative movement' as this is understood in government and social and economic development policy. Cooperatives are the outward expression of an economic religion in Eastern Africa, namely socialism, differently though this is understood in the four countries. As such, cooperatives acquire a kind of ideological, or theological, untouchability. They stand for a means that is also taken to be an end in itself, again, however differently either their propagators or participants (for they are not always the same people) interpret this. Conceived of as being greater than their parts, cooperatives defy being dismantled into them for purposes of analysis in the same way that a less ideologically charged organization can be broken down for study. For the faithful the worst that can happen is . . . a few heresies. For the faithless, cooperatives were non-starters in any event.

Putting the power of conviction of belief in agricultural cooperatives as agents for rural development in such religious and ideological terms shows just how deeply rooted it may be in present government policies in Eastern Africa at the present time. We would do badly to underrate this. This is, however, as prob-

[16] Moncef Guen, *La Coopération et l'Etat en Tunisie*, n.d. (1964).

ably in many countries where government priorities are heavily committed to central economic planning of the directive kind, not a conviction that may be shared to the same extent by both peasants and planistrators. Indeed, though it is not taken up here, at the local level there may be little knowledge of, or identification with, government objectives as stated in the officially promulgated principles of cooperative organizations. Study of this would take us into yet another aspect of the matter which may be vitally important (although on the Million Acres settlement scheme, subject to various qualifications which also have been discussed elsewhere, the level of identification with the cooperatives' objectives was relatively high). It is on the side of government policy that stated adherence to cooperatives' policies is exceptionally strong. At one level, certainly, it is more to the cooperatives than to the marketing boards (between which the nature of the connection varies considerably, however) that policy statements turn to more frequently within belief in an overall and more widely embracing administrative approach.

The far reaching implications of this latter cannot be too frequently alluded to in any Eastern African study at the present time. Private trade is often not in the hands of nationals—or, if it is, then sub-nationals—whose continued existence in the country is seen to represent remnants of the former colonial power (whether they are British nationals or not) and therefore to be politically suspect. The usual argument about private trade is that this works to the benefit of that historically[17] privileged mercantile class only by means of the special detriment of the small individual grower looking for good market prices for his crops. It is not only in Eastern Africa that ideologically 'the cooperative movement' is directed less against class and capital than against caste and commerce. The capitalist use by the members of cooperatives' revenue, accordingly, would not necessarily be regarded as a contradiction of cooperativism here as it may be elsewhere in the world.

In cooperative policy, as in many other respects, the trend is for Tanzania and Zambia to march side by side. Cooperative

[17] 'Historically', not 'racially', privileged. The anti-Asian policies the world now associates with all the Eastern African governments (if the reaction of the Tanzanian government to the economic survey of small trade made in that country by the *Economist* Intelligence Unit in the early 1960s before the development of cooperatives is remembered) are to be seen more in a historical than in an ethnic context.

principles are interpreted in those two countries as being central
to all sectors, not only the agricultural (in Zambia recently there
has been some discussion of possible cooperativization of mining
to some extent).[18] In Tanzanian planning, especially, policies
complementary to cooperatives in agriculture have been applied
in the name of the same purposes and principles in other sectors.
Indeed, Tanzania stands out, along with Guinea, perhaps from
all Africa in the emphasis put there on structural change as a
necessity for economic development, based though this is on an
ideological image of what 'traditional African society' is supposed
to be or to have been. In Uganda the private sector in agriculture,
as in industry, has showed viability of its own, and on the whole
government policy does not heavily discourage this. Much, however, is anomalous and in transition in Uganda at the present
time, and it would be difficult to find any other very convincing
single formula.[19] The political culture of Kenya is different again.
To the extent that 'organizational rationality' is one of its watch-
words and relatively more emphasis is put on this than on
structural change, the material discussed above may be very
apposite for that country.

[18] I am indebted to David Phiri for this observation. For a change in
policy in Zambia from production to service cooperative of various kinds,
see President Kaunda's speech of 12 January 1970. I am indebted to
Stephen Lombard for this reference.

[19] The allusion here is specifically to the time at the turn of the year
1969–70 which saw the politics of *The common man's charter* by A. Milton
Obote (published in October 1969), which is greatly concerned with a class
owing its privilege to wealth in the private sector.

Dov Weintraub **Rural cooperation, local government and social structure: a comparative study of village organization in different types of community in Israel[1]**

As is perhaps well known, the Jewish community in Palestine created and developed its own highly characteristic forms of rural organization, including several varieties of both the collective and the cooperative village. These basic patterns, however, were founded and developed by organized pioneering nuclei, ideologically oriented and socially highly integrated; and their problems, experience and achievements—much as they are significant for rural cooperation in general—seem thus only remotely relevant to the particular issues with which the present volume is concerned. Of greater interest to it are rather those rural communities in Israel in which cooperation has been introduced externally, and into a non-selective and insufficiently prepared population, and this paper will therefore devote itself to the analysis of recently established villages of the smallholders' cooperative type (the so-called *moshavim*; singular *moshav*), peopled exclusively by newcomers within a mass immigration and a mass settlement scheme. Owing to limitations of space, however, we shall examine in this context chiefly the relationship between cooperative organization and community structure, to the exclusion of other, no less important, factors—such as household structure, level of agricultural technology and individual orientations and motivation.[2] For the same reason we also confine ourselves primarily to the initial confrontation with or adjustment to the rural cooperative, or what may be called the stage of 'cooperative initiation' (covering in our study a period of roughly up to ten years from establishment); while further processes of consolidation and development, and factors which promote or

[1] This paper is based on a larger study by the author of new settlements in Israel, published under the title *Immigration and social change* by Manchester University Press and Israel Universities Press, 1971.

[2] For data on these aspects of the cooperative village, see D. Weintraub, *Immigration and social change*, chapters 1, 2 and 5 respectively.

impede modernization in general are mentioned only in passing towards the end.

A *moshav* is primarily a multi-purpose cooperative society with limited liability, established to promote farming as the sole occupation and source of living of its members. The nuclear family is the basic social and economic unit, but the various households—of which there are on the average seventy in a village—are closely bound together by mutual solidarity and aid, as well as by common agricultural, financial, supply, marketing and other services. The village economy differs from place to place, according to general economic considerations and local conditions (there being five basic farm types); in each *moshav*, however, an equitable division of the means of production (chiefly in respect of the size and quality of plots, water resources and capitalization) is maintained. There is also little differentiation between the target economies of the various villages themselves, all farm types being constructed so as to require a generally similar capital and manpower input, and to provide a like level of income.

Besides being an agricultural cooperative and upholding a specific way of life, the *moshav* constitutes also a unit of local government with municipal duties. The authority over this and the cooperative function is alike vested in the general assembly of the adult members, which decides upon matters of principle and lays down the general policy. The implementation of this policy is entrusted to the village council, assisted by various elected committees and a salaried administrative and professional staff. The council is chosen by the assembly in free, secret and universal elections. The two constitute, in fact, the executive and the legislative body respectively; and their separation, together with the principle of democratic representation and responsibility, are an integral part of the *Moshav* Movement's value system and constitution.

The *moshav* type of village was originally created in 1921, and by the time of the establishment of the State of Israel there were fifty-eight settlements of this type. After independence, this pattern became a major vehicle both of rural development and of immigrant absorption, and during the following years more than 270 units of this kind were established and settled with new immigrants.[3]

[3] For historical details see D. Weintraub, M. Lissak and Y. Atzmon,

As may be seen from this thumbnail sketch, a village of the *moshav* type is meant to operate a comprehensive multi-purpose cooperative framework, and to maintain a system of local government charged with the provision of modern municipal services and patterned on the 'Westminster' type of democracy. The question discussed here is thus what happens when such a distinct organizational form is superimposed upon a variety of populations and groups with different social traditions and structure.

The discussion falls into three parts. First, the normative pattern or the 'blueprint' of *moshav* organization is more systematically examined. Then the actual organizational behaviour observed in the different communities studied[4] is documented and analysed, in reference to the 'ideal type'. Finally, some general conclusions are suggested.

The organizational blueprint of the moshav

Figure 1 maps out the various tasks which form the *moshav* fabric and pinpoints their organizational locus;[5] the administrative hierarchy is then graphically presented in Fig. 2. As may be seen from these data (although most readers will probably omit the frightfully elaborate and complex list, and rely on our work),

Moshava, kibbutz, moshav: Jewish rural settlements in Palestine, Cornell University Press, Ithaca, 1969.

[4] The material included here was obtained within the first phase of the above-mentioned study (see note 1), carried out in the years 1959–62. In this phase a sample of eleven new immigrant *moshavim* was examined:

Code name of village	Origin	District	Year of establishment	Type of farm
Savel	Yemen	Lakhish	1950	Field crops
Te'ena	Persia	Lakhish	1950	Mixed dairy
Ta'amon	Central Europe	Central	1949	Dairy
Resissim	Mixed *	Jerusalem	1948	Dairy
Levanon	Yemen	Jerusalem	1949	Mountain–mixed
Azor	Yemen	Jerusalem	1951	Hill
Kavoa	Yemen	Jerusalem	1950	Mountain–mixed
Biyoun	Tunisia	Central	1950	Citrus
Shalekhet	Hadhramaut †	Central	1952	Hill
Zimriya	Morocco	Central	1949	Mixed dairy
Zeviya	Central Europe	Northern	1949	Dairy

* The two largest groups being immigrants from Rumania and Persia respectively.
† Yemenite cultural area.

[5] This organizational blueprint is based on (*a*) a job analysis carried out in two veteran *moshavim* considered prototypical; (*b*) information from the *Moshav* Movement and the Land Settlement Department.

Fig. 1 Organizational blueprint of the *moshav*: tasks and 'division of labour'

Legend:

Decision making
A Ordinary decisions
B Extraordinary decisions
C Approval and confirmation

Action
D Initiative
E Preparation
F Execution

Support and supervision
G Information
H Advice
I Supervision
K Control

Organizational bodies (columns):
1 Yearly general assembly
2 Chairman
3 Nominations and election committee
4 Extraordinary general assembly
5 Comptrollership committee
6 Village council
7 Executive committee
8 Secretariat
9 Fire-fighting and security committee (including Accounts)
10 Vocational training
11 Economic committee
12 Agricultural committee
13 Livestock and poultry committee
14 Village shop and store committee
15 Production store
16 Fruit orchards
17 Water system
18 Garage
19 Dairy
20 Village shop
21 Building store
22 Social and membership committee
23 Health committee
24 Care of individuals committee
25 Clinic
26 Education and culture
27 Youth committee
28 Religious affairs committee
29 Youth club
30 Sports stadium
31 Convention hall
32 Country club
33 Library
34 School
35 Kindergarten
36 Synagogue
37 Cemetery
38 Members

Tasks	1	2	3	4	5	6	7	8	9	10	11	12	13	14	15	16	17	18	19	20	21	22	23	24	25	26	27	28	29	30	31	32	33	34	35	36	37	38
General policy																																						
Overall policy; goals and aims	A	A		B		D	D	E			E	G		G								G	G			G		G										
General budgeting	A	A		B		C	F	E			E	G	G	G								G	G	G		E	G	G										
Organizational structure				A		C	F				D	D	D	D								D				D												
General welfare and advancement of public functionaries	A			B	K	A	I			H	CD	D	D	D								D				D												D
Basic economic policy	A			B	K	C					F	G	G	G								D				D												
Crop rotation										H	A	A	G																									
Composition of crops	A									H	A	G	G																									
Development of dairy farming	A			B		C	F			H	H	D	G																									
Development and improvement of livestock						C				H	C	D	D																									
Planning of poultry branch										H	D		EF																									
New plantations	A					C				H	D	G				F																						
Basic social policy	A	A		B	K	C	I															F	F	G		F												F
Principles of recruitment and expulsion; sanctions		A		B	K	C	I															F	D	D		D												
Basic educational policy	A			B	K	C																				D												F
Size and structure of school (continuation classes)	A			B		C																				D												
Participation in regional schools	A			B		C																																
Continuity of government — Elections																																						
Preparation of lists of candidates for council and committees			F																																			
Consideration of and discussions with prospective candidates			F																																			
Publication of list of candidates			F																																			
Elections (yearly or special) to village council						A																																
Election to committees	A			A																																		
Election of council chairman		F																																				
Election of chairman of general …																																						

Category	Item											
	functionaries											
	Acceptance of new members	A	C	A	D		G	D	G		D	D
	Cessation of membership	A	C	A	D		D	D	D		D	D
	Housing for public functionaries		F	A	F		F		G			
	Problems between individuals and council or committees	B	B	F	D		D	D	D		D	D
	Allocation of members to (salaried) public employment		F	F			D					
	Arrangements for hired labour			F			F					
	Economic analysis of individual farms			C	D		C					
	Changes in taxation	A	K	C	D		F	D				
Care of the individual	Problems between individual members			F	G		F	G				
	Problems between members and co-operative economic enterprises			G	G							
	Disciplinary problems and actions	K		A	F		C	D				
	Employment for disabled members			A								
	Visits to sick members			A	F							
	Mutual aid							E				F
	Job rotation or changes among functionaries	K		A	F		C	D	D			
	Special care of needy households and social cases	K		A	F		C	D	D			
	Special tax concessions and exemptions	B	K	A	F		C	D	D		D	
	Follow-up of work of council and committees			A								
Comptrollership	Auditing	F		F								
	Supervision of cooperative economic enterprises	F		F								
	Reports to accounting office	F		F			F					F
	Village balance sheet						F					F
	Individual accounts			F			F					F
	External accounts			F			F					F
	Salaries			EF			F					F
	Taxes and welfare deductions			F			F					F
	Cost accounting information			F			F					F
	Production accounts			F			F					F
	Suppliers' accounts			F			F					F
	Income tax payments			F			F					F
	Trial balance			F			F					F
Accounting	Village shop accounts			G			G					G
	Individual supplies accounts			F			F	G				F
	Branch (cooperative enterprises) accounts			F			F	G				F
	General accounting			F			F	G				F

Category	Function	1	2	3	4	5	6	7	8	9	10	11	12	13	14	15	16	17	18	19	20	21	22	23	24	25	26	27	28	29	30	31	32	33	34	35	36	37	38
General administration	Chairing of yearly assembly	F																																					
	Chairing of general (extraordinary) assembly					F																																	
	Activation of council and committees					F	F																																
	Order of deliberations					F	F	F																															
	Population census							F																															
	Village books (movements of people and production)							F																															
	Care of mail							F																															
	Care of village offices							F																															
	Village newsletter					F		F																															
	Follow-up of work of functionaries (administrative and economic)							F																															
Representation	Representation of village in ceremonies					F																																	
	External relations and negotiations							F																															
	Guides to casual tourists						F	F																															
	Care of and hospitality to visitors							F	I											F																			
Management of enterprises and branches	Erection of public buildings	A			B		C	F		F		D										D																	
	Instruction and training of functionaries and members						A	F		F		C	D	D		D																							
	Allocation and roster of mechanized equipment						F	F								D			D																				
	Maintenance of public buildings						C	F	I																														
	Herd books							F		F				F																									
	Special public works													I							F																		F
	Poultry books															F																							
	Packing files																		F																				
	Motorized transport files																		F	F																			
	Collection of milk from members																			F	F																		F
	Milk hygiene											H		I																									
	Distribution of chicks								F	F		H		GH																									
	Central buying of supplies						K	B		G			I		C	C																							D
	Pricing of supplies for sale to members												I					G			E	E																	G
	Maintenance of water lines and meters												I	I					F		E	F																	
	Evaluation of water use (in cases of meter failure)												F	F																									
	Analysis of marketing costs and earnings											E	F	E	E																								
	Veterinary care										H	E		H								F																	G
	Preparation of feed mixtures													D																									
	Supply of beef stock										H	C				D																							F
	Provision of agricultural and other tools												DE			D		F																					

Management of enterprises and branches	Codes
Reading of water meters	F
Industrial crops	H · DI · F
Green fodder	H · H · F
Vegetables	H · H · F
Buying and selling of beef	H · GH · F
Irrigation works	H · H · FH · F
Pest control	H · H · FH · F
Analysis of fat content in milk	I · F
Selling of consumption items to members	F
Selling of production items	F
Collection of agricultural produce	I · F · F
Marketing of milk and agricultural produce	I · F · F
Storage of empty boxes	F · F
Grading and packing of produce	DI · F · F · F
Work safety	I · F · F · F
Isolation strips	I · D · DI · F · F
Maintenance of sheds, etc.	F
Maintenance of public motorized equipment	I · FI
Cultivation	G · F

Insurance	Codes
National insurance	F
Members' insurance	F
Livestock and poultry insurance	F · F
Buildings insurance	F · F
Crop insurance	F
Mechanized equipment insurance	F

Municipal services	Codes
Maintenance of electricity network	A · F
Current security	C · F · F
Special security problems	A · F
Ecological lay-out and planning of village	F · F
Location of fire-fighting equipment	F
Maintenance of fire-fighting equipment	D · F
Planting and maintenance of public gardens, landscaping	D · D
Maintenance of cemetery	F · F · D · DI
Members' gardens	F · F
Tidiness and cleanliness of public buildings and places	I · F · F · L · L · L · L · L

		1	2	3	4	5	6	7	8	9	10	11	12	13	14	15	16	17	18	19	20	21	22	23	24	25	26	27	28	29	30	31	32	33	34	35	36	37	38
Municipal services	Maintenance of paths, ways and roads																																						
	Maintenance of sanitation							I									F						D																
	Equipment to kindergarten and school							I																															
Finance	Loans to members						A	F				G											G																
	Contributions						A	F																		G													
	Payments to institutions							F						EH											G														
	Banking							F																															
	Payments to members								EF																														
	Financial arrangements with members							F																															
	Payments to workers								EF																														
	Financial reports							F	F																														
	Agricultural credit to members						A		F																														
Recreation, adult education, information	Excursions																										CF	F						F					
	Contact with parents and pupils																										F	F											
	Public fetes and holidays																										F	F											
	Educational activities for adults																										F	I					F						
	Library and newspapers																										I												
	Cinema shows																										FI	F											
	Maintenance of clubs																										F	I											
	Youth instruction																										I	F											
	Gadna [youth corps]																										F												
	Social gatherings																										F												
	Artistic groups																										F												
	Special cultural activities																									H													
Health	Special health problems																																						
	Public health																						F																
	Hygiene																						F																
	Blood bank																						F																
	Contact with medical services																						F																
	Contact with dental services																						F																
	Convalescence for members																						F		F														
	Inoculations																						D																
Religious affairs	Religious worship accessories																												F										
	Maintenance of synagogue																												F										
	Religious activities																										T		F										

the blueprint embodies very definite precepts as regards both the *functions* which the village organization should carry out and the political–administrative *structure* through which this has to be done. As regards the former, the corporate body is vested with authority over the three essential governmental functions—that

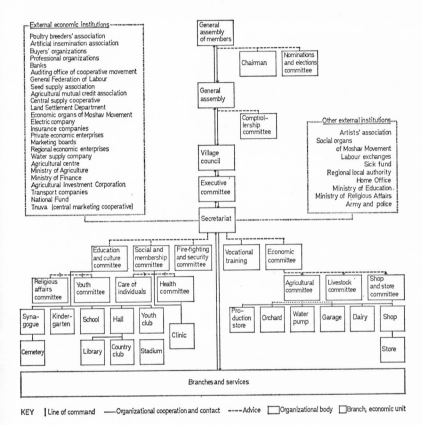

Fig. 2 Organizational hierarchy in the *moshav*

of decision-making, in terms of formation and coordination of policies; that of provision of services; and that of social control. The essential feature, however, is surely the *scope* and the *intensity* of the intervention of the corporate body; it is in fact expected to guide, regulate and sanction all the community and many of the private aspects of economic, social and cultural life.

The injunctions as to the *way* in which the carrying out of the corporate duties should be articulated emerge no less definitively. They may be formulated in the form of four principles:

1. *Political autonomy,* namely the rule that the various organizational functions should be vested in the corporate body as such, and relinquished neither to externally appointed personnel, nor to any internal sub-groups.

2. *Democratic system of government,* in the 'accepted' twofold sense of:
   (a) Institutions based on free elections, secret ballot, universal suffrage, and universal right to office.
   (b) Institutions acting on majority rule, embodying free and regular transition and rotation, recognizing the separation of governmental functions, and subordinated to the general assembly of members as the supreme legislative body.

3. *Rational–bureaucratic organizational criteria,* again in a double sense of:
   (a) A rational definition of roles, division of labour and authority structure.
   (b) Rational-efficiency or achievement-oriented recruitment of public personnel.[6]

4. *Equality of treatment and service,* that is, a universalistic orientation towards all members in respect of obligations, rewards and sanctions.

To sum up, the organizational pattern of the *moshav* is characterized by a comprehensive set of community goals, cooperative and municipal;[7] these goals are carried out by a structure which is independent and democratic on the political level, and bureaucratic–rational on the administrative one. We must now examine the confrontation between this pattern and various groups of new settlers.

[6] It should be mentioned that the democratic and the bureaucratic principles are to some extent at odds: in particular, the insistence upon rotation in office and upon the diffusion and spread of power (reflected in the inordinately large number of specialized committees) may affect experience and specialization in the executive offices, and efficient decision-making. An example of how this contradiction is resolved in practice is given later on.

[7] Needless to say, some community activities are optional, and may differ from place to place, according to the character and the wealth of the village. Some settlements are thus without a synagogue; others clearly cannot afford a 'communal hall', etc.

Moshav organization in novel forms: from variations on a theme to political cacophony

As has been mentioned above, the organizational structure of the *moshav* may be formulated in the form of four principles— autonomy, democracy, rationality of organization and recruitment, and universalism. Accepting that in the new villages none of these principles is automatically assured, and conceiving of each of them, for simplicity's sake, as an element of a dichotomous dimension, we obtain a Cartesian product of sixteen possible profiles.[8] Indeed, most of these theoretical possibilities have actually been observed in the field at one period or another; within the present context, however, we propose to focus on three types, which may be considered basic. These types are:

1. The 'normative' organization, namely autonomous, democratic, rational and universalistic.
2. The 'traditional' organization, namely autonomous, non-democratic, non-rational and particularistic.
3. The 'managed' village, namely heteronomous, non-democratic, rational and universalistic.

In our analysis we shall try to show the differential significance and 'fitness' which these patterns have for effective cooperative activity in different types of community. And we shall thus relate

[8] These profiles are as follows:

	A *Seat of power*	B *Legitimation*	C *Structure and recruitment in offices*	D *Public service*
	(*a*) Autonomous (*b*) Heteronomous	(*a*) Democratic (*b*) Non-democratic	(*a*) Rational (*b*) Non-rational	(*a*) Universalistic (*b*) Particularistic
1.	Autonomous	Democratic	Rational	Universalistic
2.	"	"	"	Particularistic
3.	"	"	Non-rational	Universalistic
4.	"	"	"	Particularistic
5.	"	Non-democratic	Rational	Universalistic
6.	"	"	"	Particularistic
7.	"	"	Non-rational	Universalistic
8.	"	"	"	Particularistic
9.	Heteronomous	Democratic	Rational	Universalistic
10.	"	"	"	Particularistic
11.	"	"	Non-rational	Universalistic
12.	"	"	"	Particularistic
13.	"	Non-democratic	Rational	Universalistic
14.	"	"	"	Particularistic
15.	"	"	Non-rational	Universalistic
16.	"	"	"	Particularistic

The profiles discussed here are thus Nos. 1, 8 and 13.

each corporate system to the social structure of the village, this structure being classified along two dimensions:

A. The *nature of the social relations in the village*. None of the new settlements has the *Gemeinschaft* type of social interaction characteristic of the veteran *moshav*, and these relations are taken to vary between the modern associational or contractual principle on the one hand, and the traditional-familistic (or ascribed) principle on the other, with this latter being based on one common framework—the *hamoula*.

Properly speaking, the origin of what is known in Israel villages today as the *hamoula* lies in the territorially defined Mediterranean patrilineage (both Arab and Jewish). In Israel, however, these criteria of membership have sometimes been blurred, and units which combine several families—not always strictly of common patrilineal descent or common former residence—still call themselves and act as *hamoulas*. This is due not only to changes in the original structure which among some groups had already begun in the country of origin, but also to the fact that these groups were sometimes splintered in the process of migration and settlement. In some of the villages, therefore, the term *hamoula* denotes reconstituted rather than original *hamoulas*.[9] In spite of these changes, however, the new organization has often been as important a unit as it used to be, at least in the initial years. The reason for this is that the process of migration has caused individuals to fall back even more upon familiar groups and accepted forms of social interaction. The *moshav*, in fact, has frequently not only strengthened links in the traditional structure which were weakened in the country of origin, but has also broadened the scope of activity of this structure, even causing it to assume new functions. This is especially so as regards economic and political activity: in the former, the *hamoula* has

---

[9] As may be seen from the sample (note 4), in the present discussion we are basing ourselves chiefly on the Yemenite Jewish lineage, which, owing to the extremely traditional nature and isolation of the overall Yemeni society, the strict, caste-like position of the Jews in it, and the total migration of this community to Israel, has maintained itself and been transplanted in the most integral form. Generally speaking, however, the kinship pattern described in our case studies represents also other traditional diasporas—notably that of Kurdistan (in Iraq, Persia and Turkey) and that of the Atlas mountains in Morocco.

For examples of such units, see charts of lineages in a *moshav* of Kurdish Jews in *Immigration and social change*, chapter 6.

gained immensely in importance, while in the latter it has even entered the new fields of local government and party politics.

In their countries of origin, members of the *hamoula* usually formed a neighbourhood group. Membership implied an obligation to afford economic help, hospitality and protection to all other members of the group whenever required. There was a strong sense of belonging to the kin group, loyalty to which was regarded as being more important than loyalty to any other group. Economic cooperation within the *hamoula* did not, however, imply arrangements of communal or even cooperative production. The unit of production was the individual household, usually comprising an extended family, but not the kinship group. Nor was the kinship group an effective political unit. Members were mobilized in case of trouble, but permanent functions of local government were not within the jurisdiction or sphere of influence of the *hamoula*.

But in the *moshav* the *hamoula* has assumed these functions. The *moshav* imposed cooperative production on the new immigrants, as well as processes of political decision-making through elected representatives and committees. The 'Oriental' immigrants, who were not used to acting as individuals, logically enough interpreted the *moshav* institutions in terms of the *hamoula*. Thus the *hamoula* took often upon itself the organization of production and cooperative marketing prescribed by the *moshav* constitution. Even more importantly, it has become the main political unit in the village, both internally (that is *vis-à-vis* other groups) and externally, as the representative and champion of its members in their relations with the absorbing society. This in turn has forced the *hamoula* organization to tighten up, has lent it new strength and has endowed it with the power to adopt sanctions. Long-'lost' members of the original groups have been sought out all over the country and 'drafted' to settle in the villages concerned; and there have even been cases of wholesale 'exchange' of populations between various *moshavim*. This process of social reconstruction and absorption by way of internal selection, and on the basis of kinship or quasi-kinship criteria, has infused the traditional orientations, divisions and strifes with new life.

In this way the social structure described here still constitutes, essentially, a characteristic traditional kinship-embedded pattern of interaction, featuring very strong attachment to ascribed and territorial groups, limitation of social interaction chiefly to these groups, and lack of confidence in, and capacity to work together with, people from outside the group.

B. *The actual social composition of the population,* i.e. whether the village is composed of a culturally and socially homogeneous group or of several heterogeneous groups. The concept of homogeneity is of course not absolute but relative to dimension A, and the more permissive and voluntary the interaction is the more tolerant it is of heterogeneity.

These two dimensions are in practice combined in a variety of types, including intermediate and 'transitional' groups. For the purpose of the present analysis, however, we concentrate on the 'modern' and the 'traditional' poles, whether homogeneous or heterogeneous.[10] Our four main types are, therefore, as follows: *the modern homogeneous, or subdivided, community* (that is, a community which includes a variety of sub-groups but which is socially integrated)—type 1; *the modern heterogeneous, or 'sectoral', community* (that is, a community whose variety of culturally distinct sub-groups prevents overall integration)—type 2; *the traditional homogeneous, or 'familistic', community*—type 3; *and the traditional heterogeneous, or 'split', community*—type 4.

Of the twelve major socio-organizational possibilities thus obtainable, we have actually observed, and document, six profiles, as follows:

1. 'Normative' organization, appearing only in combination with modern homogeneous social structure.

2. The 'managed' organization, appearing in three distinct social structures:

   (*a*) In the modern heterogeneous community.
   (*b*) In the traditional homogeneous community.
   (*c*) In the traditional heterogeneous community.

3. The autonomous traditional organization, appearing in two different social structures:

   (*a*) In the traditional homogeneous community.
   (*b*) In the traditional heterogeneous community.

[10] For a fuller discussion of this aspect, and for the analysis of 'intermediate' social types, see chiefly D. Weintraub, op. cit., chapter 3; or (for an earlier and less complete report) J. Ben-David (ed.), *Agricultural planning and village community in Israel,* Unesco, Paris, 1964, chapter VIII.

1. The 'normative' village

The 'normative' type of government, namely the autonomous, democratic, rational and universalistic one, appears in our sample in two communities—Ta'amon and Zeviya—both representing Type 1 of our social classification, namely the modern homogeneous ('sub-divided') village. Here we shall describe the former.

Ta'amon is a dairy farm situated in the southern part of Israel on fertile land, relatively far from the frontier. It is connected to a central water pipeline, a main electricity line and a good road. In addition the adjacent area is dotted with established villages and towns, and the regional local government authority is both active and very experienced. The settlement thus enjoys the most favourable conditions as regards agriculture, security and services.

It was founded by some forty Yugoslav families who settled on the land in 1949, after they had spent some time waiting in temporary quarters in an abandoned Arab village. Shortly after they settled they were joined by additional groups, also from Yugoslavia. In 1950, with the consent of both the *moshav* itself and the Settlement Department, new farm units were added and a Rumanian group settled on an area near the original centre of the village. In the course of time other families settled, partly to occupy farmsteads that had been abandoned by some of the original settlers and partly to cultivate new ones. The newcomers were also mainly Yugoslavs and Rumanians, with an admixture of other Central European, Oriental and local families. Today the Yugoslav group represents some 48 per cent of the population of Ta'amon and the Rumanians 22 per cent, the rest being individuals from other, mainly European, countries.

The Yugoslavs themselves are divided into two distinct sub-groups—the 'Ashkenazi' group, which is the larger of the two, and the 'Sephardi' group.[11] The difference between the two communities is not great, and though the former seem to be some-

---

[11] Ashkenazi ('German') are the descendants of Yiddish-speaking Jewish groups whose forebears had lived in Central and Eastern Europe until the eighteenth century and have dispersed since then over most parts of the world; the Sephardi ('Spanish') Jews are descendants of Jewish communities expelled from Spain at the end of the fifteenth century who have since lived mainly in the Middle East, the Balkans, the Netherlands and, from the seventeenth century, also in England. There are certain cultural differences between the two groups.

what more 'Westernized' than the latter, the characteristics attributed to the Yugoslav immigrants as a whole apply, in the main,
to both groups. All these settlers are of middle class urban or
semi-urban backgrounds, and have a predominantly secular outlook on life. They consist mainly of former businessmen, civil
servants and members of the free professions; among the original
founders of Ta'amon were a lawyer, an agronomist, a banker, a
diplomat, a musicologist and a few senior civil servants, and while
this elite constituted some 20 per cent of all the heads of families
in the original nucleus the rest were also predominantly composed
of men and women who had had secondary school education and
were of good social standing. Most members of the group had
some experience as active participants in the public life of the
communities to which they had once belonged. Religious tradition and practice had already become somewhat alien to them;
before world war II there had, in fact, been little Jewish consciousness among them at all, and their activity in Jewish religious and community organizations was largely marginal to the
roles they performed in society in general.

This, then, was the foundation from which the *moshav* was to
develop. Although part of this elite left Ta'amon as soon as
opportunities to resume an urban way of life arose, and although
the Yugoslavs no longer command an absolute majority in the
moshav its specific character is, nevertheless, still very much
the product of the work and character of the original founders.

The second largest group in the village, the Rumanians, is
made up of somewhat different elements. Some of these families
came from relatively developed parts of Transylvania and from
urban middle class backgrounds, and their education was more
or less similar to that of the Yugoslav settlers. Most of the
Rumanians, however, came from small towns and villages and
were of a lower socio-economic status—small merchants, artisans
and a few farmers. Almost none of them had had a secondary
education; and the majority had attended traditional Jewish religious schools. They had larger families than the Yugoslav settlers,
and had previously belonged to traditional religious communities.

However, over and above the two basic backgrounds, the village
is characterized by the multiplicity and variety of its social groups.
There are eight main lines of association over and above the
family nucleus: friendships begun abroad; friendships formed
during the period of common training; friendships based on a
mutual mother tongue; blood and family relationships; ethnic

origin; age; religious observance; similar schooling. These lines intersect and act in conjunction, yet it seems that the factors of education and language are the most decisive at present. The ethnic factor, by itself, scarcely acts as a barrier between the Ashkenazi and Sephardi Yugoslavs, while Hungarian-speaking Yugoslavs and Rumanians associate closely, and this circle also includes the few Hungarian immigrants in the village. Similarly, people with academic and secondary education tend to draw together, in clear preference to all other considerations except that previously mentioned. All in all, it can be said that these two criteria are the basic elements of the network of social relationships in the *moshav*, although significant secondary differentiation derives from the other factors.

In effect, then, this is a community formed by a plurality of distinct social crystallizations: a plurality which is an explicitly stated principle in the organization of the settlement. When it was founded, plots were assigned according to the following scheme: (*a*) the various self-defined social groups were given a number of adjoining plots, equal to the number of their members; (*b*) the raffling of the plots was then carried out by each group separately, and only determined the internal distribution within each geographical–social cluster. In this way, friendship and affinity were the cause, rather than the effect, of the ecological formation of neighbourhoods. This arrangement was upset when some families left and new families arrived in their place; but the empty farms were redistributed, to a considerable degree, by the cooptation of neighbours.

But this social plurality in no way hindered the emergence of solidarity in the *moshav*. As we have already stated, no single predominant factor determines the character of the various associations within the village; these associations are almost entirely social and do not define or reflect cultural separation; nor do they, for this reason, preclude more extensive social activities, celebrations, fetes, or meetings. On the contrary, the attempt of the elite to promote overall frameworks of contact gained support from the 'associational' groups. Social standing with these groups themselves is largely derived from, and determined by, a given member's overall success in the eyes of the village; and this is measured by his contribution to its economic, political and social life in general. Village society, in fact, is actually the decisive frame of reference, and accordingly can promote common identification and cooperation and prevent social cleavages along any of these lines.

Nor have differences in interests and ideology led to any major conflicts. Many settlers are active in Israel's intense political life, working for parties which range from the extreme Left to the moderate Right, and are traditionally at loggerheads on many issues. But even this activity does not penetrate into or disrupt the fabric of *moshav* society, nor does it bring about ideological divisions (something which happened in a number of established *collective* settlements) or sharpen already existing tensions (as was the case in several new villages).

The same is true also of economic differentiation. In fact the settlers' respective socio-economic backgrounds, aspirations and ability to support themselves outside agriculture created distinct occupational strata (agricultural and non-agricultural) in the *moshav*, as well as different economic interests and ways of life; thus some of the Yugoslav immigrants brought furniture and utensils with them and supplemented these subsequently with new purchases, while other groups not only arrived almost completely impoverished but put their money primarily into developing their farms. Although the village thus contained families whose material standards were very different for a long time, none of these differences crystallized into permanent status- or interest-group divisions.

Another area of life in which distinctions exist, but are also overcome, is religion. We have already mentioned the differences of outlook in this respect. The conspicuous absence of Jewish ritual and folklore in the Yugoslav group was originally a source of friction and conflict in its relations with the Rumanian immigrants. However, a conscious process of adjustment occurred, brought about by the desire of the majority group to meet halfway a large segment of the village and to recognize its value system: thus the general aspect of the community is still primarily secular, and this with a considerable measure of common approval; religious dicta, to the extent that they are observed at all, are confined to private life, and do not affect the freedom of action of the non-observant settlers; religious rituals, however, have become part and parcel of the activity and the tradition of the *moshav* as a whole.

That this rather loose and permissive structure is able to support common goals, policies and institutions in other areas of *moshav* life is largely due to the way in which the latter were

defined by the settlement elite. This definition has been minimal;
it has attempted to eliminate from community life all points of
actual and potential tension (explicit and implicit). Economically,
emphasis has thus been put on development of individual holdings and on their owners' right to work as they think best. The
moshav offers expert advice on agricultural matters, but each
farmer is free on the whole to decide on crops, area of cultivation,
etc., and there is considerable variation among the farms in this
respect. The same pattern emerges in terms of mutual aid. The
community takes care of the individual in so far as farming help
is needed in cases of sickness or military reserve service, household emergencies and so forth. Other such needs remain outside
the public sphere, there being a general feeling that entrusting
them to the community and to its executive organs might be an
infringement of individual dignity, and that they are better solved
within the more intimate and familiar frameworks of neighbourhood and personal relationships.

To recapitulate: Type 1 social structure, as represented by
Ta'amon, can be considered a loose but stable association of a
number of social crystallizations. It is a structure based chiefly
on interaction within sub-groups, incorporating various social
backgrounds and inclinations. Over and above these sub-groups,
social identification and participation on the village level has also
evolved, and these frameworks together have been able to support the common goals, policies and institutions of the whole
community. One necessary condition for this support has been
the *moshav's* collective values, which are so defined as to require
a relatively low social consensus and which can accommodate
different orientations.

As can be seen from the above thumbnail sketch, the modern
associational type of social integration has impinged here on both
the *scope* and the *intensity* of corporate activity, limiting some
cooperative and communal functions, and handing others over to
various social sub-systems. By its very nature, however, it has
accepted and supported also the 'modern' governmental organization, expressed in the four principles mentioned—although, as we
shall see, not without some characteristic modifications.

To begin with, Ta'amon is a consolidated[12] *moshav* which
has been running its own affairs *independently almost from the*

---

[12] Consolidation status means (*a*) the 'absorption' and utilization of the
allocated development budget, (*b*) the withdrawal of the resident team of
social and vocational instructors.

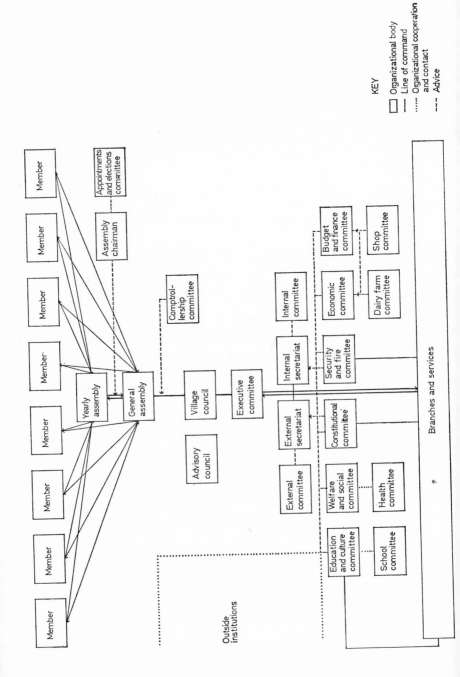

KEY

☐ Organizational body
— Line of command
⋯ Organizational cooperation and contact
--- Advice

beginning of its existence. More precisely, it became independent (except for certain agricultural branches) by the end of its first year, and has not backtracked since. The most prominent feature in Ta'amon's organizational pattern, however, is without question its modern bureaucratic structure, pushed to the very limits which are compatible with the egalitarianism and solidarity which ideally characterize *moshav* society.

This bureaucratic structure is given full expression in the realization of those organizational principles we discussed above, namely: (a) *the structure of public office and its division of labour, which are based on efficiency and rationality,* i.e. they embody a distinct hierarchy of authority, advice and supervision, clear-cut and practical definition of the competence of the various institutions, and a strong achievement orientation; (b) *a universalistic method of dealing with all clients.*

Figure 3 schematically summarizes[13] the *moshav*'s organizational bodies and their relationships and demonstrates the parallel with the 'ideal' model. Of course, the pattern of specific committees is somewhat different: institutions such as the synagogue and the cemetery are missing; the poultry committee is absent, and so on. But it is clear that these differences stem from special local features; on the other hand, Ta'amon maintains bodies which exist only in the most rigorous of old-established villages, and do not exist at all in many others. In addition to the committee, there is also a large advisory council—absent in the majority of *moshavim*, and also from the essential blueprint. Ta'amon has also special committees for internal and external affairs which are, again, not obligatory.

The spheres of activity of each of these organizational bodies are quite separate. Each has its own area of undisputed authority and standing regulations which guide its current work. The relative importance of the various institutions is inherent in the definition of functions (the welfare committee, for instance, for social reasons mentioned above, does not succeed in fulfilling a central need), and there are inevitable ebb and flow periods in the tempo of committee work. But all the committees do operate, meet regularly, deal with specific, well defined matters, and do not just constitute a formal part of the *moshav* structure but also fulfil an organic need.

[13] I.e. omitting particulars of branches and services which we detailed in the 'blueprint'.

The emphasis on effective organization can be seen also in the principles which govern appointment to public office. All the incumbents are qualified for their jobs; for the most part, they are the people best qualified for their particular tasks. Specialization and appropriate division of labour, in fact, is *more* prominent in this village than it is in the 'model' itself, and we shall discuss this phenomenon further on. Here, however, it seems appropriate to quote the chairman of the council:

The general functioning [in the classical *moshav*] of village institutions is still based too much on the irrational phenomenon of non-specialization. True, the two separate spheres, the municipal on the one hand, and the economic cooperative on the other, are interrelated. But each should be dealt with according to different criteria, and by different experts, and not through general elections to a single council. While one sphere is more public (especially in the sphere of general policy) and may properly be entrusted to politicians, the other is professional and should be organized as a regular economic and commercial company with shares, or some similar structure. At present the 'municipal' chairman can decide, on the basis of his own judgment, budgetary matters which are purely financial and economic. The same situation holds for the economic sphere itself, where specialization, though present, is insufficient. In practice, the person chosen to serve on the economic committee and on the council itself is almost always the owner of a successful farm; but he may be a dairy specialist now called upon to plan field crops or fiscal matters.

The chairman's attitude exemplifies the concept of economics as requiring a real specialization, and of the desirability of autonomy in economic decisions.

The principle of universalism in public matters is also strongly supported; each member of the *moshav* is treated equally. Personal integrity, honesty and genuine commitment are the *sine qua non* of all appointments to public office. Prevention of undue external influence or 'pull' is one of the main concerns of the *moshav*'s supervisory institutions: separation—rarely found in other villages—is maintained between elected committee members who determine general policies and between the salaried employees who implement these policies. In Ta'amon the two secretaries—one for internal and one for external affairs—who are usually council members, are non-residents, and therefore neither is likely to arrogate too much power to himself or likely to be subjected to the pressure of friends and relatives from the village itself. This determination to eliminate potential abuse was once defined for our benefit as follows: 'The secretary for internal

affairs has the committee on his back; the committee is carefully
watched by the advisory council; the village council supervises
the advisory council and the comptroller's committee has its eye
on everyone.' We witness here a complex system of managerial
and public supervision, coloured by a constitutional–legalistic
tinge.

In point of fact, Ta'amon has a quasi-constitution of its own,
over and above the organizational legislation of the *Moshav*
Movement: when it was first established, one of its members,
formerly a lawyer, was asked to study the legal forms specific to
Israel and in particular those affecting agricultural settlement,
and then to draw up a detailed internal constitution adapted to
the village's special needs.

These uncompromising organizational principles unavoidably
hampered the democratic government of the village. Most requirements associated with local democracy have been scrupulously met: free and open elections, democratic representation,
majority decisions, separation of the legislative and executive
branches, and the primacy of the former—all these are characteristic of the *moshav*. Moreover, these principles are in line with
the village's social structure (which, as we have seen, is characterized by the absence of an ascriptive or any other total crystalliza-
tion) and with the settler's own ideology. Things are different,
however, as regards changes of government and rotation of function. As mentioned, these principles always contradict to some
extent the rational division of labour and process of specialization. In Ta'amon, however, this phenomenon, in the course of
time, brought about the existence of a 'professional' elite whose
members eventually became really qualified and began, implicitly
or explicitly, to demand a monopoly of power. While the multiplicity of committees and control mechanisms helped to limit this
demand somewhat, the committee posts, too, were filled by
suitably qualified people, who also specialized in their particular
spheres of responsibility, and the reservoir of manpower again
depended on the same people, who were elected again and
again. Moreover, membership of committees was not a very important position. In terms of status as well as power it was,
perhaps, considered superior to that of the paid secretary, but
much below that of village council membership. In other words
a committee member was not, either objectively or subjectively,
a recognized leader, while the council members gradually evolved
into a small, fairly exclusive group which *de facto* ran the village

affairs by making all the important policy decisions. As we have said before, this group could certainly not be accused of poor management; its work was very successful and quite free of corruption. Also, it was constantly under the supervision of the comptrolling committee and the village assembly, both of which discharged their supervisory functions thoroughly. But even so, the power monopoly was resented. In part this hostility was created by the frustration felt and expressed by some of the politically inert settlers who realized that their agricultural work was considered less 'important' than the public activities of office-holders; additionally, at this stage, ethnic organization began to rear its head. This was initiated by the Rumanian settlers, who saw power being permanently handed over to the Yugoslavs, even though this occurred by majority vote and was clearly good for the community and the individual settler alike. The main reason, however, was the flaw in democratic government in such. The lack of rotation in public office—although it was never actually abused—reinforced the already fully acknowledged personal superiority of the *moshav* elite, a superiority which became more obvious as time went on and which, essentially, made all the democratic election mechanisms seem insignificant. Gradually the elite developed attitudes of 'benevolent absolutism'; utilizing paternalistic authority through democratic channels, it began to act on behalf of the people and to decide, by itself, what was good or bad for them. We were not able to follow this development in its early stages, but it was easy to see how much the settlers were aware of it, and to note the sharp reactions of the non-Yugoslavs. About a year before our study got under way a council had been elected from a group of 'new' men. Unlike other previous changes in function which had taken place among the same members, on this occasion offices were manned mainly by 'opposition' members who belonged to the *moshav*'s Rumanian minority. This was the result not of a 'revolution' but of the voluntary standing down of members of the former council who decided not to run for office again, although they had enjoyed majority support—quite sure, however, that the 'new men' would fail, and that the 'rebellious' settlers of little faith would thus be taught a lesson. This was exactly what happened. The new council continued the work mapped out by its predecessor, but was, as predicted, simply not sufficiently efficient or experienced. Its chief difficulty was in the realm of outside contacts, an inadequacy which led to all kinds of financial crises and management problems. This being the situation, against a background of current difficulty in comparison with past success, the new people were not really given enough time or credit. Lack of cooperation from the old elite, plus the tension and aggressiveness of the insecure new council, combined to exacerbate matters to such a pitch that, by 'popular' demand, the old council was finally re-called *en bloc*.

In this way, the need for political and managerial professional-ization and specialization was exploited by the elite in order that its power be maintained and even increased. This was not pri-marily a matter of personal ambition; practically all the members of this group already held positions in State and public institutions above village level. It was rather a question of emphasis on the use of rational and autonomous criteria in the management of financial and economic matters—a managerial de-democratization for the sake of efficiency.

2. The 'managed' village

The 'managed' village is a settlement unable[14] or unwilling to govern itself, as a consequence of which its administration is vested in external managerial personnel, appointed, as the case may be (and as will be seen below), by the village itself or by settlement institutions. As mentioned above, this type appears in our study in three distinct variants, related to the social character of the village population. Let us take up each of these variants in turn.

(*a*) *The managed village in a 'Western heterogeneous' ('sec-toral') community.* This type is exemplified, in our sample, by Moshav Resissim. Resissim, situated in the centre of the country and blessed by good settlement conditions, is, like Ta'amon, characterized by a diverse population. The socio-economic back-ground of the majority of this population is, moreover, similar to that of the Rumanian group in Ta'amon. The same is true of the pattern of interaction adopted, which is also based on association by friendship, place of origin, age, kinship, ritual, language and education, these last two criteria being the most significant. In Resissim, however, there has developed no overall solidarity be-

---

[14] Of course, sometimes the inability may lie only in the eyes of the observer, and the Settlement Agency may unjustifiably prolong an ad-ministration by its instructor.

yond emergence of several sub-groups,[15] which constitute almost
the entire social universe of the village. These do not promote
inter-group activities designed for the community as a whole but
aim only at satisfying the social needs of the individuals who
belong to them.

The reason for this relative lack of success in establishing
overall community solidarity becomes apparent when we compare
the two settlements. First of all, in Resissim the population was
much more varied. Its main groups—Rumanian, Persian, Moroc-
can, Turkish and native Israeli—came from different cultural and
social milieux, and represented very different ways of life. Thus,
although the *pattern* of interaction was free and associational,
there were few *actual* points of contact, whether in language,
religion or tradition. Furthermore, unlike Ta'amon, Resissim had
undergone no social selection or preparation of the kind which
might have minimized anxiety and encouraged social flexibility.
Finally, Resissim had no elite to set the tone for the *moshav* and
provide the necessary leadership. In the Type 1 village as represented by Ta'amon this function was fulfilled by the Yugoslav
settlers. Here, however, there were two relatively large groups
which greatly differed from each other, plus a medley of smaller
groups and individual families who had come to Israel from all
over the world. Thus, while Resissim was ecologically dispersed
no less than Ta'amon, it was much more heterogeneous; and this
heterogeneity could not be made to merge into a sense of common belonging.

Because of its composition this village never evolved any overall solidarity or sense of identification with the community as a
whole. Consequently, it was not capable of supporting the *moshav*
institutions, although the political traditions of its inhabitants
would have made this quite feasible.

We illustrate the sort of problems which kept the village organization from functioning properly from the sphere of marketing.
In Resissim, where dairy farming and fruit production were the

[15] The main sub-groups are: (*a*) the bulk of the Rumanians, characterized
by a common language as well as by a combined traditional and elementary
general education; (*b*) the Persians, Moroccans and Turks, with similar
characteristics; (*c*) a group composed of Israelis, Western and Central Europeans, Argentinians and a few Russians, distinguished by a higher general
education and by using Hebrew as their everyday language. Each of these
groups has also attached to itself some of the remaining families culturally
closest to them.

main economic branches, there was no argument about the need for, and the efficiency of, organized marketing in general, and a single marketing agency for the village as a whole. But at the level of concrete marketing policy this all became a very complicated problem which involved everyone in long discussions within the economic committee and its dairy and fruit sub-committees, at the level of the council, and in the general assembly. Questions were raised as to the marketing agency best suited for each branch; the size of payments and conditions of marketing which should be adhered to; the ratio between the amount of money which the cooperative was entitled to debit each producer's account and the minimum amount which each farm had to be paid regardless of its balance; and so on. The differences on each such point were not very large, and were not even identified with the various groups in the village; but the very need for so much negotiation, talk and effort at every one of the three levels mentioned made it virtually impossible to arrive either at quick decisions or fast action. The trouble was the participants' inability to isolate their organizational role from their social background. Since this inability was evident only in certain situations, and since it contradicted the settlers' recognized interests, to say nothing of their better judgment, the organizational structure's ability to function was not entirely destroyed, but its efficiency was certainly impaired. Decisions were reached and appropriate steps were taken, but only after enormous outlays of time and work, and long delays. As soon as this sank in, the village decided to change its organizational set-up. Some authority was removed from the assembly and council, especially in the area of economic policy and services, and handed over to an outside team of experts composed of two secretaries (one for internal and the other for external affairs) and the manager of the fruit branch. On the other hand, the need to give greater organizational autonomy to the sub-groups in matters requiring close contacts was recognized, and the marketing organization was divided into three parts, paralleling the village's three main social groups. An umbrella organization, i.e. the cooperative, was retained to represent the formal judicial interests of the village, and it determined and watched over the general 'overall' interests; but within these limitations each association or sub-cooperative was entrusted with management of its own affairs. Each such organizational framework dealt with the entire process of marketing the farm produce assigned to it; and three independent 'poultry committees'[16] were carved out of the original single committee which had disintegrated. Each of these committees, among other things, was entrusted with collecting money from its members, while the internal affairs secretary was appointed to act as the liaison officer charged with transmitting the required sums of money to and from the committee. Thus it happened that a village initially based on a system of self-government relinquished its authority in favour of professional managers, on the one hand, and its various social groups, on the other.

To sum up, Resissim's organizational structure is characterized by the following features

(i) As regards self-government there is only very limited independence; most matters which, according to the blueprint of the independent *moshav*, should be entrusted to the council are entrusted here to outside management.

(ii) The concept of full democracy does not apply. The managers of the village's affairs are responsible to a general assembly which functions properly, and are also supervised by an active control committee, but there is no division of power between the various office-holders, no real elections for offices, and no rotation in office.

(iii) Both the structure of public office, and recruitment to it, are rational and achievement-oriented; but limited by the trichotomic division which impairs the profitability of marketing and disperses the managerial potential.

The social factors determining the structure of the organizational web (given schematically in Fig. 4) of necessity limited also the *extent* of corporate activity. Resissim, like Ta'amon, had no ideology of corporate expansion or of the encroachment of the public upon the private sphere. But in Resissim the very fabric of the community served to limit non-instrumental functions, and the village organs could not contribute to social integration or to social policy.

(*b*) The *'managed' village in a traditional homogeneous ('familistic') community.* Type 3, the traditional homogeneous community, is based on *hamoula* integration, as described above. It may appear in two distinct variations: the unitary or 'pure' form

---

[16] However, for overriding technical reasons, marketing of milk continued for the village as a whole.

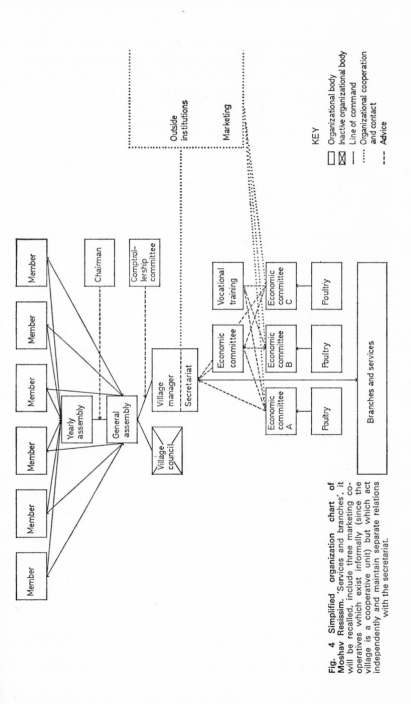

Fig. 4 Simplified organization chart of Moshav Resissim. 'Services and branches', it will be recalled, include three marketing co-operatives which exist informally (since the village is a cooperative unit) but which act independently and maintain separate relations with the secretariat.

KEY

☐ Organizational body
☒ Inactive organizational body
— Line of command
······ Organizational cooperation and contact
--- Advice

—namely a village based on one kinship group only (seen in our
sample in Moshav Levanon); and the quasi-homogeneous or
'weak' form (observed in Shalekhet and Azor)—namely a village
containing a plurality of *hamoulas*, but ones which come from a
common background and place of origin and thus have a measure
of consensus and integration. Here the solidarity is more limited,
based largely on institutionalized conflict and on basic agreement
to sustain essential community interests.

In the present section we refer to the latter of the two, as
represented by Moshav Shalekhet, while the first form serves as
an example of the autonomous traditional homogeneous village.

The entire population of Shalekhet comes from the same place.
namely the desert sultanate of Haban in the Hadhramaut part
of the former Aden protectorate. Before it immigrated to Israel
the community numbered 345 people, all of whom came to Israel,
and most of whom were settled in Shalekhet by the Settlement
Authority. In spite of the fact that in Haban they had lived in
the capital town, they had very little experience of or need of
social relations, co-operation and organization over and above
those of the extended family. Almost to a man they had worked
as silversmiths, and since they were concentrated in one very
small place they had been dependent on a large hinterland for
work, and consequently lived as itinerant hawkers. The men
(those from about thirteen to fifty years) constantly moved from
place to place, leaving the women, the small children and the
aged at home. The families were reunited only on Saturdays and
on religious holidays, and the *hamoulas* met regularly only for
Sabbath prayers or during other religious ceremonies. Roles and
relationships transcending the *hamoula* and pertaining to the
community as a whole were even more sporadic, and were undertaken for the most part in times of trouble, when head taxes had
to be paid and so forth. Although restricted in scope, the *hamoulas* served thus as the basic social and religious framework, with
little interaction and contact between them. In this way, while
the community was on the one hand highly homogeneous culturally, constituted a single ecological unit and was dependent
upon and cooperated opposite the same external political rule,
it was nevertheless organized by and large in distinct and separate kinship lines. This structural division was further strengthened
and symbolized by processes of religious 'schism' and social competition.

The first was the evolution of different prayer rituals. None of the variations was theologically important or extensive; in fact, they related only to four repetitive points in the entire prayer book. But the subjective symbolic value of the different rituals was enormous. Supporters of the opposing versions not only stopped praying together but also gradually withdrew from common attendance at prayer. Since 'ascending to the Torah' during prayers is important both religiously and socially for orthodox Jews, a multiplicity of synagogues at which this honour could be given to as many people as possible had in any case been characteristic of the traditional Jewish community. At Haban, however, this trend was not only reaffirmed; it also overlapped and emphasized an already deep social division based in kinship.

The second factor was the 'affair' of the ritual bath. Originally, the various *hamoulas* had used a common ritual bath, attached to the synagogue which belonged to the 'Hillel' *hamoula*. As relations worsened, members of the competing 'Maatuf' group proclaimed this bath ritually impure and began to send their women to a pool outside the walls of the town. This was taken as an intolerable religious as well as social slight. Revenge took the form of 'Peeping Toms' who disturbed the bathing, and the polluting of the pool by a dead camel. In turn, rotten fish was thrown into the 'Hillel' bath. These acts of retribution continued until both sides finally agreed to differ, and a second real ritual bath was built, adjoining the 'Maatuf' synagogue.

These and similar points of disagreement thus estranged the groups from one another, reinforcing kinship lines. In this way two rival camps came into existence already in Haban, each composed of one big *hamoula* and one of the two smaller lineages; and the situation has been replicated in the *moshav* in Israel. The same four *hamoulas* exist and they are still organized in what can be called two systems made up of 'a sun and a satellite':

System A

Group I	Maatuf *hamoula*	38 families
Group IV	Mifi *hamoula*	8 families
Total		46 families

System B

Group II	Hillel *hamoula*	30 families
Group III	Shamuch *hamoula*	10 families
Total		40 families

These systems cut across all the spheres of *moshav* activity. Religiously, they do not intermix. Since the Settlement Department has erected only one synagogue building in Shalekhet, additional though temporary quarters have been provided in the village club, and the two groups take turns each week at each synagogue. The authority of the Maatuf rabbi, authorized by the Ministry of Religious Affairs to serve the whole community, is not fully accepted by the opposing groups, whose members have sometimes refused to permit him to officiate at their weddings and have protested against the appointment in writing.

Economic interaction has also been reduced. The villagers support and utilize the necessary marketing and other facilities but refuse to cooperate *directly* between groups. One good example: draught animals (usually mules) are often given in joint ownership to two or three *moshav* families. In Shalekhet, however, mules were given to neighbouring families from different *hamoulas*. The tensions which then arose affected the relationship between the *hamoulas* as a whole, and led to non-cooperation with the Settlement Department. The villagers refused for months to accept any equipment or other means of production which were issued to them, thereby considerably delaying the start of efficient farm cultivation.

The same situation exists in other spheres of social interaction; apart from the school, the youth club, weddings, circumcisions, etc., there is almost no informal contact between members of the different groups.

To sum up, this kind of social integration is based on the minimal overall solidarity of ascribed groups, solidarity which derives not from positive social preferences but rather from a tradition of a common political front opposed to 'outside' rule, common history and lack of better alternatives. Each of the groups described would thus opt for living in a truly homogeneous village of its own, and sees the present arrangement, at best, as a not entirely unsatisfactory substitute. In reality, though, the stability of this structure is considerable. Not only is there a common cultural consensus, but the social situation is actually both familiar and reassuring. The antagonism and mutual suspicion of the various groups is institutionalized, as well as regulated, by tradition and long common past and position; they are by way of being the accepted rules of the game and, as such, certainly preferable to the unknown conditions obtaining in the world outside. Need we say more than that not a single family has left Shalekhet since its establishment—a unique record in the history of Israel's new villages?

The traditional patterns of social interaction described above thus affected the positional organization and the administration of the *moshav*. Support of political institutions was given only on the condition that this would be in the interests of *hamoula*. Furthermore, formal office in village government was regarded either as inferior to or as directly connected with the office-holder's status within his own *hamoula*. This prevented the creation of a too independent power elite but it also precluded the separation of the various spheres of internal government and the creation of autonomous status scales.

The following is, in fact, the relationship between the ascribed social structure and the political system in Shalekhet: the council is staffed by each faction in turn on every alternate year; the secretariat stays in the hands of the majority *hamoula* (Maatuf), but the second largest *hamoula* (Hillel) is allowed, when it sits on the council, to choose the Maatuf member it likes best as secretary. This arrangement applies also to less important functions. The list below shows how these jobs are distributed by the *hamoulas* in Shalekhet, and demonstrates the attempt to maintain a delicate intergroup balance.

Secretary	Hamoula I
Rabbi	Hamoula I
Treasurer	Hamoula II
Storekeeper	Hamoula II
Security officer	Hamoula IV
Border policemen	Hamoula I, II
Worker at the Mekoroth Water Company	Hamoula I
Recreation director	Hamoula II
Youth club instructor	Hamoula I
Cook	Hamoula III
Teachers	Hamoula I, II

In consequence, Shalekhet is a co-operative society in name only. This organizational form is, as we know, required by law, and the settlement authorities enforced it from the very outset of agricultural production,[17] since this kind of registered society

[17] We know of only one village which is not formally a cooperative society. This is a traditional heterogeneous village (settled by people from the Atlas mountains) which was unable to agree even on elections for common institutions.

satisfies the judicial and procedural conditions of village management. Hence the existence of those institutions which are insepar-
able from the cooperative's very structure: the annual assembly
which elects the cooperative's council, and the council itself,
which is registered with the Company Registrar and the signature of whose members is binding. In practice, though, these
bodies are only formally elected. They are not conceived of (nor
run) as live institutions with real administrative functions; membership in them is viewed as a source of additional income and as
a symbol of traditional, rather than modern, status which reinforces the position of the elected elders and of the kinship
groups which they represent. In fact the council, which includes
only leaders of the *hamoulas*, actually reflects the *hamoula* structure perfectly. It was appointed by this structure when the political 'cake' was cut, and all the village's ascriptive groups are proportionately represented in it. As a result, the councillors are
men whose organizational experience and managerial know-how
are very meagre and who have only partially assimilated the
village structure either on the cognitive or the normative level. In
this situation the settlement authorities are still saddled with
management of the cooperative's affairs, which, at least on the
instrumental level, have been entrusted almost entirely to the
social instructor.

This does not mean, however, that the village has no organization of its own at all. Its traditional structure determines policy in
certain spheres and exercises social control in accordance with
this policy. This arrangement was not initially supported or
legitimated by the authorities, who tried to turn the *moshav*'s
institutions into foci of genuine public power and at the same
time to imbue them with principles of democratic rule and
bureaucratic organization. The social instructor at first hoped to
staff the council with younger people who might be more mal-
leable and more interested in modernization than the older men,
but failed to do so: Shalekhet's social integration and consensus
were strong enough to keep the instructor from breaching the
traditional structure. A clear division of labour was arrived at
between the instructor and those controlling the traditional village institutions. Today the village is heterogeneous or outside-
managed in respect of its municipal and cooperative services,
economic policy and production, but 'sovereign' in its social,
religious and cultural arrangements.

Table 1 summarizes this division of organizational responsibility

Table 1

Division of organizational functions in Moshav Shalekhet

	Authority	
Task	Instructor	Village
General policy		
Overall policy—goals and aims	+	+
General budgeting	+	+
Organizational structure	+	+
General welfare and advancement of public officials		+
Basic economic policy	+	+
Crop rotation	+	
Composition of crops	+	
Development of dry farming	+	
Development and improvement of livestock	+	
Planning of poultry branch	+	
New plantations	+	
Basic social policy		+
Principles of recruitment and expulsion; sanctions		+
Basic educational policy		+
Size and structure of school		+
Participation in regional schools		+
Elections—continuity of government		
Preparation of lists of candidates for council and committees		+
Consideration of and discussions with prospective candidates		+
Publication of list of candidates	+	+
Elections (yearly or special) to village council		+
Election to committees		+
Election of council chairman		+
Election of chairman of general assemblies' members	+	+
Care of the individual		
Hiring (and dismissal) of public (salaried) officials	+	+
Acceptance of new members		
Cessation of membership		
Housing for public functionaries	+	
Problems between individuals and council or committees		
Allocation of members to (salaried) public employment		+
Arrangements for hired labour	+	+
Economic analysis of individual farms		+
Changes in taxation	+	+
Problems between individual members		+
Problems between members and cooperative economic enterprises	+	+
Disciplinary problems and actions		+
Employment for disabled members		+
Visits to sick members		+
Mutual aid		+
Job rotation or changes among functionaries		+
Special care of needy households and social cases		+
Special tax concessions and exemptions		+
Comptrollership		
Follow-up of work of council and committees		+
Auditing	+	
Supervision of cooperative economic enterprises	+	

The absence of + in both columns means that the particular activity is not carried out at all in the *moshav*.

9—T.B.O.G.

Table 1—*contd.*

Task	Authority	
	Instructor	Village
Accounting		
Reports to accounting office	+	
Village balance sheet	+	
Individual accounts	+	
External accounts	+	
Salaries	+	
Taxes and welfare deductions	+	
Cost accounting information	+	
Production accounts	+	
Suppliers' accounts	+	
Income tax payments	+	
Trial balance	+	
Village shop accounts	+	
Individual supplies accounts	+	
Branch (cooperative enterprises) accounts	+	
General accounting	+	
General administration		
Chairing of yearly assembly	+	+
Chairing of general (extraordinary) assembly	+	+
Activation of council and committees	+	
Order of deliberations	+	
Population census	+	
Village books (movements of people and production)	+	
Care of mail	+	
Care of village offices	+	
Village newsletter		
Follow-up of work of functionaries (administrative and economic)	+	+
Representation		
Representation of village in ceremonies	+	+
External relations and negotiations	+	
Guides to casual tourists		
Care of and hospitality to visitors		
Management of enterprises and branches		
Erection of public buildings	+	+
Instruction and training of functionaries and members	+	+
Allocation and roster of mechanized equipment	+	
Maintenance of public buildings	+	
Herd books	+	
Special public works	+	
Poultry books	+	
Packing files	+	
Motorized transport files	+	
Collection of milk from members	+	
Milk hygiene	+	
Distribution of chicks	+	
Central buying of supplies	+	
Pricing of supplies for sale to members	+	
Maintenance of water lines and meters	+	
Evaluation of water use (in case of meter failure)	+	
Analysis of marketing costs and earnings	+	
Veterinary care	+	
Preparation of feed mixtures	+	
Supply of beef stock	+	
Provision of agricultural and other tools	+	

Table 1—*contd.*

	Authority	
Task	Instructor	Village
Management of enterprises and branches—*contd.*		
Allocation of water quotas to households	+	
Irrigation roster	+	
Reading of water meters	+	
Industrial crops	+	
Green fodder		
Vegetables	+	
Buying and selling of beef		
Irrigation works	+	
Pest control	+	
Analysis of fat content in milk		
Selling of consumption items to members	+	
Selling of production items	+	
Collection of agricultural produce	+	
Marketing of milk and agricultural produce	+	
Storage of empty boxes	+	
Grading and packing of produce	+	
Work safety	+	
Isolation strips		
Maintenance of sheds, etc.	+	
Maintenance of public motorized equipment	+	
Cultivation		
Insurance		
National insurance	+	
Members' insurance	+	
Livestock and poultry insurance	+	
Buildings insurance	+	
Crop insurance	+	
Mechanized equipment insurance	+	
Municipal services		
Maintenance of electricity network	+	
Current security	+	+
Special security problems	+	+
Ecological lay-out and planning of village	+	+
Location of fire-fighting equipment	+	
Maintenance of fire-fighting equipment	+	
Planting and maintenance of public gardens, landscaping		
Maintenance of cemetery		+
Members' gardens		+
Tidiness and cleanliness of public buildings and places	+	
Maintenance of paths, ways and roads	+	
Maintenance of sanitation	+	
Equipment for kindergarten and school	+	
Finance		
Loans to members	+	+
Contributions	+	
Payments to institutions	+	
Banking	+	
Payments to members	+	
Financial arrangements with members	+	+
Payments to workers	+	
Financial reports	+	
Agricultural credit to members	+	+

Table 1—*contd.*

Task	Authority	
	Instructor	Village
Recreation, adult education, information		
Excursions		
Contact with parents and pupils		+
Public fetes and holidays	+	+
Educational activities for adults	+	+
Library and newspapers	+	
Cinema shows		
Maintenance of clubs		
Youth instruction		+
'Gadna' (youth corps)	+	+
Social gatherings		
Artistic groups		
Special cultural activities	+	+
Health		
Special health problems	+	
Public health	+	
Hygiene	+	
Blood bank		
Contact with medical services	+	
Contact with dental services	+	
Convalescence for members		
Inoculations	+	
Religious affairs		
Religious worship accessories		+
Maintenance of synagogue		+
Religious activities		+
Funerals		+

and shows the gaps in activities—some for traditional reasons, and others because of administrative or financial difficulties—which resulted from these characteristics. This schematic division into a polar dichotomy as between instructor and village is, of course, a simplification, and shows only the situation on the level of top policy-making. In reality the *hamoulas* enjoy considerable internal autonomy, which extends over all those traditional spheres—internal matters, religious ceremonies and ritual, and welfare—which they controlled before coming to Israel.

The most interesting fact is that this situation has, in the meantime, been given some recognition by the instructor; a quasi-institutionalization which is expressed by the informal establishment of a 'supreme' institution for the coordination of the various functions and foci of power.

The organizational features of Shalekhet can thus be summarized as follows:

(i) Division of authority, in which the instrumental sphere is handed over to external management, and the integrative and cultural spheres are internally managed.

(ii) The instrumental sphere is achievement-oriented and universalistic (though obviously non-democratic) and governed by rational methods of organization; but work is concentrated in the hands of a small staff, which must implement objectives that are divided up in other villages among several bodies. This imposes a very heavy burden, particularly on the social instructor, and may even lead to his having to neglect proper training and guidance.

(iii) The spheres entrusted to the village itself are organized according to a wholly traditional scheme:

  (*a*) The village council is elected by democratic elections, but this is only a show of democracy; in reality, the list of candidates is not the result of free political activity, but based on the *hamoulas*. The council is a 'foreign' organizational body, whose formal pattern is quite unfamiliar to the settlers; it does not actually perform any concrete organizational tasks, nor is it involved in decisions taken elsewhere; to the extent that it has any public responsibility, this is not to the general assembly but rather to the *hamoula* structure.

  (*b*) The council is elected on the basis of criteria which are conspicuously ascriptive.

  (*c*) The council is not guided by universalistic principles, but serves instead to confirm the existing particularistic division—albeit within the limitation of consensus concerning the political game.

The autonomous element in the village is therefore dual: partial independence of sub-units whose structure and activities are traditional; and a quasi-'collegium' recruited by cooptation of a non-Israeli pattern. The 'collegium' manages to exert social control and to determine social and cultural policies. With the external management, it represents the 'supreme' political authority of the *moshav*.

Figure 5 gives us a schematic picture of this structure.

(*c*) *The 'managed' traditional heterogeneous ('split') community.* We find a vivid example of this in a Yemenite village in the Lakhish area, namely Moshav Savel. This settlement had been blessed by excellent settlement conditions and regular financing,

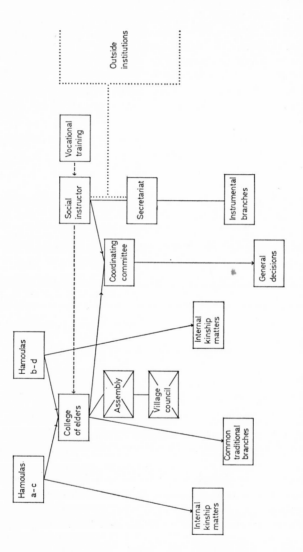

KEY   —— Line of command   ····· Organizational contact   --- Advice   ☐ Organizational body   ☒ Inactive organizational body

Fig. 5 Simplified organization chart of Moshav Shalekhet. Note: (a) 'Internal kinship matters' are, as has been mentioned, areas in the social, educational and cultural spheres which are handled by the *hamoulas* themselves, e.g. relations between kin, matters of religious ritual, welfare, etc. (b) 'Common traditional branches' are areas in the above-mentioned spheres which relate to the traditional community as a whole, e.g. relations between *hamoulas*, division of functions in the village, school, etc. (c) 'General decisions' are those which are taken jointly by the instructor and the village leaders (in the coordinating committee); see Table 1

and its settlers, with the aid of good instructors, reached a high standard of agricultural proficiency and development. In fact, within two years of reaching the intermediate stage their crops brought in an above-average income. But in the ten years of the *moshav*'s existence not even the most minimal social integration of the community had developed, and the various factions of the population have in fact grown still more hostile to each other than they used to be.

Emergence of community-wide solidarity was made impossible by the relationship between the *hamoulas*, of which there are two. But while in Moshav Shalekhet all the *hamoulas* came from the same place and brought with them a tradition of carefully balanced social cleavage and cooperation, in Savel the *hamoulas* came from different localities (though both are from central Yemen). From the very beginning, each group has had its own synagogue and assembly hall, so exclusively maintained that members of opposing factions are not even invited to such traditionally hospitable ceremonies as weddings and circumcisions. In the village's entire history there has not been one case of inter-group exogamous marriage, although this is common among the Yemenites, and serves, in fact, as a mechanism for resolving inter-kinship differences. All mixed youth activities have been forbidden, and the village youth club no longer functions. Even at the elementary school there have been many instances of friction among children of the two warring groups.

However, as long as *moshav* administration and government were vested in the absorptive team the division between the *hamoulas* was one of withdrawal rather than of open conflict. The social instructor and his small clerical staff did all the jobs which required interaction with and acceptance by all the settlers, thus concentrating the *moshav*'s economic power in their hands and allocating various resources and rewards impartially. These arrangements, though not actually legitimated by the population, nonetheless commanded compliance and prevented a bitter fight over so-called spoils.

In short, the organizational activity in the village was minimal, and autonomy was limited to a few internal *hamoula* matters. All the authority which in Shalekhet was vested in the 'collegium' of elders and in the coordinating committee here resided in the settlement personnel. This situation holds true for other villages in our sample, namely Kavoa and Levanon in the first years.

In Fig. 6 we elaborate on this phenomenon.

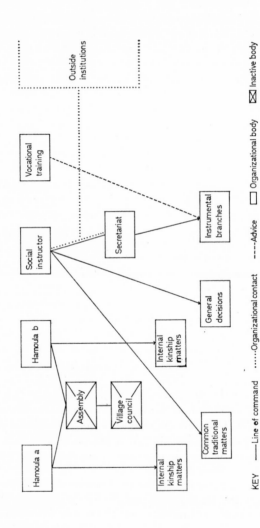

KEY ——Line of command ......Organizational contact — — —Advice □ Organizational body ⊠ Inactive body

Fig. 6 Simplified organization chart of Moshav Savel (during heteronomous period). See notes to Fig. 5

3. The traditional autonomous community

The independent traditional village is a direct continuation of the managed traditional one. Its characteristic trait is that change of government within it *is not conditional on any change in social structure or on the assimilation of new organizational principles*; it results, rather, from a projection of the traditional pattern onto the organizational structure *as a whole*. In other words, the traditional lines of organization which in the previous type existed only in a restricted sense now appear in all the village institutions. The council, once basically fictitious, becomes the real ruling body and, with the secretariat, executes all those duties which were previously the responsibility of an external management; but its work is governed by non-democratic, ascriptive and particularistic criteria. This, by its very nature, is premature autonomous rule, and is, therefore, unlikely to succeed. But there is one very significant difference between a homogeneous and a heterogeneous traditional community. While the former can function as an instrument of policy-making and social control, and may meet with difficulties mainly as the provider of services, the latter is doomed to fail in all three areas.

(a) *Autonomy in the homogeneous traditional village.* The Yemenite village of Levanon, in its more recent period, represents this type. This settlement, situated in the Jerusalem Corridor, is on the main road to the capital. The mountainous terrain has somewhat limited its agricultural development, but on the other hand, when the villagers first settled there, terraces and some fruit-bearing trees had already been prepared for them. In this respect, at least, Levanon was more fortunate than many other *moshavim* in the same area which had to start from scratch. The security situation, however, was consistently bad; not only is the *moshav* very near the frontier, but for a long time it was the only settlement in the vicinity. This, and the actual military duties entailed, were a constant drain on the physical as well as the moral resources of a far from militant group, particularly since the original nucleus comprised only twenty-five families.

These first families were actually rather haphazardly chosen and intended as an 'advance' party which represented several larger units. Initially, their homogeneity was not very important. The village and its population were small; there was still no agricultural organization or work (the villagers were engaged in ground breaking and house building); nor was there any communal or cooperative structure. In fact the village was a sort of rural workers' camp, and in no way resembled, nor was meant to resemble, a *moshav*. This should have made it easier for the new settlers to adjust and should have served as a 'breathing spell' before they faced new duties and responsibilities. We shall see, however, that when the situation did change, this preparation proved insufficient.

Within two years the settlement became a proper *moshav* (in so far as the agricultural resources of the area permitted). Its population was brought up to 130 families, each 'section' of the 'advance group' having in the meantime mobilized members throughout the country. The village now consisted of three almost complete *hamoulas,* each one originating from a different place. These three *hamoulas* crystallized into rigidly exclusive social groups which at first were almost totally isolated from each other, but after a while entered into a fierce power struggle for political and economic primacy. Since, at this point, the village had more families than had been originally planned, the Settlement Department was not interested in keeping all three units. As a result the conflict came to a head very soon, and a population upheaval left the largest group in sole 'possession' of the *moshav,* which numbered fifty households. This change meant a transition from a heterogeneous social structure to a homogeneous one, and the general cohesiveness and relative freedom from conflict which followed the *Stürm und Drang* brought significantly better social conditions in their wake.

The basic motivation of this one-lineage community seems to be the preservation of the group as such, and the cohesiveness of its members. The *hamoula* thus takes good care of its own welfare cases. The village has ten such families either entirely or partially unable to work. Their continued presence in Levanon is an incessant strain: the farms are in the hands of people incapable of developing them (this is also of concern, of course, to the Settlement Department); these settlers are exempt from various local taxes and dues, thus impoverishing the communal fund; their meagre competence provided by various welfare agencies must be supplemented by the *hamoula*; they are frequent recipients of loans which the *moshav* has to underwrite and invariably repay; and more often than not they are unable to perform any communal roles, not least among these being the heavy guard duties needed. These problems could be solved in various ways, and offers of resettlement have been made by the authorities, but the families themselves are reluctant to leave the *moshav*, and it is reluctant to let them go. This type of solidarity also binds the sceptical, the weak and the vacillating to the village at least for as long as the group as such stays there.

Common interests also underlie economic activities. As mentioned earlier, economic production in the Yemen almost never transcended the household; the *hamoula* had no duties in this respect, and no experience of any large or combined enterprise. But in Levanon the *hamoula* leaders have not only had to accept economic responsibility, they have also had to adopt some form of cooperative production. While auxiliary and livestock farming remains strictly within the control of individual households, the *hamoula* is the unit of production for orchard and field crops. These crops are not communally owned, as often happens in smallholders' villages; the idea is not attractive to the property-conscious group, and the settlers insist on having all the plots legally assigned to heads of families. However, since the greater efficiency of large-scale production is recognized, cultivation is supervised by and entrusted to the group. So is the apportioning of the produce. All in all, then, we find here a process in which a traditional structure assumes new roles and functions and redefines its ways of common action, while maintaining its essential system of authority and organization.

The principles which have shaped the social structure and behaviour of the *hamoula* in this new situation are reflected in the status system of the village. There are two distinct scales of social prestige. One expresses the old standards of the traditionally ascribed place of each family within the group. The other represents the level of adjustment to Israel in general, and to the *moshav* in particular. Currently, the traditional scale is the more important: high position on it, due to age, family and religious learning, confers more power and status than does agricultural or administrative achievement. The second scale is complementary rather than conflicting, and subordinate rather than competing.

Traditional integration in fact served as the basis for the achievement of autonomy in the village. Indeed, we can say that this settlement achieved its independence via a 'revolution', i.e. in a non-institutionalized, non-planned way—by showing the door to the social instructor. As in Shalekhet, here too the team tried to change the principles and composition of the settlers' organization, by transferring the centre of power to the council and then staffing it with young people. But while, in Shalekhet, the settlers were content to oppose the situation from within, in Levanon the outside management was removed altogether (this was done by an adamant refusal to cooperate with the instructor or to continue to put the village facilities at his disposal), and the village has not accepted an instructor since.

As a result, and owing to Levanon's social homogeneity, the following organizational web was created.

(i) 'Proper' organizational frameworks were limited to the barest minimum necessary. The only active institutions, in fact, were the council, the secretariat and the farm committee (and even that happened much later), although on paper other bodies existed too. Thus there was a comptroller's committee, which was required by the Registrar of Cooperatives in accordance with existing legislation but which had been inherited from the hetero- nomous period and no longer had any function; a security com- mittee, required by local conditions, was also formed, but it too was inactive; finally, a religious committee was created, but this was no more than an address for the receipt of grants and budgets from the Ministry of Religious Affairs. As a result of the fact that the *moshav* was run almost completely by the council and the secretary, and that there was no proper division of labour, spe- cialization could not progress and no specific functions were carried out efficiently.

(ii) There was no genuine democratic rule in the village, since no organization existed which could either encourage or develop the free play of political power. The general assembly contented itself with giving formal approval to the decisions of the tradi- tional leadership, which in any case were brought before it only to satisfy *moshav* statutes. Even this official procedure was re- sorted to only for council elections, and general policy decisions were hardly ever brought to the assembly's notice. Obviously, under such conditions there could be no question of responsibility to the general assembly as a 'supreme' legislative body, nor could there be any effective control over the council. In practice the council was answerable to the *hamoula* leadership which elected it and which it represented. It goes without saying that *moshav* women had no active or passive vote in it. However, since this form of government reflected the *moshav's* political image and had been validated by the settlers, its homogeneous social struc- ture made it possible for the functions of decision-making and control to be discharged. So despite the limitations of its insti- tutions the *moshav* enjoyed a large degree of coordination between the various spheres of activity, and the inhabitants were able to support council policy and its execution.

(iii) The situation was different where cooperative and municipal services were concerned. Although these matters were dealt with in a general way, which related to all the members of the particularistic group in a manner that was actually universalistic, they were not attended to in an efficient or achievement-oriented fashion. Farming and services, like other organizational matters, were entrusted to the traditional leadership. It would be inexact to say that this leadership was entirely ascriptive. It included two elderly men who had enjoyed positions of honour abroad, a religious leader, and men who had represented the Jewish community before the authorities of their country of origin, a responsibility which required certain gifts and qualifications. Status acquired by virtue of family and age was in this way mingled with the principle of proof by performance: within the kinship framework there was also the expectation of efficient management of public affairs, based on past intellectual and political achievement. Obviously, however, such partial achievement criteria were essentially different from those now required in Israel, and this kind of qualification was quite irrelevant to the task at hand. Despite this, the leadership demanded complete control in the sphere of organization of *moshav* services and refused to hand over to the more efficient individuals who were being pushed by the social instructor before he left Levanon. These included graduates of agricultural schools, young men who had completed their military service, and the more experienced farmers. Failure to make use of their initiative and potential organizational ability because they lacked traditional legitimation led to a series of crises in the village about the supply of services and the functioning of the cooperative; the result was a sharp decline in the efficiency of marketing and purchases, the slowing down of development, financial problems, and the dwindling of the *moshav's* credit. The situation—summarized in Fig. 7—got so bad that the settlement authorities resorted to extreme measures, such as denying the right of signature to council members. Thus the situation which obtained before the instructor left was to some extent restored, i.e. heteronomous rule was partly reinstated through tight outside control.

(b) Autonomy in the heterogeneous traditional village As might be expected, the heterogeneous independent village faced an even

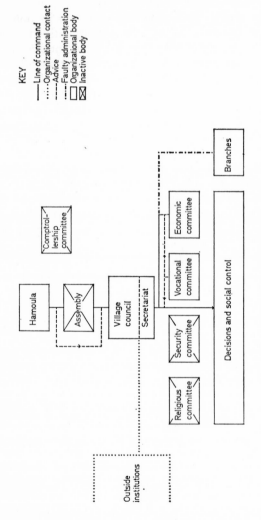

Fig. 7 Simplified organization chart of Moshav Levanon

more serious crisis. We described the situation of Savel during the time that it was heteronomously managed, and we have seen that as long as the social instructor was at the helm he was able to carry out minimal organizational functions. But the settlement authorities felt that, since the village showed no signs of progress in the course of ten years, drastic measures were called for if organizational independence was to be promoted. In accordance with this policy, it was decided at the end of 1958 to take steps described to us as 'throwing someone into the water so that he would learn to swim'. The instructor was suddenly transferred from the village without the settlers' approval and power given to the council. An organizational vacuum was created, and all corporate activity came to a stop. It was impossible for the council to adopt a common point of view; the various members and officials put forward by the two *hamoulas* invariably gave preferential treatment to their own kin; conversely, they received no co-operation from anyone but their own allies. This not only precluded efficient administration but also created acute tensions hitherto kept within limits by mutual avoidance. The resultant paralysis extended to all organizational decisions and led to a breakdown in the cooperative's activity and that of the municipal authority. Taxes were no longer collected regularly, the market mechanism was severely undermined, and the negotiation of payments and credits with outside institutions was thrown out of kilter. In other words, the council and the secretariat showed that they could not possibly function as the main executive bodies of the *moshav*, and the assembly demonstrated that it could not arrive at any decisions. In fact the only important organizational activity which went on relatively undisturbed was the village cooperative shop (run by an outsider) and the supply store. Figure 8 shows us the situation in Savel during this period.

Since these latter events occurred at the end of our study, we were unable to follow them up, but later we learnt that around 1960 the community—like Levanon—split, and half the settlers (in fact, one of the two rival *hamoulas*) left it altogether.

Conclusion

In the preceding pages we have examined the confrontation between an ambitious scheme of rural cooperation and modern municipal government, and different social groups. The material presented has, it is realized, several limitations. First, it deals

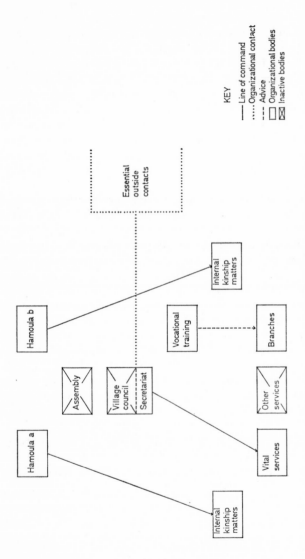

Fig. 8 **Simplified organization chart of Moshav Savel (during autonomous period).** Note (a) 'Essential outside contacts' are institutions such as the district office of the Land Settlement Department, the police station, supply company, etc. (b) 'Vital services' are, for example, the village shop, buying of supplies, etc.

KEY

——— Line of command
········ Organizational contact
– – – Advice
☐ Organizational bodies
☒ Inactive bodies

primarily with polar or 'pure' types of social structure—whether 'traditional' or 'modern'—and inevitably omits various 'transitional' and more complex communities. Second, each type described represents a few case studies at the most, so that any comparative analysis based on the village as the unit of study may be indicative or suggestive but certainly not definitive.[18] Third, this analysis deals with one highly specific pattern only— a pattern, moreover, in which cooperation and municipal government are so inextricably interdependent that it is objectively difficult to isolate problems specific to the first aspect only. In spite of these limitations, however, some general conclusions may perhaps be drawn.

At the risk of stating the obvious, the material thus clearly shows the close relationship which exists between cooperative organization and social structure, in terms of the type of interaction prevalent, as well as of concrete group composition. This interdependence was indeed demonstrated both positively or directly, and negatively or indirectly—that is, in actual case studies presented, and in the significant absence of some socio-organizational patterns—notably of the 'normative' or modern autonomous village in any community type except one.

On the concrete level, this relationship means the necessity of a differential and a gradual approach to cooperation itself. This is so as regards the *comprehensiveness* of the patterns adopted, as well as their *specificity* and *uniqueness*. As we have seen, the *moshav* blueprint combines far-reaching activities in both multi-purpose cooperation and local government. Moreover, it lays down rigid and uniform regulations affecting both goals and implementations. As a result, an overall framework of demands and requirements was created, joining many spheres of life into one integrated and highly interdependent whole; and this lack of separation between, and autonomy of, different areas of activity, with its emphasis on total change and total performance, laid a leavy burden on social resources, and in particular on conformity and consensus. Indeed, not a single village within our sample has met the requirements fully in respect to both goals

[18] To some extent, though, the effective size of the sample is increased by the fact that, because of the long period covered by the research, some villages have actually represented more than one pattern, constituting thus more than one unit of analysis. In this way, it will be recalled, Resissim, Levanon and Savel were observed in both the independent and the managed organizational form; Levanon was also seen as a heterogeneous as well as a homogeneous community.

and organization: even the sophisticated European community
—a 'natural' candidate for modern economic and political institutions—found the intensity and the scope of the pattern too much
for its liking. Elsewhere, of course, the problems were much
greater, ranging from partial and inefficient operation to a total
stand-still or disintegration. One particular step which suggested
itself in this situation was thus that by at least temporary 'sacrifice' of aims on the political-ideological level—democracy and
autonomy—some problems on the rational-instrumental level
could be solved.

The obverse side of such cooperative flexibility, including a
preparatory stage, gradual introduction and a variety of forms,
is clearly the existence of a viable social structure to sustain the
cooperative. In the 'traditional' population such a viability implies
first of all a *functioning* kinship unit (in our specific case the
lineage), without which social organization and action of members
are in general hampered. Indeed, all attempts at early 'atomiza-
tion' and dispersion of such units—attractive as such a procedure
may have seemed for speedy results—disrupted rather than promoted cooperativization. Over and above the individual kinship
unit—relevant, of course, only in the traditional population—
community viability in general has been best achieved in a context of social and cultural homogeneity. The requisite nature of
this homogeneity differs, as we have shown, according to the
pattern of social relations of the population concerned, and in the
traditional village people from the same culture and social stratum
but not from the same concrete background are still effectively
alien to each other from this point of view. This does not mean,
to be sure, that all conflicts in such a population are in terms of
kinship loyalties and obligations, and along *hamoula* lines; or
that there are no tensions within the lineage itself. The Yemenites,
for example, have in fact been characterized by considerable individual competitiveness, reflected *inter alia* in struggles for
public positions and ritual rewards, and in frequent inter-personal
litigation; nor were they free (as we have seen also in our own
data) from inter-generational tensions.[19] The crucial factor in-

[19] See chiefly Shlomo D. Goitein, 'Jewish education in the Yemen as an
archetype of traditional Jewish education' in *Between past and future*, ed.
Carl Frankenstein, Henrietta Szold Foundation for Child and Youth Welfare, Jerusalem, 1953; 'The public life of Jews in the Yemen' (in Hebrew)
in *Mordechai Kaplan jubilee volume*, New York, 1953; Percy S. Cohen,
Tension, hostility and conflict in a Yemeni immigrant community in Israel,
n.d. (mimeograph).

herent in the lineage structure, however, is that it regulates and controls such hostility, and imposes upon it its 'rules of the game'. Of course, the 'proper' intensity of the homogeneity—or the measure of solidarity and integration it has to assure—is not absolute or given but determined by the exigencies and requirements of the cooperative framework. These are particularly great in a *moshav*, and it stands to reason that in less demanding systems, such as specific single-purpose cooperatives, the necessary social basis could be narrower. All in all, however, the basic relationship described seems to be a generalized one.

Of course, the data presented in this paper refer, as was stated, chiefly to the period of 'cooperative initiation' and do not spread over extended processes of change and development. Much of what has been said, however, has elsewhere[20] been shown to obtain in the same population also at later stages. Thus while heterogeneity is of course not necessarily a lasting phenomenon, and can be overcome by prolonged common experience and effective leadership, these factors are often inversely related; a relatively homogeneous population thus provides a background for the emergence of leadership, while even able leaders may not be able to find the necessary social backing in a heterogeneous community. This and more: a strong, solidary, traditional kinship structure may—paradoxically—constitute a positive condition for the sustained development of modern cooperation and not just for the initial introduction: its assured core of genuine loyalty allows the group, as it were, to 'unfreeze' or release part of the traditional commitments in other spheres, while the lack of such a core engenders resistance to innovation. In other words, the security found in traditional frameworks is probably a prerequisite for the introduction of any novel, possibly more 'adventurous' patterns; and in situations in which the sense of belonging to such a group cannot be fulfilled, but the need for it still persists, development—cooperative or otherwise—is made more difficult.

This positive relationship between traditional structures and cooperativization stands only up to a certain level of activity and

[20] See, for instance, D. Weintraub and F. Bernstein, 'Social structure and modernization—a comparative study of two villages', *American Journal of Sociology*, No. 5, March 1966, pp. 509–21; D. Weintraub and M. Shapira, 'The traditional family in Israel in the process of change—crisis and continuity', *British Journal of Sociology*, No. 3, September 1968, pp. 284–99; D. Weintraub and T. Parnass, 'Rural life, orientation to change and modernization', *Rural Sociology*, No. 3, September 1968, pp. 285–99.

complexity, of course, and breakdown or stagnation is subsequently likely to occur if such structures remain viable when
they are no longer capable of sustaining ongoing modernization.
In other words, continued stable development depends on the
extent to which the traditional structure and solidarity recede
and hand over to other social principles in a gradual and controlled way—that is to say, neither disintegrate too soon nor
linger on too long. However, the conditions of such an inversion,
its proper timing, and the difficulties and crises inevitably
associated with it, are clearly beyond the scope of the present
paper.[21]

[21] For a close longitudinal study of such a process in a village, see Moshe
Shokeid (Minkovitz), *From lineage to association—family organization in
the process of adjustment to the moshav* (in Hebrew, with English summary),
Eliezer Kaplan School of Economics and Social Sciences, Hebrew University, Jerusalem, 1967. For a general discussion of traditional and modern
elements in village development, see D. Weintraub, 'The concepts "traditional" and "modern" in comparative social research—an empirical evaluation', *Sociologia Ruralis*, No. 1, March 1969.

Geoffrey Shillinglaw **Traditional rural cooperation and social structure: the communist Chinese collectivization of agriculture**

This paper sets out to examine two aspects of the Chinese experience in collectivizing agriculture. Part I reviews some traditional forms of collective property ownership and of cooperative work, outlines briefly the strategy of the Chinese Communist Party (CCP) in creating collective patterns of ownership and of work, and discusses how far the Party was able to draw on any of these traditional forms. Part II deals rather more explicitly with one of the most acute problems facing the Party in its rural work during the 1950s: that of the optimal size of new collective and commune units, and the relationship of these to two 'natural' (i.e. traditional) units of social organization, the 'natural village' and the standard marketing area. Both parts thus reflect the more general question of how far traditional social cohesiveness may inhibit or promote the formation of modern cooperative and/or collective agricultural organization.

It is necessary to note in passing a number of difficulties in considering China: the existence of wide regional variations in, for example, types of farming, degree of agricultural commercialization, and in the presence or absence of lineage organization; differing rates of social change as between the 'old' liberated areas where the Communist Party had been established since the middle 'thirties, and the areas liberated only in 1949; and the fact that rural China for at least the half century before 1949 had been going through a period of vast change involving the position of the family, lineage, land tenure, population, etc. Thus a generalization true of one area may not be so of another; and statements about 'traditional' practices need to be understood as applying mainly to village China since the beginning of the century. Indeed, 'traditional' should perhaps be rendered as 'transitional' throughout.

I

1. Traditional forms of collective ownership of property

The most restricted unit was, of course, the family itself: the *chia*. C. K. Yang's description of collective property ownership in the *chia* will serve our purposes here:

Although management was dominated by the head of the household, family property was collectively owned, with other family members retaining their share. Under the collective principle, family property was often legally registered in a form of corporate ownership known as *t'ang* under the direction and management of the head of the house and could not be disposed of without common consent of all the male members, each of whom held a share. . . . The Chinese system of collective ownership of family property was largely a result of the earthbound peasant economy, which required the organized labour of the entire family to till a plot of land; and the traditional distribution of property rights within the family was developed mainly from the male-dominated structure of the family as a unit of economic production.[1]

As we shall see later, this basic collective unit was to be heavily eroded in the post-1949 period.

More relevant to our purposes, however, are those forms of collective ownership based on wider units than the family. Only two main types are considered here: lineage property and village association property.

Lineage property was a far more widespread phenomenon in southern China than in the north. In the county (*hsien*) in which was located the village near Canton studied by C. K. Yang in the late 'forties, lineage land constituted 30 per cent of all cultivated land. In a neighbouring village it amounted to 70 per cent of the cultivated area. The economic functions of lineage land were varied. Income from such property was used to finance the village school, for maintenance of temples, public works such as construction and repair of roads and bridges, military defence of the village, and at times relief for the poor. Many lineages in the region of Canton apportioned land to poor members at nominal rent. A very important economic function of the lineage was the collective

[1] C. K. Yang, *Chinese communist society: the family and the village*, 1965, Part I, pp. 140–1. The term *t'ang* (most commonly translated as 'hall') denotes corporateness of ownership, and may be used for non-familial business or religious associations as well as family property. In the usage above, the title deed to the peasant family's land and house would carry the 'hall name' of the family, not the name of any individual.

undertaking of irrigation and water control projects, and the control of irrigation.[2]

I have read of no case where such land was collectively worked for common profit. Rather, communal lineage benefit came from renting the land to individual tenants. In one case cited by Yang, the land went to the highest bidder (although it is not clear whether he had to be a lineage member); in another, the land was rented to male members at nominal rates. 'In such cases', Yang observes, 'collective ownership of land by the clan had the obvious effect of equalizing the right of clan members to use the land and preventing concentration of land ownership in private hands, a situation particularly beneficial to the poor peasants. . . .'[3]

Against this picture of collective benefit through individual exploitation must be put, however, the considerable evidence of diversion of communal profit into private hands, the monopolizing of lineage-land proceeds by lineage managers, and the outright acquisition of such land by influential groups in the village. Thus a Chinese investigator in 1933 could write that 'almost everywhere in China [lineage land] is quickly becoming the private property of the family, or in some cases, of the individual'. Managers of such land frequently monopolized rent collection and kept accounts secret.[4] A detailed analysis of lineage-land management has not yet been made.

A second type of collectively owned property was that of the *village associations*. Gamble, in his study of eleven northern village in Hopei, Shansi, Honan and Shantung, covering the period *c*. 1900–33, has noted the existence of village associations which directed all the affairs of the village and took direct charge of social and economic matters. Their leaders usually, although not always, 'did not represent any specific sections, clans or classes'. In the Honan and Shansi sample villages, family heads served in rotation on these associations.[5] Associations disposed of village land and ponds, the sale of the produce of these going to support schools, local administration, crop watching, local defence and religious activities. The main source of revenue came from a land levy charged for (frequently collective) crop watching. During the period of Gamble's study, however, the position and activities of many of these village associations seemed

[2] C. K. Yang, op. cit., I, p. 194.
[3] Ibid., II, p. 43.
[4] In R. H. Tawney, *Agrarian China*, p. 23.
[5] S. D. Gamble, *North China villages*, 1963, p. 35.

to be declining. Gamble has explicitly contrasted the picture of
what he found to the judgment of Hsiao Kung-Chuan (in *Rural
China: imperial control in the nineteenth century*):

... communal activities were limited in scope and were rarely if ever
conducted by all the inhabitants on a basis of equality. It is difficult
to find an instance in which associative efforts were conducted by a
village-wide organization for the welfare of the inhabitants ... Commoners were not precluded from participation or even leadership in
village undertakings, but the gentry usually dominated them.[6]

2. Mutual aid labour

Apart from these structural units of collective ownership of
property, other forms of cooperative relationships among the
peasantry, revolving essentially around patterns of agricultural
work, were also to be found in traditional China. These may be
termed *mutual aid labour*, and will concern us rather more
directly, since it was in part, although only in part, on such forms
that the communists placed their hopes for the transition to the
eventual collectivization of agriculture.

There was apparently a wide variety of such cooperative labour
forms, and they existed widely in China. 'War, famine and hard-
ship,' as Schurmann notes, 'have always prodded the Chinese
peasant towards co-operation.'[7] Some were of a temporary, seasonal nature, where peasants worked in rotation on each other's
land at peak agricultural periods; others were more durable. Some
involved the interchange of human labour, others the exchange
of labour power with draught animal power. Some were based
on kinship, others not. Nor is the question of who dominated these
cooperative work forms simple. In some areas they had the
character of gang workers hired by rich peasants or landlords; in
others they were clearly much more egalitarian.

Two descriptions of traditional mutual-aid labour have been
chosen to illustrate the complexity of forms. The first is from one
of the innumerable surveys of rural China during the 1930s:

In many localities [in north China] where the system of exchanging
labour power prevails, there is no wage payment whatsoever for farm
labour.... [Such arrangements are made] for the exchange of labour
power with a rich peasant family or even middle peasant family own-

[6] Cited in S. D. Gamble, op. cit., p. 9.
[7] F. Schurmann, *Ideology and organization in communist China*, 1966,
p. 413.

ing field animals. The contract for such exchange of labour power . . .
lasts anywhere from several months to several years.[8]

In Kwangsi

during busy seasons of farm work, the fairly well-to-do middle peasant
and even some poor peasants often find it necessary to hire one or
several day workers, but at other times of the year they themselves
are hired out. . . . They are in reality assisting in a system of labour
exchange. Sometimes they dispense with the payment of wages entirely
and adopt a direct exchange of labour. . . . There is also a system of
cooperative labour. When some big engineering work necessitates the
participation of a large number of workers at the same time, this
system is used. The peasants are called together by the beating of
gongs, and, while no wages are paid, they are given their meals in
return for their work.

The second description is summarized from a report on traditional rural mutual aid made to the North East Bureau of the
Central Committee of the CCP in 1952.[9] The report distinguishes
three types of such cooperative labour:

(a) Mutual transfer of human labour, or the mutual use of large
implements. The general term was *huan kung*. This was
found in provinces close to the sea or to rivers and hence
prone to natural calamities—thus the peasants naturally
had something of this sort, i.e. the peasants voluntarily
organized in crisis periods. Often there was joint ploughing,
planting and harvesting, i.e. collective production.

(b) Cattle mutual-aid teams, where individuals pooled their
cattle for joint cultivation.

(c) Collective selling of labour: this involved a transfer of
labour over a wide area. Because the agricultural season
varied throughout and beyond the province, the poor
peasants came together to sell their labour collectively
elsewhere.

In southern Kiangsu, the report notes, all three types existed—
and in certain areas, between 50 and 80 per cent of households par-
ticipated. The reasons were that many peasants had drifted to well
developed commercial towns, so that the remainder had to combine to solve their production difficulties; that much agricultural

[8] In Tawney, op. cit., p. 72.
[9] 'The original situation and characteristics of rural mutual aid', in *Collection of material on agricultural cooperation in the period of people's
economic reconstruction* (in Chinese), two vols., Peking, 1957, pp. 733–49.

work could not be done by individuals; and, third, that land was not plentiful, so the peasants had to take on sidelines, and to look after both they had to combine.

Finally, the report notes three aspects of such mutual aid:

(a) The social strata who joined these groups: the majority were middle peasants (with implements, but lacking labour power and unable to hire workers) and poor peasants (with labour power but lacking implements). Very few rich peasants joined. Thus they were a sort of 'poor help poor' organization. Because, however, middle peasants had implements and cattle they often became the central elements in mutual aid groups.

(b) Such forms were usually small-scale (two to five households), and generally seasonal.

(c) Inequitable aspects of these mutual-aid teams: the poor peasants were often at a disadvantage—for example, cattle labour was often exchanged at a higher rate than human labour.

We shall be returning to the question of mutual aid in the next section, but a final passage, again drawn from one of the rural surveys of the 1930s, indicates the pervasiveness of various forms of general social cooperation in China prior to 1949:

Long before the introduction of modern co-operative societies into China there were, in Chinese rural communities, various forms of organization for self-help. Being in principle similar to the modern movement [i.e. the Chinese co-operative movement of the 1920s and 1930s], these traditional co-operative societies still exist in almost every district throughout the country. . . . Recent field investigations around Tsinan, the capital of [Shantung], have revealed that in twenty-seven districts there are eighteen types and fifty-seven kinds of traditional co-operative societies. The purposes for which these societies have arisen include cultivation, marketing, loans, savings, general labour, self-defence, famine prevention, and . . . mutual help for weddings, funerals, care of children, band music, common temple worship and travel.

All these forms of social cooperation sprang from the necessity of either finding outside labour or meeting unavoidable expenditure.[10]

To summarize briefly, then, the foregoing: collective ownership of property was found in the family, the lineage and the village

[10] In Tawney, op. cit., pp. 204–5.

association. Income from lineage land was used, in principle, for lineage economic and social purposes, but was derived from individual economic exploitation, not from the lineage members' collective labour. In practice, such income might frequently be diverted to the benefit of powerful social groups or individuals in the village community. Income from village association property was, in the villages studied by Gamble, applied for the benefit of the village as a whole, and leadership of such groups seemed to have been fairly open. This general picture, must, however, be put beside the judgment that in practice most such public land was controlled by landlords and rich peasants, and few peasants had any say in its administration. Finally, a wide variety of forms of labour mutual aid and general cooperative social practices were traditionally found throughout China.

3. The communist strategy for the transition to collectivized agriculture

It is not the purpose here to deal in any detail with the communist strategy for this transition. But, in outline, we may note that four stages were to be passed through before the distant achievement of communism. These were, in order:

(a) The individualization of land relations, to be achieved through land reform.

(b) The creation of mutual aid teams.

(c) The creation of low-level agricultural producers' co-operatives.

(d) The creation of high-level agricultural producers' co-operatives (i.e. collectives).

In this section we shall deal only with the first two of these stages.

(a) Land reform and the individualization of property relationships We may assume that it was not out of a sensitive regard for the niceties of Marxist doctrine about the stage of private property which led the Party to carry out the sweeping and violent land reform of 1949 to 1952/1953—a land reform which was to abolish all the traditional collective forms of property ownership. The Chinese land reform must be understood in its social and political context. One principal aspect of this context was directed to the destruction of the existing rural power structure as expressed in the influence and prestige of the landlord class (both at village and supra-village levels) and of the large-scale lineage organization analysed by Freedman for Kwangtung and Fukien.[11] With the new State power committed to going beyond the traditional functions of exploitation and control, towards an increasingly managerial role in society, clearly the existence of intermediate and oppositional socio-political groupings could not be tolerated. Land reform, then, was primarily an attempt to 'break open' the structure of traditional Chinese society and restructure it on new lines, by confiscating lineage property, village association property, temple property and the property of the landlord class.[12] Such property was to be distributed to the landless and poor peasants. Land titles could be issued to individuals, including women and children on request (although to what extent this was actually carried out is unknown). Finally, we may note that one argument advanced in favour of a radical redistribution of land and the consequent move towards equalization of land ownership (although extremes of ownership remained considerable) was that this would facilitate the subsequent pooling of land by the peasants in cooperatives.

The point for our argument here is simply that, by its commitment to a *drastic* restructuring of rural society along more egalitarian lines, as a means to destroying the power of oppositional social groups, the new Chinese leadership foreclosed on the possibility of using any of the forms of traditional corporate ownership of property which might have existed.

(b) *The creation of mutual aid teams* The second stage in the collectivization of agriculture, begun in 1951 and pursued actively between 1953 and 1955, was the creation of mutual aid teams (MAT). It was here that the Party drew explicitly and consciously on some of the traditional forms of mutual aid cooperation in labour described earlier. Briefly, the argument ran as follows. Where traditional forms existed, they should be built upon. Their exploitative aspects should be rapidly abolished. Where they were based upon kinship groupings, they should be expanded to cut across kinship lines. 'The inherent mutual aid habits of the peasants', to use the words of the Central Committee Decision on Cooperation of 1951, would provide a firm basis for the gradual development of cooperatives. Progressively, seasonal mutual aid

[11] M. Freedman, *Lineage organization in south-eastern China*, London, 1958.

[12] Some property of the rich peasantry was subject to 'requisition', but in general the 'rich peasant economy' was preserved in the post-1949 land reform.

groupings should be developed into whole-year teams, which might also begin to acquire collectively owned property. Thus MAT contained, as it were, the 'buds of socialism'. But, of course, such teams would be work cooperation on a basis of individual farming. Such work cooperation must only be created by mutual agreement and on the basis of benefit to all its members. Teams were to group only a few households, and to remain within the scope of the village.

It is difficult to determine to what degree in actual fact new-style MAT were developed on the basis of traditional mutual aid practices in the post-1949 period. By 1952 some 40 per cent of households throughout China were organized in either seasonal or whole-year teams, although there was wide regional variation: in the north, up to 70 per cent; in the south, as low as 10 per cent. But both the potential and limitations of traditional mutual aid forms in the eyes of the Party can be seen from an earlier editorial of 1943 on work in the border area of Shensi-Kansu-Ningsia—an editorial which launched the labour cooperativization movement of the Yenan period.

In the villages of the border regions [the editorial notes] there have traditionally existed all ways for pulling together a labour force, such as the *pienkung* [a kind of labour co-operation] and *chakung* [collective hiring out of labour], which are methods rather widely used. These voluntary *pienkung* and *chakung*, though rather narrow in scope, and only restricted to relatives, friends, neighbours, are nevertheless suited to the concrete conditions of villages in the border regions. If they can be effectively utilized and directed, and organized and led in a planned way, then they can be transformed into organizations for developing productivity . . . Precisely because this kind of mutual aid collective labour organization makes it possible not to violate the seasons, to save men and animal power, to raise production enthusiasm . . . to develop the spirit of solidarity and mutual aid among the masses, therefore it will be sufficiently supported by the masses . . . Practices such as *huoniu* [joint use of draft animals] or *huochung ti* [joint tilling] all have a mutual aid character. These forms of labour mutual aid are in content very active and suited to real conditions. All must be promptly encouraged and broadened . . . from the old rather narrow and small-scale organizations we must transform them into new organized brigades.[13]

Finally, the editorial laid down one important condition:

We must absolutely give heed to the concrete conditions in the areas concerned, and not regard them as uniform. Thus if we today strive to expand one kind of mutual aid labour among the people, the brigades

organized must not be too large. Neither the *hsiang* nor the administrative village must be taken as production units. It is best to take the
natural village as the unit.[13]

From this and other documents it is clear that in the eyes of
the Party the potential of traditional practices was considerable.
The limitations lay in the fact that such groups were particularistic, in the sense of being either frequently kinship-oriented
or else centred on the natural village as distinct from any wider
unit. To go beyond the natural village was to risk losing the
cohesiveness of the traditional cooperative-labour form.

During the period of the anti-Japanese war the Party had had
to accept a 'minimum programme' of promoting 'organizations
for developing productivity', since the overriding aim was national
unity and the minimum of rural disruption and class warfare.
(The Party's extreme programme of land confiscation had been
suspended as early as 1935.) Thus the limitations inherent in
taking the natural village as the unit of mutual aid labour organization were accepted for the duration. After land reform, the
Party continued a gradualist strategy of building on mutual aid
cooperation, within the framework of the natural village. But
increasingly it was to find that this strategy and framework
placed its organizational and economic goals in jeopardy. It is to
the Party's attempt in the middle 'fifties to break out of the particularism of traditional rural social structure that we now turn.

II

The problem of the system size of collective units

An analysis which attempts to relate 'predisposition to cooperative success' to traditional social structure might well take as one
avenue of exploration the relationship between the *system size* of
the 'modern' organizational unit and that of the traditional community. During the middle 'fifties the Chinese communists encountered in acute form the tension between their collectivist
goals and certain traditional units of social cohesion. In this
section our discussion will focus on how the collective and commune related to two of these units, the natural village and the
standard marketing area, during the period 1956–58.[14]

[13] Cited in Schurmann, op. cit., pp. 420–2. The terms *hsiang* and 'administrative village' refer to administrative groupings of the basic settlement
pattern in China, the 'natural village' (*tzu jan ti ts'un*).
[14] This section draws largely on G. W. Skinner's important analysis of

G. W. Skinner has analysed late traditional and transitional rural China[15] in terms of marketing structures (considered both as spatial and economic systems, and as social and cultural systems) which integrate the primary village community into a wider economic and social network. A necessarily brief review of certain aspects of his analysis will precede our discussion of the CCP's collectivization of agriculture.

Skinner distinguishes three principal levels of market areas existing above the simple 'village community'. These are, in ascending and increasingly inclusive order: the standard (SM), the intermediate (IM), and the central markets (CM). Each market, at each level, has distinctive and vital economic and social functions. The market town at the lowest level (the SM) served as the point of exchange of goods and services between the villages which constituted its standard marketing area, and also as the starting point for the upward flow, and the terminal point of the downward flow, of goods and services of the wider economic system. It served as a centre for financial transactions between peasantry of the SM area and shopkeepers or landlords in the SM town. To its regularly scheduled market came, in addition to the peasants, itinerant traders who circuited all the standard market towns within the higher intermediate market. The modal SM area contained some eighteen villages and 1,500 households distributed over fifty square kilometres (33). For the majority of SM areas, the most disadvantaged villager was within easy walking distance of his market town (i.e. 3·4–6·1 kilometres). The SM area was discrete, that is, all its component villages were oriented toward a single market town.

The SM was, however, but a sub-system (in spatial and economic terms) of a wider trading area, the intermediate marketing area (IMA), which functioned as an intermediate point in the supply and purchase of goods and services between the SM area and the central market. Unlike the SM area, the IMA was not spatially or economically discrete: that is, its component SM areas were typically oriented toward two or three IM towns. Finally, the CM, handling merchandise in bulk and providing goods and services not found at the lower marketing levels, func-

---

marketing patterns in China, 'Marketing and social structure in China', *Journal of Asian Studies*, vol. xxiv, Nos. 1–3, November 1964–May 1965). Bracketed references in the text are to pages of this article.

[15] Skinner confines his analysis to 'agricultural China', i.e. to the approximate half which excludes the inner Asian provinces.

tioned as an economic link between those levels and wider regional trading systems. Like the IM, the CM area was not a discrete system.

Only at the higher levels of these traditional marketing systems was there any marked tendency for coincidence with administrative systems (discrete units). Thus, only a minority of IM towns traditionally served as *hsien* (county)[16] seats, whereas a majority of the higher level marketing towns had administrative status.

Marketing structures, unlike administrative structures, take the form of interlocking networks. It is the joint participation of standard markets in two or three intermediate marketing systems, of intermediate markets in two or three central markets, and so on, which articulates and unites the little local economies centred on each market town into, first, regional economic structures and eventually into a single society-wide economy. Thus, marketing had a significance for societal integration in traditional China which at once paralleled and surpassed—which both reinforced and complemented—that of administration. [31]

Marketing systems were, however, more than economic systems: they were also social systems and 'culture-bearing units'. 'In so far as the Chinese peasant can be said to live in a self-contained world, that world is not the village but the standard marketing community. The effective social field of the peasant... is delimited not by the narrow horizons of his village but rather by the boundaries of his standard marketing area' (32). The SM community tended to be endogamous for the peasant. It possibly served as the framework for the formation of the composite lineage. It could serve as a source of peasant credit and finance beyond the village, and also as a focus for secret society organization. The power structure of the community was 'unlikely to be divorced from [economic] control of the market itself'. Recruitment to the market town's temple committee was from leading villagers throughout the SM area, which also corresponded to the earthly domain of the temple deity. Occupational groups, voluntary occasions (e.g. crop watching) and peasant recreation could all take the SM area as their unit of organization. In the sense that religious folklore, language, weights and measures tended to vary with the SM area, it can be seen also as the unit of a distinctive 'little tradition'.

[16] In very simplified outline, the levels of administration below the province (both before and after 1949) were the *hsien* (county) and *hsiang* (township).

Thus, traditional marketing systems, in this analysis, emerge as formidable social structures with important integrative functions for the village. Specifically, the standard marketing area is seen as one of the basic elements defining the peasant's community and delimiting his cultural world. It could be expected that the CCP, in moving towards the collectivization of rural China, would need to reckon seriously with the particularism of the village, and of the marketing community as analysed by Skinner.

The Party's drive towards full cooperativization of the Chinese peasantry was announced by Mao's speech of July 1955, 'On the question of cooperativization in agriculture'.[17] Prior to that date, progress in the formation of both mutual aid teams and cooperatives had been slow. By mid-year only some 14 per cent of all households were in cooperatives, and this figure concealed wide regional variation. There were compelling economic reasons for the renewed campaign (chiefly, the inability of agriculture to provide the requisite surplus for industrial growth), but an important factor, in the Party's view, was an increasing class polarization in the villages, and the re-emergence of traditional intra-village leaders. Reports throughout the early 'fifties indicated that many of the existing cooperative organizations had been infiltrated by rich peasants and former landlords 'who diverted them to the particularistic interests of the village',[18] cadres were tending to accommodate Party policy to local interests, or were joining 'rich peasant cooperatives' and teams which exploited the labour of hired peasants.

The results of the campaign far exceeded the official projections. In the event, the peasantry was not only cooperativized but collectivized, i.e. private land ownership and interest payments on land shares were abolished. By December 1955 63 per cent of all households were members of cooperatives; by February 1956 51 per cent were in fully socialist *collectives*; by June, 63 per cent; and by December 1956, 88 per cent.[19] Whatever the reasons for the move into full collectivization,[20] not only the rate of formation but

[17] A series of directives on the formation of cooperatives had, however, been issued from 1951.

[18] Schurmann, op. cit., p. 445.

[19] Figures in K. R. Walker, *Planning in Chinese agriculture*, 1965, p. 14.

[20] One factor was undoubtedly the inability of cooperative cadres to manage the complicated accounting involved in apportioning season-end output (after deductions for tax, State grain purchases, capital investment, etc.) between labour and land-share interest. By pressing for full collectivization of land, cadres abolished the problem at one stroke.

also the *size* of the new collective units surpassed that of the earlier campaigns. Where, in the early 'fifties, mutual aid teams and cooperatives had encompassed only segments of the village,[21] the new units now in many cases far surpassed the bounds of the natural village. Can we see in these new multi-village units an attempt by the Party to break the peasants' social and economic organization out of the confines of the particularistic natural village —that is, an attempt to undermine traditional bonds of solidarity by creating new foci of organization and ownership?

Certainly, in autumn 1956 the Party had not discouraged the formation of multi-village collectives. A Central Committee directive of September 1956 advocated the following figures for households per collective: 100 in mountainous regions, 200 for hilly areas, and 300 for plains regions—figures which, as Skinner notes (385), 'far exceed the average size of Chinese villages in each type of terrain'. Whatever reasons existed for this permissive attitude to multi-village units other than an attempt to cut across traditional ties of solidarity, the result was clearly, in many cases, an eruption of inter-village factionalism. Within a year, the Party had issued a new directive which called for a general reduction in size to the level of one village per collective. 'Henceforth, the scale of operation of [collectives] should in general take the village of 100 households or more as its unit, and set up one [collective] for each village.'[22]

Thus by early 1958 there had been a fresh 'down-swing' in unit size, with a majority of collective farms consisting of a single natural village. This in effect meant that the natural village now operated as a single unified economy, and that the collective included practically the whole village population. It is not difficult to imagine that this invited just that resurgence of village self-sufficiency and particularism which the Party had sought to obviate a year earlier with the multi-village collective. In the context, for example of those villages in Kwangtung noted by C. K. Yang (see above, part 1), where lineage land holding had formerly constituted a very high proportion of total cultivated area, reunification of the village as a collective unit would come close to restoring the *status quo ante*. In single-surname villages collectivization of the village as such would serve to reinforce its

---

[21] Mutual aid teams typically grouped six to eight households; cooperatives, twenty-eight to forty households. Figures in Walker, op. cit., pp. 16–17.

[22] *Jen min shouts'e*, 1958, p. 519; extract in Schurmann, p. 456.

traditional cohesion. J. W. Lewis has argued that 'when the communists encountered the pooling of land ... they inadvertently recreated the critical ingredient of lineage and village power, the collective land holdings. Moreover, by the unrelenting stress on the proletarian collective, Party leaders enforced obligations to the village and consciously re-established ... defunct village activities ... such as the village meeting. ...'[23]

The dimensions of the problem are clear. If we accept that during the mid 'fifties the Party had experienced in acute form the tension between its organizational goals and the claims of the particularistic village, we must also assume that any attempt to create still *larger* organizational units which took as their basis the standard marketing community in which the village was embedded *would simply recreate that tension at a wider level.* The suggestion, then, is that the communes of summer and autumn 1958 may be seen as an option, suddenly presented to the Party leadership, which led it to an attempt, born of the experience of the previous years, to create at one blow new units which would bypass and eventually destroy all particularism of village or the wider community to which it traditionally belonged, the standard marketing area. (For, in the event, communes in very many areas either exceeded the size of the SM area by as much as three times or cut entirely across the boundaries of traditional marketing systems.)

Certainly, other factors, such as the continuing poor performance of the agricultural sector[24] and the increase in the territorial mobility of the rural labour force during the water conservancy campaign of winter 1957–8, with its resulting demand for larger units of work organization, were important elements in the move towards the formation of communes. But, as Skinner argues:

The decision to make communes larger than basic marketing systems may well have been deliberate, and if so, it is not unreasonable to surmise that one objective was to circumscribe and diminish the pernicious particularisms of traditional social relations. In this regard, of course, the communist planners faced a dilemma whose twin horns had become only too familiar during the formation of collective farms. When units of collectivization are made to coincide with natural social

[23] *Asian Survey*, III, No. 10, p. 463.
[24] For example, grain output per head, 1952–7, had increased by only 6·9 per cent in five years. State tax plus grain purchase fell by 13·5 per cent in 1956–7 (see *T'ung chi kung tso*, 19, pp. 28, 31–2). Soviet aid and credit declined and stopped in 1956–7. By that date the burden on agriculture was bound to be important if imports of capital goods were to be sustained.

systems, the organizational task is greatly simplified by the ease with which traditional bonds can be used to reinforce the solidarity of the new unit, but at the same time that task is complicated by the inappropriateness of those bonds to the very nature and objectives of modern organization. On the other hand, when units of collectivization are made to crosscut or envelop natural systems, the advantage which accrues from escaping the constraints of traditional ties is necessarily coupled with serious disadvantages, in particular the need to build up organizational strength and to develop solidarity not simply *de novo* but in the face of mutually antagonistic loyalties to the component natural groups. There is some evidence that, having been nicked by the second horn, communist cadre men in 1957 veered back toward the first, and that by the summer of 1958 they were finding it painfully sharp. [384–5]

Space does not allow any full review of the nature and subsequent fate of the communes. But some details of their size and function will show how far they went beyond the peasants' traditional units of work organization and community. First, we should note that the commune was conceived of as a fully integrated administrative and economic unit. Ownership of the means of production was (at the height of the period) in the hands of the commune, as was responsibility for education, public works, militia organization, finance and much rural industry. For agricultural China as a whole, the average area per commune was three times that of the modal SM area in September 1958, and almost four times by August 1959. In the eastern provinces the average number of households per commune was 7,500 (although in other areas considerably less).[25] Some communes, Skinner notes, 'bore no relation to any possible trading system at whatever level'—for example, a Honan commune with over 20,000 households included at least five SM systems which formed part of two IM systems.

At the same time the traditional institutions of peasant marketing were entirely dispensed with. Vast numbers of rural standard markets simply ceased operating. Supply and marketing cooperatives, which hitherto had operated as quasi-autonomous units at the level of the standard marketing town, linking the cooperative/collective on one hand with the State trading companies on the other, were rapidly absorbed into the commune structure. As a result, commodity flows were channelled no longer through traditional marketing systems but through the 'artificial' adminis-

[25] In August 1958 the Party had praised 2,000-household communes as 'better', but all reference to such modest figures rapidly disappeared!

trative systems of the commune. The result was a widespread breakdown in commodity supply.

Two further aspects of the rural commune as a collective organization are relevant to our discussion of the tension between the Party's organization goals and traditional social relations. The first concerns changes in work organization.[26] Until 1958, the work patterns of the peasantry had changed very little from their traditional forms; they were still diffuse, unrationalized, and followed a total agricultural cycle of ploughing, planting, irrigating and harvesting. By early 1958, however, perhaps as a result of their experience in organizing large groups of peasantry for the massive water conservancy campaign of the preceding winter, cadres began pressing for more rationalized systems of work. Where, earlier, the peasant had maintained informal ties of work organization, he increasingly became a member of a group drafted for specialized purposes, such as planting, irrigation or running rural industries, far outside the bounds of his village or his marketing area. This drive to transform traditional labour patterns is reflected in an editorial of August, 1958:

> The working people in their drive forward have advanced the following slogans which fulfil the revolutionary spirit: Militarize Organization, Turn Action into Struggle, Collectivize Life! What is meant by the militarization of organization of course does not mean that they are really going to organize military companies . . . The rapid development of agriculture simply demands that they greatly emphasize their own organizational character, demands that in their work they act faster in a more disciplined and efficient way, that they can be better shifted around within a broad framework, like the workers in a factory or the soldiers in a military unit. Thus they have recognized that their organization requires militarization.
>
> It is possible that the leaders of the peasants who have raised these slogans are not aware of the fact that Marx and Engels long ago in the Communist Manifesto set out a general programme 'of forming production armies, particularly in agriculture.'[27]

The fact that payment for work was now to be made to individuals rather than to the head of the household as hitherto,[27] while entirely consistent with a pattern in which the peasant was no longer to continue working in his primary group on collectively-

[26] For a fuller discussion, see Schurmann, op. cit., pp. 467–72.
[27] *Hungch'i (Red Flag)*, No. 7, August 1958, pp. 14–15. Cited in Schurmann, p. 479.
[28] Wu Chih-p'u, 'From agricultural producers' cooperative to people's commune', *Hungch'i*, No. 8, September 1958.

owned land, represented the final individualization (in economic terms) of the traditional *chia*.

The second aspect of the rural commune concerns, in rather wider terms, its integrative role between State and society. Historically, Chinese administration had rarely extended below the level of the *hsien*. Beneath that level, society largely organized itself—around work, family, lineage, the village and marketing structures. The general acceptance by the State of its role as 'hovering above' society reflected in turn its conception of itself as having primarily exploitative and control functions. During the republican period, the Kuomintang (Nationalist Party) had endeavoured (largely for purposes of greater political control) to extend State power down to the *hsiang* level and beyond. The CCP preserved the *hsiang* level of administration, but throughout the early 'fifties the cooperative and village continued to exist beyond the limits of formal administrative organization. The new State was, however, committed to an increasingly managerial role in society, and with the creation of the communes the dichotomy between State and society was to be finally abolished. The commune was merged with the (grossly enlarged) *hsiang*, thereby, in the words of the First Secretary of Honan, fusing 'the organ of State power with the economic organization. [The commune] is both a basic social organization and a basic political organization'.[28]

The commune was thus a vast, administratively rationalized collective unit which aimed at full integration of State and society. Its labour organization was to be 'militarized' or 'like a factory'. In a large proportion of cases it cut across all traditional marketing patterns, with disastrous results for rural trade. Its effective life was, however, brief.[29] By the beginning of 1959 Party reports suggested that, as with the multi-village collective, the 'localism' (*pen-wei chu-i*) of the commune's component brigades (which corresponded largely with the former natural village-cum-collective of 1957) was beginning to assert itself against the 'universalism' of the commune. For example, the Li-wu brigade in a Kwangtung commune 'hid 17,000 catties of unhusked rice. According to them, the unhusked rice was hidden [so that] ... the brigade could be assured of food in case the commune could not

[29] The cautious December 1958 communique of the Central Committee in fact marked the beginning of the retreat in this phase, although a new attempt was made during 1959 to reinvigorate the commune campaign.

afford free meals . . . and could attain a position [from which] to surpass the other brigades'.[30] Other reports indicate that the assigning of peasants to work outside both native village and marketing community aroused very deep resentment.

By late 1960 and early 1961 the retreat was in full swing. Communes were, on average, reduced to a third of their 1959 size, and by 1963 apparently corresponded frequently to natural marketing systems. A series of decisions after August 1959 effectively decentralized the commune, leaving it only residual powers of administration, banking and internal security, and responsibility for some small industries. The unit of ownership became first the brigade (i.e. the natural village-cum-collective) and, by late 1960, the team (i.e. small villages or 'neighbourhoods' of larger villages). The team (and in some areas, the household) seems to have become in many cases the basic unit of accounting in production.

The revival of traditional marketing systems was slower. Only in late 1962 did the government formally admit the value of traditional trading structures:

. . . the logical, historical supply relations must be rediscovered. People may prefer a certain product from a certain place because of facility of transport or simply because that is what the people were used to . . . These conditions still persist today . . . Therefore, this must be studied, and these traditional relations re-established, of course not completely and not in every detail, because not all traditions . . . are logical today.[31]

At the same time renewed stress was laid on traditional leaders at the local level who, as distinct from 'outsider' commune cadres,

---

[30] T'ao Chu, 'Report of an investigation of Hu-men commune', cited in Skinner, pp. 394–5.

[31] Cited in Skinner, p. 376. In late 1968, during the closing stages of the cultural revolution, moves were again made to bring the supply and marketing cooperatives under tighter control by 'revolutionary committees' (successors to Party committees) at the local level. On his occasion, however, the leadership in one province at least (Honan) showed it was aware of the significance of traditional marketing systems: 'Some comrades were worried that unified leadership by the revolutionary committees of the *hsien*, commune and brigade would result in stress on setting up points of the commercial network *in accordance with administrative districts, thus impeding the circulation of commodities in accordance with the economic areas*. After study . . . all understood that the purchase of goods from other areas and the direction of the flow of goods, which were *practices formed naturally in accordance with the economic areas*, were an objective law which should not be violated.' *Survey of the Chinese mainland Press*, No. 4379, 19 March 1969; emphasis added. The term 'economic areas' clearly refers to the marketing area.

were 'familiar with local conditions pertaining to social relations, ... [since] the local villagers are all either relatives or friends'.[32] By some time in the early 'sixties the basic socio-economic unit in rural China was effectively either the natural village or its component 'neighbourhoods'. Within the confines of the village the peasant divided his labour between his own private plot and team work on collective land. Reports indicated that 'rich peasants' were appearing again, which, in Schurmann's phrase, 'suggests that "kulakization" may be endemic to an imperfectly collectivized rural economy such as that of China'.[33]

Conclusion

By its commitment to radical social change through land reform the CCP had foreclosed on any adaptation of traditional forms of corporate property ownership to 'modern' collectivist agricultural organization. But during the early 'fifties it sought, where possible, to work *through* certain traditional forms of labour cooperation, and *within* the framework of the natural village, as a means to laying the foundation for eventual cooperative and collective organization. Faced, however, with the localism of the natural village, which constantly deflected organization from its 'universalistic' goals, the Party changed course. The formation of collectives may be seen *inter alia*, as an attempt to break out of the constraints of traditional village solidarity by creating multi-village units, an attempt which foundered precisely on village localism. By early 1958 a majority of collectives had been reduced in size to align with the natural village, and this tended in effect to re-unify the village as an integrated economic and social unit. The communization of summer and autumn 1958 was in part a response to the continuing problems posed by traditional solidarities. The Party sought, in one leap, to go right outside all particularism of village or traditional marketing community, to induct the peasant into a vast, administratively rationalized, collective unit which would fully integrate state and society. At the same time, it attempted to radically alter work patterns through an intensification of division of labour. The failure to align the new unit with the natural marketing system produced paralysis in commodity exchange; the attempt to 'de-

[32] Cited in Skinner, p. 396.
[33] Schurmann, p. 492.

structure' the peasant from the ties of his community produced a resurgence of localism. By the early 'sixties the Party was again seeking to work through, rather than against, traditional solidarities and social structure.

This paper has not attempted any extensive analysis of the reasons for, and the results of, the vast changes in the organization of Chinese agriculture and rural social life during the decade of the 'fifties. Nor has mention been made of the role of ideological education in changing existing peasant attitudes and fostering loyalty to new organizational units, or of the sanctions employed by Party cadres to secure compliance. A scholarly attempt to account for relative degrees of success or failure in various regions of China in implementing collectivist policies would, if the evidence were available, properly have to consider variables such as type of farming, dispersal or concentration of the settlement patterns concerned (e.g. as between the nucleated villages of much of China and the dispersed villages of the Szechwan basin), the presence of ethnic minority groups, the extent of previous lineage land holdings (if they existed), as well as many other factors. Clearly, on the evidence available this would be impossible. But, in general terms, the Chinese experience is suggestive of the continuing strength of traditional social systems as against 'modern' organization. It reveals something of the dilemma in choosing, or choosing to dispense with, traditional solidarities as a basis for cooperative and collectivist organization.

Ronald G. Crocombe Social aspects of cooperative and other corporate land-holding in the Pacific islands

This is not a scientific paper, as the necessary data are not available, but is based on personal evaluations and a limited number of facts. I have visited almost all the institutions and places referred to, talked with people concerned with them, and studied the very limited writings about them, but only in a few cases has research been undertaken by myself or others.

Whereas land-holding by foreigners in the Pacific is almost all by joint stock companies, partnerships or individual entrepreneurs, almost none of the land is held by islanders in these ways. Most of their land is held under a diversity of customary tenures, and a little under various forms of leasehold and freehold.[1] The rest is held under various cooperative and other corporate forms, which have the advantage, from a research point of view, that each instance has been created and developed in relative isolation.[2] However, the possibility of scientific comparison between them is limited, as both the structures and the context in which they operate differ so widely. It may be more profitable to contrast each organization with other institutional forms in the same place.

The nature and relative importance attached to the various goals of the institutions mentioned in this paper vary greatly, although none was set up with simply economic goals of maximizing productivity per unit of land, capital or labour. Some have grown from inaccurate notions by colonial governments about the nature of indigenous land tenure. These I have termed 'institutionalized misunderstandings', fossilized by colonial law and practice. Second are those established primarily to protect underprivileged minorities. Third are the formal cooperatives, descendants of Rochdale. Fourth are cooperative or other corporate

[1] None of these concerns us here, and they are discussed more fully in Crocombe (1970).

[2] Only the cooperatives (a term reserved here for Rochdale-type cooperatives) have a common ancestry and some current interaction (through common journals and occasional regional cooperative conferences).

ventures set up, voluntarily or compulsorily, mainly to overcome
problems of traditional land tenure and work organization. Fifth
is a State-owned land corporation, of which only one major example exists. Finally, a wide range of informal group enterprises
involving land have been formed by Pacific islanders to achieve
improved economic and social standards.

1. Group land-holding as an institutionalized misunderstanding

Most indigenous people in New Caledonia, Fiji, New Zealand,
the Cook Islands and the Society Islands find themselves joint
members of legally determined land-owning groups as a result
of misunderstandings by colonial land authorities about the
nature of their traditional land tenure.

New Caledonia In 1868 Governor Guillain mistakenly declared
that indigenous land ownership was collective, that the unit of
collective ownership was the tribe, which was represented by its
chief. As a result of this misunderstanding 'the administrative
fiction of collective common property was born . . . [and] has been
the basis of government policy ever since' (Saussol, 1970). The
problem was greatly exacerbated by the reduction in size of
Melanesian reserves, often by force, and after 1897 by the compulsory resettlement of Melanesians to make way for French
settlers.[3] Entire groups were transplanted to lands which 'far from
being unoccupied or collectively owned, belonged traditionally
to clans which still owned them' (Saussol, 1970). Both immigrants
and traditional residents accepted that the latter still owned the
land and that the former had only the most tenuous rights. The
original owners had no choice but to make land available to their
forced guests for subsistence, but new problems arose when the
compulsory planting of a commercial tree crop, coffee, was enforced by the *gendarmerie* after 1925. Where immigrants and
local clans were related or had extensively intermarried, the
forced compromise was less traumatic, but everywhere it was
difficult.

There are several sociological morals to be drawn from the
New Caledonia experience. First, the results of logical planning
(and the logic of the French planners cannot be faulted) are likely
to be tragic if based on false premises. Perhaps this is axiomatic,
but a century of frustration and despair is only now leading to

---

[3] A good example is contained in Guiart (1961).

official reassessment of basic assumptions. Second, effective co-operation requires a degree of cultural identity among members (and some who were forced to live 'communally' had no common language, let alone customs) as well as felt identity (for both immigrants and residents considered it unjust and inappropriate that they should have to live together). There was no traditional basis for their communal living, but since government thought there was, no alternative structure was provided. The social and political context could scarcely have been less conducive to pro-ductivity or harmony, even after the colonial government con-sciously sought to promote these goals. The Melanesian reaction of repressed hostility and long periods of despondent apathy periodically erupting into violent rebellion is not surprising.

A century of 'experience' of this experiment in group land-holding has resulted in an understandable increase in demand for individual ownership.

Fiji Here the traditional leadership structure of kin groups was formalized by the colonial government and given unprecedented powers. The leaders, whose positions are hereditary in the male line, have been legally guaranteed security of position, prestige, power and economic advantages.[4]

Fijian commercial agriculture in this context has been most unproductive. With some notable exceptions the hereditary aris-tocracy had neither skills nor motivation to maximize commercial agriculture; rather, their aim in maximizing income was for con-sumption or distribution (i.e. for social rather than economic investments). Commoners, on the other hand, had two good reasons for not producing more than a limited surplus. The first was due to the institution of *kerekere* whereby a person is obliged to grant personal property to a kinsman who requests it. It is impolite to request the necessities of others, but very common to request their surpluses (i.e. surplus to the average of that class and kindred). The second reason was that chiefs are entitled to an unspecified proportion of surpluses,[5] and it is considered dis-courteous for a commoner to possess things which his chief does not. Both factors derive from a value system in which humility is virtue and attempting to rise above one's status is considered improper.

[4] For details see Belshaw (1964), Groves (1963), Nayacakalou (1965, 1970) and Sahlins (1962).
[5] For land leases the proportion is specified at law.

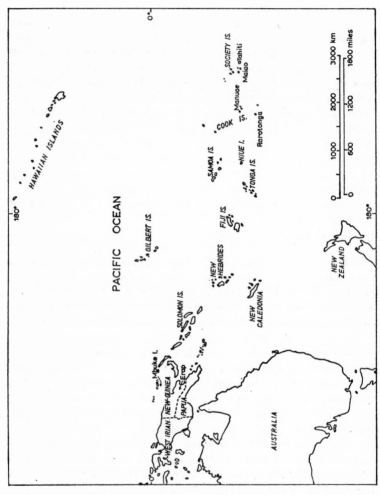

Fig. 9   The Pacific islands

The Fiji *mataqali* holding can be described as successful in its own terms. Although not fully congruent with either traditional precedent or current need, it did provide a working basis for leadership and group action in relation to land, and for the transfer of land to outsiders in need, though this was achieved only by direct government action to record and lease land to collect and distribute the revenue from it.

New Zealand, the Cook Islands and the Society Islands In all three areas traditional leadership was, in effect, abolished, for it was given no role and was prohibited from applying sanctions.[6] Thus although productivity had risen in the Cook Islands while groups remained traditionally cohesive and leadership effective, it fell after the turn of the century, by which time the sanctions of traditional leadership were no longer legally supported, and bilineal inheritance had turned the traditionally small and localized land-holding groups into large, amorphous, non-localized groups.[7]

One of the social prerequisites for the effective functioning of such systems is the existence not only of appropriate procedures but also of political action to remedy structural defects. For example, in both the Cook Islands and New Zealand, bilineal inheritance, though introduced through misunderstanding, became accepted after several generations as based on hallowed tradition, and the owners of uneconomic fragments would not tolerate change. In New Zealand the ruling National Party dared not pass comprehensive legislation on Maori land problems for fear of not gaining Maori seats in Parliament. But despite this caution and despite increasing investment in election campaigns among Maoris, all successful Maori candidates belonged to the Opposition (Labour) party. This fact, and the proposals of senior officials, persuaded the government that it had nothing to lose and it has therefore proceeded to legislate to overcome the problem of fragmentation.[8] In the Cook Islands the opposite

[6] For the Society Islands see Panoff (1964); for the Cook Islands see Crocombe (1964a); for New Zealand see Kawharu (1970).

[7] Crocombe (1964a, pp. 129–42). In the Society Islands, however, where land was a saleable commodity, multiple ownership of single lands by large numbers of people living on many islands was the best protection against foreign alienation. The process of acquiring the minute rights of so many people on so many places was too cumbersome for most would-be buyers (Panoff, 1964, p. 138).

[8] Under the new legislation (Maori Purposes Act, 1967) Maori land which

power relationship obtains, i.e. the ruling party depends for its support on the conservative land-owning majority and thus it is reluctant to institute reforms which the party leadership favours.

2. Corporate land-holding to protect underprivileged minorities

The peoples of the Pacific, with subsistence technologies and small-scale polities, were at a disadvantage in relation to bearers of industrial technology and centralized government from Europe. Some local governments protected themselves by prohibiting land sales (e.g. the kingdom of Tonga) but the cases we are concerned with here are at the other end of the scale—those in which dominant foreign groups have acquired most of the land, but where some lands have been set aside for indigenous minorities, under the control of their representatives.

Maori land corporations In the 1850s many Maori tribes, under the leadership of traditional chiefs, engaged in extensive commercial agriculture both for sale to settlers in New Zealand and for export to Australia and California. The Maori wars of the 1860s and 1870s left European settlers in control of the markets. Peace and the Maoris' withdrawal from commercial activity atrophied traditional leadership.

Most high quality lands had been acquired by Europeans by the 1890s, when Mr (later Sir) Apirana Ngata and other Maori leaders sought to establish an institutional structure which would preserve the remaining Maori lands in Maori hands and enable them to be turned into productive assets. The first Maori corporations, formed to lease tribal lands to Europeans, date from the 1890s. These were extended in 1903 to permit large-scale farming by Maori owners also. Progress was limited until Sir Apirana Ngata, then Minister for Maori Affairs, initiated the Maori Land Act of 1931, which provided for governmental loan finance and farmer training for corporations.[9] The largest of the one hundred

---

is owned by four persons or fewer automatically becomes ordinary freehold land (this is expected to result in a reduction of 20–30 per cent of separate Maori land titles) and is thus saleable on the open market. There are extensive provisions for consolidation of fragmented holdings and compulsory acquisition by government of uneconomic shares in Maori land for resale to co-owners or other Maoris.

[9] Extensive provision was also made for the development of individual owner-operated farms, in which the fragmented land holdings were consolidated, developed as large single units under government control and

or so Maori land corporations is the Mangatu corporation, which has 112,000 acres, assets (including land) of about $nz3 million, about 1,900 'owners', a permanent staff of 125 and a fluctuating number of casual staff. Most corporations own several thousand acres, but the land is not of high quality.

There are seven major roles with respect to any corporation: those of the members, the committee of management, the secretary, manager, workers, the Maori Land Court and the Department of Maori and Island Affairs.

The members, numbering from a dozen to several thousand, are the original land-holders and their descendants, who hold shares in proportion to the value of the land surrendered to the corporation. Many owners have emigrated to urban or other rural areas,[10] but this is not considered by any party to be a problem. In fact many consider it an advantage, for they get their share of profits without becoming involved in the corporation's day-to-day affairs or in factional disputes (usually between kin-based segments of owners), which are a considerable problem for some corporations. A possible disadvantage is that the more energetic and innovative tend to emigrate, but this applies to farm workers anywhere.

The committee of management is elected by members and meets at monthly or other intervals. In the early years committee members were almost invariably chiefs or their nominees: chiefly families were better educated and accepted as leaders. The spread of education gave chiefs less technical advantage and the weakening tribal structure gave them less automatic access to leadership roles, and conflict between chiefly roles and corporation goals increased. Nevertheless, seniority and genealogical connection remain influential in determining election to many committees, and some conflict between traditional Maori values, principles and goals in organization, and those of the corporations as commercial ventures remains.

Most management committees consist of members of the cor-

---

then subdivided into individual farms. This has been widely undertaken with reasonable success.

[10] It was originally intended that all owners would reside on the lands and work them communally, but though this partially happened in the early days it no longer does. As Kawharu (1969) points out, there has been a gradual shift away from traditional patterns of cooperation and 'the latest synthesis may owe more to the joint-stock trading pattern than to the tribal system'.

poration concerned, but many of the most successful corporations included one or two non-members who were seldom involved in internal factions and who tended to emphasize the long-term well-being of the enterprise rather than the short-term goals of individual members. But the main advantage of outsiders is that they are chosen for their personal qualities and knowledge of farm management. Corporations are more willing to elect non-members to committees of management today than several decades ago, the criterion increasingly being one of long-term financial success. Although most committees of management are exclusively Maori, it is not uncommon for a European with appropriate skills to be elected.

There is sometimes conflict between corporation members and the committee of management over the disposal of profits. Members generally press for maximum pay-out and committees (especially the more experienced ones) for re-investment. As committees which do not pay out enough may not be re-elected, there is a tendency for land to be 'milked' and the enterprise starved of development capital. The pressure for immediate payment is due not only to preference for short- rather than long-term gratification[11] (which is in part related to a lack of appreciation of the savings and investment process) but also to mistrust of the future and mistrust of people—the former because depressions and pests have deprived them of assets in the past, the latter because of instances of embezzlement and mismanagement. As the management committees are paid for attendance at meetings, it is feared that they may devote excessive time and thus money to this rather than to development.

A secretary is not mandatory but almost all corporations have one. He is usually a corporation member and, if so, usually a committee member. The secretary is a key figure not because of any statutory powers but because of his ready access to, and familiarity with, both the people and the information, which is crucial to the affairs of the corporation. Most corporations today appoint independent commercial accountants and auditors.

Managers are full-time, salaried employees of the corporation, appointed by the committee of management. Many informants inside and outside corporations rated their personal integrity and managerial and technical skill as the most important factor in

[11] Development of marginal land is, of course, a very slow process, and the investment may not bring substantial returns during the lifetime of the persons originally responsible for management.

the success or otherwise of corporations. Managers appointed from outside the membership have a much better overall record than those appointed from within: partly because one is statistically less likely to obtain a high-quality man within the small group of owners than within the country as a whole, and partly because the advantages of being a member (in terms of motivation and links with workers) seem to be outweighed by the disadvantages of the non-economic obligations of member-managers. Many managers have been appointed because of their social or political position in the hierarchy of owners, or according to such criteria as skill in oratory, which is justly valued for many leadership roles, though it is not particularly appropriate for this one. The managerial record of such people has generally been poor.

An additional problem for some Maori managers[12] is that workers expect to be accorded Maori tenets of generosity when they want time off for social commitments or when their work is not of adequate standard. The manager may be faced by a dilemma, as the two value systems differ in some important respects: applying the one leads to short-term harmony but reduced productivity, whereas the other is likely to result in more conflict but higher production. In so far as the manager employs positive sanctions such as persuasion and encouragement, their common heritage and common interest in profits is an advantage. But in so far as he has to employ negative sanctions (issue orders, deny privileges or threaten dismissal) these are not congruent with his kinship with them. Thus it becomes difficult to remove inefficient workers, and there is strong pressure within the owning group to employ the closer kin of the manager. This problem is steadily declining, partly as a result of government schemes for training managers and partly because the Maori value system is accommodating itself to the dominant commercially-oriented model.

Perhaps the greatest difficulty in the selection of managers has been that prestige (and usually financial reward) is much greater for farm owners than for farm managers, and the best farmers are thus often not available as managers.[13] The rewards from pastoral

[12] A minority of managers are European.
[13] The development of rough land in New Zealand has been undertaken mainly by individual men (mainly European) working extremely long hours for minimal income with the prospect of individual ownership and high income in a decade or two. If this effort has to be paid for at ruling rates of pay to employees it creates a vast debt, the interest on which doubles or trebles the debt, by the time substantial revenue is derived.

farming (and most corporations are sheep and cattle farms) are very closely related to the effort invested, which depends mainly on the quality of management.

Workers are appointed by the manager, mainly from among members, who are usually given preference both as a privilege of membership and because they may be motivated to work more efficiently. They are paid award rates of pay (in addition to their normal share of profits if they are members).

The Maori Land Court has power to check the disposition of assets of corporations and to disapprove the inclusion of any person in the committee of management.[14] There is much disagreement about the Court having these powers today, though some corporations still need an independent agency with power to protect the interests of shareholders. If corporations were ordinary companies, any failures could be wound up and their assets sold. But these corporations have two additional functions: to retain the lands in Maori hands and to ensure that the owners gain maximum benefit from them.

One of the most serious difficulties[15] for corporations was the lack of external check on their operations unless they were in financial difficulty, when it was often too late for remedial action. In this respect they were like private companies, but private companies have internal non-statutory checks in the form of shareholders, directors and management whose interests are much more exclusively economic and whose knowledge of commercial operations is more extensive. Since 1965, however, corporations must submit their audited annual accounts and balance sheet to the Land Court registry. The Land Court has statutory power, though it is seldom necessary to use it, to remedy defects in management or other aspects of corporations.

The Department of Maori and Island Affairs is responsible for promoting the development of Maori land, including the provision of credit, extension services and training. Those corporations

[14] The court normally approves the elected committee, but a committee member with a history of incompetence or dishonesty is likely to be rejected. The court occasionally appoints a person (sometimes a Departmental official) to the committee of a corporation in financial difficulty.

[15] In addition to social difficulties, a major physical difficulty has been that as corporations were not begun until most high-quality land was alienated, many are on land of medium or marginal quality. Scale, too, has been important: despite such cases as a profitable 400 acre dairying corporation, few corporations below 5,000 acres in area have been very successful.

which borrow government finance[16] must have their annual farming programmes, and dividend payouts, approved by the government.

Despite their difficulties and disadvantages, the Maori land corporations have achieved a great deal.[17] They have held in Maori hands lands which would probably otherwise have been alienated. They have provided a means by which uneconomic units have been consolidated into effective farms, not only for economic operation but also to make maximal use of limited skills. They have provided a structure which meets the needs of numerous right-holders while achieving reasonable managerial standards, more long-term planning than would otherwise be likely, and an institution to which banks will provide development finance. The corporations have also facilitated mobility of the people, who could benefit from their lands while working at full-time posts elsewhere.[18] Those remaining on the land have been fully and quite profitably employed. This may be a factor underlying the more rational distribution of Maori population than occurs in most of the Pacific, where people tend to be tied to ancestral lands, irrespective of suitability of the land, either because they can obtain no other or because if they leave the land to which they have traditional rights they gain no benefit from it. Psychologically, successful corporations have made their shareholders partners in a large and valuable enterprise rather than in a small, often unidentified, portion of undeveloped land.

David Bettison, in a personal communication, observes that the land corporations come closer to providing an egalitarian relationship between immigrant and indigenous people, as well as within the indigenous community, than any institutional structure he has seen in the world. They also give the indigenous people some of the institutional implements to become owners and users of capital rather than merely workers.

[16] As at 31 March 1968 $NZ640,000 was on loan to corporations from the Department (in addition to normal loans from commercial sources).

[17] Though many have been less successful than neighbouring European farms, this is not the issue. European farmers have had much greater access to loan finance and training, as well as having cultural and psychological patterns which were much more conducive to successful commercial farming. The Maori corporations, then, must be compared with other approaches to Maori land development and with other approaches to land-holding by cultural minorities.

[18] Retention of rights on lands which the right-holder does not use has disadvantages too.

Princess Bernice Pauahi Bishop's estate A different means of
protecting and managing a minority group's lands is presented
by the Bishop estate, the lands of which comprise 368,226 acres
or about nine per cent of the area of the State of Hawaii. Princess
Bernice Pauahi (Mrs Bishop) was the last direct descendant of
King Kamehameha, who united Hawaii into a single kingdom in
1795. Land became a saleable commodity in 1852 and most was
soon acquired by foreigners. Princess Pauahi was distressed by
this loss and by the lack of compensating skills to compete in the
new environment, in which Hawaiians had become a minority.
In 1884, therefore, she willed her landed estate, by far the largest
in Hawaii, to be managed in perpetuity to finance education for
Hawaiians (for details see Black and Mellen, 1965). From a capital
value of $us300,000 in 1884 the estate rose in value to $us248
million by 1965 through the use of the land for a wide range of
agricultural and commercial purposes (Bishop Estate, 1965, p. 10).
Had this trust not been formed, these lands would almost certainly
have been acquired by foreigners.

    This trust is by far the largest and most profitable corporate
land-holding enterprise in the Pacific islands. Why has it achieved
its goals so fully? First, I think, because it has limited decision-
making to a very small group of five trustees and has given them
full powers.[19] Second, because the trustees are chosen by the
Supreme Court, which, though far from completely so, is as independent of direct political pressure as is possible in Hawaii.
Third, the trustees have generally been personally qualified by
extensive business experience (and have operated in a context of
rising commercial prosperity). Fourth, the goal has been simple
and precise—to make money and to use it to educate Hawaiian
children. Finally, joint action has been limited to specific tasks,
and the day-to-day exploitation of the land has been delegated to
those corporate groups, whether Hawaiian or other, which are
most competent to carry out the operation concerned. All five
factors have much wider relevance to cooperative forms of land-
holding in the Pacific.

South Australia's Aboriginal Lands Trust This experiment began
only in 1966, so that it is far too early to assess it. The Trust
consists entirely of aboriginal representatives with very little commercial experience, who will administer about twenty million
acres of aboriginal reserve lands formerly administered by the

[19] Many, but not all, trustees have been of Hawaiian ancestry.

state. They represent diverse aboriginal groups with different languages and cultures, and their success may depend in part on the strength of their common rejection of a century of white domination. Vital issues for future study include the formal structure of relations in the operation of each reserve, and the relationship between members of the Trust and other aboriginal people in the state.

3. Formal (Rochdale-type) cooperatives

These have become widespread only since world war II. Based on Rochdale principles, they have been grafted in their transmission through United Nations agencies, the South Pacific Commission and various colonial governments onto diverse traditional group structures and sentiments. Although none saw land-holding or land-working as a goal, this has resulted in some cases. Most of the land used by these cooperatives was purchased from foreign companies, usually as going concerns. In some cases the cooperative has worked them as a single unit, in others they are subdivided into individual farms (though still owned by the cooperative) with varying degrees of cooperative action between farmers.

M'buke cooperative plantation, New Guinea[20] In Manus, which has about twenty language groups, early proposals for control by the large, multi-language local government council were dropped in favour of small, localized cooperatives. The M'buke cooperative plantation consists of thirteen small islands within ten miles of the main island (M'buke), on which all 450 of the group's inhabitants live in a single village. The plantation, by which many of these people were formerly employed, was bought by the pre-existing trading cooperative in 1961 for $A12,000. Only the cooperative could raise the necessary deposit (*per capita* cash income at the time was perhaps $5 a year) and it was the only form of business organization with which the people had experience.

The great cohesive force in the early years was the strong and unanimous drive to retrieve the plantation, alienated over fifty years before, from foreign ownership. Once that goal was

---

[20] There are about six cooperative plantations in New Guinea but only M'buke has been studied. Government policy does not favour this form of enterprise.

achieved, divisive forces became stronger, perhaps the greatest being the desire on the part of sub-groups who would gain from such a division to abandon the cooperatives and return the land to the 'original' owners. There is such uncertainty about these rights that this policy would have created chronic disputes, and, because of differential fertility and the movement of population over the past fifty years, many would have been left landless while others would have had more land than they could have farmed.

Management is by an elected committee of five members, including the manager. Each committee member is assigned a segment of the plantation and eight workers for periods of three months. To avoid discipline problems and concentration of too much power in management, each worker is paid by output rather than by the hour. As each man works about six months annually on the plantation, and the rest of the year on subsistence and minor cash-producing activities, this has meant that the supply of labour has been adequate and that discipline has not been a serious problem. Replanting is an unpaid (but inadequately met) obligation on all workers, but clearing every four months is by contract (usually let to women members of the cooperative). The secretary, store man and inspectors are paid wages. The present government assistance, through its cooperative officer,[21] appears to be needed.

Despite the intention to rotate committee members and workers around the various islands of the cooperative, both have tended to associate much more with the areas to which they have a traditional attachment. Where men have long identified with specific locations, those very strong psychological bonds must be given serious consideration in any cooperative farming enterprise located on such land. The recent work of ethologists is increasingly demonstrating the mechanisms by which these strong associations with locality operate in various animal species,[22] and much greater research is needed to determine their nature in human societies. Insufficient awareness of this strong biological force may be one of the basic reasons for the difficulties of many cooperative farming ventures.

[21] A cooperatives inspector pays a brief visit each month or two, the district cooperatives officer visits twice a year for a day or two each time, and the cooperatives office in Lorengau is available for advice on marketing, etc.

[22] Carpenter (1958) gives the best summary of these mechanisms and Wynne-Edwards (1962) the fullest detailed exposition of the facts.

The advantage of cooperative organization in this and similar situations is that it provides the only institution for many people to accumulate capital to acquire large farming areas and assets. It also makes maximum use of very scarce technical skills, including book-keeping, skilled husbandry practices and management techniques, and facilitates linkage with external sources of finance and skilled advice.

Fiji's land-holding cooperatives The first of these was established in 1962 and involved thirty-eight farmers who, as a cooperative, acquired a 453 acre block. The second involved twenty-seven farmers and 2,000 acres of land worth $F154,000. There are now sixteen such cooperatives covering 18,000 acres with a land value, including land development costs, of about $F2·3 million (Nand, 1969; p. 4). In 1966 cooperatives acquired the land on which the bulk of export bananas have been grown, and the 400 members each farm a plot which they hold under occupancy agreement from the cooperative.

Almost all these cooperatives were born in crisis—leases were about to expire and were not to be renewed or landlords were about to sell to speculators. The tenants' survival at existing standards of living depended upon group action (they had neither the skills nor the finance to acquire land individually) and the existing cooperatives' legislation and advisory service constituted a convenient structure. Motivation for unity was thus high, at least until the properties were paid off. The land acquired is subdivided into family units, each of which holds a certificate of occupation from the owning cooperative.[23] Other cooperative actions include bulk buying and produce marketing for members.

All the societies are mono-cultural and mono-racial (most involving persons of Indian ancestry), except the Lovoni land-holding cooperative, which, with forty families and 2,253 acres, has about equal numbers of Indian, Fijian and European members. There is scope for interesting research on the degree of cultural unity necessary for cooperation between members.

Nand (1969, p. 5) sees cooperative land-holding becoming an important form of tenure among Pacific islanders. He claims further that social and economic isolation has been too great in settlement schemes based on individually owned plots, and that cooperatives provide a necessary degree of group support and

[23] In one case sugar cane is grown cooperatively by twenty-seven Fijian farmers at Natalau.

group action without inhibiting individual or family allotments. This is an interesting hypothesis which merits research.

Cook Islands cooperative plantations The two largest agricultural enterprises in the Cook Islands are both cooperatives, one a single copra plantation[24] and the other sub-divided for individual truck farming among members. One reason for the different organization is the crop—copra production involves simple, continuous routines and centralized drying, whereas truck gardening depends on frequent adaptation to varying ecological and market conditions.

In both cases the land is leased (and has been leased for over two generations) from some hundreds of owners of fragmented rights. In both cases the land-owners want it back, but this would almost certainly cause production to drop to a fraction of its present level, for their other land produces only a minute proportion of its potential.

The problems of multiple ownership set out in section 1 above have been overcome by these cooperatives. Multiple ownership is overcome in a different way by a government citrus scheme whereby individuals get occupation rights to sites for citrus orchards. In this case, however, government has had to invest very large sums in capital and management, for the assumption that farmers would manage their farms efficiently, if only they were simply given individual title, turned out to be false.

Land held by individuals with occupation rights, or by cooperatives, is many times more productive per man and per acre than land which is held—as most land is—by bilateral descent groups. Some reasons for this are obvious: whereas one belongs to the kin group by ascription, and cannot either relinquish or transfer membership, one belongs to the cooperative by choice. Individuals can make this decision for themselves and the cooperatives have adequate decision-making structures, but the bilineal kindreds have no traditional or modern precedent and no effective structure for decision-making. Cooperatives, moreover, can apply sanctions; bilateral descent groups cannot.

Maiao, French Polynesia. This is the oldest functioning cooperative in French Polynesia and the only one for which research data are available (Finney, 1968 a and b). There is no coopera-

---

[24] An early proposal to sub-divide it into ten-acre individual blocks was not accepted.

tives officer and no bureau in French Polynesia and, with little official support and active hostility from entrepreneurs, cooperatives have been of little consequence. Most cooperatives were sponsored by individual administrative officers on the assumption that they would 'naturally take hold and flourish', ignoring the fact that traditional Polynesian cooperation occurred within smaller kin-based groups with different functions (Finney, 1968a, p. 67).

The cooperative was formed in 1935 to enable the people of Maiao island to acquire the half of the island which a deceased foreign planter had bought piecemeal over the previous decade from various islanders. Owing to confusion over the precise rights of particular claimants the government decided to transfer all the estate lands of the deceased planter to a cooperative to be run as a group enterprise. The cooperative began with all Maiao men as members, but only just over half belong today, partly because the Maiao treat cooperative membership as an inherited good, usually to only one son.

Copra production from private holdings increased, while that from the cooperative plantation—though it occupied the best lands and had great expansion potential—remained static. The cooperative inefficiently produced about twenty tons of copra a year, but did succeed in keeping the land in local hands. Husbandry was negligible and cooperative members maintained their private coconut holdings in much better order.

This is understandable. Individual effort on copra production led to immediate visible returns to the individual but investment in replanting and maintenance brought uncertain returns only years later and largely to other people. The people are thus motivated against actions with long-term group pay-off in favour of immediate personal gain. This results in 'mining', or short-term exploitation of the asset. The cooperative could probably have overcome this problem if it had deducted a proportion of income from all current output and used it to pay for maintenance and replanting.

The cooperative continued with very limited success until 1963, when the islanders desperately needed a boat to provide transport to market. The governmental credit agency would lend only to the cooperative. Finney (1968, p. 82) states that the great need and desire for the boat lifted the cooperative to a new level of production after thirty years of inefficient operation. The confidence and energy mobilized spilled over to the plantation, and large-scale planting of new coconuts was undertaken for the first time.

Since it was established by external adminstrative decision rather than local choice, the Maiao people still regard the co-operative as a foreign institution and the acquisition of land by other than traditional processes as to some extent improper. The overwhelming sentiment, according to Finney, is for the alloca-tion of land so that each man can 'work as he chooses and be rewarded according to the work he does'. The import of Finney's research is that the extent of cooperative action was taken a little too far and that greater social and economic advantage would have resulted if the cooperative had continued its transport and marketing functions but reorganized production 'to make it more individually oriented . . . within the framework of the coopera-tive'.

The final social problem in the Maiao cooperative is leadership. The surge of activity since 1965 was facilitated by the personal interest and skill of a *demi* (person of mixed ancestry living after a predominantly French style) administrator who has supervised the trading operations and finances of the society. As an outsider he has the advantage of not being closely associated with internal factions. Little progress has been made in training Maiao people in management functions, leaving the cooperative vulnerable if the administrator is transferred elsewhere. The government has no agency for promoting or assisting cooperatives. Lack of effi-cient and honest management has been responsible for the failure of many cooperatives in French Polynesia (as throughout the Pacific). An adequate ethic and adequate management skills re-main major problems for effective cooperative action.

Ouitchambo cooperative farm, New Caledonia In 1958 the gov-ernment acquired an estate of 175 hectares for use as a 'coopera-tive' farm, though the work was to be communal, on the fallacious assumption that the Melanesians were 'naturally' disposed to 'collective' agriculture. Twenty families joined the cooperative, but, lacking either traditional precedent or adequate current incentive or sanctions, it was impossible to create a functioning organization. It was abandoned in 1964, some families having left and others remaining as independent subsistence cultivators (Saussol, personal communication).[25]

[25] The only other 'cooperative' farm using 'communal' labour to my know-ledge is the equally unsuccessful one in Jamaica. According to the *Economist*

Nonouti, Gilbert Islands Land-owners in 1969 began leasing their tiny fragmented plots to cooperative societies. Clearing, planting and harvesting of crops will be handled cooperatively. This interesting experiment, which aims to facilitate higher productivity, will merit future study if it continues to spread as at present indicated.

4. Corporate land-holding to overcome traditional tenure problems

Communal cash-cropping in Papua The most extensive experiment of this kind was with communal plantations in Papua, which from 1918 to 1940 were the main agencies through which the government carried out its programme to extend commercial agriculture.[26] The government bought areas of land and allotted each to a dozen or so surrounding villages as their communal plantation for cash crops (subsistence crops continued to be grown on traditional lands). Every able-bodied man was required by law to work a minimum of sixty days per year on the plantation, but in practice many villagers had to work five mornings a week, supervised by the local policeman. Official reports emphasized people's lack of enthusiasm for the scheme, and government officers applied heavy sanctions (usually three months' imprisonment with hard labour) to enforce it.

Nor did enthusiasm rise once the crop (most commonly coffee) came into being. Half the income went as tax to pay for administration and education, and the other half in equal amounts which were paid to each producer. This was paid only once a year and amounted to only ten to forty shillings per man (labour for foreign plantations at that time was paid 120 shillings per year plus minimal subsistence).

Plantation work ceased during world war II but was resumed compulsorily thereafter. Annual payouts increased, and tax deductions ceased. From 1950 immediate payment for coffee was made upon delivery to the government buying centre. Penal sanctions for non-attendance were abolished, and within a few years production had ceased on most plantations and was infini-

---

of 6 August 1966 the experiment with fully cooperative farming in Ghana had failed.

[26] For details of the communal plantations see Crocombe (1964b) and Miles (1956).

tesimal on the others. Other earlier and later experiments with
the communal growing of coconuts, rice, rubber and cocoa failed
within a few years of commencement. Reasons for failure have
been traced to problems of land tenure, work organization, income distribution and motivation (Crocombe, 1964b). Let us deal
with each of these predominantly social problems in turn.

When the land of a descent group was bought by the government for communal projects, the traditional land rights of the
vendors continued to be recognized by both the vendors and the
other communal users despite the legal annulment of such rights.
I know no instance of truly communal agriculture by a single
descent group on its own land. Security of tenure in such a situation depends more on belief than on law and, unless supervised,
the 'land-owners' either got a larger share of proceeds or denied
non-owners access to the land, for all local parties considered
this to be proper.

A basic problem of work organization was that the people of
mainland Papua were not accustomed to large groups under
unified leadership. This did not preclude the formation of such
groups in the colonial situation, provided people wanted them
and developed the institutions to direct them. But the new groupings were based exclusively on external direction and external
sanctions, through a local policeman under the authoritarian
control of a foreign colonial official. When sanctions were withdrawn in the post-war period the coffee price was ten times
higher than in the period of complete government control. Many
villagers wanted to continue coffee production but could not, as
they had no traditional precedent to ensure the efficient allocation
of work and the law specifically forbade the exercise of sanctions
by any indigenous individual or group. The moral of this for our
purposes is that sanction systems must be built primarily into the
local community and geared also into those of central government.

The main problem of income distribution was to relate reward
to effort. As almost all participants were illiterate, it was not
possible to keep sufficiently accurate records of work done by
individuals.

As far as motivation is concerned, many of the people began
the communal projects willingly enough, in the hope of substantial financial reward. But continued operation was achieved only
by force. When motivation is lacking, strict government supervision and heavy penalties can ensure some production, but as

supervision by force results in very high overhead costs as well as producing resistance, it does not result in high output.

The Christian cooperative farms In 1946 an Anglican missionary began to organize cooperative farming among the Orokaiva of Papua (for details see Dakeyne, 1966). The movement spread very rapidly to include perhaps 20,000 people at its height, but the greater the distance from the source of the technique the less precise the knowledge of the system and the greater the religious content.

Statuses were clearly set out—chairman, secretaries, committee men, job masters, farm leaders, tool-keepers, time-keepers and so on. The usual unit of cooperative activity was the village. There were attendance registers, but there was no attempt to discriminate between hard workers and slackers, and the person who was present for eight hours but worked only one received the same credit as one who worked all eight.

Status levels were clearly set out, but the roles that went with them were not so clearly specified. Religious ritual was involved at all stages, and cult associations were so strong in some areas that many people considered that mere participation would result mystically in great economic and spiritual rewards. This was no doubt important for cohesion and motivation but was no compensation for lack of planning and many other essential skills. Nor did cult activity bring about the major reorientations of behaviour patterns which were laid down and needed but not effectively adopted.

A major divergence of goals existed between the missionary, who saw cooperative living as the goal, and as a way of life growing 'naturally out of the teachings of the Christian faith', and the people, who expected great increases in material prosperity.

In the fringe areas the cooperative farming was tried only for a year and then abandoned. In the central areas some cooperative farming continued until 1951, when the missionary became seriously ill. Within a year of his departure all cooperative farming ceased.

In 1947 the most prominent member of the cooperative movement broke away, as a result of disagreement with the mission over his taking another wife. He led a group of between 100 and 200 people, almost all related by kinship and marriage, and formed what was probably the most successful and active cooperative of all. This group lived during the week in houses they

built in the gardens, returning to their villages for the weekend.
This cooperative prospered for four years (but did not spread)
until its leader was killed in a volcanic eruption. Then it collapsed
almost immediately. It had been focused upon its leader, who
was highly intelligent, literate and possessed of a charismatic
personality which vested him with considerable authority. But
if this was the main reason for the success of the movement it
was also the reason for its failure. As authority centred on a
person rather than an institutional role, it could not survive his
demise. The same problem has beset many small ventures of this
kind in various parts of the Pacific.

Niue In Niue Island (a locally self-governing territory of New
Zealand) agricultural productivity has been declining as a result
of increasing and more lucrative opportunities for employment,
and of extensive remittances from Niueans working in New Zealand. The major land problems on the island are, first, that the
best potential is for cattle and coconuts in combination on large
holdings, but the lands are divided traditionally (for subsistence
purposes) into small, fragmented, odd-shaped lots. Second, as
many Niueans live off the island as on it, and most absentees
object to others using their lands except for short-term crops.
    The government of Niue seeks to overcome these problems by
persuading the multiple owners to surrender their rights to blocks
of 100 acres or more of unused or little-used land to cooperative
or corporate groups for large-scale operation. It will be some
years before the success of the scheme can be assessed.

5. State-owned land corporations

WESTEC (Western Samoa Trust Estates Corporation) This is by
far the largest agricultural enterprise in Western Samoa, with
assets totalling about $ws2 million. It operates ten major planta-
tions producing coconuts, cocoa, coffee, rubber and cattle.[27] These
were separate German plantations which, by the Treaty of Ver-
sailles (1920), were taken by the New Zealand government as war
reparations and run as a State enterprise. With the approach of
independence the New Zealand government decided to give the
estates, together with all improvements and assets, to the people

[27] As well as an hotel, wholesale and retail stores, engineering, furniture
and carpentry shops and a sawmill.

of Western Samoa.[28] There were competing pressures to return the lands to the villages from which they were originally acquired, to sell them as plantation units, and to sub-divide them for the resettlement of Samoans who wanted to leave the village economy and become individual commercial farmers. The elected Samoan legislature decided to maintain them as a national asset controlled and managed by WESTEC, 'as trustee for and on behalf of the people of Western Samoa'.[29]

The main reasons for this were economic, for WESTEC has made substantial contributions in taxes, customs duties, profits (mainly used for government development projects), employment and foreign exchange.[30] But the main problems of WESTEC have been basically social, and derive from divergence between Samoan patterns of social action and expectation and some highly desirable prerequisites of large-scale commercial operations.

WESTEC claims to be analogous to the basic traditional Samoan unit of land-holding and social organization (the *aiga*, or ambilateral kin group under a chief) in that the chief manages the group estate, in the same way as WESTEC does, for all who belong to it (in the latter case, all Samoans). This is politically wise but scientifically inexact except in a very general sense. Moreover, to the extent that WESTEC is run on the lines of an *aiga*, this detracts from its efficacy as a commercial enterprise.

An *aiga* is based on bonds of close kinship (and, to a much lesser extent, of marriage) and its main functions are to provide for the subsistence needs of members and to enhance its prestige and influence *vis-à-vis* other like groups. This is achieved largely by the relatively short-term accumulation and distribution of certain kinds of food and property, which is antithetical to using long-term investment as a means of achieving maximum cash benefit. Social relations within the *aiga* are determined by personal status and by highly structured reciprocal obligations which

[28] Profits from the estates had always been used to finance educational, medical or other services.

[29] Samoa Amendment Act (No. 2), 1956, sections 22–3. WESTEC was to be autonomous, self-governing and self-financing, and was to pay taxes like a company. Nevertheless, linkage with the government is close, as the Prime Minister (Hon. Mata'afa Fiame II) is chairman of directors and several of the other six directors are members of Parliament.

[30] In the year ended 31 March 1958, the first year of WESTEC's independent existence, taxes amounted to $ws11,320, import and export duties $ws140,000, profits $ws141,440, wage labour cost $ws199,796 and salaries an unspecified amount; export earnings were $ws770,844.

emphasize status and prestige. Ethical principles are not absolute nor general, but specific to certain kin or statuses.

WESTEC's major management problem has been that its supervisory staff have to operate within two often conflicting frames of reference. All plantation workers operate mainly within a Samoan frame of reference whereby relationships should be highly personalized, and time and resources allocated to maximize the position of the kin group (WESTEC's attempts to persuade its employees to regard it as a national *aiga* have not been very successful). Top management personnel work largely within an impersonal corporate frame of reference, but those between are caught in a position of acute role conflict between the expectations of their kin and their work subordinates on the one hand and those of their management superiors on the other.[31]

Directors are probably more subject than top management to the conflict between traditional (and modern political) pressures on the one hand and corporation interests on the other.

6. Informal group land-holding enterprises

There has been a wide range of projects of this category, mostly initiated by officials or missionaries. The only case to be described here was initiated by a New Guinean named Numbuk.

The Erap mechanical farming project Drawing capital from contributors in forty-one villages with a total population of about 2,000, Numbuk raised \$A3,144 during about five years.[32] Tractors were bought to assist the production of cash crops, mainly potatoes and peanuts, and land was acquired from outside the area of the participating villages.

For the first few years the project employed up to a hundred workers per day drawn on a roster system from about four hundred available workers in the main participating villages. It continues today, twelve years later, on a smaller scale and in modified form, despite difficulties and changes of leadership and other personnel. For an organization of almost illiterate people, involving technical operations of which the participants had no former knowledge, institutional structures with little traditional

---

[31] Middle-level staffing was mentioned in every annual report as the major non-agricultural problem facing the corporation.

[32] This is a very large sum relative to the *per capita* income of perhaps \$A32 per year in the villages concerned.

precedents, and complex external relations for which they had no model, its survival is a considerable achievement.

Before discussing social factors within the movement, a major governmental obstruction must be mentioned. The participants were mountain-dwellers and had no land suited to mechanical cultivation. They therefore purchased unoccupied land from a local group in the Markham valley, with governmental approval. It was later discovered that the land had previously been bought by the government. Government land in the area was mainly leased to foreign plantation operators and, owing to what appear to me to have been fallacious assumptions about the capacities and 'proper place' of New Guinean villagers, the government would not give the mechanical farming group any secure title. They were in fact under periodic threat of eviction. There was considerable conflict between officials directly concerned with the project, who were extremely sympathetic, and some more senior officials, who were decidedly hostile. After years of uncertainty the project was formally denied the use of adjacent unused government land for a cattle and coconut enterprise, and was given only an annual permit to occupy what it was currently using. Foreign planters in the area were given extensive government loan finance for development but the mechanical farming group was not. With such serious operational frustrations it is surprising indeed that the project survived at all. Had it been given prompt and secure rights to the land, some guidance in book-keeping and farm management, and preferably but not essentially some loan finance, it would have had excellent prospects. But the colonial government was not, at that time at least, sufficiently flexible to adapt Australian precedents to the needs of New Guinean people.

The project was seen by the participants as a revolution in their way of life. Numbuk had been away for some years, seen a model for economic and social change, and returned with a message.[33] There was considerable supernatural activity as people sought the 'true' way to conduct their enterprise, but the basic model was the leaders' perception of the way of life of Europeans in the area. There would have been great receptivity to assistance or advice about book-keeping and management planning. Dore (1969, p. 7) rightly notes that 'institutionalized sus-

[33] The model was initiated by another New Guinean of a different language group some hundreds of miles away. (For details see Crocombe and Hogbin, 1963.)

picion' (by book-keeping, audit, policy-making committees and annual and other reports) is likely to be resisted where it is needed most, but in this and a number of other instances I think it would have been welcomed as an essential ingredient of the 'true' way.

The crucial factors in the degree of success which the project achieved seem to me to have been as follows. First it was not on the participants' traditional land. I know of no major successful group enterprise in the Pacific which is on the traditional lands of a participant sub-group. I know of many on other lands. Traditional lands are inevitably associated with the assertion of superior rights or status by the sub-groups or individuals primarily associated with that land. The other participants are embarrassed by the conflict in personal relations which thus arise when working the land of others *within their community*. When working land which is equally neutral or equally foreign to all, the tension otherwise caused by uncertainty as to which of several competing behaviour patterns to adopt is avoided (provided they have reasonably secure tenure). Some of the most productive village areas I know of in New Guinea are on land outside the traditional lands of the participants.[34]

Second, the project followed a model and the people had a way to achieve it. The organizational structure adopted (based on the hierarchy of government officers Numbuk had been associated with as a policeman) and the pattern of work organization (using an eight-hour day with a big gong for starting and stopping, as on neighbouring plantations) were reasonably effective.

Third, a sufficient degree of cultural cohesion. They were all of one language-group, though one cluster of villages at one extremity constituted a distinct sub-group. Whereas the initial impetus came from the major group, but with the sub-group participating, the sub-group has now taken over the project, with minimal participation by members of the major group.

Fourth, a sufficiently strong and persistent collective motivation to reach the goal they had set.

Fifth, a greater number of people anxious to participate than able to participate. This facilitated relatively easy discipline (by denying job opportunities to those who did not work well), and the availability of some cash-cropping in home villages and some wage labour elsewhere gave ready alternatives to the dissatisfied.

[34] E.g. Bakoiudu in the Central district, Naura in the Milne Bay district, Kapurahambo in the Northern district, Silanga and Uasilau in the East New Britain district, Langandrowa in the Manus district.

Disintegration of such projects seems to set in quicker when *everyone must* cooperate, when dissidents have no easy escape, and when opportunities are better outside the cooperative than within it.

The main problems the project has faced relate to increasing dissatisfaction with charisma and personal leadership as the project became established and profitable. When nobody else had a 'way' almost everyone was prepared to follow the man who had. His authority stemmed in part from his knowledge of a system and in part from assumed mystic characteristics of the system. Once the immediate goals of continuing cash income and expensive mechanical equipment (mainly the tractors) had been achieved, and the knowledge of how to perform various tasks became widespread, opinions on how the project should be run began to differ. What had been regarded as inspired guidance tended to be seen as unjustified authoritarian control. The leader, aware of having led the people to a new way of life, was upset by their diminishing gratitude.[35]

At that stage it would have been helpful if the personal leader could have achieved an institutionalized status with a clear-cut role, even if the same person had occupied the new status. This transition from the one form of leadership to the other is a very major one. With certain technical tasks (book-keeper, time-keeper, foreman, mechanical overseer, driver, etc.) it did happen to a considerable extent, and these people were often known by their job descriptions. But it did not happen to nearly the same extent with the leader. The reason may be partly cultural, for leadership in New Guinea is more personal and achieved than in the vast majority of human societies. This may not be such a disadvantage, for societies with complex systems of chieftainship (e.g. Samoa) seem to find even more difficulty in dissociating traditional from commercial roles.[36]

As a result of the lack of institutional leadership the organization suffered a severe setback in 1964 when the leader was

[35] There are some interesting parallels with the phasing out of foreign colonial officers. In the early stages of introducing a radically new system a strong case can be made for authoritarian or paternalistic management, but such are the effects on the personality of the man exercising these powers that it seems rare indeed for him to make a successful transition to democratic leadership.

[36] Finney (1968) suggests that the exploitation of modern opportunities is not opposed to, but combines with, traditional achievement behaviour in the New Guinea highlands.

seriously ill for nine months. Not only was there no one to replace him, and there were consequent heavy financial losses, but the illness was interpreted as a weakening of his potency and effectiveness.

When the government refused to make additional land and capital available, and with his followers dissatisfied with the lack of growth, Numbuk accepted a government offer to take an individual family farm plot in a new resettlement scheme.[37] Leadership fell to Sea, the leader of the other main group in the project (see Crocombe and Hogbin, 1963, p. 16), and employment opportunities mainly to his followers. Numbuk's people mostly diverted their support to his nephew, Wagiming, who they believed had received divine guidance on the running of successful business enterprise. This group has now been formalized as a marketing cooperative which transports and sells the individually produced coffee and tobacco of members. Its membership now approaches 1,000 people.[38] Some of the lieutenants of Numbuk's organization have taken equivalent roles in the new organization, which does not at present extend its cooperative activities to land-holding.

Another important problem in the late stages of Numbuk's leadership was the lack of information on the financial status of the project and a lack of distinction between his personal finances and those of the project. In the early stages the two were almost identical, but when, towards the end, he used $A200 to sponsor a great feast there was dissatisfaction among some followers, who assumed it to have been project money rather than personal finance. Numbuk probably did not make a clear distinction, and the feast probably involved mostly project members, but the institution had not yet provided the necessary facilities for differentiating between personal and group interest.

7. Cultural context and cooperative success

Here we attempt to relate cooperative success to particular forms of cooperative organization, and to economic and political

---

[37] Government practice was to limit indigenous farmers to family farms and to provide large-scale plantations, and facilities to operate them, only to foreigners. The government sincerely believed in the fallacies on which it based this policy.

[38] See Hannett (1969).

factors. The answers for cooperative land-holding institutions in the Pacific would appear to be:[39]

(a) Exposure to 'strong commercial influence' has generally created a demand for the property and prestige that the commercial operators are seen to enjoy but gives little or no access to the skills and linkages that are the basis of the commercial prosperity. There seems to be a level of assumed achievability by the subordinate group, above which it will attempt to emulate the bearers of commerce and below which it will reject them either by force (or attempted force) or by withdrawal. The history of the Pacific shows all three to have been common—and in that order. First comes the attempt to emulate, then the attempt to reject, and last—usually as a result of the almost inevitable failure of the first two—comes withdrawal. Only since the turn of this century in Hawaii and New Zealand, and since world war II in the rest of the Pacific, has a second attempt at emulation or competition emerged.[40]

Almost all instances of formal cooperative land-holding in the Pacific involve the purchase of already functioning plantations from foreign individuals or companies, i.e. exposure to successful enterprises of this kind has frequently led to attempts to acquire the existing ones but seldom to attempts to create others like them. Cooperative success is positively associated with exposure to commercial influences, but people also need extensive experience of the techniques of commercial operation.

(b) The extent to which traditional precedents favour modern cooperative forms cannot be determined with any certainty. Group land rights are widespread in Polynesia, and are based on a number of functional criteria (residence, sex, seniority, need, etc.) operating within a framework of kin ties. In all cases it involved group land-holdings: frequently, too, *ad hoc* groups cooperated for specific tasks, particularly in the clearing of forest prior to planting. But in few cases did it involve joint cultivation and sharing of produce. The most extensive instances of the latter occurred in Hawaii and New Zealand, and were based on a

---

[39] See table 2 for a subjective assessment of relationship between commercial success and aspects of cooperation. Items (a)–(e) are based on Joy's queries, items (f)–(h) are other factors which appear from the data to be of possible significance.

[40] Insufficient weight is often given to the disruptive effects of commerce on the pre-existing cultures, and to the fact that, particularly for many of the more isolated peoples, extensive involvement in commerce has often brought more disadvantages than benefits.

hierarchy of chieftainship and powerful natural as well as supernatural sanctions. All three were greatly weakened if not gone
completely by the time formal cooperatives came to the Pacific.
To replace hereditary with elective leaders, and to replace the
traditional sanctions with new ones adapted to the new structure,
involves creating a new culture and a new ideology. This is a
tremendous task. The vast pressures from Europe over the last
century and more have not led to the adoption of a European
way of life by the islanders, though they have led to the adoption
of large portions of European culture and ideology. We cannot
know what the result would have been if the dominant immigrant
culture had been cooperatively organized.

Formal cooperative land-holding has been tried only among
Pacific islanders who are literate (or have sufficient literate members), accustomed to regular wage or salary employment, familiar
with cash-cropping, and have the support of a reasonably efficient
governmental organization. I doubt whether they could do with
less, and almost all need more formal training and more capital.

Cooperatives are based on a complex structure of relationships,
with interaction between statuses rather than individuals, and
with a rigid hierarchy of decision-making and authority. It might
appear that a society with such characteristics (e.g. Samoa) is
better adapted to cooperation than a society which has minimal
structuring (e.g. New Guinea), but I think not. When a Samoan
operates in the cooperative structure he carries over much of the
idiom associated with parallel roles in the traditional structure,
and this conflicts seriously with the principles of formal cooperatives.[41] A New Guinean has to learn all the features of cooperative
activity without much help from traditional precedents, but also
without too much hindrance from them. In a sense Samoans do
take naturally to cooperative organizations, but their traditional
forms of cooperation are designed to serve quite different ends,
and hinder the achievement of commercial goals.[42]

[41] Dr Ben Finney is studying congruence between traditional values and
modern entrepreneurial success in various Pacific island societies, but no
parallel study concerned with cooperative activity has been attempted.
Dr Anton Ploeg has suggested that New Guinea cultures may have been
adjusted to such constant change and adaptation and such a range of
alternative choices that acceptance of any long-term, stable structures may
involve considerable difficulty.

[42] Formal cooperatives were introduced to Samoa during the 1950s. Almost
all failed within a year or two of commencement, and the government
abandoned the policy.

Before we draw too many conclusions from the failure of the cooperatives and related experiments it should be noted that in New Guinea, for example, the government has emphasized individual cash-crop farming for more than a decade as a means of overcoming the assumed sociological disadvantages associated with the group experiments. Despite vastly increased resources to promote individual cash cropping, the results (in terms of productivity at least) are not much more encouraging. There is much that we do not understand about the nature of cultural, social, psychological and other factors, let alone the causal relations between them. Facile answers based on limited perspectives of any one are likely to slow down, rather than speed up, our understanding of the processes involved.

(c) Kin-based units appear less well adapted to cooperative activity than territorially based units. In Maiao the group could not function when kinship was dominant. Only since kinship has been subordinated to a stronger external authority has the cooperative become an economic success. The successful land-working cooperatives in the Cook Islands involve non-kin from many different islands. In M'buke kinship is perhaps the most divisive factor, and in New Zealand the increasing success of land corporations appear to be causally associated with a reduced intensity of kinship ties.

The sociological principle is clear. Membership of a cooperative bestows *identical* rights on members, and requires the acceptance of certain elective authority roles as common to all, i.e. they are institution-centred. Kinship systems, by contrast, are ego-centred. They necessitate individuals recognizing others as different in varying degrees according to the proximity of genealogical connection, whether the attachment is through males or females, seniority of birth, or other criteria. In kin-based authority structures the leadership roles are usually held by seniority of descent, and such systems necessitate deference to persons on grounds of inherited rank. This is inimical to cooperative success, which depends on quite different selective criteria and on what Dore so aptly terms 'institutionalized suspicion'.

(d) The data are too limited to determine whether diffuse interpersonal ties lead to greater or less success in cooperative activity than activities manifesting more specific ties. Those Pacific land-holding cooperatives with more diffuse ties are more successful, but whether it is because of the diffuse ties remains an open question.

Tight-knit communities, in my experience, are created not so much by the people in them as by people outside them. They might more appropriately be called 'tight-split' communities because, despite deep splits within them, they are bound together by common need in a hostile environment. This common hostility acts as a motivating force only while the outer hostility is greater than that within. Centralized government and stable administration usually lead to a relaxation of hostility to the external world, which results in a reduction of the extent to which local communities are prepared to, or need to, cooperate.

The fact that few Maori corporations of under 5,000 acres have been successful may be only partly due to historical and economic factors. The small units seem to involve too few people, and their interests come into contact (in conflict as much as in congruence) too often. The larger units not only have a larger pool from which to select talented persons, but the individuals bump into one another less frequently. The answer does not seem to lie in maximum diffuseness, nor in maximum specificity, but in a middle situation in which there is sufficient specificity for common interests to hold the unit together but sufficient diffuseness to ensure that the contacts are not too frequent, too oppressive or too comprehensive.[43] It seems that cooperative and corporate landholding organizations in which the same individuals have to cooperate in too many ways within the same structure are likely to experience great inter-personal tension. In the most successful enterprises discussed in this paper the owners and/or workers have few overlapping roles and all the least successful ones have many overlapping roles.[44] Likewise, in the four most 'successful' enterprises daily face-to-face contact between owners is minimal or non-existent, whereas in all 'low productivity' enterprises such daily contact is extensive.

(e) I am not aware of any traditional authority structures in the Pacific which could be carried over intact to cooperatives. The traditional goal of family self-sufficiency in subsistence needs, with minimal exchange of small items, has little to offer for

---

[43] Kawharu (1970) notes that kinship has 'been at the root of such factionalism in management as has arisen' but has also acted to contain the more extreme effects of factionalism.

[44] Within the Maori land corporations, too, some of the most successful are those in which the corporate action is concerned only with ownership and leasing, and the exploitation of forest or farms is left to entrepreneurs. The extent of overlapping roles could be rated as low for items 1, 2 and 4 in table 2, medium for items 3 and 5, and high for items 6–15.

market-oriented, technically complex cooperatives. The stronger
the traditional organization the more hierarchical it was and thus
the less well adapted to cooperative action.

The circumstances under which hierarchical authority structures
become more egalitarian in cooperative activity may be illustrated in both the Cook Islands cooperatives and the Maori land
corporations. In the Cook Islands all joint ventures in the nineteenth and early twentieth centuries were run by chiefs, usually
exploiting traditional criteria of authority. These economic
activities enhanced the power of the chiefs until it was broken, in
land matters at least, by the Land Court and by the colonial
government in the early twentieth century. Chiefly roles remain
important in some respects, but in the formal cooperative plantations (which were not set up until the 1950s and bear no relationship to the joint tribal enterprises in the previous century) they
have no role whatever. In Maori land corporations half a century
ago, chiefs played the dominant role, but today their role is
minor, owing to external circumstances, not to the corporations.

The difference between the Cook Islanders and the Maoris is
interesting, for they have the same cultural origins and many
similarities in social structure and values. In both cases early
post-contact economic ventures were dominated by chiefs by
virtue of their powers over both land and people. The Land
Court diminished the powers of the chiefs in both cases. The
Cook Islands cooperatives, however, are owned by a great
diversity of people from many islands and rent their lands, and
thus consider it inappropriate for chiefs to have any say in them.
The Maori corporations, on the other hand, are on the traditional
lands of the corporate owners, and the strength of chiefs has
lasted longer there than in other spheres of activity.

These examples strongly suggest that where traditional
authority was based on land as well as on an occupying descent
group, cooperative use of that land will perpetuate rather than
eliminate the hierarchical authority structure.

(f) *Work organization.* The four most successful categories of
enterprise in table 2 work the land using paid employees; the
next category is worked by individuals farming separate plots
leased from the cooperatives, which also provide certain services.
All those in the 'moderate success' category and the first four in
'low productivity' are worked under various customary arrangements, and the last two (which are the only two to have been
completely abandoned) were worked communally. As none of the

'correlations' was plotted until the institutions were listed in order of commercial success, the apparent relationship between success and work organization may be very significant, and merits further study. Similarly, worker participation in decision-making is low or absent in five of the six 'successful' institutions (M'buke cooperative being the exception) and relatively high in all other cases.

(g) A crude index of scale incorporating area and value of land held by each enterprise would correlate very closely with commercial success. The enterprises listed as 'successful' in table 2 are all relatively large-scale, those listed as 'moderate success' somewhat smaller, and those of 'low productivity' are of the smallest average area and value. Related to scale is the quality of managerial skills, which may be rated as relatively high for the three institutions listed in the table as most successful commercially, and for the fifth; as medium for the fourth, sixth and eighth, and as low for the seventh, ninth and below. This is roughly similar to educational levels in the societies concerned, the two marked exceptions being Samoa, where general education is low but management of estates relatively efficient, and New Zealand, where general education is high but management of land held under customary tenure is far below average standards.

(h) *Income distribution.* It is probable that all the institutions dealt with resulted in more even income distribution than entrepreneurial structures would have achieved, but it is likely that entrepreneurial forms would have produced much more total income than any of the customary and communal forms dealt with, though not necessarily more than the formal corporate or cooperative forms among the same peoples.

8. A tentative evaluation of social preconditions

Governments in many developing countries are promoting cooperative enterprise in various forms, and we need to improve our understanding of what kinds of social structures, subject to what kinds of change in environmental conditions, conduce to what kinds of cooperation.

It is extremely difficult to prove that something is a precondition. We can only say that it is probably so if its total or relative absence is associated with shortcomings in the achievement of the set goals. Factors can be regarded as preconditions only on the basis of assumptions about the goals of the institution, and

Table 2. Subjective assessment of relationship between commercial success * and aspects of cooperation

In decreasing order of commercial success	(a) Exposure to commercial influence			(b) Traditional cooperation (at time of establishing enterprise)			(c) Kinship or territory as primary basis for cooperation		(d) Degree of cultural diffuseness			(e) Degree of traditional hierarchy in the society			(f) Method of work organization				
	Low	Medium	High	Low	Medium	High	Kin-based	Territory-based	Low	Medium	High	Low	Medium	High	Paid workers	Individual farmers	Coop	Customary	Communal
A. Successful																			
1 Bishop estate			+	++†								+			+				
2 WESTEC			+	+							+			+	+				
3 NZ land corporations			+			+		++			+	++			+				
4 Manuae cooperative, Cook Is.		+			++			++		++		++			+				
5 Fiji cooperatives		+			++		+			++				+		+			
6 M'buke cooperative		+				+		++	+			+					+		
B. Moderate success																			
7 New Zealand kindreds	++				+		+				+	+						+	
8 Maiao cooperative	++					++		++	++				+				+		
9 Erap project						++		++	++			+						+	
C. Low productivity																			
10 Fiji *mataqali*	++					+	++		++			++						+	
11 Cook Is. kindreds	++				++		++		++			++						+	
12 Society Is. kindreds	++				++		++		++			++						+	
13 New Caledonia reserves						++		++	++			++						+	
14 Papua communal		+				++		++	++			++							++
15 Ouitchambo (NC)	+			+								+							

* Commercial success relative to potential for that land use in that environment.
† Hawaiian forms of traditional cooperation were almost completely extinguished by the time the estate was set up.

different goals lead to different measures of what constitutes success.

As far as Oceania is concerned, there is not a sufficient range of situations which have enough in common to enable scientific conclusions to be drawn, but the limited data that are available have led me to the tentative view that the major social preconditions which are conducive to successful land-holding cooperatives in the Pacific are as follows:[45]

(a) *An accepted or acceptable set of status relations* is essential, as participants must accept, to a large degree, the validity or legitimacy of their articulation with others. The problem is seldom one of non-acceptance (of managers, chairmen, foremen, shareholders, etc.) but is often one of an inadequate degree of acceptance. The Western Samoan Trust Estates Corporation has a particular problem in this matter. Samoan society is extremely conscious of status relations, and Samoan people are highly skilled in the courtesies and reciprocal obligations constantly involved in personal interaction. But this is within a particular system of rank titles and village living. The Trust Estates do not come within this system. Thus while the formal status of foremen, managers and other superior ranks is acknowledged, this acknowledgement is not sufficiently reinforced by behaviour patterns, which are geared to a quite different system. Likewise, the problems of some managers and other leaders in the Maori Land Corporations, the Maiao cooperative or the Erap project.

(b) *An appropriate socio-legal and political context.* Not only must those who conform to the norms of the organization be supported, and the deviants pressured into conformity (or punished for deviance), there must be a degree of congruence between the structure and functioning of the land-holding corporation and that of the wider society. There must be an enforceable legal framework, and it must be enforced. Newly formed cooperatives are unlikely to succeed when they have to compete with long-established, highly capitalized business corporations (usually foreign-owned), and naturally (but unlike Erap) the organizations must have secure tenure of the land they work.

(c) *A relevant set of technical skills is essential* to enable the tasks to be carried out effectively. The skills must be continually available—many Pacific cooperatives have failed because of the

---

[45] Many preconditions may seem almost platitudinous, but it is in fact through the misunderstanding of such simple principles that many 'reform' programmes have gone awry.

loss of one or two men with crucial scarce skills. Some of the institutions referred to in this paper (notably the Western Samoa Trust Estates Corporation and the Maori land corporations) make better use of scarce skills than would probably otherwise have occurred, but few have provided extensive technical or managerial training. Nor have they been used much as institutions through which to inject development capital from outside, though many have been useful institutions for internal capital accumulation.

Formal cooperative enterprises in the Pacific presuppose such different values and structures from traditional forms of cooperation that they necessitate extensive training in new techniques and major adaptation of deep-seated cultural behaviour patterns.[46] Thus if governments want to introduce successful cooperative enterprises on a wide scale they will need to invest substantial time, skills and money in providing the framework and sustaining it for some years until the new patterns are effectively established. Moreover, they will need to explore carefully the particular forms of ownership, production, processing and marketing that are most likely to be conducive to maximum advantage from cooperation as against other forms of organization.

(*d*) *An effective ethical system* is needed to ensure that adequate consideration is given to the needs and interests of other members of the group. If cooperatives were to be widely established in the Pacific the greatest need might be for a stronger ethic related specifically to the needs of cooperative organization and large-scale society. The traditional ethical systems were designed for the needs of small, kin-based, self-depending societies, and thus involve principles which conflict with the universalistic orientation needed in effective cooperative action.

(*e*) *An adequate system of incentives and motivation* is needed to ensure that participants devote sufficient energy and time to the operation of the institution, but I have no data on the vital ques-

---

[46] Finney (1968a, p. 84) notes the paradoxical fact that cooperatives have usually been introduced in the Pacific among the isolated rural people who are least able to make them function successfully, and have seldom been introduced in urban and peri-urban areas among people more familiar with the social and economic prerequisites of formal cooperation. A common reason for this has been that highly capitalized, highly skilled foreign enclaves have effective control of entrepreneurial activity in and around the towns and a new enterprise like a cooperative with untrained staff and little capital is at a serious disadvantage in open competition with them. In rural areas such competition is much less, or may be non-existent. Moreover, the towns were built by foreign immigrants who also, in many cases, acquired the best peri-urban lands.

tion of the relative satisfactions (to members, management, workers and the public) accruing from cooperative as against other forms of land-holding.

(f) *Internal agreement on the aims and operation of the enterprise* is of course highly desirable, and a substantial lack of it will threaten the survival of the enterprise (as in the Papuan communal plantations after the withdrawal of external sanctions). This can probably be achieved only if the membership of the organization is relatively homogeneous.

Conclusion

Pacific island societies have neither the degree of internal cohesion provided by powerful common religious and defensive goals, which facilitate extremely comprehensive cooperative action, as in Israeli *kibbutzim*, nor the powerful external sanctions of the Russian *kolkhoz*. There is, nevertheless, a strong disposition towards joint action, usually by kin-based groups, for particular purposes. There may be a case for cooperative land-holding, with independent family farms held from the cooperative, giving security of group cohesion combined with freedom of individual action in relation to operation of the farm. There seems also to be a case for large-scale corporate or cooperatively owned enterprises run as single units on commercial lines. The evidence suggests, however, that exploitation of farms by a joint or cooperative work force is unlikely to be as successful in most circumstances, despite its effectiveness in the rather unusual social and physical environment of M'buke.

References

Belshaw, C. S. (1964), *Under the ivi tree: society and economic growth in rural Fiji*, London.

Bishop estate (1965), *Bishop estate: foundation of the Kamehameha schools: a five-year report, 1959–64*, Honolulu.

Black, C., and Mellen, K. D. (1965), *Princess Bernice Pauahi Bishop and her legacy*, Honolulu.

Carpenter, C. R. (1958), 'Territoriality: a review of concepts and problems' in *Behaviour and evolution*, ed. Ann Rae and George G. Simpson, New Haven.

Crocombe, R. G. (1964a), *Land tenure in the Cook Islands*, Melbourne.
— (1964b), 'Communal cash cropping among the Orokaiva', *New Guinea Research Bulletin* No. 4, Canberra.
— (1965), 'The M'buke cooperative plantation', *New Guinea Research Bulletin* No. 7, Canberra.
— (ed.) (1970), *Land tenure in the Pacific*, Melbourne.
Crocombe, R. G., and Hogbin, G. R. (1963), 'The Erap mechanical farming project', *New Guinea Research Bulletin* No. 1, Canberra.
Dakeyne, R. B. (1966), 'Cooperatives at Yega', *New Guinea Research Bulletin* No. 13, pp. 53–68, Canberra.
Dore, R. F. (1969), 'Traditional communities and modern cooperatives', paper presented to a conference on social prerequisites for agricultural cooperation held at the Institute of Development Studies, Sussex, March 1969.   See pp. 43–60 of this volume.
Finney, Ben R. (1968a), 'A successful French Polynesian co-operative?' *Journal of Pacific History*, 3, pp. 65–84.
— (1968b), 'Big fellow man belong business', *Ethnology*, 7, pp. 394–410.
Groves, Murray (1963), 'The nature of Fijian society', *Journal of the Polynesian Society*, 72, pp. 272–91.
Guiart, Jean (1961), 'Un problème foncier exemplaire en Nouvelle Calédonie: la Vallée de Tchamba', *Le monde non-Chrétien*, No. 55–56, pp. 1–15.
Hannett, Leo (1969), 'A successful small business born from thunder-clap', *New Guinea*, vol. 5, September 1969.
Kawharu, I. H. (1970), 'Maori land tenure in New Zealand' in Crocombe (1970).
Maori Affairs Act, 1953, Wellington.
Miles, J. (1956), 'Native commercial agriculture in Papua', *South Pacific*, 9, pp. 318–28.
Nand, Sharda (1964), 'Land settlement cooperatives in the Fiji Islands', *Spectrum*, 1964–65, pp. 40–5.
— (1969), 'Co-operative land-holding experiments in Fiji', paper presented to the third Waigani Seminar, Port Moresby, May 1969 (mimeograph).
Nayacakalou, R. R. (1965), 'The bifurcation and amalgamation of Fijian lineages over a period of fifty years', *Proceedings of the Fiji Society, 1961–62*, pp. 122–33, Suva.
— (1970), 'Manipulating the system' in Crocombe (1970).
New Zealand Government, Department of Maori and Island Affairs. Files and reports relating to land.
Ngata, Sir Apirana (1946), *Native land development*, Wellington.

Panoff, Michel (1964), *Les structures agraires en Polynésie française,* ORSTOM, Paris.

— (1966), 'Un demi-siècle de contorsions juridiques; le régime foncier en Polynésie française de 1842 à 1892', *Journal of Pacific History,* 1, pp. 115–28.

Sahlins, Marshall D. (1962), *Moala: culture and nature on a Fijian island,* Ann Arbor.

Saussol, Alain (1970), 'Melanesian land tenure in New Caledonia' in Crocombe (1970).

Schwartz, Theodore (1966), 'The cooperatives: ol i bagarapim mani', *New Guinea,* 1, 8, pp. 36–47.

Smith, Norman (1962), *Maori land corporations,* Wellington.

Western Samoa Trust Estates Corporation (1958–61), annual reports and balance sheets, Apia, Western Samoa.

Wynne-Edwards, V. C. (1962), *Animal dispersion in relation to social behaviour,* New York.

Acknowledgements

Advice, assistance or information from the following persons is acknowledged with gratitude: Mr J. H. W. Barber, Professor D. G. Bettison, Mr John Booth, Mr L. J. Davis, Dr Ben Finney, Hon. Albert Henry, Mr Robin Hide, Dr I. H. Kawharu, Mr P. W. Kelly, Mr J. M. McEwen, Mr Sharda Nand, Dr R. R. Nayacakalou, Dr Anton Ploeg, Miss Susan Reeves, Dr Alain Saussol, Dr Sumer Singh and Professor Peter Worsley.

Thomas F. Carroll Peasant cooperation in Latin America

This paper attempts to review some of the experiences with peasant economic cooperatives in Latin American countries. The main purpose is to identify some strategic policy issues in the successful introduction, growth and viable functioning of cooperative-type arrangements among peasant cultivators. The emphasis is on the various alternative organizational forms and structures of group activity. For this purpose the term 'cooperative' is broadly interpreted to include all kinds of institutions in which peasants join together for common economic purposes.[1] Attempts to organize pre-cooperatives and experiences with various joint agricultural activities in which the role of outside agencies is predominant are also included. On the other hand, little attempt is made to review situations involving mature, business-type cooperatives in the more advanced countries or sub-zones of the region.

Throughout the paper the stress is on types of peasant cooperation which have shown elements of success or viability. It would indeed be very easy to compile a list of failures and, while many of these negative experiences have important lessons for future policies, a deliberate attempt has been made to stress success elements, however rare and unrepresentative they may be. It is believed by the reviewer that, at this stage of Latin American experimentation with various forms of cooperative organizations, these positive elements in relatively successful cases have a substantial policy value. However, the many internal and external difficulties that beset cooperatives, or indeed the generally indifferent or hostile atmosphere in which they must function, are not to be minimized.

[1] The term 'institution' in this paper is further defined as arrangements which have a substantial degree of continuity and regularity. Occasional joint activity, common in community development projects, is not covered. Also excluded from this review are organizations whose field of activity is not concerned with agriculture, such as consumer-oriented associations or housing cooperatives.

Among the many aspects and variables which play a role in rural cooperation, the human, organizational, and institutional elements are stressed over technological and more narrowly economic variables.

It appears that at this juncture of Latin American development the subject of rural cooperation is particularly relevant. The agrarian situation, which at the beginning of this century had been based on a rigid semi-feudal structure, is now increasingly in a state of flux. While agrarian reforms are not yet widespread, there are many planned and unplanned ways in which the old structures have been changing. At the same time sporadic commercialization, technification and market-orientation of agriculture have taken place, frequently accompanied by new and growing inequalities among the peasantry and further 'marginalization' of peasant groups.

The gradual shift from traditional land tenure systems, the increased capitalistic and individualistic development of commercial agriculture, and the inroads of advanced technology have been accompanied by an increased awareness and mobility on the part of the peasants. Governments and other power groups are becoming increasingly aware of the political potential of the peasantry. There are also incipient struggles for its allegiance. There is an increasing desire to stimulate local participation of peasants in the development process. All these factors are affecting the concept of development planning in domestic and international agencies.

While the writer is under no illusion that the orientation of change will turn decidedly in favour of rural cooperation and that drastic departures from current power constellations could be expected which would be more sympathetic to communal and strongly egalitarian rural development, the framework of this review is positive and cautiously optimistic. It is the writer's belief that, given the overall fluid situation, new political opportunities for more rational, egalitarian and humanistic agrarian policies are likely to arise in the medium run in a number of countries. Hence one can and should take advantage of these opportunities to suggest new and fresh approaches and lines of strategy.

In this perspective, rural cooperation would become important in the following cases:

1. The first situation is characterized by the prevalence of relatively static, semi-feudal systems in which strongly tra-

ditional agrarian groups coexist. Cooperation, while necessarily limited, may assist peasants to organize (or be organized) more effectively to compete with landlords, money-
lenders, or other groups of superior power.
2. The second situation is more dynamic and fluid, especially
in cases of increasing market-orientation and labour mobility.
Cooperation can here enable peasants and small farmers to
participate more fully in an increasingly commercial environment and obtain a better distribution of the benefits of
investment and new technology.
3. The third situation is represented by post-revolutionary systems in which the semi-feudal land tenure arrangements have
been displaced and power has been shifted more decisively
toward workers and peasants. Under these circumstances
cooperation can assist in the planning and consolidation of
the new agrarian structures and can represent a 'buffer'
between the peasants and the new official bureaucracy, to
preserve a degree of freedom and self-management.

The body of this paper is presented in two parts. In the first
a taxonomy is developed to classify different kinds of cooperatives
and similar peasant groupings according to their main economic
functions. Whenever possible, case studies are used to illustrate
each function and important problems in cooperative organization. In the second a number of issues are analysed which appear
to be strategic for cooperative policy in peasant areas in Latin
American countries. Some of these issues are identified as mainly
'internal' and revolve around the predisposition of communities or
groups for successful cooperative activity, while others are described as mainly 'external' to these local collectivities. However,
as both are integral parts of the system, what really matters is
their interaction.

I. *Review of case studies by type of activity*

1. *Joint management of supplies and services*

(a) *Purchasing associations* Group purchasing of farm requisites
is often the first joint function undertaken in the realm of economic activity when cooperatives emerge in the countryside. In
recent years promotional activity has increased the number of
savings and loan associations which eventually may lead to joint
buying and selling for farm members. In Peru membership of

these associations has increased from 259,000 in 1956 to 359,000 in 1968. In Colombia between 1963 and 1966 membership of credit societies nearly doubled to 200,000. However, the overwhelming majority of these new associations benefit urban groups and middle class rural families in smaller rural districts, but are not very effective among the peasantry. Moreover, they operate in the realm of personal finance or housing and have almost no effect on productive activity. Nevertheless, such societies, when operating in rural areas, sooner or later tend to affect the farm business purchases of its members and may function as the foundation for other cooperatives. Many of the associations originally formed for purposes of consumer cooperation or some aspects of community improvement gradually branch out from the buying of food, household items and other articles of family consumption into the purchase of fertilizers, pesticides, veterinary supplies, tools and other supplies which are needed in the agricultural process.

Experience has shown that in cases where the introduction of cooperatives meets with considerable distrust, group purchasing can be the opening wedge for associations which ultimately fulfil multiple economic functions.

The major problem with a primarily supply-oriented cooperative in its formative years is its limited ability to extend credit and compete with merchants and money lenders. Therefore the expansion potential of such an association depends largely on how effectively its operations can be supplemented by credit from development programmes. If the supply association is not able to expand into fields in which it can make a more fundamental and innovative contribution, it can easily lapse into a routine, relatively marginal role.

Some purchasing associations remain specialized and function effectively as long as other parallel organizations exist which satisfy the other needs of their members. One of the largest specialized purchasing cooperatives is INSUCOOP (Union Nacional de Cooperativas de Insumos Agropecuarios) which was created by the Chilean government in 1965 to be the exclusive distributor of superphosphate fertilizer and to attempt to secure a 20 per cent reduction in prices farmers paid for other agricultural inputs. It has quickly become the most important Chilean cooperative organization in terms of sales (Foytick and Faris, 1967). Similar central supply organizations exist in Brazil among coffee cooperatives. Although they also perform other functions in connection with sales, credit and technical assistance, one of the main purposes of the regional *centrais* is the bulk purchase of productive requisites.

(*b*) *Marketing associations* The second major type of cooperative deals with joint marketing of farm products. Marketing is the leading function of Latin American agricultural cooperatives. Cooperatives marketing the same products frequently join into commodity groupings (coffee, dairy, wine, citrus). Examples, such as the coffee cooperatives in São Paulo and Paraná in Brazil, the cotton cooperatives in Formosa and Chaco in Argentina, the wheat cooperatives which are important in Rio Grande do Sul in Brazil, and the dairy cooperatives in Chile, are common (Foytick and Faris, 1967). Where processing is an important part of the marketing sequence, vertically integrated cooperatives are the rule, organized around a processing plant. The plant itself may or may not be cooperatively owned.

One of the most important initial factors influencing the success of marketing coops is the timing of their establishment. In principle, it is advantageous to create marketing associations simultaneously with the introduction of new crops or intensification of the production process.[2] Yet there are dangers in prematurely insisting on cooperative marketing when the production process is still in its experimental or formative stage.

On the other hand, the introduction of marketing coops at a later stage, when middlemen are already well entrenched, may also be extremely difficult. There are many reports of failures due, to a large extent, to the impossibility of overcoming competition. For example, the Tarma marketing association in Peru, although in an extremely favourable situation to supply vegetables to the Lima market, could not overcome the well organized 'mafia' of the wholesalers. After an initial unsuccessful effort (in which the coop was 'locked out') the cooperative relapsed into the operation of a supply store (Scott and Fletcher, 1967).

The disadvantages of a delayed cooperative organization or late start of new cooperative ventures are particularly evident in the Mexican *ejidos*. While the communitarian aspects of the new land tenure system have not been supplemented by cooperation in market arrangements, the individualization of farming and

---

[2] Opportunities for such 'package projects' are offered by land reform and land settlement schemes, especially as part of massive programmes such as the La Laguna experience in Mexico during the 'thirties.

private commercial arrangements have evolved to such an extent that any effort at this stage to introduce a more egalitarian marketing system based on the original *ejido* concept faces near-insurmountable difficulties.

Thus the proper strategy of timing seems to call for a gradual development of marketing cooperation *pari passu* with other development efforts. The disadvantages of being early may be eased by a certain amount of assistance in transport, credit, price guarantees by government agencies, or the construction of a strategically placed warehouse prior to the creation of a full-fledged cooperative marketing system. To late-comers, Scott and Fletcher (1967) make the following suggestions:

(i) Co-operatives are most disadvantaged when they try to enter the marketing system for traditional crops. It is easier to enter the marketing process with new crops or new areas (irrigation) to reduce competition. If traditional markets are entered, those activities should be selected which have the highest income potential.[3]

(ii) Unless a whole new agrarian structure is created (as in land reform), it is not advisable to by-pass too many steps in the existing market channels, as this will align more people against the new enterprise. Instead, when a new venture is vulnerable, one or two steps at a time should be displaced, especially when the new cooperative controls only a few products and during only part of the year. Coops can best be established at a single stage in the marketing system, usually in assembly markets at the point of first sale by producers—this seems the crucial stage for initial success.

One could add the observation that success is predicated on strong financial and political support from institutions outside the local organization. Failure to overcome middlemen's opposition and other early problems is a question of external assistance rather than any specific line of operating strategy at the local level. Where such support has been available, in many instances,

[3] Not all observers agree on such a narrowly focused strategy. John T. Westbrook, who organized the Alpaca peasant association in Peru, believes that the marketing cooperative should handle any and all available products in the area (with the possible exception of notorious problem crops) in order to satisfy its members, who usually provide various items. A wider variety of produce also may facilitate obtaining outlets. (Personal communication.)

spectacular improvement in farmers' income has been reported through the coop's ability to increase volume and improve quality.

Marketing associations achieve their more sophisticated form and derive their best economic justification in a vertically integrated structure in which the processing of farm products becomes an essential part of the joint marketing system. In such situations, control over the processing part of the operation is central to the functioning of the whole system. The manner in which such control is shared by the participating farmers becomes a factor in determining the degree of 'cooperativeness'. Many processing systems operating under the cooperative label, as shown by the Frutillar dairy coop in southern Chile, are simple business associations operating along corporate lines. Some systems, such as the Mexican sugar *ejidos,* are not recognized as cooperatives but contain certain features of shared control and membership participation. The prevailing agrarian structure and social stratification determine the manner in which control is shared.

(*c*) *Cooperative farm credit* As mentioned earlier, Latin American countries demonstrate a notable upsurge in credit associations in recent years. Although most of these are not directly connected with farming, some of the new credit associations are beginning to penetrate rural areas and are often an opening wedge into other types of technically innovative activity.

It is widely recognized that cooperatively managed farm credit can have the following advantages over individually administered credit: (i) reduction in the costs of supervision and assistance; (ii) efficiency in administration by providing stimuli for group control and sanctions for non-compliance; (iii) opportunities for building economic and social infrastructure as well as farm capital on a community-wide basis. Promotion and experimentation with methods of joint credit are especially noticeable in land settlement and land reform projects in which either there is some important element of joint production, or in cases where the requirements of planning the new or reorganized farm structure appear especially favourable for operating farm credit programmes on a group basis.

Historically the most important types of credit association are the Mexican *sociedades locales de crédito ejidal.* Because of the fact that *ejido* lands[4] cannot be mortgaged, the Banco Nacional

---

[4] The history of the *ejido* movement in Mexico is outlined below.

de Crédito Ejidal was created as an essential complement to the
Mexican agrarian reform. The Banco operates *vis-à-vis* its clients,
who are members of *ejidos*, through the credit associations. The
structure of these associations (which parallels, but is not identical with, the *ejido* organization) includes a general assembly, a
comité de vigilancia and a *socio delegado*. It is not necessary for
each *ejido* member to be a member of a credit society, but membership of the societies is a condition for receipt of credit from
the Ejido Bank. The Bank, through its exclusive controlling
position, has acquired a decisive role in the farm operations of
its client groups.

More than 9,000 credit societies have been formed since the
establishment of the Ejido Bank, and 5,000 continue to be active.
While a number of these societies are said to exist for the sole
purpose of obtaining credit by fulfilling legal requirements, others
do fulfil important cooperative functions and are often a more
dynamic form of organization than the *ejido* itself. This is
especially true of the still surviving collective *ejidos* and for those
semi-collectives which have given up joint land use for individual
cultivation while conserving some joint features of management.

Credit societies are important in the irrigation districts of
north-west Mexico. In this region ploughing and planting with
machinery, disease control and other activities are carried on
jointly among members of credit societies, who frequently have
adjoining parcels, although most *ejidatarios* cultivate and harvest
their own plots of land. Uniformity of cropping and the joint use
of machinery are facilitated by the central planning of the Ejido
Bank. Group responsibility for the management of credits was
originally part of the objectives of the Bank, which granted credit
through the societies for further reallocation to its members.

However, the gradual disfavour of collectives and the shift of
policy away from strong cooperative management in the *ejidos*
has caused the Bank to favour individual accounts. It is now
by-passing the societies, except in the northern irrigated regions
of La Laguna and Yaqui and in other special cases. The sugar
ejidos—generally integrated with a government-managed processing plant—exemplify the latter. In these situations the Bank
can reduce its costs of supervision and its risk by relying on the
cooperative for bringing pressure to bear on lazy or careless
members. In this manner the Bank relieves itself of the need to
sanction debtors. If the inefficient member does not mend his

ways the credit society may take over his parcel and operate it collectively until his debt to them has been repaid.

As mentioned earlier, credit associations are also becoming more significant in connection with agrarian reform and settlement programmes. INCORA, the Colombian land reform agency, has organized cooperatives in each of its new settlements. The programme supervises credit arrangements and gradually branches into marketing and processing. In Chile CORA supplies credit to its reform settlements, the success of which will depend heavily on the viability of cooperative management now being introduced.

A special case of group financing which may become more important in certain agrarian reform programmes involves the purchase of land. In cases of collective settlements or partially communal land, villages assume joint responsibility for amortizing the cost of the land. This has been the history of the Vicos project, where part of the surplus accumulated through the use of credit has been set aside by the community towards the purchase price of the *hacienda*. Apparently, the process of buying themselves out of bondage has provided the peasants with incentives which might not have been present had the *hacienda* been given to them free of charge (Vasquez and Dobyns, 1964). Similarly, great interest and remarkable capital accumulation have been observed in Bolivia, where many peasant communities in the post-reform period have offered substantial cash payments for the landlord's remaining parcels (*consolidaciones*).

Such projects can also be an effective instrument for capital building by the community as a whole. Once members feel they are obtaining sufficient material benefits from group financing, the withholding of a certain percentage of sales proceeds appears easier than accumulating either land costs or financing other capital improvements through repeated collections. Clearly, once a cooperative has become a full-fledged business enterprise, setting aside non-distributed profits for capital expansion becomes a standard procedure.

But apart from the economic objective of establishing a flow of controlled credit for productive purposes, an important aspect of most cooperative projects is the gradual development of grass-roots institutions capable of managing some of the *asentamiento* (reform settlement) affairs. Group discussions and shared decisions between extension, bank personnel and the union members regarding farm operations are means used for achieving these objectives. Farm plans are then formalized into definite annual programmes, including the choice of seed and the amount of land each member is to devote to the crop. Unions are responsible for all the marketing, management of credit in kind and storage of the inputs.

Because the management of funds requires a certain capacity for competent, honest management, the initial phase of such a programme is uncommonly difficult. This phase tests not only the community's ability to mobilize managerial talent but also the complex and delicate relationship between the new group and the lending or control institution.

Some of the lessons which seem to emerge from experiences in several countries are:

(i) Credit, offered through the association and used both individually by members and communally in a joint venture, was an adequate opening wedge for technical and institutional innovations and led to a process of economic organization in the community.

(ii) In spite of strained relations with the lending institution, which insisted on control and compliance, cooperative members have rapidly assumed responsibilities and performed well in situations according to the rules. This is true even for rules set up by 'outside agencies'. The members did not comply with rules pertaining to technical and 'internal' matters. These rules and their corresponding sanctions were too diffuse for people who were accustomed to clear-cut relationships.

(iii) The sympathetic assistance of an outside agency (extension) was crucial for success, as was the 'legitimizing' function of some of the local political authorities who acquired an interest in the project's performance.

(d) *Multi-purpose cooperatives* As we have seen, associations which often start out with a single purpose, such as purchasing, marketing or credit, sooner or later become multi-purpose societies, especially if their initial operations are successful. In many cases the assumption of important market and processing functions leads to cooperative activity in a series of interrelated fields. At full maturity a number of Latin American cooperatives have reached a degree of complexity found in highly developed cooperatives in industrialized countries. Clearly, most of the successful multi-purpose associations are in the richer Latin American countries and in the more highly developed regions. Never-

theless, some multi-purpose societies function within an environment of general under-development and without benefit of a
supporting governmental network. This testifies to the extraordinary efforts of their founders and promoters.

The Victoria cooperative in Costa Rica is one example of a
successful multi-purpose cooperative, but perhaps the most
notable success story is the Cotia group in the state of São Paulo,
Brazil (Cooperativa Agrícola de Cotia). This society developed
from an early initiative of small Japanese vegetable farmers and
agricultural workers in 1927 for the purpose of transporting produce to city markets. From an original nucleus of seventy members it had grown by 1960 into a giant complex of over 10,000
families directly benefiting a total population of about 100,000
persons (Saito, 1964). The history of Cotia shows the strongly
cohesive force and economic behaviour of the Japanese immigrants as the motive power behind this organization. By the early
'sixties the membership did become more diversified and is now
about forty per cent Brazilian. An overwhelming proportion of
the membership consists of small farmers operating very intensive
vegetable farms and growing other high-value commercial crops.
Three-quarters of the members own farms of 1–25 hectares and
twenty per cent have farms of 25–100 hectares.

Cotia's members produce a third of the sweet potato output
of the entire state of São Paulo and a quarter of its tomato production. Operations are decentralized into smaller specialized
groupings such as transport groups, production groups and other
'micro-cooperatives' covering the entire state. The cooperative
operates 3,000 tractors and 1,800 trucks.

It is notable that Cotia has been the source of an exceptional
number of technological innovations among its membership and
is constantly improving the quality and yields of its members'
farming operations through up-to-date central installations and
services. For example, in the field of coffee production, members
of Cotia can count on a full network of credit and technical
services, including soil testing, seed selection, a rigorous classification of quality coffees, a supply of fertilizer and complete
processing and marketing facilities.

Another example of a multi-purpose association is the Juan
XXIII cooperative in the Veraguas region of Panama. It is part
of a comprehensive programme of rural development sponsored
by a Catholic church group under the leadership of Bishop
McGrath. Through intensive educational effort and simple field

demonstrations, illiterate peasants were gradually trained for more complex forms of organization. Juan XXIII now operates its own storage facilities and rice mill, but there is also some communal land use and a central agricultural machinery pool. The cooperative store sells agricultural supplies and food. The positive results achieved by this programme have been ascribed to the decisive promotional and training effort of the church group. This group utilized methods which included the gradual introduction of new ideas and techniques and the training of local leaders, and it provided financial assistance for infrastructure and capital installations (Lodge and Guderman, 1967).

A more recent development is the emergence of multi-purpose cooperatives which have their origin in rural community development programmes. Such is the case of Cogua on the Sabana de Bogotá in Colombia (Edel, 1968). The first step was the formation of local community action groups (*juntas de acción communal*). After the juntas successfully tackled some simple tasks based on the 'felt needs' of the villagers a meeting of all the groups reached an agreement to construct facilities for a purchasing society. The juntas agreed to subscribe the initial capital, which was to be partly in cash and partly in supplies. Additional funds were collected which enabled a fertilizer section to be opened. Within two years Cogua entered into marketing and processing activities.

As this experience shows, there can be a close sequential relationship between community development and the organization of agricultural cooperatives. A gradual strategy appears in which peasants, through initial experience with community organizations such as the Colombian juntas, learn to form more complex organizations. Skills acquired in conducting meetings, keeping records and organizing projects can be thereafter transferred to more difficult tasks. Successful completion of joint village projects has an important effect on the peasants' perception of the possibility of change and on their degree of trust of outsiders. Moreover, the confidence of members of the community is increased by the completion of community tasks: 'a job in which each was only risking some of his time may become great enough for them to trust one another with their savings', Edel remarks.

2. *Cooperation in the production process*

We now turn to different forms of rural cooperation which more directly affect the production process itself. There is no sharp line which separates some of the input–output and service co-operatives discussed in the previous section from those in which production facilities are pooled. (The credit system has a strong influence on the cropping pattern, while marketing or processing arrangements may have a decisive influence on the whole farm-ing system.) Production cooperatives are distinguished by the fact that they directly involve the internal organization and pro-ductive operations of the participating farm units, while service cooperatives affect only the farm's relations with the 'outside' world. Production associations fall into two main categories: in the first category, joint production decisions and common opera-tions are carried out without affecting the distinction of the individual farm units; in the second, the association is character-ized by the merger or absence of individual farms in favour of a larger collective in which the link between the membership and specific parcels of land disappears.

(a) *Cooperative farming with individual land parcels* Productive cooperation, in cases where the individual ownership and control of the members' farms are preserved, can range from informal arrangements involving selected aspects, such as the pooling of some equipment, to complex systems of joint management of most of the key operations. Irrigation and machinery are most frequently operated in a centralized fashion because of techno-logical necessity.

While some central authority is necessarily present for the management of every water system, its 'cooperativeness' depends on the relationship between the irrigation agency and the farmers. In some cases, as in the Peruvian community of Huaylas, there appears to be a degree of self-management and democratic con-trol. This is marred by some corruption owing to the fact that none of the water administration in Peru receives compensation other than sporadic payments based on fines. Therefore it is not surprising that some officials, especially the *repartidor*, occasion-ally resort to bribery and collusion with more affluent clients (Doughty, 1968).

Another type of farm production group is the wool improve-ment association in the villages around Huancayo, Peru (*junta de fomento lanar*). Central treatment facilities, including sheep dips to control pests, have been constructed by village labour. A veterinary service has also been installed. The junta then pro-cesses and markets the wool. In a similar Bolivian association the animals continue to be individually owned but, through the traditional use of communal pasture and the central treatment and marketing facilities, practically all aspects of wool production are carried out jointly. The costs of wool improvements are covered from higher revenues.

(b) *Cooperation with joint land management* Joint or pooled land management is the most difficult form of agricultural cooperation. It is also subject to considerable ideological controversy. In Latin America land use cooperatives appear to be important in at least three contexts:

(i) A considerable amount of land is currently operated under various forms of communal or semi-communal management, especially in areas of traditional culture. There are also systems in which individuals have or own private plots and, in addition, also jointly operate considerable acreages of communal property, especially pasture and forest land. The modernization of these systems may be accomplished in a more satisfactory way by maintaining some joint land use, especially where ecological and technical factors favour it.

(ii) Land pooling and consolidation is seen as one of the solutions to the *minifundia* problem, through which economies of scale may be achieved.

(iii) Various agrarian reform efforts are faced with the problem of taking over large estates which are difficult or inconvenient to divide. In such situations temporary or permanent models of joint land use have been created. Experimentation to find viable solutions are likely to continue under different ideologies and political systems.

The most important experience in Latin America with production cooperatives is that of the collective *ejidos* in Mexico. Most of the collective *ejidos* were organized in regions of intensive farming and commercial crops, where rather highly developed private estates employing both resident and seasonal wage workers were expropriated. Strong and militant peasant unions organized on the estates were responsible in great part for the original reform process in these regions and for the cohesive spirit on which the collectives were founded. Through the requirement of forming collective credit societies (*sociedades locales de crédito colectivo ejidal*) the Ejido Bank has acquired special responsibilities for collectives and control over them. The bulk of the collectives were formed between 1936 and 1939. In the peak year of

1940 approximately 1,000 collective *ejidos* were in existence. The history of these novel types of organization is intimately bound up with ideological and political struggles in Mexico during the past three decades. Their initial success and later decline are closely associated with the course of official policies. These policies have fluctuated between encouragement and support of collectives, especially under the Cárdenas regime, to indifference and outright hostility in later periods. At the present time, out of approximately 18,700 *ejidos* with 1·5 million members, there are only a little over 300 collective *ejidos* with a membership of 32,000. Some of the surviving collective *ejidos* are operating in the field of livestock, while agricultural collectives are concentrated in the Laguna region of northern Mexico and in the Yucatan peninsula. In the former case they specialize in cotton and, in the latter, henequen.

Although the economic viability of the collective *ejidos* under conditions of intensive irrigated farming has been repeatedly demonstrated, the issues of internal organization of the collectives have, from the beginning, created serious problems. The creation of an effectively functioning 'collective discipline' has been difficult. The establishment among unlettered peons of collective types of organization, requiring management of a high order, has not been accompanied by sufficient cooperative-type education, or training of local leaders. The authority of the *jefe de trabajo* or the *socio delegado* was frequently not recognized nor accepted by all the members, and in many cases it has been difficult for the leaders to impose the necessary discipline. Part of the difficulty of achieving effective leadership has been due to the prevalence of certain cultural traits such as the system of *compadrazgo* (godfatherhood) and the entrenched beliefs in the dishonesty of leaders, even in cases without substantiating evidence. The fact that accounting was not always open and available for inspection often aggravated this atmosphere of suspicion. A number of leaders abused their power, which caused frequently documented situations of graft and corruption. However, most commentators agree that the major supporting sources of corruption were external.

Another major internal problem was the inability of the collectives to reward effort in proportion to the members' actual contribution. The system of *anticipos* (advanced sales proceeds) which the Ejido Bank paid to the beneficiaries frequently degenerated into simple wage payments. In some instances these became com-

15—T.B.O.G.

pletely dissociated from effort and reward for exceptional contributions, and in others fostered an atmosphere of dependency and a feeling of being employees rather than co-participants in a system. The institutionalization of the *anticipos* often fostered a negative attitude toward hard work and initiative and, worse, prevented most of the *ejido* members from developing behaviour which would have favoured the long-run economic success of their joint undertaking over short-run personal benefits.

These internal reasons were doubtless important; but the disintegration of the collective *ejido* system was due essentially to an external reason, i.e. the unfavourable government policy after 1940. The Ejido Bank, which had previously been assigned the double function of organizing and assisting the *ejidos* in their economic and productive systems and administering the credit, has gradually abandoned the development objective and concentrated on the control function. This has produced an adverse effect in the young local societies, most of which had not yet become firmly established. The withdrawal of official assistance and the rigid tightening of credit controls have caused many of them to collapse. These unfavourable official policies have exposed the struggling collectives to all sorts of divisive forces. The main detrimental effects were the dissemination of doubt and uncertainty and the weakening of social cohesion.

Part of the official hostility was due to ideological struggles. Many of the collective leaders and their peasant associations have identified themselves with leftist parties. These parties were then considered dangerous by the national power hierarchy, especially by the private commercial interests of the non-*ejido* agricultural sector. Every effort was made to penetrate, split and weaken the collective ejidos and their supporting institutions, such as the regional peasant associations and some of the second-level cooperative unions. New rival factions were created and splinter groups were encouraged to break up the collectives. These efforts encouraged and accentuated the latent or underlying divisive factors within the *ejidos* and created a vicious circle of adverse forces. The withdrawal of official support has frequently forced *ejido* leaders to adopt even more radical policies than they otherwise might have adopted (Eckstein, 1966).

One of the few surviving and successfully functioning collective *ejidos* is Quechehueca in the state of Sonora, which started in 1937. Another example of a successful cooperative *ejido* is the San Miguel *ejido* near Torreón. One of the reasons for San

Miguel's survival is said to be the cohesiveness of its membership, greatly strengthened by the many battles they have fought and won during its history.

Part of San Miguel's strength is attributed to the fact that this *ejido* is financially independent and not indebted to the Bank, as are most of the others whose financial weakness has led them increasingly into a position of dependency. Recently a minority group provoked an internal struggle which resulted in the assassination of the *comisariado ejidal* and threatened the survival of the *ejido*. However, the dissidents were given land elsewhere and the *ejido* survives (Huizer, 1968).

A third example of functioning collective *ejidos* is the case of Cananea, a livestock collective in the state of Sonora. In Cananea one can see the beginning of separation between a politically sensitive leadership and a technically competent management. A similar separation can be observed in the case of the Sinaloa *ejidos* mentioned under 'Marketing associations'. Here the more pros·perous *ejidos* separate ownership from management by hiring professional *agrónomos* and machine pool managers. This separation may involve the gradual limitation of the government's role to more narrow technical aspects.

As long as the role of the government is so important, serious conflicts are bound to arise in the process of restricting outside policy influence. For example, as the income of technicians and their subordinate personnel comes from the interest paid on the official loans by the societies rather than from profits, government technicians may acquire a vested interest in credit operations that appear of doubtful value to the farmers.

In spite of these occasional conflicts it is reported that the *ejidatarios* at Cananea have a great sense of participation in their own affairs and enjoy considerable political independence. Although some members continue to press toward individualization, the collective experience seems to be satisfactory to most participants. Other policies which strengthen the system include granting small garden plots for each family, and creating small industries to increase diversification (Huizer, 1968).

(*c*) *Semi-collectives* These are systems in which some features remain individual while others are carried out on a collective basis. Generally, peasants hold some private land for subsistence (as a sort of 'floor' or income security) and operate other acreage jointly for commercial production. The degree of mechanization often determines the land areas and specific operations which remain in the hands of individual families. Often the semi-collectives are comprised of small voluntary groupings of farmers for specific tasks.

Recent experiments in collective farming have emerged from the Venezuelan agrarian reform. The successful cooperatives within the Venezuelan reform settlements (*asentamientos*) have resulted from local circumstances (such as the taking over of coffee and cocoa estates which could not be sub-divided) rather than from a strong central policy (Erasmus, 1964).

The Mondragón cooperative in the state of Portuguesa is a good example of a spontaneous cooperative. After the membership had become a homogeneous and compatible group the peasants decided to operate their ten-hectare parcels collectively, although their plots are not contiguous. Members have obtained credit and purchased machinery, and are working their plots in rotation by exchanging labour among one another, a well known practice in the region. Each owner acts as a foreman on the days when the group is working on his parcel and each man's benefit is determined by the harvest of his own parcel. Weekly advances are paid prior to harvest based on the number of days worked. Any member who does not do his full share of work is threatened with expulsion. If this occurs he is reimbursed only for his share of the equipment.

It is believed that the most successful of the production societies are those which concentrate on the collective production and marketing of highly specialized crops such as coffee, cocoa and tomatoes. Difficulties arise and members become disillusioned when the profits are divided merely on the basis of land contributed, i.e. without taking into account the individual labour input (which, of course, has already been compensated in the form of wages). Failure to observe this simple principle seems to be a frequently encountered defect of similar initiatives in other countries as well.[5]

---

[5] One of the serious risks of these semi-collectives is that if the work is not well organized and controlled a kind of a *hacienda* system may become gradually established under cooperative cover: the settlers withdraw their labour contribution toward the joint enterprise, which is then run with salaried workers. For example, in a rather prosperous semi-collective CIARA has found that of a total membership of fifty-three, only twenty-eight are willing to devote part of their time to the joint part of the enterprise: only four work regularly all year, fourteen work irregularly for some months, and the rest only a few days. All in all, about two-thirds of the total labour bill

A recent variant of the joint land use cooperative, at least in a transitional form, is provided by the Chilean land reform. As initially conceived, the Chilean reform envisaged the expropriation of large estates (many of which were centrally managed commercial farms rather than traditional *haciendas*) and their redistribution to about 100,000 peasant families over an eight-year period. Each beneficiary family received a plot of about six irrigated hectares or the equivalent in non-irrigated land.

Although the expropriated holdings could have been legally assigned to *campesino* (peasant) families on an individual basis, in practice the old *fundo* was converted intact into a collectively managed enterprise or *asentamiento* formally known as a *sociedad agrícola de reforma agraria*. The land reform agency, CORA, retains title to the land for a period not exceeding three years (five years under exceptional circumstances). After this transitory period, CORA, together with the peasants, will decide if the *asentamiento* is to be operated as a permanently cooperative enterprise or sub-divided into individual farms. Even then it is envisaged that the new structure will be strongly cooperative in many aspects.

Each settlement is governed by an elected committee of peasants and two technicians appointed by CORA. One of the technicians, a middle-level extension agent, is permanently assigned to the *asentamiento*, personifies the government's 'partnership' in the operations, and provides the link to the reform agency.

Work on the *asentamientos* is carried out by field crews, much as it was before the reform, except that individual peasants can keep a small plot for household crops and livestock. In some *asentamientos*, the fields are under individual ownership but subject to land use planning by the settlement committee. Investments and short-term credits provided by CORA are channelled through the *asentamiento* committees. Marketing is also undertaken collectively.

The peasants receive monthly wage advances with differential wages for special skills. At the end of the year the farm's net income is divided according to a pre-arranged formula. CORA, as the transitional land-owner, usually takes an average of twenty per cent for investment, administrative expenses, and interest. The remaining eighty per cent is divided among the peasants

---

was paid to workers from outside the cooperative. (Personal communication from J. M. Texier.)

according to the number of days worked by each, with the subsistence advances subtracted from the final settlement.

Under this system nearly 14,000 peasant families became members of about 350 *asentamientos* by the end of 1968. The *asentamientos* contained about 1·3 million hectares of farmland, of
which 136,000 were irrigated.

The change of status and prospect of future individual or collective ownership seem to be adequate stimuli for the peasants
to save, invest, and actively participate in the *asentamiento*
system. Although the land reform agency has virtual control over
credit and marketing, there is a tacit *quid pro quo* between it
and members of the *asentamientos* that seems mutually satisfactory. Thus although there is at this point an almost total dependence on CORA for most external services, the rudiments of
cooperative behaviour are actively developed and the transitional
nature of the relationship generally understood by both the government and the peasants.

II. *Issues*

1. *Possibilities of utilizing traditional forms of cooperation*

For some time the possibility of modernizing traditional forms of
cooperation, especially as found in Andean Indian societies, has
intrigued commentators and development strategists alike. The
cooperative movement in Western industrialized countries came
after a long individualistic phase of agricultural development.
However, forms of mutual help and communal use of resources
frequently exist in traditional and only weakly market-oriented
peasant communities. The question is then asked: can these traditional institutions be expected to evolve (or be deliberately
converted) into modern, more technology- and market-oriented
cooperatives without passing through the individualistic phase?

Available experience and the opinions of scholars diverge, but
the weight of the evidence is on the pessimistic side. Texier
(1967), for example, after extensive review of traditional forms of
rural cooperation, concludes that the organization and functioning of traditional communitarian institutions are so fundamentally
different from modern structures that they cannot be considered
as parts of the same continuum. He characterizes the traditional
systems of work organization and exchange of services (*mita,
faena, minga, ayni,* etc.) as 'consensus' types and authoritarian in
character, which 'more often than not promotes the institutional-

ization of inequality'. He further concludes that the factors of cohesion manifest in such communities are neither spontaneous nor voluntary, but are a form of collective behaviour which is accepted and agreed upon as the 'only possible alternative for the survival of the group.' Hence efforts at a smooth transformation are bound to fail as the binding ties disintegrate or disappear once the traditional system is broached. Texier takes almost the same sombre view with regard to the possibility of introducing production cooperatives based on traditional communal land use. He emphasizes the motivational differences between 'communitarian solidarity' in traditional joint land use and 'co-operative solidarity' required in the modern management of land resources. Furthermore, he points out that historically important systems of joint land use such as the *ayllu* have already given way to individual cultivation. Thus attempts to transform these systems into modern production collectives, as was the case with the *zadruga* in Europe, may well be futile.

Similar ideas are expressed by Vellard (1963), who concludes that because of the different milieu in Indian communities, where cooperation is based on traditional social obligations rather than on economic interests, there appears to be no functional equivalence between the traditional and modern forms of associations. Moreover, he believes that the creation of a modern cooperative meets with fewer obstacles in a completely new community organized through agrarian reform or settlement than in well established traditional areas. Texier (1967) holds similar views on production associations and reports that in Venezuela he noted greater success of joint farming among *asentamientos* which were 'detribalized or uprooted' and at the same time composed of more heterogeneous elements.

Vasquez and Dobyns (1964) stress the point that traditional Andean Indian cooperation is based on principles of reciprocity in kind or in labour services between competitive individuals, while they see modern cooperation requiring behaviour in which 'the internalized ethic of group cohesiveness' subordinates individual interests.

Pearse (1966) and others interpret the rationale of traditional communal labour in terms of a wealth-distributing function, rather than a wealth-producing one. After surveying the contemporary trend of agrarian change affecting the peasantry in Latin America, he is exceptionally pessimistic in stressing 'the incompatibility of the traditional rural systems and the extending modern society . . .'

Behind these gloomy views are some well documented observations that many communities are really neither cohesive nor egalitarian and that the traditional systems are weakening and in process of dissolving. Among forces disintegrating the old system are the following: (a) the accelerated, selectively individualist market involvement of peasant families (both as consumers and producers); (b) the opportunities for earning money wages instead of exchanging labour; (c) the increasing disaffection of young people with collective forms of work from which they do not benefit individually, and (d) the unremitting individualization of society under the influence of prevailing forces of development. The working of these factors may be illustrated by the disappearance of the Haitian *combite* system and other similar institutions of reciprocal farm labour. According to Erasmus (1965), individualization is an inevitable sequence to traditional communality. While the latter is based on reciprocal or 'centripetal–personal' behaviour, individualization produces a 'centrifugal–impersonal' type of behaviour in which social approbation is achieved through conspicuous consumption rather than conspicuous giving. He further reports that in Haiti many social planners looked upon the *combite* as a practice on which to base cooperative self-help projects, but 'its disintegration everywhere seemed to correlate with the very socio-economic changes which the planners were endeavouring to accelerate'.

Texier thinks that the only hopeful sign is the sporadic emergence of 'new factors' or situations which have the capability of 'being substituted for the old systems or being superimposed on them'. This view of functional discontinuity has been expressed by a great many observers of the highland-type *hacienda-comunidad* pattern, such as Vasquez and Dobyns (1964), Metraux (1959) and Bjornberg (1959).

Turning now to more hopeful views, we have Ritter's conclusions drawn from his work in Peru. While he acknowledges and documents the disintegration of Indian communities, he firmly believes that cooperative attitudes have been sufficiently preserved or modified to serve as connecting links (*Ansatzpunkte*) for new economic institutions organized along cooperative lines. He sees the causes of the many failures and frustrations of previous programmes more in the inappropriateness of promotional approaches rather than in the incompatibility of the peasants' present institutions. Thus while it is inappropriate to think of models of collective land use on the *kibbutz* pattern for highland Latin America, there are many perfectly viable opportunities for modernizing communal pasture arrangements. As crops are generally consumed, while animal products are sold, the already existing market orientation of livestock production could be a base for the expansion of output through modernized *granjas comunales.* Indeed, such collective livestock enterprises are already functioning, and profits are involved in communal projects. Similarly, the existing practices of common work on some crop land can be utilized for demonstration plots or for promoting such innovations as sheep dips or tree nurseries.

Ritter (1966) is also more hopeful that the traditional community leadership can be transformed into a vehicle for modernization on a community-wide basis. He feels that one of the errors of previous programmes was the deliberate attempt to by-pass the existing village institutions and the creation of different channels for planned change. In view of the scarcity of managerial talent and the distrust with which new institutions are faced, he recommends using the present community structure wherever possible and imparting to the leadership a set of fresh and positive orientations by a gradual transfer to them of new responsibilities. In the Yaqui valley of Mexico, small credit societies (with twenty to twenty-five members) are successfully operated by a special agency of the Ejido Bank by making use of the authority of traditional tribal organization.

After an evaluation of the cooperative activity which has grown up around the 'bases' of the Andean Action Programme in Bolivia, Ecuador and Peru, the ILO in a 1961 report arrived at some favourable conclusions. While the early experience of this programme shows a series of failures or near-failures (Leonard, 1966), subsequent development is more encouraging. Joint enterprises which were difficult to maintain without constant pressure have become routinely accepted, and some of the dissolved production associations have been reconstituted by the peasants themselves. Invariably previous group experience by the *comunarios* was helpful to them in comprehending and adjusting to new and in many cases more complicated forms of organization, such as operating a grain mill at Otavi in Bolivia or farm machinery stations and repair shops in Riobamba, Ecuador. The conclusion of the evaluation is that the traditional collaboration, cohesiveness and solidarity of the communities represented a favourable condition for the successful organization of economically-oriented cooperatives.

The Vicos/Cornell case offers support for these relatively optimistic views. In this case successful modernization can be partially explained by the adaptation of previous communal practices which formed the basis for specific innovation. However, it must be pointed out that the liberalization process, from quasi-serfdom to a state of self-management, was perhaps of overriding importance. Nevertheless, the Vicos experience is congruent with the view that traditional communitarianism may serve as a springboard for modern cooperative-type organization. In Vicos the gradual, adaptive and sensitively administered techniques of modernization took advantage of already existing joint activities so that (even in the controversial case of joint land use) the estate's modernized structure emerged as a strongly cooperative model.[6] This was accomplished by utilizing the available community structure in building and re-orienting its functions rather than by adding new institutions (Holmberg, 1960, 1965; Doughty, 1965; Dobyns, 1965).

There is evidence, then, that some continuity of community organization is possible and even desirable without waiting for Erasmus's 'individualization phase' to be completed. The Mexican data also indicate some successful cases in which traditional behaviour has facilitated the adoption of innovations such as modern irrigation (Chonchol, 1957), pasture and forest management (Maturana, 1968), and some of the economic community development activities such as those sponsored by CREFAL among Tarascan highland Indians (Smith, 1961; Foster, 1967). It must be pointed out, however, that the contemporary Mexican

---

[6] 'The Vicos experience is showing that it is possible to create out of manors with peonage a new type of community or peasant association . . . where the use of the land base does not benefit only a single individual or a faction, but the entire community and each one of its members, as well as the region and the country.

The 'Vicos model' has as its ultimate objective the establishment of an economically viable and socially rewarding modern rural community. It constitutes in its present stage, however, a socio-economic transition model for a backward population on the way toward modern producers' cooperative organization. In commercial terms, Vicos has at the present time the characteristics of an informal corporation or joint stock company in which the household heads are shareholders and proprietors of Vicos as a production enterprise. Vicos may be conceived as currently in a preliminary stage of organization preceding modern cooperative operation . . .' (Vazquez and Dobyns, 1964).

agrarian situation is dominated by sharp conflicts between the Indian and the *mestizo* worlds, between agrarianism and technological capitalism. Most students of Mexican peasant villages report the persistence of a strikingly conflict-ridden and essentially non-cooperative community structure, with few elements of modernization based on any group activity (Foster, 1967; Lewis, 1951; Belshaw, 1967). However, it appears that the lack of rural cooperation in Mexico may not be entirely due to the failure of transforming traditional communitarianism, but also to external constraints as discussed elsewhere in this paper.

One of the most interesting recent success stories of almost spontaneous community organization is the case of Huaylas, as reported by Doughty. Here the Vicos experience seems to have been repeated without much outside expertise. In reviewing the factors which may be related to the progress of Huaylas, Doughty strongly emphasizes the capability of the village to maintain communal institutions and convert them to new purposes. Thus the viability of various joint labour arrangements (*repúblicas*) has been preserved for a large number of new economic tasks.[7]

Doughty also stresses the fact that Huaylinos always had to cooperate with one another to a certain extent in order to assure reasonable success in their individual farming enterprises. Because of the scarcity of water, constant conflicts arise over its use, but practical necessity appears to have overridden such disagreements and there is considerable cooperation in keeping the irrigation system operative. In general 'the firm and positive sense of belonging to the community' is emphasized as a unifying force. In spite of the existence of the same disruptive and divisive forces which operate in similar communities, this unifying force, which may be traced to its traditional origins, has clearly provided the vital sustaining element in Huaylas.

How are the two views on the possibilities of utilizing traditional forms of cooperation reconciled? First, it is evident that owing to differences of emphasis the debate may not be fully joined. Many of the pessimists' arguments are directed against the chances of establishing 'Rochedalian' or idealized Western-type

---

[7] 'Most Huaylinos can and do feel that the benefits from work on *repúblicas* and committees accrue to the community at large and not merely to a small group or clique. The fact that Huaylas is able to utilize almost all of its human resources for community enterprises is of a major significance, considering the limited monetary, technological, and other resources at its disposal' (Doughty, 1968).

democratic cooperatives rapidly and directly. The optimists, on the other hand, stress the possibilities for the introduction of less formal and imperfect types of system. While the emphasis of the two 'schools of thought' is respectively gloomy and hopeful, the real difference between them may not be quite as great. Thus after dramatizing the apparent incongruences and even incompatibilities between the two systems Texier does finally admit that there really are opportunities for certain types of cooperative institution (but which he and other specialists are reluctant to identify as 'true' cooperatives). These 'pre-cooperatives' or 'para-cooperatives' are described as differing from the pure forms in that they are purposefully planned and partly controlled by 'intervening organs' from the outside. They are said to represent imperfect models of free, democratic and participating groups.

Most of the examples of successful linkage with traditional systems cited by the more optimistic commentators are intermediary or quasi-cooperative types of structures, rather than the fully self-managed, democratic models. Thus, even the severest critics admit the transmutability of certain aspects of traditional structures as long as gradualistic strategies and intermediate modes are used.

Next, one has to consider what stage of development and type of peasant group is being discussed. It seems that the pessimists generally deal with peasant groupings in which the traditional community organization is in an advanced process of disintegration and where the outside commercial world (mostly *mestizo* and white) represents a strongly threatening environment. In such situations, it is not surprising that neither the outward-aspiring mobile individuals, nor those who may have reacted to the hostile world by withdrawing into non-functional traditional behaviour, represent good bases for egalitarian, economically progressive organizations. One would think such circumstances present the following alternatives:

(a) The emergence of a 'closed corporate community' described by Wolf (1966), in which a self-imposed cohesion exists, reinforced by expulsion of those individuals who do not conform to group patterns and who gain too much wealth. In this case cooperative promoters would have to gain the confidence of the community as a whole, thus opening the path for a variety of pre-cooperative or quasi-cooperative undertakings based on village consensus and the re-articulation of group needs.

(b) The traditional community gives way to a collection of more or less independent smallholders. In this case, while there may be few of the old mutual aid traditions left, perhaps 'purer' models of cooperation may be successfully introduced. Certain technological requirements such as irrigation might provide special incentives for such group management.

The fact that appropriate strategies for transitional economic cooperation can be designed does not deny that powerful barriers are undoubtedly present in traditional peasant societies, especially when modernization requires new types of economic organization with a fairly sophisticated management component. Such new institutions must sooner or later acquire a dual type of structure, made up by the membership meetings on the one hand and by the administration, on the other, and based on the 'coordination of parallel flowing individual interests' (Ritter, 1966). This duality, in which there is a functional specialization between (a) management and (b) policy-making by the body of membership, is an unfamiliar form of organization for peasant communities. It has no parallel, nor any visible connecting link with the traditional community, no matter how cooperative it may have been in its primitive form. Many of the grave problems encountered in modern cooperatives, such as the difficulty of differentiating the role of paid supervisor from that of 'elder' or village leader, can be traced to this type of basic conflict with the traditional behaviour patterns. Yet, when one takes a larger and longer view, there is no reason why these new requirements cannot be learned and eventually institutionalized. It is fair to say that successful strategies for discontinuous changes of this sort depend on other factors and not primarily on fundamental cultural resistances or incongruities.

2. Problem of egalitarianism

The issue of egalitarianism becomes critical at least at two main stages of cooperative development: in the formative stage, which requires the extremely difficult step of mobilizing group motivation, and at a later stage, when more mature cooperatives must choose between exclusive, elitist behaviour and more expansionist democratic alternatives. With respect to the initial step there appear to be various dilemmas. One is the mobilization for egalitarian goals of essentially passive or closed communities, more or less hostile to outside intervention. It was previously mentioned that such traditional peasant communities may not be egalitarian at all.

Foster's image of the 'limited good' is frequently cited as one of the main constraints for group mobilization. According to this view, individual success in societies in which the consequences of an expanded economy are understood and accepted need not be perceived by neighbours as a threat against the community. Under such conditions voluntary cooperation can function as an effective mechanism for promoting social and economic progress for the group. However, in a society where members believe that their economic system is static and non-expandable (resources are held to be strictly limited, so that if some get more others have to get less), voluntary cooperation can be expected to function only under exceptional circumstances. Extreme individualism is chosen over cooperation in preserving peasant security because cooperation assumes effective leadership, and peasants who accept leadership are vulnerable to criticism and sanctions from envious neighbours (Foster, 1965).

While Foster's static concept is a real and important deterrent as far as cooperative organization is concerned, his inclusion of the fear of individual accumulation at the expense of other members of the community does not appear to be applicable to the concept of cooperative progress, in which the membership could benefit as a whole from joint activity. Perhaps the image of the limited good does apply also to group progress, but one would think that it is precisely the avoidance of disproportionate individual enrichment in the process of change which provides one of the strongest arguments and possible motivating sources for cooperative effort. One must also consider that Foster's model tends to represent the most traditional and isolated communities, while cooperative promotion is best started in more progressive areas, whence it may radiate into the hinterland.

Mangin too takes Foster to task for making his pessimistic theory too general and for de-emphasizing (a) the influence of outside forces on the peasant community and (b) the role of the more powerful members of society in his explanation of the peasants' outlook. For example, in Vicos the Indians were blocked from changing their agricultural technology by middle-class Peruvians who prevented them from buying fertilizers and pesticides. Because they were Indians they had no access to extension services. Once these things became available through the outside pressure of the Cornell/Vicos project the Vicosinos willingly improved their economic position through a primarily cooperative effort. All too common is the case, reported by Harris (1964), of the introduction of merino sheep of much better class than the local variety in an Ecuadorian community. When suspicion was overcome and the sheep were accepted by the local peasants, wool production improved so much that the *mestizos* came and stole all the sheep (Mangin, 1966). Leadership can also emerge and operate effectively if these outside constraints are removed or weakened. Both the squatter invasions around Lima and the land invasions in the Peruvian sierra show evidence of planning, cooperation and leadership of the highest quality; yet many of them were organized by men and women who had recently left peasant communities. There is hope that the leadership of peasant associations may come increasingly from average community members rather than charismatic outsiders (Mangin, 1966).

A different dilemma is posed by a factor which has been commonly emphasized: the individualism of peasants as an obstacle to cooperative organization. The argument seems to be that once the static passivity of a community is broken by outside stimuli, economic progress is made by individual entrepreneurs rather than by organized peasants. How can cooperatives flourish in an environment of rampant individualism, especially when it expresses itself in capitalistic entrepreneurship?

Erasmus, who believes that the 'individual egotist' is the source of development, is extremely critical of all government efforts to promote egalitarian cooperation in the face of this rising commercialism. He views with concern the efforts of official organizations that result in 'dependent peasants' who feed on paternalism and throttle individualist entrepreneurs:

> True natural leaders spring up very readily in communities not dominated by social welfare administrations, although . . . they are often resented by the latter. The able farmer who improves his lot through his own skill and initiative is a thorn in the side of the government technician who seeks dependents—not independent 'egotists'. The 'egotists', however, appear everywhere in an environment made fertile for their managerial abilities and entrepreneurial creativity through social overhead, capital developments . . . such projects as roads, irrigation and public power. [Erasmus, 1964.]

This view of development appears excessively biased and downgrades the influence of the ideological framework. Obviously, the social environment of rewards and sanctions in which these observed motivations are formed is of crucial importance. If the model of development is individual capitalism, with the social system offering little reward for collective or cooperative leadership as a means of personal gratification, it is not surprising that individualistic economic behaviour will predominate. From the point of view of Latin American development strategy the dilemma is precisely in the problem of how to channel the emerging energies and initiatives of the community leaders and members toward joint rather than individual action so that the majority rather than the minority would benefit from the infrastructure and other public investment.

One possible model which attempts to present a middle way is Alpaca, formed in the Peruvian sierra around Huancayo with assistance from the International Development Foundation. Essentially Alpaca is a multi-purpose service association, with some assistance available to all, but other types of assistance restricted to the more able farmers; in general, however, it offers individual success through an independent large-scale organization which can negotiate with outside market outlets and act as a channel for external resources (Henley, 1969).

Belshaw believes that many communities, including Huecorico in Mexico, which he studied, are divided and stymied by the mistrust of 'negative individualism'. He describes such a state as one in which there is no pride in accomplishment or achievement and in which persons exhibit an ego-focused rather than a group-focused image of change. Here, only activities bringing direct benefit to the self will be undertaken. This is contrasted with 'positive individualism', in which the desire for independence is tempered by a sense of social responsibility and the acceptance of some restraints for the benefit of the community at large. He argues that most of the successful examples of cooperation have occurred in places where the preconditions for positive individualism have been created (Belshaw, 1967).

But it may be a long time before Erasmus's individual egotist is finally replaced by Belshaw's positive individualist. In the meantime we may already be well on the way toward a kulak-type rural development, based on the better educated, more affluent, middle-level farmers. (Dore, for example, is highly sceptical whether political opportunities and administrative resources for cooperative rural strategies would indeed become available in Latin America. Hence he reluctantly accepts the kulak-based path, hoping it would generate enough general welfare. See Dore's 'Comment', following Pearse, 1966.)

3. Cohesion v. creative factionalism

How much cohesion in the community is required for successful cooperative organization and how much factionalism may be tolerated or even encouraged? There seems to be no doubt that the formation of cooperatives requires a minimum degree of similarity of thought and that sufficient cohesion for the subsequent survival of the cooperative is needed to produce acceptable decisions or consent in order to avoid disruption and open quarrels. Cohesion may be achieved by limiting membership to kinsmen or by selecting for membership only those who are already strongly committed to a single ideology. Often, a mechanism to permit secession by dissenters is required to maintain unity (Dobyns, 1967).

The Quechehueca collective in Mexico survived many disruptive attempts by the elimination of dissenting groups until membership was sufficiently homogeneous for effective functioning. (Clearly, in the case of a land use collective cohesion of the group is even more crucial than in that of a credit or marketing association.) The Mexican data generally indicate that small associations are more efficient and durable than larger ones (Eckstein, 1968). In Cotoca, at one of the Bolivian Andean Indian Programme bases, all settlers were originally required to belong to the cooperative. The association proved much too heterogeneous and soon failed. However, a minority group of the original cooperative voluntarily agreed to continue joint livestock operations and has since prospered (ILO, 1961).

In a number of exceptionally successful cases these cohesive traits have been associated with minority or deviant groups, such as ethnically distinct immigrants, religious sects or revolutionary political parties. For almost twenty years the communist enclave of Viota in Cundinamarca, Colombia, amidst constant official hostility, has managed its own affairs, including communal production and marketing, on coffee estates that were occupied between 1934 and 1936 (Hirschman, 1963). In the Choapa valley of northern Chile a similar enclave of a left-wing group has formed an effective local government and network of land use collectives which, by fighting for labour and occupancy rights, laid the groundwork for a production cooperative (Eckstein, 1965). Most

16—T.B.O.G.

of the surviving collective *ejidos* have a membership bound together by radical ideological ties (Huizer, 1968). More often than
not these are exclusive and even 'elitist' groups set off from mass
organizations by choice or by necessity. In a number of regions
in Latin America the earliest and most vigorous cooperatives have
been set up by immigrants, such as the Japanese in southern
Brazil and the Germans in southern Chile and Rio Grande do
Sul (although elsewhere the innovative behaviour of immigrant
entrepreneurs has been strongly individualistic, such as that of
the Canary Islanders in Venezuela).

The relative success of cooperative organization among immigrants, which has also been reported from other parts of the
world, can be explained not only by their previous homeland
experience and enforced need to stick together but also by what
Cohen terms their 'socially destructured' state, that is, by the fact
that they are no longer involved in an ongoing system. Thus
they have been forced to abandon many sets of rights, obligations
and powers which define relationships both among themselves
and between themselves and others. But, while such immigrant
groups may be 'destructured' they are not 'decultured'. Thus
while they have preserved some aspects of cultural cohesion,
their potential for social and cultural change is not as circum-
scribed as that of people 'who are still involved in a system of
external constraints, which strengthen and maintain internal ones,
and which predisposes them to accept the external ones' (Cohen,
1966).

Relatively few of the cooperatives organized by immigrants
have a 'spread effect'. (The giant Japanese cooperative, Cotia, in
São Paulo, seems to be an exception.) Moreover, once liberated
from fraternal bonds the strongly motivated immigrant may be
socially even more outwardly-oriented than his domestic counterpart. He would then be even less concerned about joining or
working with other peasants and more eager to enter an urban
career.

Almost as important as homogeneity of belief is uniformity of
status. Great differences in the economic and social status of
association members are particularly damaging to the cooperative
spirit. While such heterogeneous associations may continue to
operate, they frequently fall under the domination of the high-
status richer members. Erasmus has cited some cases from Colombia in which coffee farmers have refused to cooperate in maintaining a local water system after the Coffee Growers' Federation

turned it over to them. The better-off settlers preferred to hire caretakers to maintain the irrigation system because they felt degraded by working together with some fellow members who, in their eyes, were of a lower status (Erasmus, 1961). Dobyns believes that 'democratic determinism', which is an essential element in economic cooperation, is feasible only among peers. The manorial system, such as the one found at Vicos, fosters interpersonal interactions based on subordination or superordination of individuals and needs to be changed before cooperation becomes possible.

However, several commentators have emphasized the importance of a certain amount of heterogeneity or factionalism in a healthy cooperative movement. For example, Vellard (1963) has pointed out that in Venezuela there is less resistance to cooperatives in heterogeneous settlements than in more unified communities. He explains that this has occurred because the phenomenon of uprooting has broken traditional ties and has given rise to a more experimental and open mentality among the peasants. Cohen (1966) reminds us that some very cohesive communities may indeed reject outside assistance and prove impermeable to such essential services as bookkeeping.

Edel (1967) also reports, from Colombia, that a certain amount of fragmentation among cooperative groups belonging to different parties and having different allegiances might be favourable, since it makes political control by a single government agency less likely and also allows for more successful bargaining to obtain appropriations.[8]

Another aspect of cohesive behaviour which at certain times seems favourable to cooperative organization is common hostility towards rival interests. An example of this is given by Schwartz of the Zacatepec sugar area. In this area an atmosphere of distrust, suspicion and acceptance of corruption prevailed because of troubled relations between the government-controlled sugar mill management and the farmers. On the initiative of one of the village leaders who refused to become part of the system of

[8] The Alpaca experience, mentioned previously, supports this idea. The organizers endeavoured to have the initial nucleus group evenly divided between adherents to the rival Acción Popular and APRA parties. Each group tended to check the other, while at the same time the organization as a whole received moral and other support from both political powers (John T. Westbrook, in a personal communication).

financial collusion with the mill management, the peasants established a society for the common exploitation of a mineral water
spring located on their lands and waged a successful legal battle
to maintain their rights to this resource.[9]

A similar phenomenon has been observed by Padget (1966) in
his case study of factional strife in the Ignacio Romero Vargas
ejido of Puebla. Headed by an old agrarian leader, the peasants
got together against their corrupt *comisariado ejidal*, who had
been controlling the village with the help of federal officials. As
a result of the struggle, waged at various levels of the hierarchy
of local and state government to replace the *comisariado* and the
officials who backed him, the *ejido* had no difficulties in obtaining
credit for a tractor and help for a new school which was partly
built by community effort.

The cohesion problem also has a territorial or geographic
dimension, which can be posed in the following way: successful
cooperation demands free association of like-minded individuals
which can best be satisfied by selective or exclusive groupings.
But the village or rural community structure is generally composed of many heterogeneous family units with divergent
interests and resources whose mobility, and therefore choice, is
extremely restricted. Thus the settlement pattern itself limits the
possibilities of selective free associations. If all or most are to
benefit from cooperatives, then all-inclusive types of association
or compulsory grouping of villagers or holders of land rights are
needed. One possible solution lies in the use of multiple associations—some of which, by geographic necessity, would have to be
all-inclusive (*ejidos, asentamientos, sindicatos*), while others would
have to be more selective or limited, i.e. credit associations, commodity marketing associations, etc. The experience of Mexico
indicates a certain amount of successful adaptation to the problem. While membership is available to farmers in a number of
overlapping associations, some of which may be specialized and
exclusive and others more general and inclusive, advantage is
offered to all (Landsberger and Hewitt, 1967).

---

[9] 'The extent of the involvement, the degree of cultivation of unity
through common hostility, illustrates the potentiality of this kind of organization and the importance of shared feelings of hostility for the creation of
groupings, for cohesion and solidarity above a base of inter-personal conflict, hostility and malice that we have described' (Schwartz, 1962, as quoted
by Huizer, 1968).

4. *External factors*

The issues reviewed in the preceding sections, which deal with traditional communities, cohesion and egalitarianism, focus on the 'internal' problems of cooperative organization. We now turn to an examination of the role of some of the more external forces, especially those related to the broader socio-economic structure. The discussion of these interrelationships is greatly complicated by the circles of causality and the reciprocities between the various systems. At the beginning of this paper the hope was expressed that large-scale cooperative movements would, by allowing the peasants to enter the economic and political process, liberalize the broader system and make it more responsive to the peasants' aspirations. But much of the subsequent evidence seems to indicate that the direction and speed of cooperative development itself depends to a great extent on the permissiveness and evolution of the broader social system, and indeed on active stimulation from above.

(a) *Ideology and legitimacy* Ideological commitment seems to be an essential ingredient for a successful cooperative movement. Such positive value orientation, except for such relatively brief periods in history as the Cárdenas period in Mexico and the emergence of certain more recent political groups such as the left wing of the Chilean Christian Democratic party, has been rare in Latin America. While 'modernization' has been accepted as an important national goal in most countries, and a great deal of intellectual effort has gone into the debate over models of industrial development (especially along the corporate State pattern), almost nothing has been heard about desirable models of agricultural reorganization and modernization. In the meantime the image of rural progress, somewhat anachronistically, remains either the classical family farm or the commercial plantation. Apart from the strongly commodity-oriented cooperative movement in the Southern Tier, temperate zone countries—which involve mostly fully commercial middle or upper level farmers —one cannot really speak of 'movement', much less of a universal commitment. The cases described in the first part of this paper (with the exception of Mexico, Bolivia and Venezuela) are either isolated and localized programmes, or the work of emergent influence groups struggling for recognition within or at the fringes of the national power hierarchy. In countries of massive land reforms, peasant cooperatives clearly enjoy greater institutionalized legitimacy, but in no country is there sufficiently strong and sustained ideological commitment to transcend short-term partisan political struggles.

Under such conditions cooperatives, bent on improving the position and bargaining power of peasant groups, sooner or later become involved in a power struggle with established interests. When, as is frequently the case, there are no existing channels for reform in the power system, those who support cooperative development and their clients soon find themselves in the position of having to oppose the established order to be heard.

The fact that cooperatives and other kinds of peasant association can undermine local power relations and often threaten the existing order can be demonstrated by many of the case histories. In Veraguas, after the need for rice storage facilities was identified as the key element for effective assistance to peasants, one of the earliest achievements of the cooperators was the building of a storage bin which allowed members to store their own rice rather than pay the *tienda* (store) for this service. The storekeeper's wife recruited a number of other women in the village and one night burned the bin down. In this case the cooperative, through effective help from its outside sponsors, recovered from the disaster quickly and was able to build a new and better bin. The incident was thus converted from a defeat into a definite motivational challenge, and the new organization gained confidence that it could not only change its environment but also withstand more intensely hostile attacks upon its new power position (Lodge and Gudeman, 1967).

The violent reaction of displaced coffee buyers in Yungas against the peasants has already been mentioned (Barnes, 1968). The Vicos project also went through an extremely critical phase of attacks by neighbouring *hacienda* owners and their allies. In Mexico the history of the collective *ejidos* is replete with stories of violence from organized interest groups who felt threatened by these new associations (Huizer, 1968). Two such cases, Zacatepec and Puebla, were reviewed in the preceding section.

With this potential for militant opposition to the cooperative movement, the question of legitimacy becomes an important issue. Some commentators believe that the rebelliousness of cooperative founders is an essential ingredient in the effective initiation of the movement (Dobyns, 1967). Such rebelliousness directed against economic monopoly, exploitation and low status may explain the success of many of the strongly radical groups such as those in Quechehueca and Choapa. This active opposition is also an important focus for rallying smaller cohesive groups into larger movements which could be mobilized against the establishment. The questions of when and how such a minority rebellion could strengthen the cooperative movement, and how, in the process, it could acquire enough legitimacy to survive without being captured or 'coopted', becomes important. In such cases as Mexico the movement must also sustain sufficient counter-force to allow it to mature.

Rebellious ideology can even become an effective substitute for, or complement to, traditional solidarity in maintaining commitments to communal goals where peasants can be mobilized in opposition to a system of domination and exploitation. This has been achieved in a number of agrarian reforms in Latin America. Cohen (1966) thinks that it may well be that the peasants 'need the disruptive effects of opposition to the State and/or internal struggles for power in order to dissolve the traditional system so that modern contractual relations can be accepted'. If coexistence of rebellious groups with established regimes is not possible, bridges to more or less legitimate power structures are needed. The left wing of the Church in Latin America is now attempting to fulfil this role of 'legitimizer' for otherwise subversive peasant groups. In a number of countries cooperatives and peasant associations have been established under Catholic and other Christian Church sponsorship and certain Church groups have fulfilled the important role of protectors for these new associations. The same role in some cases has been fulfilled by certain political parties, such as APRA in Peru and COPEI in Venezuela, through their *sindicato* and cooperative adherents during their period as opposition parties.

As long as outside threats can further unite peasants and some mechanism for building up and extending allegiances exists, such conflict situations may not necessarily be detrimental to the cooperative movement, which, as we have indicated, may benefit from a certain amount of stress or conflict to achieve the right cohesive motivation. The key question is: what congruence may be achieved between the interests of the nascent power structure of the peasants and those of other established power hierarchies? In this respect the relationship between the cooperative movement and the peasant associations becomes crucial.

Peasant associations that are essentially political pressure groups without an economic base can be effectively supplemented by strongly anchored cooperatives which do have economic functions but lack upward linkages. This complementarity has not been generally recognized by policy-markers. In such countries as Bolivia and Venezuela, where strong peasant associations have emerged through agrarian reforms, little has been done to take advantage of this opportunity to strengthen simultaneously and cumulatively the political and economic position of peasants. Nationally strong and independent peasant movements seem to be required for the effective support of locally rooted cooperatives. The ability of cooperatives to provide their members with income, economic independence and market power is clearly one of the essential underpinnings of an effective peasant union movement.

However, in the absence of a strong ideological commitment which transcends partisan politics this suggested symbiosis between cooperatives and peasant associations entails considerable dangers. If the essential external support depends mainly on established party loyalty a shift of power to other parties may result in the withdrawal of such support. Happily, this does not seem to be the case in the recent shift of the Venezuelan government from AD to COPEI control; the associations have for some time been accepted as a part of the national land reform goal. The degree of independent economic power that peasant cooperatives can acquire in Venezuela remains to be seen; previous attempts by the Federación Campesina to enter the fields of marketing and machinery supply for its members on a massive scale have not yet been very successful.

The foregoing suggests these general conclusions: sporadic successes notwithstanding, large-scale peasant cooperative movements will have to await the emergence of strong, ideologically committed peasant unions, usually in the aftermath of agrarian reforms. Through such a link-up to national power sources cooperatives can obtain essential external support. The economic base of cooperatives can, in turn, offer peasant associations independence and continued viability. However, there is danger that unless the ideological commitment is deep, political and economic support may be withdrawn from peasant cooperatives before they can overcome the many internal obstacles they face and before they are able to consolidate their position.

(b) *Structural problems and upward linkages* We will now review briefly a number of important external constraints on successful peasant cooperation. Consideration of land tenure and *municipio* power structure will be followed by references to regional markets and finally to employment and technology issues. All of these have been touched upon earlier in this paper.

It was seen that cooperatives have a very special and perhaps crucial role in the follow-up and consolidation phase of agrarian reforms, as the recent programmes in Chile and Venezuela demonstrate. However, the persistence of inequitable and onerous land tenure arrangements is one of the chief obstacles to the successful development of cooperatives. On a very elementary level this may involve giving security of tenure to squatters, tenant-workers and other types of small cultivators whose ownership arrangements are uncertain and precarious. But in areas of domination by large traditional estates more fundamental transformations are necessary in terms of land distribution and improving the status of the peasants who are tied to or dependent on the estates. Agrarian systems characterized by domination and subservience relationships, widely different income levels and differences of status do not provide the egalitarian prerequisites for effective cooperation. Whenever cooperatives manage to establish themselves in areas of severe inequalities in regard to tenure—as shown by the studies of García and his co-workers in Chile—neither those associations in which the lower strata peasants are exclusive members, nor cooperatives which include both large and small farmers, are likely to function in a satisfactory manner.

This problem is most serious where tenure-related social stratification within a community is very rigid. If landlords and other upper-status individuals are admitted to cooperatives, the cohesion of the group suffers and the whole impulse of the organization may be impaired. If membership is denied to landlords and richer farmers, more cohesion may be achieved, but often at the cost of efficiency and market access.

At any rate, it seems clear that where the tenure system is grossly inequitable cooperatives, even if they manage to get established and survive, are not expected to become a force for structural reform. In such a situation the best that can be expected is successful adaptation to the existing social system and some protection of its members from the more onerous forms of exploitation. Membership, in such cases, seldom includes landless workers or tenant-labourers.

One of the related obstacles, closely linked with the absence of strong orientation towards reform, is the legislative system itself. In many Latin American countries cooperative legislation is non-existent or inadequate, but even where it has been designed with some care it may impede rather than facilitate peasant coopera-tion. A case is cited from Peru in which the rigid legal prerequi-sites of minimum paid-in capital prevented a peasant group from forming an association. Members of the group, on the other hand, wanted legal recognition as a *prior* guarantee for their capital contributions.

Legal provisions frequently favour the 'pseudo-cooperatives' of larger commercial farmers, who may derive tax rebates and other financial benefits from forming associations which are modelled on strictly commercial or corporate structures (the Frutillar dairy group in southern Chile is an example). Legislation which facili-tates the formation of pre-cooperatives or transitional informal arrangements is generally lacking. The creation of multi-purpose societies is often impeded or made more difficult by legal restric-tions.

Perhaps it should be added that while the resolution of the land tenure problems is certainly a necessary precondition for coopera-tive success, the existence of land reform may not be a guarantee that cooperation will flower, as the Bolivian experience demon-strates.

Cooperation in independent peasant communities which are based on small family holdings and are not tied to large estates faces a different kind of outside constraint. Such communities are exploited not only by local middlemen but also by the power structure of the towns and villages on which they are economi-cally and socially dependent. Pearse, Wolfe, Stavenhagen and others stress the increasing domination of the municipality and the local market centre over the smallholders and the inhibiting effect of these new decision-making foci on the organization of peasant groups. Even new, official programmes designed to bring credit, extension and other benefits to the peasants are often intercepted by the local municipal power structure, that is, those 'who live by the agriculturist rather than by agriculture' (Pearse, 1966). The political domination of the local centre (*cabecera*) and the consequences of lack of participatory local government have been vividly described by Wolfe (1965). In a typical rural munici-pality political power is exercised by one or several cliques which derive their influence from a combination of land-holding, trade and clientele relationships with persons holding office at the departmental or national level. The administrative apparatus is upward and outward-oriented and has little responsibility towards the surrounding agrarian community and few roots in it. A comprehensive regional study in the south of Peru describes the situation in the following terms:

> In the middle and upper classes, attitudes of dependency are manifested in an almost total expectation that local administrative affairs will be resolved by the Government and its functionaries, combined with a lack of confidence in the capacity of these functionaries and a lack of interest and initiative in solving collective local problems. . . . One consequence is formalism or ritualism in public activity, which respects legal forms while believing that to reach individual ends what is needed is *vara* (influence), or patrons in a strategic part of the relevant hierarchy. [While cooperation is formally given a high value by these classes, this overt attitude is contradicted by] attitudes of conformism and fatalism accompanied by passivity in action and scepticism as to the possibility of reaching social and economic ends through cooperation. A kind of self-fulfilling prophecy leads to the failure of attempts at local organization. [*Plan regional para et desarrollo del sur del Perú*, vol. xxii, as quoted by Wolfe, 1965.]

Should some cooperatives become established locally, their consolidation and expansion are often strictly limited by the absence of upward channels of communication and linkage with the broader economic system. There are very few effective regional cooperative associations which might provide these channels. Exceptions are the Brazilian and Colombian regional coffee coops and the national marketing boards assisting Carmenpampa in Bolivia. The lack of these 'second-level' structures is regarded as a very serious obstacle to the expansion of the cooperative movement in Chile (García, 1968a), in Mexico (Durán, 1967) and in Colombia (Vélez and Feder, 1961). In Mexico part of the official resistance to encouraging the emerging cooperatives in the Laguna may be explained by the fear that second-level federations may turn into powerful political organizations.

Upward economic linkage is also essential to wholesale outlets or processing plants. Without effective two-way arrangements with such central facilities, local market cooperation has very strict limits. Once such working arrangements between local group and marketing or processing centres have been established, the key to continuous, effective and democratic functioning of the cooperative system is the degree of shared control over central facilities and politics. The detrimental effects of excessive dependence on the decision-making apparatus at higher levels are clearly demonstrated in the case of the Mexican sugar *ejidos*, the Chilean grape growers and the Peruvian Highland potato farmers. In this connection, the advantages—mentioned earlier—of pluralistic regional and national associations, instead of single, politically controlled confederations, becomes clear.

There may also be some minimum effective size of the cooperative system, especially with respect to the area of influence of regional associations and their market power. This issue of minimum size is also related to strategies for regional development in general, in which complementary employment opportunities and effectively decentralized technical services form a coordinated matrix for local groups (Wolfe, 1965). At stages of greater maturity a minimum amount of independent control over these broader economic bases also seems necessary as a defence against subversive influences, as shown by the history of the collective *ejidos* in Mexico.

Finally there is the employment dilemma. In many Latin American areas the increasing pressure of rural population is a serious obstacle to cooperative development. Yet unless the economy is dynamic enough to provide more jobs outside farming it will become increasingly difficult to find the necessary compromise between egalitarianism and economic efficiency. As the cooperative develops there is bound to be an increasing economic and social distance between members and non-members unless the above-mentioned complementary job opportunities can be provided by multi-sectoral cooperative units or by decentralized regional development. Even while farmers' associations may achieve certain egalitarian goals among their members, as technology improves they may simply accentuate the contrast between members and outsiders. Obviously, the problem of the gradual exodus of marginal producers is much smaller in a service cooperative than in a production enterprise. But the affluence of large numbers of landless workers and squatters has already complicated the organization of cooperatives in Mexico, Chile and Central America; in some cases, as in the Laguna region of Mexico, it may have contributed to the disintegration of promising collectives.

5. *Leadership and paternalism*

The concluding section deals with the interplay between internal and external factors in cooperative organization. Special attention will be devoted to the delicate position of the promoters, technicians and leaders.

It was seen that the role of 'outside' groups, institutions and individuals is crucial for motivating and energizing peasant communities towards organized economic cooperation. Such initial managerial and technical assistance provides the first link of the nascent cooperatives with outside forces. While in some cases this function has been accomplished by foreign promoters or by specialized non-governmental institutions, most of the responsibility for promotion and assistance falls on national governments. However, until very recently governments have not been set up to provide service for peasants. Their staffs have been urban-oriented and generally ill-prepared to play an effective role in rural cooperative organization and assistance. When governments have become involved with cooperatives or cooperation-type institutions a paternalistic type of relationship has frequently emerged in which dependence, control and continued reliance on outside resources overshadow and frequently prevent local initiative, self-management and effective organization. Non-official agencies are often no better in this respect.

The dilemma, therefore, is how to achieve a working compromise between the essential role of the outside agencies as stimulators and assistants of the cooperative movement—especially in its initial stages—and the local initiative and democratic control which is so essential for the success of the movement.

To a great extent the prevalence of paternalistic attitudes, even in post-reform situations, as in Mexico and Bolivia, can be explained through the tenacity of the very system of social relationships which the cooperative is supposed to modify. In such a system personal relations and guarantees, rather than legal and contractual relationships, predominate. The *'patrón* syndrome', in which the 'boss' is relied upon for protection and special favours in exchange for loyalties and services, is too easily transferred to the government–peasant relationship. The education and previous experience of technicians and other functionaries reinforce their prejudices towards peasants in such hold-over *patrón*–client relationships.[10]

[10] One of the strongest criticisms of this persistent symbiotic relationship in the context of community development is found in a recent article by Erasmus (1968). He calls it the *'encogido* syndrome', based on the attitude of insecurity and withdrawal of the disadvantaged peasants, who easily establish new dependency relationships with community development personnel.

Another dimension of the same problem is implicit in Hirschman's dual model of the 'image of economic change', which is particularly applicable in Latin America. In the 'group-focused' image of progress, individuals think of economic change as something that must affect all members of the group equally, with everyone remaining at his previously assigned place. This is contrasted with the 'ego-focused' image of change, in which the individual conceives progress only in terms of improving his own lot while dismissing such a possibility for society as a whole. The relevance of this analysis to the *patrón* syndrome is clear. Latin American peasant societies are often characterized by this duality; for example, the submissive resignation characteristic of the Andean Indian way of life is contrasted with the active concern with self-promotion and manipulation of the *ladino* and *mestizo* elements. The latter are strongly competitive individuals who show domineering attitudes toward persons of lower status. Hirschman sees in the ego-focused conception of progress one of the important limitations of the cooperative component of entrepreneurship—the act of agreement-reaching and cooperation-enlisting—until the image of change has shifted to one which takes cognizance of the possibility of mutual benefits (Hirschman, 1958).

At this point something should also be said about corruption. Economic corruption is an extremely widespread and debilitating phenomenon in Latin American rural organizations. Clearly, cooperatives, even the most rudimentary kind, cannot survive without a substantial degree of honesty in their leadership. Where corruption is endemic even large-scale agrarian reforms can do little more than 'democratize graft', i.e. open up the possibility of peasant participation in bribery and misuse of resources, previously enjoyed by the privileged groups (Senior, 1958). Most probably, the stronger the ideological commitment of an organization and its leaders the less is the likelihood of economic corruption. This would signify a lower degree of corruption in more radical movements (Eckstein, 1966; Landsberger and Hewitt, 1968). But apart from such commitment, the most effective remedy appears to be the creation of an independent economic base. This would ensure that the local officials, as well as the regional and national representatives, are paid by the membership and are accountable to it rather than dependent on the outside hierarchy.

Under these conditions it is extremely difficult to create systems

with a more sensitive and reciprocally trustful relationship between administrators and groups of peasants. The problem is
particularly acute in the so-called 'forced-decision cooperative'
(Dobyns, 1968); by its very nature, this kind of cooperative
requires a certain degree of coerciveness or strong initial control
without which it could not function. Irrigation associations, in
which competent joint water management is crucial, and many
agrarian reform projects involving the reorganization of complex
commercial units, are examples of such 'forced-decision' situations. Credit societies also seem to require strong outside intervention and control, even in more highly developed countries.

But even in the case of service cooperatives outside financial
and managerial assistance is crucial. Excessive reliance on local
resources in the early stages may simply deliver control of the
cooperative to already existing dominant groups of large producers or merchants.

The circularity in this situation may be seen in the following
sequence: (a) the absolute necessity for initial outside competence
and material assistance, (b) the lack of initial responsibility and
knowledge by client groups, (c) the subsequent need for the
authorities to keep control of their investment and political
commitment and to reduce risk of failure, and (d) the scarce
opportunities for peasants to learn managerial skills and assume
responsibilities, and their continued expectation that someone
else will take care of matters, etc. etc.

The key issue, then, is how to 'let go' gradually, while training,
encouraging and stimulating effective internal leadership. The
Vicos experience is one illustration in which power was intelligently shared in the course of gradual withdrawal or devolution.
At any rate, systems are required in which responsive local participation in the decision process and 'positively individualistic'
leadership is rewarded.

CORA is tackling the same problem in the Chilian *asentamientos*, which, as we have seen, must be independent at the end
of the transitional three-to-five-year period. CORA is discovering
that (a) the reform agency cannot properly control each settlement,
(b) agency technicians unfamiliar with local conditions can make
big mistakes, (c) the peasants must simply be allowed to learn by
being allowed to make their own mistakes, and (d) the short-run
gains in marketable surplus extracted through tight government
direction might be followed by long-run problems unless the

reform beneficiaries are rapidly given opportunities to learn (Thiesenhusen, 1968).

In Venezuela CIARA is trying an imaginative approach of multi-faceted assistance combined with simultaneous partici-patory education. It is interesting to note that CIARA consciously places responsibilities on its clients for planning and programme operation *which exceed their present capacities.* Tolerance and even encouragement of such situations of deliberate imbalance may well prove to be an effective way to deal with this dilemma.

References

Alers-Montalvo, Manuel (1960), 'Social systems analysis of supervised credit in an Andean community', *Rural Sociology*, vol. xxv, No. 1 (March), pp. 51–64.

Avram, Percy (1965), *A report on the development of a pilot project in directed agricultural production credit through the 'Santa Teresita Ltda' Credit Union at Julio Andrade, Carchi, Ecuador*. AID/Ecua-dor/CUNA csd—236, Quito, Ecuador (September).

Barnes, Katherine (1967), *Results of the agrarian reform in the Bolivian Yungas, LTC/CIDA*, Study of the Bolivian Agrarian Reform, La Paz (October) (mimeographed draft report).

Belshaw, Michael (1967), *A village economy—land and people of Huecorico*, Columbia University Press, New York and London.

Bergmann, Theodor (1968), 'Factors influencing optimum size and decision making in cooperative farms', paper prepared for second World Congress of Rural Sociology, Enschede, 1968.

Bjornberg, Arne (1959), *Las poblaciones indígenas y el cooperati-vismo: observaciones y experiencias del desarrollo del programa andino en Bolivia*, Instituto de Estudios Ibero-Americanos de la Escuela de Ciencias Económicas, Stockholm.

Chaves, Fernando (1962), *The agricultural cooperative movement in Latin America*, Pan American Union, Washington, D.C.

[Chonchol, Jacques] (1957), *Los distritos de riego del noroeste—tenen-cia y aprovechamiento de la tierra*, Centro de Investigaciones Agrarias [publicado por] Instituto Mexicano de Investigaciones Económicas, Mexico City.

Cohen, Percy S. (1966), 'Traditional societies and modern cooperatives', paper prepared for the Sixth World Congress of Sociology, Evian, 1966 (mimeograph).

Dobyns, Henry F. (1965), 'The strategic importance of enlightenment and skill for power', *The American Behavioral Scientist*, vol. viii, No. 7 (March), pp. 23–27.

— (1967), 'Sociological and anthropological approaches to engineering successful economic organizations', paper presented at the Agricul-tural Development Council seminar at the University of Kentucky, April 1967 (manuscript).

Doughty, Paul L. (1968), *Huaylas: an Andean district in search of progress*, Cornell University Press, Ithaca, N.Y.

Duran, Marco Antonio (1965), 'El estancamiento en la organización interna de los ejidos'. *El Trimestre Económico*, vol. xxxii (3), No. 127 (julio–septiembre), Mexico D.F., pp. 455–67.

— (1967), *El agrarismo mexicano*, Siglo Veintiuno Editores, Mexico D.F.

Eckstein, Shlomo (1965), *Notas sobre una gira por la zona del Choapa*. Santiago (julio) (mimeographed report).

— (1966), *El ejido colectivo en México*, Fondo de Cultura Económica, Mexico D.F.

— (1968), 'La comarca lagunera', draft report prepared for the Centro de Investigaciones Agrarias de México (manuscript).

Edel, Matthew D. (1968), 'An economic evaluation of the Colombian community action program', Ph.D. dissertation presented to Yale University.

Erasmus, Charles (1961), *Man takes control*, University of Minnesota Press.

— (1964), 'Agrarian reform: a comparative study of Venezuela, Bolivia and Mexico' in Dwight B. Heath, Charles J. Erasmus and Hans Buechler, 'Land reform and social revolution in Bolivia' (unpublished manuscript), University of Wisconsin, Madison, Wisc.

— (1965), 'The occurrence and disappearance of reciprocal farm labor in Latin America' in *Contemporary cultures and societies of Latin America*, ed. Dwight B. Heath and Richard N. Adams, Random House, New York, pp. 173–99.

— (1967), 'Culture change in northwest Mexico', *Contemporary change in traditional societies*, vol. iii: *Mexican and Peruvian communities*, ed. Julian H. Steward, University of Illinois Press, pp. 1–131.

— (1968), 'Community development and the *encogido* syndrome'. *Human Organization*, vol. 27, No. 1 (spring), pp. 65–74.

Fals-Borda, Orlando (1961), 'Acción Comunal en una vereda colombiana', *Monografías Sociológicas* No. 4, Universidad Nacional, Bogotá.

Feder, Ernest (1966), 'Societal opposition to peasant movements and its effects on farm people in Latin America', paper prepared for seminar on 'Latin American peasant movements', December 1966, Cornell University (Mimeograph).

Foster, George M. (1960–61), 'Interpersonal relations in peasant society', *Human Organization*, vol. xx, No. 4, pp. 174–78.

— (1965), 'Peasant society and the image of limited good', *American Anthropologist*, vol. 67, pp. 293–315.

— 1967), *Tzintzuntzan—Mexican peasants in a changing world*, Little, Brown, Boston, Mass.

Foytick, Jerry, and J. Edwin Faris (1967), 'Agricultural cooperatives in Latin America: the Chilean case', paper presented at Agricultural Development seminar held at the University of Kentucky, April 1967 (mimeograph).

García, Antonio (1968a), *Cooperativas y financiamiento agrícola en Aconcaqua*, ICIRA, Departamento de Cooperativas y Crédito, Santiago (March) (mimeograph).

— (1968b), *Las cooperativas pesqueras del valle de Elqui*, ICIRA, Departamento de Cooperativas y Crédito, Santiago (mimeograph).

García, Antonio, Enrique Astorga, Pedro Hidalgo R. and Enrique Contreras S. (1966), *Cooperativas y financiamiento agrícola en un area lechera y forestal de Llanquihue*, ICIRA, Departamento de Cooperativas y Comercialización, Santiago (September) (mimeograph).

Harris, Marvin (1964), *Patterns of race in the Americas*. Walker, New York.

Henley, Llewellyn (1969), 'Alpaca—a *campesino* organization in the Peruvian Sierra', research paper prepared in seminar on 'Land policy problems in Latin America', George Washington University, Washington, D.C. (manuscript).

Hirschman, Albert O. (1958), *The strategy of economic development*, Yale University Press, New Haven, Conn.

— (1963), *Journeys toward progress*. The Twentieth Century Fund, New York.

Holmberg, Allan R. (1960), 'Changing community attitudes and values in Peru: a case study in guided change' in *Social change in Latin America today*, Harper, New York, for Council of Foreign Relations.

Holmberg, Allan R. (1965), 'The changing values and institutions of Vicos in the context of national development', *The American Behavioral Scientist*, vol. viii, No. 7 (March), pp. 3–27.

Holmberg, Allan R. and Henry F. Dobyn (1962), 'The process of accelerating community change', *Human Organization*, vol. 21 (2), pp. 107–24.

Huizer, Gerrit (1968), 'The role of peasant organizations in the process of agrarian reform in Mexico', Comité Interamericano de Desarrollo Agrícola. (March) (unpublished mimeographed draft).

International Development Foundation (1968), *Cuyuta Association sesame seed commercialization program*, IDS special report No. 6 (Guatemala) (processed).

International Labour Office (ILO/OIT) (1961), *Informe al Director General sobre las posibilidades de organización cooperativa entre las comunidades indígenas*, Geneva (manuscript).

Kirschbaum, Alfred, J. A. Navarro Ochoa and Oscar Ali Pino (1967), *El cooperativismo en el sector rural—análisis en el estado Aragua*, Oficina Central de Coordinación de la Presidencia de la República, Caracas (mimeograph).

Lancelin, Marcel (1966), 'Los movimientos cooperativos en América del sul', *Comunidades*, No. 2 (May–August); publication of the Instituto de Estudios Sindicales, Sociales y Cooperativos, Madrid.

Landsberger, Henry A. and Cynthia N. Hewitt (1967), *Preliminary report on a case study of Mexican peasant associations*, Cornell University, Ithaca, N.Y.

— (1968), 'Ten sources of weakness and cleavage in Latin American peasant movements', paper prepared for the second World Congress of Rural Sociology, Enschede, Holland, August 1968 (mimeograph).

Leonard, Olen E. (1966), *El cambio económico y social en cuatro comunidades del altiplano de Bolivia*, Instituto Indigenista Interamericano, Mexico D.F.

Lewis, Oscar (1951), *Life in a Mexican village: Tepoztlan revisited*. University of Illinois Press, Urbana, Ill.

Lodge, George C. and Stephen F. Gudeman (1967), *The Veraguas report: a study of the organization of change in rural Latin America*, Harvard University Graduate School of Business Administration, Division of International Activities, Boston, Mass. (June) (ICH-ii G103).

Mangin, William A. (1966), 'Classification of highland communities in Latin America', paper presented at the conference on 'The development of highland communities in Latin America', Cornell University, Ithaca, N.Y. (March) (processed).

Mathiason, John R. and Eric B. Shearer (1967), *Caicara de Maturin* (case study of an agrarian reform settlement in Venezuela), CIDA Research Papers on Land Tenure and Agrarian Reform, Research Paper No. 1, Washington D.C. (November).

Mattson, Frederick S. (1968), *The Banco Agrícola–IDB cooperative in the CBF–IDB project of colonization in the Alto Beni, 1964–6*, Washington, D.C. (July) (manuscript).

[Maturana, Sergio] (1968), *Paracho–estado de Michoacán, México, las comunidades agrarias y el desarrollo*, Comité Interamericano de Desarrollo Agrícola (CIDA), Trabajos de Investigación Sobre Tenencia de la Tierra y Reforma Agraria, Trabajo No. 4, Washington, D.C.

Métraux, Alfred (1959), 'The social and economic structure of the Indian communities of the Andean Region', *International Labour Review*, vol. 89, No. 3 (March), pp. 225–43.

Nordby, Michael (1966), *Socio-economic study of the following cooperatives . . .* (report on seven cooperatives prepared for the Peace Corps) Lima (mimeograph).

Padgett, L. Vincent (1966), *The Mexican political system*, Houghton Mifflin, Boston, Mass.

Patch, Richard W. (1965), *Social aspects of the CBF–BID colonization program in Bolivia*, report prepared for the Inter-American Development Bank (July) (manuscript).

Paulson, Belden (1964), "Difficulties and prospects for community development in north-east Brazil', *Inter-American Economic Affairs*,
vol. 17, No. 4, spring, pp. 37–58. (Land Tenure Center, Reprint
Series No. 4, University of Wisconsin, Madison, 1964.)

Pearse, Andrew (1966), 'Agrarian change trends in Latin America',
Latin American Research Review, vol. 1, No. 3, pp. 45–69.

Peace Corps–CLUSA (1966), *Once upon a cooperative: studies of
seventeen cooperatives in Colombia*, The Cooperative League of
the USA (CLUSA), Chicago, Ill (February) (mimeograph).

Pinho, Diva Bevevides (1966), 'O cooperativismo na cafeicultura
brasileira', *Communidades*, Madrid, I, January–April, No. 1, pp.
141–67.

Plunkett Foundation for Cooperative Studies (ed.) (1963), 'Problems
of Latin American cooperative development', *Yearbook of agricultural cooperation, 1963*, Blackwell, Oxford.

Ritter, Ulrich Peter (1966), *Dorfgemeinschaften und Genossenschaften
in Peru*, Göttinger Wirtschafts-und socialwissenschaftliche Studien,
Band 4, Verlag Otto Schwartz, Göttingen, 1966 (published in
Spanish as *Comunidades indígenas y cooperativismo en el Perú*,
Ediciones Deusto, Bilbao.

Ruiz, Rodrigo and Antonio Vega (1964), 'Cooperativa de producción
agrícola industrial Victoria R.L. de Costa Rica', *Las cooperativas
como método de desarrollo de regiones y comunidades*, Unión Panamericana, Estudios y Monografías xıv, Washington, D.C.

Saito, Hiroshi (1964), 'Cooperativa agrícola de Cotia do Brazil', *Las
cooperativas como método de desarrollo de regiones y comunidades*,
Unión Panamericana, Estudios y Monografías xıv, Washington,
D.C.

Schiller, Otto (1966a), 'Gemeinschaftsformen im landwirtschaftlichen
Produktionsbereich', *Zeitschrift für Ausländische Landwirtschaft*,
Sonderheft 5, DLG-Verlag, Frankfurt am Main.

— (1966b), 'Kollektive Landbewirtschaftung in Mexiko', *Zeitschrift für
Ausländische Landwirtschaft*, vol. 2, No. 2.

Schwartz, Lola Romanucchi (1962), 'Morality, conflict and violence in
a Mexican mestizo village', Ph.D. dissertation, Indiana University.

Scott, J. T. and Lehman B. Fletcher (1967), 'Potential and feasibility
of cooperatives as instruments of market reform in underdeveloped
areas—the economist's view', paper presented at Agricultural Development seminar at the University of Kentucky, Lexington, Ky.,
April 1967 (manuscript).

Senior, Clarence (1958), *Land reform and democracy*, University of
Florida Press, Gainesville, Fla.

Smith, William C. (1961), 'Hens that laid golden eggs', *International
Development Review*, vol. 3, No. 3, pp. 2–5.

Texier, J. M. (1967), *Etude sur les formes non-conventionelles de coopération*. Geneva (February) (manuscript).

Thiesenhusen, William C. (1968), 'Cooperative tenure system plays role in Chilean agrarian reform', paper prepared for *International Cooperative Training Journal* (August) (manuscript).

Thiesenhusen, William C., Ricardo Alezones, Ramon Pugh and John Mathiason (1968), *Leonardo Ruiz Pineda (case study of a Venezuelan agrarian reform settlement)*, CIDA Research Papers on Land Tenure and Agrarian Reform, Research Paper No. 7, Washington, D.C.

Vasquez, Mario C. and Henry F. Dobyns (1964), *The transformation of manors into producers' cooperatives*, Comparative Studies of Cultural Change, Department of Anthropology, Cornell University, Ithaca, N.Y. (January) (mimeograph).

Velez, Ernesto and Ernest Feder (1961), *The lagging growth of the cooperative movement in Colombia: a preliminary survey of its development and obstacles*, Ministerio de Agricultura, Servicio Técnico Agrícola Colombiano Americano, Bogotá (August) (mimeograph).

Vellard, J. (1963), *Civilisation des Andes*, NRF, Paris, France.

Wolf, Eric (1965), 'Aspects of group relations in a complex society: Mexico' in *Contemporary cultures and societies of Latin America*, ed. Dwight B. Heath and Richard N. Adams, Random House, New York [reprinted from *American Anthropologist*, 1956, vol. 58, pp. 1065–78].

— (1966) *Peasants*, 'Foundations of Modern Anthropology' series, Prentice-Hall, Englewood Cliffs, N.J.

Wolfe, Marshall (1965), 'Rural settlement patterns and social change in Latin America', *Latin American Research Review*, vol. i, No. 2, pp. 5–64.

Part II

Boguslaw Galeski Types of collective farm in Poland

Poland's collective farms are generally classified according to the statutes they follow. Until 1954 there were three model statutes from which farmers forming cooperatives could choose. Type I maintained individual control of the means of production: while some operations were carried out in common and over the entire area (e.g. ploughing), others (e.g. cultivation) were carried out by individual families on their own land. The product was also disposed of individually by each family, after settling for the work contributed by the cooperative. In Type II the entire farm (except the individual garden plots) was cultivated in common; income was distributed in proportion to work done and contributions of land and capital. Type III differed from the preceding in that income was distributed only according to the input of labour. Another statute was added after 1954, the so-called I*b*. It provided for common grain production and for fixed income according to the amount of land, capital and labour contributed, while animal husbandry was to be carried on by each family individually.

This classification is thus based on the criterion of differences in the statutory regulations which determine the cooperative's socio-economic organization. Independently of that division, collective farms are also classified, for the purposes of economic analysis, by size, volume and composition of output and of machinery, equipment, livestock, productivity per head, etc.

Statutory Types I and II are virtually non-existent today, while agricultural cooperatives are of little interest because they are only marginally important in contemporary Polish agriculture (in 1967 there were 1,170 production cooperatives with 32,000 members, producing 1·1 per cent of gross agricultural output on the same percentage of the total arable land, and these indices remain virtually the same today).

Without questioning the utility of the above classification, its inadequacy for sociological analysis is obvious. It takes no account, for example, of the motives for establishing collective farms, or the social origin of the founding members. For these factors essentially determine the functioning of the farms and their members' problems. They are all the more important when the members cannot freely control the economic and organizational principles guiding these economic institutions, but have to accept those ordered by the management or the authorities. Conflicts between values recognized by the members, on the one hand —i.e. their views of what is right and what is not—and the statutes imposed upon them, on the other, may be so sharp as to lead to decline or social disorganization. More frequently, however, there is some adaptation of the collective farm's economic and organizational principles to the aspirations of the members and to their cultural standards. The result is the emergence of a quite stable institution which does not actually correspond to the statutes formally adopted by the members.

Among the motives for founding collective farms the following are most typical: (1) ideological; (2) economic, i.e. expectations of greater or more easily acquired income than on individual farms; (3) awareness of the special difficulties of running an individual farm under contemporary conditions; (4) administrative or economic pressure on the part of the authorities to overcome aversion to collective farming and disbelief in its effectiveness.

Each of these motivations may occur with different degrees of intensity, and may be linked to one another. But there are no sharp divisions between them, and borderline cases lend themselves to conventional solutions. Thus ideological motives include religious or political ones, adherence to egalitarian ideas, or beliefs in racial, class or national mission or destiny, etc. Such motives always entail the members of the group distinguishing themselves from others. It may be difficult to include desires for economic success or economic rationality among such motives, although these too are a kind of ideology.

Reference to the particular difficulties of organizing and operating an individual farm includes the situation where the members of a cooperative would gladly do so but lack the necessary prerequisites: machinery, equipment or know-how. (The former cowbarn attendant or the coachman on the manorial estate who acquires land from agrarian reform may, for example, consider it beyond his capacity to run a farm.) In this group of motivations we may also include situations where farming requires improvement of the soil, e.g. via irrigation, which exceed the resources of individual farm families. But difficulties created by government agrarian policy (prices, taxes, etc.) are of another, non-technical order. If, for example, the State enforces compulsory deliveries or levies such high taxes as to threaten individual farmers with bankruptcy, while it places collective farms in a privileged position, then the motivation for forming cooperatives must be not in the third but in the fourth of the above groups.

With regard to the classification of the social origins of collective farmers, at least four groups should be noted: (1) non-farmers, (2) former agricultural labourers, (3) peasant owners of subsistence farms, (4) operators of market-oriented farms or, more generally, farms with 'entrepreneurial' characteristics. Even this classification is not exact, for there are a number of intermediate groups, between peasants and farmers in particular. Furthermore, besides collective farms with a homogeneous class character there are also those which include some of or all the above groups. Cooperatives with a heterogeneous social structure present a number of interesting theoretical and practical problems. But farms with a homogeneous structure are more common, and reflect class differences in the groups to which their members belonged.

Cross-classifying the two divisions—i.e. motivation and social composition—would theoretically require sixteen types of collective farm. Although they are all theoretically possible, in practice the majority are exceedingly rare. It is thus unlikely that 'commercial' farmers would form a collective on ideological grounds. Geared to the maximization of profit and full exploitation of market opportunities, this type would consider it absurd to subordinate economic considerations to religious, national or egalitarian ones. Nor is collective farming imposed upon such groups simply by technical considerations, since they are *ex definitione* market-oriented independent farmers operating functioning farms. Apart from strong external pressures, their only real motive for opting for collective farming would be economic benefit or considerations of economic rationality—particularly if they were to occupy posts in the collective enterprise.

The literature, as well as observation in various countries, provides a basis for distinguishing four most frequent types of cooperative bond. The first is the collective farm established primarily with ideological objectives. This type is most often founded by non-farmers and sometimes by agricultural labourers. Even if there are individuals or groups of rural origin among the founders, they are usually of minor importance. Such collectives most frequently occur in the form of unions of advocates of social justice, or of religious groups or persons dedicated to some historic mission in protest against the worldly lust for money, the alienation of the individual or the decline of morality. Such agricultural communes are rare in the modern world, of course. Examples are the communes of agricultural labourers in the Soviet Union immediately after the revolution, the socialist communes before world war I, the *kibbutzim* (at least, a considerable number of them), the 'utopian' communities formed by religious sects in the USA, and so forth.

This type of collective farm is, on the whole, characterized by a high degree of group cohesion and by a reasonable economic income from dedicated labour, which is regarded as of high value and is stimulated by non-economic incentives. As a social group it is marked by great exclusiveness and many-sidedness, like a family, since it takes over almost all the functions of the family except the biological. A serious weakness of this type of collective is its need for moral rigour over a long period, which calls for the unremitting stimulus of ideological incentives. This, however, either forces the group into cultural isolation or leads to constant conflict with its neighbouring communities. Moreover, many of the ideas which inspire the founding of such cooperatives (notions of equality, for instance) are exceptionally difficult to maintain consistently without even minor and unavoidable deviations leading to a state of constant conflict in the life of the group which sooner or later becomes an insoluble problem. It is equally difficult to bring up disciples who fully share the founders' ideas, particularly since economic development (and, with it, the desire for specialization and hierarchical leadership), as well as ideas penetrating from the outside world, exert a disintegrating influence on the group's ideological foundations. Nevertheless, collective economies based on ideological motives have displayed the greatest perseverance, despite these weaknesses.

The second most frequent type is the collective farm founded by agricultural labourers, rural day labourers or peasant owners of dwarf farms, on land they have acquired but which they are unable to run individually. This pertains primarily to settlers on reclaimed or irrigated land, to territories newly brought under cultivation, to abandoned or unpopulated lands, etc. Most typical of this category are former labourers on landed estates who are allotted land by agrarian reforms but not the means of production or capital; nor do they possess the experience and know-how needed in farming. Accustomed to the division of labour and convinced that they could work as well without the land-owner, but unable to change their manner of working, they gladly respond to the idea of farming in common. They also accept outside direction (government agencies, banks, etc.), since they lack adequate knowledge to operate a large farm. The organizational and economic principles of this type of collective farm are often the same as those of the former estate, since that pattern is best known to the members. Hence the farm retains the character of a large agricultural enterprise (usually a backward one in the case of countries or regions faced with the need for agrarian reform). Modernization here depends on the employment of expert managers from outside. The members prefer a system of permanent cash advances in the division of income, as this is closest to the wage system. There are also clear tendencies towards the equalization of pay regardless of the type of work. These issues, moreover, are the most frequent causes of internal conflict. The most enterprising individuals, those most capable of managing a family farm, after a preliminary period of some economic recovery usually leave the collective to start individual farming, unless they occupy some leading post. The cooperators see no future for their children on the collective farm and try to assure them of other occupations. While farms of this type are able to maintain themselves as large farms, with modernization they tend to lose their cooperative features and come to resemble State farms in socialist countries.

The third type of collective farm is the producers' cooperative established by peasants who formerly operated traditional family farms. They often do so under pressure from the government, which seeks to ensure the structural uniformity of the national economy, to extend economic planning to agriculture, and eventually to draw from agriculture resources which are mainly invested in the industrialization programme. An essential element of this type is the individual garden plot which retains the character of a small family farm. It usually plays an important economic role, since it is exploited intensively and is geared to vegetable or animal production, while the collective farm has an auxiliary role. Since income is mainly distributed in kind, the produce obtained by the family is processed on the individual plot and then sold. Often the organization of work takes the form of family teams, with the result that the former village structure finds expression in the division of labour on the cooperative. Thus, for example, older and generally more experienced ex-farmers form groups which take on the highest-paid jobs (sugar beet cultivation groups, for instance); former landless peasants and agricultural labourers establish technical services (tractor drivers, chauffeurs), while former poor farmers constitute the lowest-paid field teams employed on the simplest field chores.

On such collective farms the administrative–specialist personnel generally come from outside. It depends upon them whether the cooperative will evolve into a large enterprise (usually accompanied by the weakening of the cooperative's self-governing prerogatives) or whether it will remain in fact an aggregate of peasant family-farms. The difficulties of transforming this type of collective into a commercial enterprise flow from the inflexibility of the old social structure based on the family as the production unit, and the unavoidable quarrels between families and groups of families as well as between members and management. As with all types of collective farm, there is a flight of young people away from farming, though in milder form, depending on the general social and economic conditions prevailing in the country. This type has a good chance of developing into a modern enterprise, but the process is rather slow and encounters strong resistance. Without pressure from the authorities it would generally tend to fall apart.

The last is the collective farm set up by modern farm operators who are convinced that this is the way to attain better economic results and primarily higher incomes. This type is usually formed by joining together a small number of farms, each of which suffers from some deficiency (for instance, lack of capital for modernization, lack of manpower, etc.) which is complemented by the others. It is generally a kind of joint stock company which hires labour and estimates income scrupulously according to land, labour and capital—in short, a clear case of common or joint stock enterprise. These cooperatives generally tend to limit the number of partners, and to pay off or eliminate some of them from production. Hence they are unstable and constantly threatened by dissolution or by the withdrawal of some members with their land and capital. In different circumstances these constitute transitional forms which give way to large private enterprises based on individual or share capital.

The above is, of course, a highly simplified classification. Each of the four types may exist within considerably varied situations. One essential influence, firstly, is the effect of the general socio-economic system of the country where the collective farm arises. Farms formed on land acquired from agrarian reform or settlement will differ according to whether they are founded by agricultural labourers, non-farmers (the *kibbutz*) or by the rural poor. Ideological incentives may also produce varied reactions. Collective farms organized as a result of pressure may be more or less resented by their members, or they may or may not be appropriate under given general social conditions. Thus where there is high rate of migration of the rural population into non-agricultural occupations (e.g. Czechoslovakia, the German Democratic Republic), collective farming may be acknowledged as the only solution. Here collective farms do not dissolve when the economic pressure is relaxed, for no one wishes to withdraw his land and return to individual farming. Shareholding farms are, in general, impossible, or at least extremely rare, in countries without market incentives. But this type may have other forms of economic calculation, oriented to the acquisition of privileges which assure higher income rather than to reducing production costs. Despite this great variety of possible situations the types distinguished above provide at least an elementary orientation. It often turns out that collective farms appear in varied economic and structural conditions, as if they were an essentially homogeneous phenomenon. But greatly differing phenomena are involved here, and on the basis of the types we have distinguished even the name 'collective farm' appears to be misleading as a generic term embracing all types.

What they have in common is the fact that all collective farms represent an attempt to go over from the peasant family farm to the large, industrial-type agricultural enterprise. As a transitional form the collective farm is distinguished by great plasticity. It may be the beginning of a large agricultural enterprise (with certain elements of autonomy) or the instrument for liquidating *latifundia* and bringing about a change to family farming (with marked elements of cooperation between the farms). It may also be a form for creating bases of auxiliary aggregrates of peasant family farms, and an element of vertical integration. The collective farm is without doubt one of the elements of the future structure of agriculture, but a structure which will be probably polymorphous, since it is the most recent.

Because of the special conditions of Poland, all these types have made their appearance although few of them have been based on ideological motivations. Some of these did emerge immediately after the war but they disintegrated or lost their binding ideological links when their most active founders left. The most numerous were collective farms of the third type described above. However, with the change of agricultural policy in 1956 they were dissolved, and their members returned to individual farming. The most lasting proved to be those of the second type, which may be divided into two sub-types: (1) cooperative farms established for the purpose of cultivating the reclaimed and settled lands in the Western Territories; these were transitional in nature—the so-called 'parcelized settlement cooperatives'—and although they eventually adopted the permanent statutes of cooperatives the vast majority were dissolved after 1956; (2) farms formed on land acquired during the agrarian reform by former labourers on the landed estates. The latter sometimes arose during the course of the reform even when the authorities did not agree to retaining the estates intact for collective farming because they wished to divide the land. But objective necessity forced a collective economy upon the settlers and they often proceeded without permission. Later they continued cooperative farming with full State support and even retained their farms after 1956. Today the majority of Poland's collective farmers are of this kind.

Owing to the nature of the economic and social system there has been no basis in Poland for the fourth type described above. Those which did arise owed their existence to the business and organizational talents of their initiators and, later, their directors. A number of concessions and privileges granted to producer cooperatives provide appreciable economic opportunities for resourceful individuals. These cooperatives are generally based on high-priced output (hot-house culture, for instance), or even on non-agricultural services. The small numbers of their members, the camouflaged used of hired labour, government credit, and the speculative opportunities afforded by a market short of supply, assure income levels never attained by individual farming. More rigorous economic controls will most certainly limit this type of cooperative in Poland, for they are not considered desirable. The growth of competition on the market can also be expected to make them less 'speculative' while reducing their members' incomes.

The existing cooperative farms (mainly of the second type) do not provide any real clues as to Poland's future economic structure. It may be that the differences between the existing collective

farms and the State farms will be reduced, and that an intermediate form of organization will emerge combining elements of
directive leadership and elements of autonomy. But it is hardly
to be expected that this form will come to embrace the greater
part of the country's farms. It may turn out, rather, that the cooperative institution of Poland's individual farmers, the Agricultural Circle, will create a form of collective which will initially
fulfil an auxiliary function *vis-à-vis* the individual farm, i.e. an
individual–collective form which will gradually evolve towards
agricultural enterprises of an individual type with certain elements
of autonomy.

Teodor Shanin Cooperation and collectivization: the case of Eastern Europe

One of the major components of social life and of contemporary sociological thought is, to use a fashionable word, reification. Consciousness reflecting specific circumstances congeals into ideology and 'self-evident' truth, becomes a 'social fact' and then in turn shapes social life. What's more, such reifications travel far and fast in the kitbags of merchants, soldiers, scholars and ... 'cooperators'. At times the initial rationale has been lost, the genesis long forgotten, yet explanations once made continue to exert a powerful influence on social life, especially if related to the interests of power elites and to the policies of States.

The reason for the attempts at collectivization in Eastern Europe was the simple fact that the same thing had already happened in Russia. It was consequently accepted by the communist movement as a self-evident and necessary step on the road to socialism. Since then rural cooperation in Eastern Europe has become increasingly synonymous with collectivization on Soviet lines. Numerous pronouncements, declarations and resolutions of each of the ruling communist parties of Eastern Europe have repeatedly hailed collectivization. Only Yugoslavia and Gomulka's Poland opted out, eventually, from the general euphoria concerning collectivization, but even there belief in collectivization as the 'correct' and self-evidently socialist way to improve agriculture still exists.

Enthusiasm for collectivization had a triple root. First, a rapid increase in agricultural productivity and production was obviously a necessity both for the national economy and for the peasant majority of the population. This need, reinforced by the ideology of 'modernization' and by the essentially urban political experience of the European socialists, led to acceptance of the industrialization of agriculture as the major way for rural Eastern Europe to escape from its sorry state of low productivity and low incomes. The short-lived 'agricultural factories' of the Soviet

1920s caricature the essence of this idea.[1] The threefold recipe
which proved such a staggering success in urban industry—large-
scale production units, high capital investment (in particular,
mechanization) and effective utilization of the achievements of
scientific research in the production process—was now to be put
to work in the villages.

Second, collectivization would eliminate the exploitation of
peasant communities by their wealthier members, thus complet-
ing the equalizing process started by the abolition of the huge
estates and by revolutionary changes in land tenure. 'To each
according to his labour', in the agricultural world, would bring
to an end the last remnants of the capitalist strata and mark a
crucial step towards a classless, just society.

Third, a development of this kind would reflect the genuine
wishes of the bulk of the peasantry and was thus assured of
success. On the one hand, the peasants would be deeply interested
both in increasing agricultural production and in the more just
and progressive society promised by collectivization. On the
other, the communal life of the village had already given the
peasants experience of local cooperation (though the forces of
production were on a low level of development, and therefore
primitive and traditional in form). Now, instead of being pushed
straight into factory conditions, the peasant was to enjoy a long
intermediate stage. The life of the peasant commune would continue, while technological and social reforms closed the gap between socialist town and collectivized village. Meanwhile the
young generation, and those with new ideas and skills, would
have plenty of scope in the new large-scale agricultural units,
Collectivization was seen as a judicious blend of modernization
and socialism, productivity and justice, rapid reform and communal continuity, Party guidance and popular will.

Yet the actual results of collectivization have been, on the
whole, disappointing.[2] The productivity of collectivized agriculture is miles behind that of Western farming, and the gap does
not seem to close. The Soviet 'private plots', which take up a
small fraction of farming land, produce a remarkably large pro-

[1] See in particular *Otchet Narkomzema IX S'ezdu Sovetov* ('Report of the
People's Commissariat for Agriculture to the eleventh Congress of the
Soviets'), Moscow, 1921.

[2] See in particular N. Jasny, *The socialized agriculture of the USSR*, Stanford, 1949. For the contemporary position see J. F. Karcz, *Soviet and East
European agriculture*, Berkeley, 1967, and R. A. Clark, 'Soviet agricultural
reforms since Khrushchev', *Soviet Studies*, vol. xx, No. 2, 1969.

portion of total agricultural production.[3] In the whole 'socialist camp' the flight from the collective farms has led to various kinds of restrictive legislation. In fully collectivized, industrially advanced Czechoslovakia the villages have been practically emptied of young people, whilst the collective farms have turned into economic backwaters of slackening productivity. In Yugoslavia and in Gomulka's Poland, where the right to choose was restored to the peasantry, about 99 per cent opted out of collective farming, 'voting with their feet' their lack of confidence in the collectivized future. Nearly every year, throughout collectivized Eastern Europe, crises of food supply and administrative changes and campaigns to set agriculture to rights shake society, with serious consequences for the whole national economy. The grotesque difference between the rapid rate of industrial progress and that of food production (which still absorbs one-third of the Soviet labour force) was well captured in the recent Muscovite joke about the child's explanation to visitors: 'Both parents are out. Father has flown to the moon, Mother is queueing for sugar.'

The explanation of these reasonably well known facts is anything but obvious. After all, large-scale specialization and mechanization *did* produce a rapid increase in industrial production, while cooperative effort was not hailed as emancipation only by the 'communist bureaucrats'. The collectivizers themselves have blamed such difficulties (always 'temporary' and 'despite general advance') on anything from peasant conservative bloody-mindedness to straight sabotage by rich kulaks and imperialist agents. One also finds the recurrent belief (basically 'marginalist') that agriculture has an inherent tendency towards backwardness and is therefore doomed to drag behind industrial progress. On the other hand, the 'free Europe' type of analysis has found in it a proof of the natural and eternal preference of every human being for a free market democracy, as well as a reminder of the stupidity and wickedness of the Reds.

Some demystification of the rhetoric of collectivization may be both useful and timely. The historians have, in fact, already done much valuable work on the genesis of collectivization. The basic reason for the resort to collectivization in the Russia of 1920–36 was barely mentioned by those who advocated it, though it had already been brilliantly spelt out by Preobrazhenskii in 1922.

[3] Those plots which account for 3 per cent of the total agricultural land in the USSR produced up to one-third of the total agricultural output in 1958–65: *Soviet Studies*, vol. xx, No. 1, 1969, pp. 52–3.

In his book *The new economics* (currently reprinted by Nove) Preobrazhenskii argued that a stage of 'primitive accumulation of capital' must precede the necessary industrialization.[4] This process, in England, had involved the exploitation of the colonies, the creation of monopolies in foreign trade and the expropriation of the peasantry by enclosures. Soviet Russia could not use the first two methods and was therefore left with the exploitation of the peasantry as the only way to secure a 'take-off' until the self-generation of capital within industry had become sufficient to secure further development. The collectivization of 1929–33 in fact did precisely that—i.e. within the context of a drive to industrialization, peasant surpluses were acquired through total control of means of production. Furthermore, M. Lewin's recent study has demonstrated how little of this was pre-planned and 'rational' and how much of it grew out of a crisis of food supply due to lack of foresight and administrative skill, a crisis solved only by the use of naked force which caused severe destruction of resources.[5] The justification, 'rationalization' and glorification of this process came later.

However, the basically repressive and relatively accidental roots of collectivization still do not explain the whole of the matter. The question remains: why did the increase in size of the agricultural units, mechanization, etc., not produce rapid and considerable increases in production? Moreover, later on, with the stage of the 'primitive accumulation of capital' over and industry booming, why did the promised justification of collectivization not now mature and lead to a much more successful development of collective agriculture? Furthermore, why did it not work in those East European countries in which industry was more advanced than in the USSR in 1928, and to which industrial as well as political support could come from the USSR? In short, why did it not, at least belatedly, work better?

Interestingly enough, Russia has produced not only the world's first 'collectivization of agriculture' but also some basic conceptual tools for its critical comprehension. In fact after a generation of ideological platitudes this analysis still provides us with a fresh and more sophisticated view of the issue. I refer in the main to the work of Chayanov and his group,[6] and to their discussion of

[4] E. Preobrazhenskii, *The new economics*, introduced and edited by A. Nove, London, 1965.
[5] M. Lewin, *Russian peasants and Soviet power*, London, 1968.
[6] N. Makarov, A. Chelintsev, N. Svavitskii, etc.

'vertical' and 'horizontal' concentration of resources and co-operation as possible alternatives in the modernization of the traditional peasant communities.

This school drew most of its inspiration from the collective
experiences of local agronomists, rural sociologists and economists
during the period in which Russia led the world in the field of
rural studies. Chayanov's group started by re-analysing the
cooperative characteristics of the traditional village communities,
via what amounted to a thorough critique of orthodox 'Populist'
beliefs. The threefold rotation system, the common lands in forest
and pasture, in local services, etc., provided the basis for extensive
local cooperation. It also led to a rudimentary democracy (or
would oligarchy be a better word?) in which an assembly of heads
of peasant households and/or peasant elders ruled by what
amounted to common consent. In much of Russia a land commune also operated, i.e. land belonged to the commune and was
periodically redivided on an egalitarian basis. This further increased the extent of the peasant's involvement in his community.
Common descent, essentially similar life experience, lack of
anonymity and extensive common interests made for deep con-
formism and some basic ideological egalitarianism in the members of peasant communities. Yet these social relations also
engendered the deep self-centredness of the patriarchal peasant
family farm (or, to use Banfield's recent expression, extensive
'amoral familialism'), hostility towards outsiders and an attitude
of suspicion towards common ventures outside traditionally
accepted spheres. The stubborn narrow-mindedness of the village
assemblies, and the viciousness of inter-family and inter-village
feuds, indicated how far removed the peasant community was
from the heaven of brotherly love in which the traditional
Populists tended to believe.

The early stages of Russian industrialization, and the spread
of market relations, were associated with a crisis in traditional
peasant social structure and peasant agriculture. The pulveriza-
tion of peasant land-holdings, and the desperate shortage of
capital equipment and skills, blocked intensification of agriculture
and seemed to indicate the necessity for some type of concentration of the limited and limiting factors of production. Stolypin's
reforms of 1906–10 attempted to achieve this by the promotion of
the wealthy farmers, 'the sturdy and strong' of rural society, who
were to 'secure the development of the country on strong mon-

archic foundations'.[7] The revolution of 1917–19 wiped all that out. Industrialization was too feeble to draw off excessive rural labour and there was very little town-to-village flow of capital and skills (the opposite in fact took place). Hence some type of rural cooperation in production was increasingly looked to as the only realistic way out. The search for an optimal road to such cooperation within the framework of the existing structure of the peasant community forms the crux of Chayanov's analysis and of the dual conceptual scheme of 'horizontal' v. 'vertical' cooperation.[8]

Horizontal cooperation, in this usage, meant pooling the village's resources, in particular the land, thereby increasing the size of the production unit. This was seen as leading to a better use of the factors of production: it would facilitate mechanization and, in consequence, would increase productivity. Such developments would also promote democracy and egalitarianism if control of the enterprise were placed in the hands of the general assembly of its working population. In fact 'horizontal cooperation' quite accurately anticipated Soviet collective farming and East European collectivization.

Chayanov's group produced a thoroughgoing critique of the 'horizontal' solution, which came to stress the need to take the particular characteristics of agricultural production and of rural society into account. Its main elements are as follows.

1. Maximization of size of an agricultural enterprise does not automatically lead to an increase in production. Above a certain point, concentration of land, equipment and labour will lead to severe difficulties in transport, division of labour, availability of leadership, etc., and will make the increase in size counter-productive. The issue is therefore not *maximization* of size but *optimal* size, which will be much lower in agriculture than in industry. To make things worse, such an optimum lies at different points in different branches of agriculture; what might be considered a good size for a grain-producing enterprise might be badly overgrown for the efficient production of vegetables. (In defining the optimum, a certain level of agricultural technology, certain types of transport, etc., are assumed; changes in these

[7] Quotations from Stolypin's speech in 1907. See G. T. Robinson, *Rural Russia under the old regime*, New York, 1969.

[8] A. Chayanov, *Osnovnye idei i formy organizatsii sel'skokhozyaistennoi kooperatskii* ('The basic ideas and forms of agricultural co-operation'), Moscow, 1927, reprinted in *Oeuvres Choisies de A. V. Chayanov*, Paris, 1967, vol. 5.

factors would make for changes in the optimum sizes. This does not, however, destroy the validity of this type of analysis.)

2. The ostensibly egalitarian step of placing authority over the enterprise in the hands of the general assembly of producers would mean, given the conditions of the time, that a small bureaucratic elite would take over extremely broad administrative functions. The shortage of educated people (even those possessing bare literacy) and of organizational tradition, experience and skill would necessarily be reflected in low standards of competence and openness to corruption; such feeble local authorities would easily succumb to huge national bureaucracies and become their local plenipotentiaries instead of being representative of local interests and aspirations. For the individual peasant the patriarchal, personal and autocratic administration of the traditional peasant household and commune would therefore be replaced by alienation, anonymity and powerlessness in huge semi-industrial complexes.

3. The horizontally organized cooperative would cut across the 'vertical' lines of social organization typical of the traditional peasant community. The traditional peasant lines of authority, division of labour and support (e.g. the typical peasant household, patriarchal patron–client relations between neighbour, etc.) would be transgressed. The cooperative would therefore operate against the type of social organization to which the peasant had been accustomed, without showing clear economic benefits on the credit side. Horizontal cooperation would consequently have to be carried out in the teeth of peasant opposition. It would jeopardize basic incentives in peasant labour—a particularly dangerous situation in agriculture, where the types of control of production typical of industry, both quantitative and qualitative, are on the whole impossible. It would lead, furthermore, to a head-on clash between outsiders—plenipotentiaries of the State and local peasant leaders. Destruction of already scarce resources and of organizational and farming skills—no less scarce—would result.

4. Somewhat more implicitly, an additional point was made— finally stated in full in Poland a generation later, after Gomulka's arrival in power in 1957. In a 'horizontal' cooperative of the Soviet type a peasant was bound to lose both ways. On the one hand he lost the relative freedom of the smallholder, while on the other he did not gain an eight-hour working day, the security of wages, sickness benefits or the retirement pensions provided by industry for its employees.

Vertical cooperation was therefore the answer of Chayanov's group to the need for change which would nevertheless take forms acceptable to the peasants. The practically unlimited concentration of capital typical of industry would not work the same way in agriculture. The spontaneous development of peasant agriculture in a market economy led, rather, to a 'vertical' process of social division of labour, and to concentration and specialization: i.e. various aspects of production were taken out of the hands of the small producers and organized on a regional or national scale by merchant capitalists (e.g. credit, sales, etc.) This led to severe exploitation of the farmers by the capitalist entrepreneurs (Makarov, for example, has pointed out that US farmers in the 1920s lost 65 per cent of their income this way). Vertical cooperation should accept and promote the general tendency towards social division of labour and specialization, but place the new services in the hands of cooperative organizations which would not have any other interests than that of their members. Such cooperatives would promote agriculture while defending the peasants from exploitation by both capitalists and national bureaucracies.

Vertical cooperation, furthermore, was to provide a much more flexible solution to the problem of optimal size (the 'theory of differential optimums'). The various branches of agricultural production could be divided into those which were to be organized on a broader-than-village level, those which should be organized on a village basis, and finally those which would operate best at the level of family farm. Cooperation of this kind would then ensure production at optimal levels which would best benefit both the members and the national economy as a whole. Development along lines known and accepted as natural by the peasants, together with obvious and immediate benefits, would ensure the acceptance of such schemes in the villages. In the second edition of his book on cooperation, published in 1927, Chayanov called for an essentially vertical rural cooperation and warned that the possible advantages of the *kolkhoz* (e.g. better use of stores and buildings) would in the long run be outbalanced by the limitations of such a scheme.

The analysis developed by Chayanov's group undoubtedly has serious limitations. Their belief in the essentially egalitarian character of their schemes could be easily challenged; in reality, such forms of organization might well strengthen some of the exploitive patron–client relations between richer and poorer members of the rural communities. Cooperation in production would require large capital investment, and would necessarily therefore bring in either private capital or the State. Yet the essence of Chayanov's analysis, especially its critical parts, seems remarkably relevant. The difficulties of collectivized East European agriculture seem to be very much of the structural type predicted in the analytical model developed by Chayanov's group.

By now even the most stolid of East European officials must be aware of the fact that agriculture has developed into a major bottleneck of the national economy, and that the troubles are not simply transitory and will not disappear of their own accord. Indeed, a debate on the ways and means to improve matters rages continuously and quite openly, at least since Khrushchev. The prescriptions vary between massive capital investments in agriculture, the production of fertilizers or 'infrastructure' (roads, warehouses), increase in agricultural know-how (and/or general education), and appeal to the farmer's self-interest by greatly raising agricultural prices. What remains outside the scope of this discussion as a rule is the social structure as a determinant of agricultural production. Furthermore, the solutions suggested by the economist, workable as they may be, might apply in the administration of steel mills or shops, but reflect remarkably little awareness of the special characteristics of agriculture in real society.

On the other hand, Galeski's analytical typology of collective farms in the present volume strikes me as a lucid exploration of the causal factors underlying those cases of voluntary 'horizontal' cooperation which have proved successful. The main weakness of his paper lies not in its content but in the fact that collective farms account for only 1·1 per cent of the Polish family population. It is the discussion of the 'vertical' cooperative experience of the 98·9 per cent of the Polish farmers which one misses.

In our superdynamic times any discussion of the past or even of the present is generally related to attempts to clarify the future. What, then, is the future pattern of social organization of agriculture in the Eastern European countries? The answer seems to be twofold. On the one hand, Gomulka's disregard for dogma, as well as the extensive studies done by the Polish rural sociologists, seem to provide an important postscript to a Russian debate of a generation ago. Under conditions of free choice, 99 per cent of the Polish peasants have opted out of the collective farms. Yet

the socio-economic polarization of these peasants has not occurred, and this not only because of the anti-capitalist policies
of the government. Rapid industrialization led to the emigration
of the poorest, the disappearance of cheap and exploited rural
labour, and the development of a new stratum of peasant-workers.
All these developments, as well as 'vertical' cooperation ('Agricultural Circles' etc.) and State policy, have led to a remarkable
levelling in the village community, coupled with an increase in
agricultural productivity. This practical lesson has clearly been
learnt by most politicians in Eastern Europe. Collectivization on
Soviet lines is still hailed as the 'correct' long-term solution of the
problems of socialist agriculture, but there is very little chance
that any government will repeat it ever in Europe. For the
moment, there seems to be no takers elsewhere either.

But what about those countries in which collectivization has
been pushed through? Could they, would they or should they
declare the experiment void, build a memorial to Chayanov (and
possibly Bukharin) and start all over again? In real life is the
naked king of Hans Andersen's story likely to run for cover, or
will the child who cried out 'The king has no clothes' be disposed
of in the sacred interest of the State? Leaving aside the question
of the ability of rulers to look critically at their own policies,
'reverse moves' cannot occur in history. By the time a policy has
been tested, alternative roads have, on the whole, been blocked,
and future possibilities are shaped by the position already
reached. That is why so many dogmas have a self-validating
quality in political life. Reversal of this deeply entrenched collectivization is by now no more than a utopian dream. With the
local farming elites destroyed, the continuity of the peasant
households severed and its young members committed elsewhere,
with complex new technologies on the increase; even the older
peasants of Bohemia or East Germany (not to say the USSR)
would find it difficult to envisage going back.

What then seems in the long run to be the way out of the
difficulties which beset collectivized agriculture and which turn
it into a major bottleneck of national economies? In so far as
extrapolations can teach, one should probably look for answers,
once again, to Soviet agriculture, in which the issues have
'matured' most. The most important change which took place in
Soviet agriculture during the last two decades seems to have been
the development in the general direction of State farms. During
this period the numbers as well as the share of production and

the labour force of the State farms rose steeply, while a decrease in all these was reported in collectivized agriculture.[9] This trend resulted both from the transformation of the weaker collective farms into State farms and the setting up of State farms as the main method of colonization of new areas. At the same time the size, complexity and bureaucratic character of the collective farms increased, and since 1966 minimum regular wages for members (similar to those of the State farms) have been introduced.[10]

Yet such a development would be yet another flight of bureaucratic imagination imposed on the countryside. Is it not another assault on the peasant's natural inclination towards cooperative development? If large-scale agricultural units were to operate in accordance with the peasants' wishes, what form would they take? It may be that the peasant's rough common sense has once again outstripped the over-sophisticated theorizing of the intellectuals. The only comprehensive and reliable large-scale studies of peasant attitudes undertaken in Eastern Europe were carried out in Poland in the early 1960s. The majority of these studies declared the existing system of smallholdings (with some additional 'vertical' cooperation) to be the only serious possibility for the future of Polish agriculture. Yet, of the important minority which saw the need for a future increase in the size and complexity of agricultural enterprises, two-thirds supported State farms rather than collective farms.[11] The reason for this was spelled out quite explicitly: the advantages of security of wages, the eight-hour working day, pensions, etc., outweighed the smallholder's desire for independence and his suspicion of change. To these peasants an 'agricultural factory', not a collective farm nor any other form of cooperation, was the alternative to peasant smallholding farming. Should we not learn from those to whom agriculture is not a bother nor a problem but a way of life? If

[9] See Soviet statistical yearbooks, for example *Narodnoe khozyaistvo SSSR v 1968 g.* ('The national economy of the USSR in 1968'), Moscow, 1969, pp. 313, 438, etc. During the decade 1953–63 the land sown by collective farms decreased from 84 to 54 per cent of the total, while the share of State farms went up from less than 10 per cent to about 43 per cent. The trend has since 'evened up'. For discussion see Clark, loc. cit.; also A. B. Ballard in *Soviet Studies*, vol. XVII, No. 3, 1966.

[10] Attempts at tackling the counter-productive results of the increase in size were made by the introduction of *zvenos* (small, autonomous production teams) in some collective farms. These experiments were never fully legalized or accepted. See Karcz, op. cit., pp. 42–3; Clark, loc. cit., p. 177.

[11] B. Galeski, *Chlopi i zawod rolnika* ('Peasants and farming as an occupation'), Warsaw, 1963, p. 118.

large-scale enterprises and collective effort are to be the order
of the day in agriculture should we not challenge the very idea
of the cooperative as the best solution to it?

B. S. Baviskar Cooperatives and caste in Maharashtra: a case study

The modern cooperative movement was formally introduced in India in 1904 with the promulgation of the Cooperative Societies Act. Initially, it was confined mainly to agricultural credit; its objective was to free the peasants from exploitation by money lenders, by providing the former with alternative sources of credit. Since 1904 the number of cooperatives and their membership and capital investment have grown many times. Gradually, cooperative activity was also extended to several other spheres such as marketing, processing, farming, banking and housing.

A distinctive feature of modern cooperatives is that they are organized on the basis of certain principles, the most important of which, from the sociologist's point of view, are equality among members and the democratic principle in management. It is well known that the caste system was one of the major bases of the organization of the traditional Indian society, and it continues to be important in many spheres of life even in modern times. Individuals acquired their caste by birth and the system was characterized by a certain hierarchy among the different caste groups based mainly on the principles of purity and pollution. The system not only implied superiority of certain groups over others in the social, economic and political fields, but it also underlined the acceptance of superiority and inequality by the other groups irrespective of the fact that the different unequal groups cooperated with each other in different spheres of life. It would appear, then, that the basic principles underlying the caste system and the cooperative movement are inconsistent with each other. The same is the case with the relation between the caste system and parliamentary democracy based on adult franchise.

A number of social scientists have analysed the role of caste in politics.[1] Some of them have also examined its role in the eco-

---

[1] Some of the important studies on this theme are: Srinivas (1962), Bailey (1963), Beteille (1969), Mayer (1967) and Rao (1964, 1968).

nomic field.[2] But although cooperative activity is a part of the wider economic field, not much work has been done on the relationship between caste and cooperatives in general or agricultural cooperatives in particular. The aim of this paper is to analyse the role of caste in a cooperative sugar factory. In this connection I should like to discuss the following questions. How far do members of different castes differ in their attitudes towards participation in a particular cooperative activity? What are the reasons underlying these differences? How far do members of different castes differ in their behaviour while participating in the cooperative activity? What are the factors underlying these differences? And finally, what role does caste play in the success or failure of a cooperative activity? I should like to discuss these questions in relation to three aspects of the cooperative sugar factory; the establishment of the factory, leadership and control of the factory, and industrial relations in the factory.

The background

Maharashtra is considered to be one of the leading states in India in the cooperative field. Among the twenty-six districts in Maharashtra, Ahmednagar district, in which the factory under study is located, is recognized as a centre of successful cooperative activity. The district has an extensive network of primary cooperatives covering almost every village. Out of twenty-eight cooperative sugar factories in the state, this district alone has eight. The District Central Cooperative Bank of Ahmednagar is acclaimed as the model not only in Maharashtra but in other states as well. The district has also a cooperative sale and purchase union which is the second largest in the state, with an annual turnover of about seven crores[3] of rupees.

The whole district, although characterized by a rich soil, was once a famine-stricken area owing to inadequate and uncertain rains. The completion of irrigation canals from the Godavari and Pravara rivers in 1916 and 1922 respectively was a major landmark in the process of economic development of the region. The canals brought about a shift from the subsistence to cash crops, the principal among the latter being sugar cane. Ahmednagar leads all other districts in Maharashtra in sugar cane production

---

[2] The contributions of Bailey (1957) and Epstein (1962) are significant in this field.

[3] *Crore*=ten million.

in terms of acreage as well as yield per acre. There are thirteen sugar factories in the district, eight of which are cooperatives while the remaining five are joint stock companies. These factories together provide regular employment for over 13,000 workers and crush over twenty-five *lakh*[4] tons of sugar cane annually. The surplus sugar cane, if any, left with the grower is converted into *gur* (jaggery)[5] by the grower himself. The social, economic and political life in the district, particularly in its northern part, revolves mainly around the cultivation of sugar cane and the manufacture of sugar and *gur*.

Most of the castes found in Maharashtra are represented in Ahmednagar district. Prominent among them are the Brahmin, the cultivator castes of Maratha, Mali, Dhangar and Vanjari, the artisan and servicing castes, such as Sutar (carpenter), Lohar (blacksmith), Nhar (barber) and Dhobi (washerman), and the ex-untouchable castes such as Mahar, Chambhar and Mang. Since 1956, following the call of the late Dr B. R. Ambedkar, the majority of the Mahars have become converted to Buddhism and are now called Neo-Buddhists. Maratha is the 'dominant caste'[6] in the region. They are numerically preponderant and enjoy economic and political power as well as a high, though not the highest, ritual status.

Modern sugar industry started in India at the beginning of this century, but it made real headway only after 1932, when the government imposed a protective duty on the import of sugar. Five sugar factories were established in Ahmednagar district within a period of about ten years after 1932. They were organized as joint stock companies controlled mainly by Marwari and Gujarati industrialists from Bombay. However, the establishment of these factories did not contribute much to the improvement of the economic condition of the local sugar cane growers. It was felt by the local peasant leaders and enlightened cooperators that the establishment of a sugar factory on a cooperative basis was the only way to improve the lot of the sugar cane growers, who had suffered from fluctuations in the *gur* market and exploitation by the joint stock sugar factories. Although efforts in this direction were begun in 1946, the first factory was established only in 1950. It was the first successful cooperative sugar factory not only in

[4] *Lakh* = 100,000.

[5] A coarse, dark sugar made from palm sap.

[6] The Marathas are dominant in the area in the sense in which Srinivas (1959) uses the term.

19—T.B.O.G.

Maharashtra but also in the country as a whole. The factory that
I studied was established in 1953—the second in the series—and
it went into production in 1955–56. I shall call this factory Kisan
(a pseudonym).

The factory

Kisan is located near a village in Kopargaon *taluka*[7] of Ahmednagar district. There are six sugar factories in the *taluka*, three
of which are cooperatives and the rest joint stock companies. The
shareholders of Kisan (1,044 in June 1963) are sugar cane growers

Table 3
Distribution of shareholders by caste and size of shareholding

	Size of shareholding				Percentage of the total shareholders
Caste	Small (1–6)	Medium (7–19)	Large (20–50)	Total	
1. Maratha	387	208	32	627	60·0
2. Mali	49	66	28	143	13·7
3. Karekar (peasant from Kare)	100	21	4	125	11·9
4. Brahmin	31	15	4	50	4·8
5. Dhangar	15	2	—	17	1·6
6. Vanjari	12	4	1	17	1·6
7. Marwari Bania (trader)	7	3	—	10	
8. Lingayat Wani (trader)	6	3	1	10	
9. Mahar (Neo-Buddhist)	8	1	—	9	
10. Chambhar	6	2	—	8	
11. Dhobi (washerman)	3	4	—	7	
12. Gujarati Bania (trader)	—	1	2	3	
13. Lonari (lime and charcoal burner)	1	1	—	2	6·4
14. Koli (water carrier)	1	1	—	2	
15. Bairagi (mendicant)	2	—	—	2	
16. Sutar (carpenter)	1	—	—	1	
17. Vadar (earth worker)	—	1	—	1	
18. Muslim	4	4	—	8	
19. Public bodies	1	1	—	2	
Total	634	338	72	1,044	100·0

Note: each share is of the value of R 500. The shareholder is obliged to supply sugar cane to
the factory at the rate of half an acre of sugar cane per share held by him.

spread over fifty-nine villages in the 'area of operation' of the
factory. Most of them belong to the local peasant castes, mainly
Maratha, Mali and Karekar. Among them the locally dominant
Marathas constitute over 60 per cent of the shareholders (see
table 3). The Malis, who constitute 13·7 per cent, are numerically

[7] A *taluka* is a sub-division of a district. Ahmednagar district consists of
thirteen *talukas*. Kopargaon *taluka* comprises 100 villages.

next to the Marathas. The former migrated from the neighbouring Poona district to this area after the completion of the irrigation canals and are recognized as the pioneers in sugar cane cultivation. The Malis are relatively well-to-do among the shareholders of Kisan, a fact reflected in the proportion of the shares held by them (see table 4). It is important to note that the majority of the shareholders—over 60 per cent—are small growers with not more than three acres of land under sugar cane.

Table 4
Distribution of shareholders of important castes according to shareholding

Size of shareholding	Caste					All shareholders
	Maratha	Mali	Karekar	Brahmin	Others	
Small (1–6)	61·8	34·2	80·0	62·0	67·4	60·7
Medium (7–19)	33·1	46·2	16·8	30·0	28·3	32·4
Large (20–50)	5·1	19·6	3·2	8·0	4·3	6 9
Total	100·0	100·0	100·0	100·0	100·0	100·0
N	(627)	(143)	(125)	(50)	(99)	(1,044)

The management of the factory rests with the board of directors—thirteen in all—elected from amongst the shareholders. The elected members of the board may co-opt two additional members as experts. As considerable prestige, material gains and power of patronage are associated with the position of director, there is intense competition among the local peasant leaders to become directors of the factory. The directors often try to use the resources of the factory to strengthen their position in local politics. The leading directors have been closely associated with the local units of political parties, particularly the ruling Congress Party and the factions within it.

In 1963–64, when field work for this study was carried out, Kisan employed 885 workers, including the supervisory and managerial staff. Among them 450 workers were permanent and the rest seasonal. The majority of the workers were semi-skilled and unskilled. About 30 per cent of the workers were local, in the sense that they came from the fifty-nine villages in the area of operation of the factory. Most of the local workers had caste, kinship and village ties with shareholders and directors. There were only ninety-two workers who came from other states, mainly Uttar Pradesh and Bihar. The numerically significant caste groups among the workers were Marathas (258), Neo-Buddhists (148), Brahmins (72), Dhangars (28), Malis (17), and Karekars (16). The

remaining 346 workers were distributed in small numbers among
a large number of castes and among Christians and Muslims.
There was a broad correlation between the caste affiliation of a
worker and the nature of the job held by him. The Brahmins were
engaged mainly in the clerical, skilled and supervisory work,
while the Neo-Buddhists were engaged mainly in unskilled and
semi-skilled work. The Marathas were found in all the occupational categories.

The factory works for about 200 days in a year. It has a crushing capacity of 1,200 tons per day. It crushes annually over two
lakh tons of sugar cane supplied by the shareholders and produces over 23,000 tons of sugar. In economic terms the factory
has been a great success. It has paid all its 'block capital' loans,
amounting to forty *lakhs* of rupees, four years in advance of the
stipulated date. In addition, it has created permanent assets worth
more than a *crore* of rupees. Recently it has been granted expansion in its crushing capacity to 1,750 tons a day. It has been able
to pay increasingly higher prices for the sugar cane supplied by
shareholders. Starting with a rate of only 37·25 rupees per ton
of sugar cane in the first year (1955–56), it paid 61·25 rupees per
ton during the year of my field work (1963–64). In 1967–68 it was
able to pay 169·50 rupees per ton. Furthermore, through its extension services it has helped the shareholders, directly or indirectly, to increase the yield of sugar cane. The average yield of
cane per acre cultivated by the shareholders increased from 36·4
tons in 1955–56 to 54·8 tons in 1965–66. During the last ten years
the factory has constructed and maintained a network of roads
in its area of operation. For its workers and staff it has developed
a small township with many modern civic amenities. It has also
helped to start and maintain two colleges and five secondary
schools in the area. In short, the factory has contributed a great
deal to the transformation of economic and social life in the
surrounding area. It also occupies an important place in the local
politics.

Establishment of the factory

The initiative for the establishment of the factory came from
Kaka, a local Maratha leader. He had been active in organizing a
number of cooperative societies of different types in the region
for over twenty-five years. Through this work he had also built

up contacts with influential cooperators and various officials in the cooperative field in the state.

When Kaka started collecting the share capital for the proposed factory in 1948, he realized that he could not do it with the support of the Marathas only, and the support of the other castes was essential. Although the Marathas were numerically preponderant, the majority of them, being small growers, did not have enough resources to become shareholders. Kaka did not find it easy to enlist the support of the other castes. His proposal was strongly opposed by the rich Marwari and Gujarati Bania traders, who considered it a threat to their vested interest, viz. their trade in *gur*. They also tried to dissuade the minority castes of Malis and Karekars from buying shares in the proposed factory. The latter were not very enthusiastic about Kaka's proposal for other reasons too. The cane growers of these castes had retained close links with the local traders in order to meet their credit needs even after cooperative credit societies had been established in the region. They feared that the new factory, like the other cooperatives, would be dominated by the numerically strong Marathas. They were also suspicious of Kaka, who had earlier antagonized these groups. The traders were opposed to Kaka because he had already undermined their monopoly in the local market by organizing a cooperative sale and purchase union. He had come into conflict with the Karekars in neighbouring villages, owing to disputes over the ownership of land and the distribution of canal waters. The Malis were opposed to him because he had earlier campaigned against their getting lands on lease from the local Maratha land-owners and also against the irrigation facilities they enjoyed. As immigrants, dependent mainly on sugar cane cultivation, the Malis felt insecure with the increasing influence of Kaka, whom they considered an open protagonist of the local Maratha peasants.

The opposition of the Malis to the establishment of the factory is worth noting, as it brings out the relevance of the caste factor. Their opposition did not arise from any doubts about the utility of the proposed factory. In fact they were the first among the sugar cane growers to realize the need for starting a sugar factory instead of being at the mercy of the fluctuating *gur* market. They had established a factory of their own in the neighbouring district on similar lines in the 'thirties, although it was not registered as a cooperative. All the shareholders in that factory were Malis.

Their opposition to Kaka's proposal arose mainly out of fear of increasing domination by the Marathas.

The new proposal required both share capital and an adequate acreage of cane with the shareholders. The Malis had both. They were bigger cane growers and also possessed resources to buy shares. But the indifference and, to some extent, hostility on the part of the Malis and other minority castes frustrated Kaka. He had to give up the idea of starting a sugar cooperative and return whatever money he had collected from the people.

In the meanwhile another Maratha leader succeeded in starting a sugar cooperative in a neighbouring *taluka* in 1950, which was the first factory of its kind in the state. This inspired Kaka to make another attempt, and this time he succeeded. A number of factors contributed to his success. In order to allay the suspicions of the trading and other minority castes, Kaka persuaded a local Marwari Bania trader to become one of the promoters of the factory. Two announcements by the state government also helped him: first, the policy of favouring the licensing of sugar factories in the cooperative sector and, second, the policy of disallowing the sugar cane growers in the canal-irrigated areas from cultivating more than six acres of cane. However, those who joined a cooperative sugar factory were to be exempted from this rule and allowed to cultivate up to twenty-five acres of cane. As most of the Malis were big cane growers, they saw the threat to their cane growing operations and joined the factory as shareholders without delay. Thus Kaka succeeded in collecting enough share capital to register the proposed factory as a cooperative, and the factory was soon erected.

It is significant that the initiative and leadership in the establishment of Kisan emerged from the dominant group of the Marathas. This was true of most of the sugar cooperatives in Maharashtra. Members belonging to the other castes have rarely taken a leading part in starting such ambitious cooperative ventures. Organizing a big cooperative such as a sugar factory required the mobilization of human and material resources on a large scale. The leaders of the dominant caste were in a better position than the others to mobilize such resources. The minority caste groups were not as enthusiastic in starting Kisan as the Marathas. This was due more to fear of the growth of the power of the dominant caste than to any doubts regarding the economic and other advantages of joining such ventures. The minority castes joined Kisan ultimately when they realized that they could not prevent its emergence.

Leadership and control of the factory

Authority in the factory vests in the board of directors, which takes all important policy decisions. The directors are elected by the shareholders, each of whom enjoys an equal number of votes irrespective of the number of shares he holds. For the first three years after the establishment of the factory there was a nominated board. Subsequently regular periodical elections have been held. There had been keen contests in all the elections, except during 1960–62, when the directors were elected unopposed. I was able to observe the elections of the board held in December 1963, and I have also collected information about all the previous as well as subsequent elections through other sources.

The history of the struggle for power in Kisan is associated with two rival factions. Factions are called *gats* in the local language, and each *gat* is known by the name of its main leader. Each faction puts up a separate 'panel' of candidates and approaches the voters supporting the panel as a whole. Each faction is led by a Maratha. Its members are, however, drawn from all the castes among the shareholders, though not in equal proportion. Over a period of time there has developed a two-party system in Kisan as well as in other similar structures of power in the area. Nobody comes forward to contest the elections as an 'independent' candidate outside of the panels put up by rival factions. The factions function almost on party lines, although the leaders of rival factions may belong to the same political party. The factions also use the party idiom in their organization and activities. Terms such as 'parliamentary board', 'party meeting', 'party discipline', and 'party line' are frequently used by them.

Before 1960 the factions in Kisan were organized largely on the basis of allegiance to rival political parties. While one faction was led by the members of the ruling Congress Party, the other was led by the members of the opposition parties, mainly the Peasants and Workers Party and the Communist Party. After 1960 most of the opposition leaders joined Congress. For a period of two or three years there was complete unity in the board of Kisan as well as in the boards of other cooperatives in the area. As a result, there were no contests in the elections to the different boards. Candidates were approved by the leaders and they were elected unopposed during this 'period of unity', as local people refer to it. At the end of 1962 serious differences developed among the leaders, and two rival factions re-emerged, by and large pitting the 'old' Congressmen against the new entrants to the party. I do not discuss here the factors contributing to the unity and those leading to the reappearance of the split, as I do not consider it relevant to this paper.

The candidates are selected by the rival factions mainly on the basis of their 'vote-catching' ability. Formal education or other qualifications for managing the affairs of the factory are secondary. Both the factions try to give proportional representation to the different caste groups among the shareholders. Over a period of time a convention has developed that the minority castes of Malis and Karekars should have at least two directors on the board. The Brahmins are given one seat, as they have a smaller number of shareholders. Members of other minority castes who do not have many shareholders may get a representation occasionally if there is an influential leader among them. The candidates are selected by the respective 'parliamentary boards' of the rival factions. However, the selection of representatives from the minority castes is made in consultation with the acknowledged leaders of those castes within the faction. The factions also try to distribute their tickets evenly among the different villages, depending on the number of shareholders in them.

All the candidates of a faction pool their resources and organize the campaign jointly. However, the candidates of the minority castes tend to approach the voters belonging to their castes individually. The issues in the campaign are not confined to those connected with the affairs of the factory. The actions of the rival factions in the factory as well as in other cooperatives, *panchayat* bodies and similar other structures are criticized during the campaign. Leading personalities and their actions are also subjected to criticism. However, the issues, of whatever kind, are not so decisive in influencing the voters. What matters most is the personal following of the leaders, based on previous obligations and future promises. Politics at this level is 'a system of reciprocal personal obligations', as described by Whyte in his study of Cornerville (1943, p. 240).

Voting is by and large on factional lines. Usually more than 95 per cent of the members exercise their franchise. Normally the panel as a whole wins or loses. This does not mean that there are no differences in the votes polled by individual candidates in the same panel. Some candidates get more votes than the others in the same panel, owing to their personal following or popularity among the voters. The candidates belonging to the minority castes often get more votes than the Marathas in the same panel, as the minority caste voters tend to vote for their caste-men across the panel. As a result, sometimes a minority caste may be slightly over-represented. Such a tendency is, however, criticized by the leaders of the dominant caste.

After the election of directors, the chairman and the vice-chairman of the factory are elected by the directors from amongst themselves. Here again, barring one or two exceptions, the chairmanship has always gone to a Maratha and the vice-chairmanship to one of the minority caste leaders, either a Mali or a Karekar.

The elections are often influenced by events remotely connected with the management of the factory. The strength of the rival factions in the District Central Cooperative Bank, other cooperative sugar factories in the district, cooperative sale–purchase unions, the *panchayati raj* bodies, the Congress Party, and the state Cabinet, influences the fortunes of rival groups in the factory. Thus control over these other organizations helps a faction to secure control over the factory. And control over the factory, in turn, helps a faction to secure control over the other organizations.[8]

Since the factions are multi-caste alliances, they do not fight with each other on caste lines or caste issues. This is because factions, not castes, form the basis of organization, competition and rivalry; and they operate more with the objective of capturing power in the cooperatives than for any ideological considerations. The caste factor enters into the 'calculus' for achieving this objective. Caste is relevant here to the extent that the rival factions are led by the leaders belonging to the dominant Maratha caste and they try to secure support of all the numerically significant castes among the shareholders. In the process almost all the castes are divided, though not equally, along factional line. The leaders realize the importance of caste in voting and try to provide representation to different castes in proportion to

[8] I have discussed in another paper (1968b) the part played by co-operatives in Maharashtra politics. It is also discussed in detail in my 'Factions and party politics: general elections in an Assembly constituency in Maharashtra' in a forthcoming volume being edited by M. N. Srinivas and A. M. Shah at the University of Delhi.

their numerical strength. The candidates belonging to the minority castes appeal to their caste-men on the basis of loyalty. The Marathas continue to dominate in spite of the divisions among them, mainly because of their decisive numerical strength as compared to the other castes. They have also the advantage of having links with other Marathas who are powerful in other cooperatives, in the Congress Party and in the government. This creates in them a tremendous sense of confidence. Much of the recent progress in the cooperative field in Maharashtra is due to the bold actions of the Maratha leaders in different parts of the state who have far more political resources at their disposal than the leaders of the minority castes.

Industrial relations

Relations among the Kisan workers themselves, between the workers and the union, and between workers and the union on the one hand and the management on the other, were influenced largely by the divisions among the workers on the basis of 'locality', political party and, to some extent, caste. The caste background of the workers and the divisions of 'local' and 'outsiders' among them have already been mentioned. The employment of a large number of 'outside' workers, many of whom belonged to castes other than those of the shareholders, needs an explanation. A large number of unskilled and semi-skilled workers were employed in the factory in 1953 when it was being erected. Initially, wages and working conditions were not sufficiently attractive for local labour to seek employment in it. The management also discouraged the recruitment of local labour for fear that it would create scarcity of agricultural labour and adversely affect sugar cane cultivation in the area. The senior officials of the factory having influence over the recruitment of workers were mainly Brahmins from outside the area. They too favoured the appointment of 'outside' workers in the hope that they would be more obedient as compared to local workers, who had access to the directors and shareholders. The outside workers, in turn, took avidly to employment in Kisan. The ex-untouchables were attracted by the prospect of regular employment free from the disabilities of village society. Workers from Uttar Pradesh and Bihar, who had experience of working in sugar factories elsewhere, joined Kisan because it offered relatively better jobs and higher wages on account of their past experience.

The Taluka Sugar Workers' Union (TSU), affiliated to Hind Mazdoor Sabha (HMS),[9] enjoys the legal status of the 'representative' union for all the six sugar factories in Kopargaon *taluka*. There are close links between the TSU and the local branch of the Praja Socialist Party (PSP). The Kisan branch of the TSU has been active since the factory went into production. Outside workers largely belonging to the minority castes were the first to join the union and constituted the hard core of its supporters. The composition of the TSU's membership in Kisan influenced significantly the management's attitude towards the union. More than 60 per cent of the workers in Kisan had been organized by the TSU. The proportion of union members was higher among the unskilled and semi-skilled workers than among employees in higher categories. Similarly, it was higher among the ex-untouchables and other minority castes than among the locally dominant Maratha caste. Moreover, the outside workers were proportionately more numerous in the union than local ones. For instance, almost all the workers from Uttar Pradesh and Bihar were loyal members of the union. The main reason for this situation was that while the local workers, particularly from the dominant and other peasant castes, could count on their caste, kinship and village ties with the shareholders and directors to safeguard their interests, the other workers had to depend exclusively on their union strength. The local workers resented the dominance of outsiders in the union and felt that the union discriminated against them.

The major source of friction within the union and also between the union and the management was the existence of a large number of outside workers. It may be mentioned here that the provision of employment for local people was also one of the objectives in starting the cooperative sugar factories. However, outside workers were recruited in the initial period for the reasons stated above. Soon after the initial period was over there was considerable improvement in the wages and working conditions. As a result, the local people began pressing the directors for jobs in the factory. At this stage the management could not recruit new

[9] HMS is an all-India trade union organization closely associated with the Praja Socialist Party. In India the major trade union organizations are closely linked with different political parties, e.g. the All India Trade Union Congress (AITUC) is associated with the Communist Party of India, while the Indian National Trade Union Congress (INTUC) is linked with the Congress Party.

workers without removing the old ones. It also realized that any such attempt on its part would be strongly opposed by the union. The management also resented the close association between the TSU and the PSP, as most of the directors were members of the Congress Party.

In order to deal with this situation the directors decided to sponsor a union which would cooperate with the management and be closer to the Congress. They encouraged the local workers to establish a rival union affiliated to the Indian National Trade Union Congress (INTUC) controlled by the Congress. The emergence of the 'company union' sharpened the division among the workers. The loyal supporters of the TSU who stood by it during this period were mostly outside workers, including those from the other states. The Maharashtrians among them were mostly ex-untouchables or belonged to other minority castes. The open supporters of the INTUC union were mostly local workers belonging to the peasant castes. Many of them had close ties with the shareholders and directors.

The rivalry between the two unions led the INTUC union and the management to take a bold step having far-reaching consequences for both the unions. The step involved the removal of 105 workers by the management on the advice of the INTUC union's leaders. All these workers were loyal supporters of the TSU. Over 90 per cent of them were outsiders and the overwhelming majority of them consisted of ex-untouchables. The vacancies arising out of the removal of these workers were filled by appointing local men, most of whom belonged to peasant castes and were connected with the shareholders and directors through caste, kinship and village ties. All of them joined the INTUC union.[10]

The TSU fought the cases of the dismissed workers in the courts and succeeded in getting them reinstated. This boosted the confidence of the TSU and weakened the hold of the INTUC union. The directors also lost interest in the latter and wondered if they had done the right thing in interfering in union matters. The INTUC union soon became a defunct body. Although this has strengthened the TSU, it does not mean that it is completely secure in its position. The Neo-Buddhist workers in the factory are constantly under pressure from the Republican Party, founded by the late Dr B. R. Ambedkar, to secede from the TSU

[10] I have discussed these developments in greater detail elsewhere (1968a).

and form a union of their own. The ruling faction in the management has been encouraging this move.

Thus we find that 'locality' and, to some extent, caste were the two important factors which determined the workers' affiliation to the rival unions. They were also the major source of friction in the union's relationship with the management. The conflict between the TSU and the management was accentuated due to their association with rival political parties.

Summary and conclusion

The fact that the sugar cane growers belonged to different castes influenced the course of the establishment of the factory. While the dominant Marathas were keen to start the factory, the minority castes were hesitant to join hands with them. Their hesitation was not due to doubts about the economic utility of such a venture. They were quite aware of the benefits derived from joining a sugar cooperative, but they feared it would make the Marathas more powerful and dominant. They joined the factory ultimately when they realized that they could not prevent its emergence.

The fear of the minority castes was not entirely imaginary. The Marathas do dominate the affairs of the factory, and to some extent it has added to their power as compared to the other castes. The Marathas enjoy cumulative advantages. Controlling the factory helps them to control other organizations, which in turn helps them to retain their hold over the factory. However, the minority castes are helped, to some extent, by factional divisions among the Marathas. The former try to take advantage of this in securing greater representation in the board and in getting their voice heard. They also try to achieve this objective by voting in favour of candidates of their own caste across the panel.

Caste is one of the factors influencing the workers' attitude and behaviour towards the union and management in Kisan. The local workers belonging to peasant castes—preferably Maratha—and having kinship ties with shareholders and directors feel more secure in their jobs and entertain greater hopes of rising in their career in the factory. This does not, however, mean that caste decides everything in one's favour. Factional divisions among directors may at times harm the interests of the local workers. For the other workers the union is the main protector of their interests.

Thus we find that although caste divisions among shareholders, directors and workers influence their attitudes and behaviour in certain ways, it has not affected the successful working of the factory. The factory was established in spite of reservations on the part of the minority castes. The board manages to function on democratic lines and a smooth transfer of power has taken place between the rival factions in spite of the divisions among directors on caste lines. The very fact that the rival factions are multi-caste alliances is an indication that caste plays a minor part in their organization. Similarly, the existence of the TSU has helped to create a certain sense of security among the workers who do not belong to the dominant caste or who do not have supporters in the management. Seen in this perspective, it would appear that the traditional institution of caste has not prevented the successful working of a cooperative. The latter, it is true, had to make an adjustment to the former in the given environment. This finding goes against those who believe that caste is a major barrier in the process of economic development, industrialization and the growth of democratic institutions in so-called traditional Indian society.

I should like to say a word about the role of the dominant caste in this process. It cannot be denied that the ventures like Kisan have emerged and succeeded largely through the dynamic leadership provided by the Marathas. This contribution of the Marathas is facilitated by the fact that they enjoy a decisive dominance in the social, economic and political fields. They control not only the cooperatives but also the *panchayat* bodies, the ruling party, and through it the state government. Their position of power in wider politics has helped them to take a successful lead in cooperatives. This leading position of the Marathas certainly bestows greater benefits and advantages upon them. In the process, however, other caste groups also gain something. This gain would not have accrued to them without the leadership of the Marathas. The question may be raised here as to whether this process will not widen the gap between the Marathas and the others. Will this not make the Marathas more powerful? It may be argued that cooperatives should aim at safeguarding the interests of the weaker sections in society and should strive to improve their lot. They should not, at least, make stronger those who are already strong. The answer to this argument would be that the establishment of equality among the different sections in a society cannot be achieved only or mainly through cooperatives.

It has to be achieved on several fronts through many other measures. I would also like to point out that the role of the dominant caste in the social, economic and political development of Indian society still awaits a fuller analysis.

The point may be raised whether cooperatives like Kisan are not permeated with a capitalist spirit. Without going into a detailed discussion, I would say that the study of Kisan does not support such a conclusion. One has to compare here the part played by the cooperative sugar factories in the life of the people in the area with that played by the private sector factories which have existed for a much longer period in the same area. The observation that these cooperatives are capitalistic in spirit is often based on a partial view of their being dominated by a few well-to-do peasants and the intense struggle for power which goes on in them. If one viewed the functions performed by these cooperatives in their totality one may not reach such a hasty conclusion.

References

Bailey, F. G. (1957), *Caste and the economic frontier*, Manchester University Press.
— (1963), *Politics and social change: Orissa in 1959*, California University Press.
Baviskar, B. S. (1968a), 'Union politics and management politics', *Indian Journal of Industrial Relations*, 3, pp. 300–315.
— (1968b), 'Cooperatives and politics', *Economic and Political Weekly*, III, pp. 490–5.
Béteille, André (1969), 'Caste and politics in Tamilnad' in *Castes: old and new*, Asia Publishing House, Bombay.
Epstein, T. S. (1962), *Economic development and social change in South India*, Manchester University Press.
Mayer, A. C. (1967), 'Caste and local politics in India' in *India and Ceylon: unity and diversity*, ed. Philip Mason, Oxford University Press, London.
Rao, M. S. A. (1964), 'Caste and the Indian army', *Economic Weekly*, XVI, pp. 1439–43.
— (1968), 'Political elite and caste association', *Economic and Political Weekly*, III, pp. 779–82.
Srinivas, M. N. (1959), 'The dominant caste in Rampura', *American Anthropologist*, 61, pp. 1–16.
— (1962), 'Caste in modern India' in *Caste in modern India and other essays*, Asia Publishing House, Bombay.
Whyte, W. F. (1943), *Street corner society*, Chicago University Press.

Acknowledgements

I am grateful to Professor R. P. Dore of the Institute of Development Studies, University of Sussex, for many acts of kindness, and to the Institute for giving me the opportunity to participate in the conference. Professor M. S. A. Rao guided me through all the stages of this study. Professors A. M. Shah and P. M. Worsley made valuable suggestions on the earlier draft; I am grateful to both of them.

Henry Landsberger & Cynthia Hewitt de Alcantara
From violence to pressure-group politics and cooperation: a Mexican case study

The break-up of a *hacienda* and its replacement by a complex, though still fragile, web of peasant organizations is the story which we shall recount and analyse in this chapter. It is a case study limited to one *municipio*.[1] This naturally prevents us from generalizing with much confidence, so that our conclusions are little more than hypotheses for further exploration. Primarily, we hope that the facts we have covered, and our analysis of them, will stimulate discussion of two major issues. First, we hope to raise questions about the multiplicity of conditions that may need to be fulfilled at the grass-roots level before an agrarian reform programme can be put into practice against tenacious local resistance, even after it has become the law of the land at the national level. Second, we hope to portray the web of organizations which may emerge after land reform has taken place, and to raise questions about the conditions under which such an organizational web may grow. We had expected to find little more than a single, government-sponsored peasant federation, imposed at the time of reform and stable thereafter. In fact we found neither stability over time nor a single monolithic structure, but a much richer and more complex situation.

The study itself was conducted in the *municipio* of Taretan, an area devoted to the cultivation of sugar cane in the state of Michoacán, south-west of Mexico City. Information on the history of the agrarian movement in the region was obtained in large part from unstructured interviews with residents of Taretan and with former leaders of the movement. Documents in the archives of the Confederación Nacional Campesina (CNC)[2] and the De-

---

[1] A *municipio* is equivalent to a 'township' or a small 'county' in the US; a 'rural district' in Britain, i.e. it is smaller than an English county. A *hacienda* is, or was, a large landed estate usually employing many peasants in practically serf-like conditions of dependence. Its owner is a *hacendado*.

[2] National Peasant Confederation. *Campesino* is the Spanish term for

20—T.B.O.G.

partment of Agrarian Affairs[3] in Mexico City were also consulted. The data obtained from these sources were predictably complex and in part contradictory. Nevertheless, the following sketch of the struggle for land in Taretan should provide some basis for comparison with other regions of Mexico and Latin America.

Information on the current status of peasant organizations in the *municipio*, their demands, resources, structure and effectiveness, was gathered in several ways. First, and perhaps most important, we were participant observers: we attended a decisive meeting in the struggle to replace the leadership of the Regional Union of Cane Producers; we watched the election of a new ejidal committee (*comisariado ejidal*);[4] we were often present when delegates of credit societies received weekly payments from the Banco Ejidal (the government bank specifically established to give credit to *ejidatarios*); and we sat in the offices of *campesino* organizations while problems of various kinds were discussed.

A second way in which we gained impressions about the current state of *campesino* organizations in Taretan was simply through unstructured interviews with leaders and members of various associations. In other instances, interviews with leaders were structured by using a very broad interview guide, including such topics as the history of the organization, its finances, contact with state and national entities, and current programmes. These interviews were supplemented by an analysis of documents found in the files of the Regional Union of Cane Producers, the local

---

'peasant', perhaps conveying somewhat more the flavours of poverty and generalized low status than does the English term. Certainly the English 'farmer' has a more substantial and prosperous ring than does *campesino*.

[3] The Department of Agrarian Affairs is the government agency specifically charged with administering claims to land under the various applicable statutes; the setting up of *ejidos*, including the holding of elections; the adjudication of disputes within *ejidos*, etc. It is therefore not a 'Ministry of Agriculture' in the usual sense.

[4] *Ejido* is the basic, collective, land-holding unit in the Mexican agrarian reform system, as the ownership of land is not given to the individual *campesino* but to the *ejido*, a collective entity which has an elected executive board (*comisariado ejidal*) to govern it. The individual who is a member of an *ejido* (the individual *ejidatario*) does, however, have the right to use the plot of land assigned to him, even though he cannot sell it or, in theory, rent it. Moreover, farm operations are for the most part individually managed: there are only a few *ejidos colectivos* left in Mexico, even though this had been the fundamental idea in the minds of many who advocated agrarian reform. Nevertheless, while totally collective operations are rare, 'mixed' systems are not uncommon, e.g. common ploughing, perhaps crop dusting, etc.

Union of Sugar Mill Workers, the sugar mill (*ingenio*) 'Taretan' itself, the Liga de Comunidades Agrarias de Michoacán,[5] the CNC in Mexico City, and the Department of Agrarian affairs.

We shall now trace the early history of the efforts of peasants and other local residents to organize themselves in order to expropriate the huge *hacienda* which dominated the Taretan area; then examine the struggle for leadership of the organizations which sprang up in the process; and finally go on to analyse how the different interest groups which now exist in the zone articulate with each other.

I. *Historical development*

1. *Agrarian agitation and change in the system of land tenure in Taretan, 1917–37*

Land in the *municipio* of Taretan is now divided between nine *ejidos* (including 640 *ejidatarios*) and approximately 100 small privately owned properties. The average size of each *ejidal* parcel is about six hectares (fifteen acres),[6] private properties are in general even smaller, although a few land-owners have as many as thirty-seven hectares (almost 100 acres). Such a pattern of land tenure was created during the period 1920–37, and a brief look at its historical roots will provide some bases for generalization on the role of peasant organizations in promoting agrarian reform.

Until 1932 almost all the land of Taretan was part of the Hacienda de Taretan y Anexos—an estate reputedly covering more than 30,000 acres, owned by a Spanish family. The *hacienda* was managed by a Mexican. A large part of its irrigated land was devoted to the cultivation of sugar cane, refined in a *trapiche*, or primitive mill, on the outskirts of the little town of Taretan, which was the centre of the *municipio* of the same name. A few

[5] The League of Agrarian Communities: the state level in the organizational structure of the CNC, as will be further explained below. Each *ejido* belongs to a regional committee; the latter to a state 'league'; these in turn to the Confederación Nacional Campesina (CNC); and the latter, finally, is one of the three main bases of the dominant Mexican party: the Institutionalized Revolutionary Party (PRI), which generally obtains between 80 and 90% of the votes cast in national presidential elections.

[6] One hectare is approximately two and a half acres, i.e. each *ejidatario* cultivates about fifteen acres. It is, of course, extremely difficult to estimate the number of people belonging to *ejidos*, and of small land-owners, who rent land. Nevertheless, it is safe to say that renting does not fundamentally alter the predominant pattern of small parcels, individually farmed. The average size of ejidal plots is based on a sample of forty *ejido* members.

well-to-do owners of orchards joined the retinue of the *hacienda*
and the business–professional class of the town to constitute the
privileged group of the region. In its heyday the little town of
Taretan was quite alive, supporting its own newspaper and even
a concert band. The rest of the population of the region provided
the work-force of the estate and servants for the town.

The first challenge to the *hacienda* system in Taretan came
not as the result of peasant agitation but as a response to the
promulgation of the constitution of 1917,[7] and the passage of
subsequent agrarian laws and decrees at the national level. In
1920 135 petitioners presented a request to the Department of
Agrarian Affairs for the establishment of an *ejido* in the *municipio* of Taretan. By no means were all the petitioners landless
labourers. The large range of interests represented within the
group of petitioners is illustrated by the results of a later census
taken by the Department of Agrarian Affairs. Almost one-third
of the petitioners for land in Taretan were not peasants at all
but businessmen, craftsmen or professionals from the town itself.
The remaining two-thirds of the group were predominantly day
labourers on the *hacienda*, with a few small land-owners also
included.

The owner of the *hacienda* engaged in a double strategy to
protect his land from claims under the new laws. First, beginning in 1926, land of the estate was offered for sale in parcels
of twelve to seventeen acres. The price of each acre may have
been sufficiently high to ensure that buyers would have to come
from the urban middle class, not from the day labourers on the
hacienda.[8] The majority of the small land-owners found in the

---

[7] The constitution of 1917 was a milestone in the Mexican revolution. It
by no means ended the prolonged period of turmoil which began with the
fall of the dictator Porfirio Diaz in 1910. But key articles formed the basis
for the expropriation of *haciendas*; the establishment of *ejidos*, the right of
industrial labour to organize, etc. What had begun as a middle class revolt
to acquire political rights thus deepened into a slow but reasonably substantial, though not complete, change in social and economic structure. The
Mexican revolution is a highly complex phenomenon, so that finding the
right adjectives to describe it is correspondingly difficult! The slowness of
change, in the face of overt opposition and other obstacles, is precisely
what this study hopes to illustrate.

[8] Letters from the estate owner in the files of the Department of Agrarian
Affairs show that irrigated land was offered for sale at prices ranging from
thirty to a hundred pesos per hectare, and non-irrigated land at prices from
ten to fifty pesos per hectare. Several former leaders of the agrarian movement stated in interviews that the price in fact demanded by the owner was
too high for any day labourer to pay.

municipio today seem to have inherited or bought parcels originally obtained from the *hacienda* during that period.[9]

A second strategy of the owner for the defence of his property was the donation of 1,500 hectares of poor land to the government, to be used for the foundation of *ejidos*. He was then able to argue that the later petitions for land were in fact not so-called 'original claims', under the law, but a request for an *ampliación* (or 'additional grant of land') and as such legally untenable because it did not fulfil certain required conditions. Representatives of the petitioners had, however, very shrewdly refused to accept the poor land offered by the *hacienda*; hence they regarded themselves as making an 'original' claim and demanded the division of the entire estate. Thus began here—as was so typical all over in Mexico—a prolonged legal and administrative battle, of sole (but actually little) benefit to the land-owner, while immensely frustrating to the peasantry.

Processing of the 1920 petition by the Department of Agrarian Affairs went on for twelve years before permission to found an *ejido* in Taretan was granted. In the meantime the economy of the *municipio* declined markedly. The manager of the *hacienda* retrenched, converting more and more of the cane-fields into pasture for cattle. Unemployment among day labourers was the result. At the same time the town of Taretan lost most of the commercial and cultural patronage of the *hacienda*: stores closed, the concert band and newspaper disappeared. Inhabitants of the town even found it difficult to obtain water and wood, usually supplied by the *hacienda*.

The delay in processing the petition for an *ejido* in Taretan was no doubt encouraged by a lack of grass-roots support for the claim. It is a fact (lamented in several interviews by men who led the agrarian movement in the zone) that there was no open agitation by peasants for the destruction of the *hacienda* until 1929. Revolutionaries who passed through the region from time to time were unable to convince day labourers of the estate that they should, or could, divide the land. And such hesitation was encouraged by the local clergy, who campaigned hard for the primacy of heavenly over earthly rewards for the faithful.

It was only after a long period of decline in the strength of the *hacienda*, briefly described above, that peasant organizations appeared in Taretan. The first of those organizations were two

---

[9] A generalization made by former leaders of the agrarian movement.

unions (*sindicatos*) of day labourers, one in Taretan itself and one in the outlying settlement of Purisima. These *sindicatos* were established in 1929 under the aegis of the newly formed CRMT, the Confederación Revolucionaria Michoacana de Trabajo, a state-wide labour and peasant federation founded by the then governor of the state of Michoacán, Lázaro Cárdenas. Cárdenas was to be President of Mexico from 1934 to 1940 and from then on a legendary figure and a hero to the non-communist left precisely because of the vigorous agrarian reform policy he pursued in those years, and his nationalization of foreign-owned oil companies. At this time, as governor of the state of Michoacán in the late 'twenties, his aim was to unite peasants and industrial workers in the struggle against exploitative employers and *hacendados* in the state of Michoacán. The purpose of the Taretan unions in the late 'twenties was not so much to petition for land as to demand higher wages and better living conditions for members. They encountered immediate opposition from armed squads organized by the *hacienda*, and the first 'martyr' of the movement died shortly after their founding. His picture still appears in a mural over the doorway of the old Confederación building in Morelia—now the headquarters of the state league of the National Campesino Confederation (CNC).

The real turning point in the struggle for land came in 1930, when a group of outstanding leaders gained control of the two existing unions of day labourers and began to organize other groups of peasants into committees to petition for the establishment of *ejidos*. Those leaders, for purposes of this report, will be called the four 'L' brothers and their close friend 'S.R.' They were the sons of well-to-do local owners of orchards; they had recently graduated from a School of Agronomy in Morelia; and they were inspired by the radical agrarian philosophy of General Múgica, whom they describe as their 'ideological father'. In any discussion of the agrarian movement in Taretan, and the later formation of peasant pressure groups there, the names of the 'L' brothers and 'S.R.' appear constantly. For over twenty years (1932–55) they controlled municipal politics, and in fact held important offices in state federations and national directorates of peasant organizations.

The 'Ls' not only organized peasants to support the long delayed petition for an *ejido* in Taretan, they also established important political contacts with the Partido Nacional Revolucionario (PNR), the predecessor of the PRI, and with the Confederación

Revolucionaria Michoacana (CRMT). Thus, after the 'Ls' assumed leadership of the struggle for land in 1930, letters from the PRN and the CRMT appear in the files of the Department of Agrarian Affairs in support of the Taretan petition. It is also clear that Cárdenas, who was then governor of Michoacán, took a personal interest in the 'Ls'' work. Within two years of the initiation of the 'Ls'' campaign for land in Taretan, Cárdenas signed documents expropriating approximately 6,300 acres of *hacienda* land (about 2,500 of which were irrigated) to be divided among 353 *ejidatarios*.

The victory of the 'Ls' over representatives of the *hacienda* signalled the beginning of a new and more critical period in the history of the agrarian movement in Taretan. The 'Ls' organized other groups of petitioners for *hacienda* land, often convincing members of established peasant *sindicatos* to stop agitating merely for high wages and to join the ranks of those who wanted a complete change in the agrarian structure of the region, i.e. to demand land for themselves and the expropriation of the *haciendas*. Letters like the following were sent to the office of the state governor:

Up till now we have fought for our economic independence through unions [*sindicatos*]. But we now realize that while the land and the other means of production continue to be in the hands of the privileged classes our efforts will come to naught. We have therefore decided to transform ourselves from unions into agrarian groups. . . .[10]

Those petitioners were forced to fight pitched battles with the *guardias blancas* ('white guards', the armed squads hired by large land-owners) of the *hacienda*, as well as to combat the more subtle tactics of the *hacendados*. One of the most serious obstacles to successful peasant organization throughout the period of struggle for land in Taretan continued to be the cautiousness of many peasants—their inability to believe that organization could really better their lot. One of the 'L' brothers recalls, for instance, that within a group of a hundred day labourers on a *hacienda* he considered himself lucky to find ten who would agree to sign a petition for land. The following excerpt from a letter sent to the Department of Agrarian Affairs indicates the difficulties which organizers encountered. Signed by eighty-four *campesinos*, it

[10] A letter dated 9 July 1936, found in the files of the Department of Agrarian Affairs. The letter-head reads 'Sindicato de Campesinos "Julio Antonio Mella".'

protested against the presentation of a petition to establish an
ejido in the little hamlet of Purisima, in the township of Taretan:

We have the broadest imaginable guarantees in our work and great
possibilities for improving our economic situation. But above all, we
have freedom to work and freedom of action, which we never had
while the leaders [presumably: union leaders] of the region were living
off our dues and exploiting our peasant ingenuousness.[11]

The owner's hand was also strengthened by the new governor
of Michoacán, Benigno Serrato. Elected to succeed Cárdenas in
1932, Serrato tried to undo the work of his predecessor and to
protect estate owners against the demands of petitioners for land.
Real repression of agrarian organizations apparently took place
under his administration and probably with his connivance.

Faced with the open hostility of the governor of the state, the
legal manoeuvres of estate owners and the reluctance of the
peasants themselves, the 'L' brothers might well have failed in
their programme of organizing peasants to request land. That
they did not fail must be credited in large measure to the assistance of General Cárdenas, who soon became President of the
Republic (1934–40). He authorized the commanding general of
the unit of the national army stationed in Michoacán to supply
the 'Ls' with arms and ammunition. And after the 'Ls' and 'S.R.'
had talked personally with him about the situation in Taretan,
Cárdenas issued a presidential decree in 1937 expropriating
2,500 acres from the Hacienda 'Patuan', a similar quantity from
the Hacienda 'Taretan', and slightly less from the Hacienda 'Purisima' (all were part of the Taretan complex).

The initial stage in the agrarian reform of the region was
thereby brought to a close. The power of the estate owner was
effectively broken; it required little violence to acquire the land
for the remaining *ejidos* in the *municipio*—a process completed
by 1944. In fact many former members of the *guardias blancas*
were converted to the agrarian cause by the success of the 'Ls',
and asked to receive land in the new *ejidos*.

This sketch of the history of agrarianism in Taretan suggests
that the active participation of organized peasants was really of
only secondary importance in the success of the movement in
Taretan. The first stimulus to agrarian reform was the passage
of a national law—which, as Albert Hirschman has noted, often

[11] A letter dated 27 August 1936, found in the files of the Department of
Agrarian Affairs.

allows the development of far more radical programmes than its sponsors ever intended. Originally, however, the possibility of obtaining land was seized upon by a group which included a large number of persons who were not peasants at all but business and professional men from the town.

Several factors appear to have been of primary importance later in the eventual establishment of a much more radical and aggressive peasant organization. First, of course, was the arrival of young, ideologically-oriented leaders who certainly did not come from the peasant class. Second, the previous long period of decline in the strength of the *hacienda* encouraged organization, and the early victories of the 'Ls' added followers to the movement. However, it is important to note that the agrarian movement in Taretan was throughout its history supported only by a minority of the peasants in the region.

Perhaps the single most important cause of the eventual success of the movement was the assistance of General Cárdenas. It was he who transmitted the original petition for the Ejido 'Taretan' to the Department of Agrarian Affairs as early as 1920, during his term as provisional governor of Michoacán. It was also Cárdenas who, as constitutional governor of the state, approved the original grant of land to Taretan in 1932. And, as President of the Republic in 1937, Cárdenas decreed the division of a substantial part of the land still remaining in the *hacienda*. It is doubtful whether the agrarian movement in Taretan would have succeeded if a less interested man had occupied these high positions.

2. The founding of peasant interest-groups in Taretan, 1937–55

Perhaps the most outstanding characteristic of the peasant movement in Taretan today is the sheer number of organizational units which exist there. Briefly, these units include nine *ejidos*, an equal number of ejidal credit societies,[12] one smallholders' credit society, a cattle-men's association, a smallholders' protective association, a union of mill workers and a regional association of cane producers. Reasons for their founding will be discussed below.

Leadership in the establishment of peasant organizations after

[12] *Ejidatarios* may, generally do, but need not form credit societies. Only such societies are given credit by the Ejido Bank.

the division of the *hacienda*, as before, came from the 'L' family
and their close friends. The efforts of that group may be divided
into two distinct periods. The first, from 1937 to 1946, was
characterized by the consolidation of gains won during the recent
agrarian struggle. During this period they founded *ejidos* and
credit societies, and integrated them into the existing national
system of political representation and economic assistance. The
second period, from 1947 to roughly 1955, was shaped, first, by
the construction of a sugar mill in the region—which encouraged
the growth of new kinds of pressure group—and, second, by the
decision of the 'Ls' to withdraw from the dominant national party
in order to establish a new central organization of peasants and
workers.

The first period of organization, 1937–46. Given the relatively
radical political philosophy of the 'Ls', it seems certain that they
would have organized new recipients of land in some form, even
had they received no encouragement from above to do so. In fact,
however, their efforts were shaped by Mexican agrarian legislation, which defined the formal structure of groups receiving land
from the government. Separate laws later incorporated in the
Agrarian Code provided that an executive board (*comisariado
ejidal*) of six peasants had to be elected in each *ejido*, and defined
the functions of that board, as well as the rights and duties of
individual members of the *ejido*. Thus neither the 'Ls' nor individual peasants influenced the form taken by initial post-revolutionary organizations.

Given the lack of previous experience on the part of *ejido*
members with managing their own land and their own government, it is not surprising that numerous problems plagued the
new organizations. Attempts to farm ejidal land collectively,
encouraged by the law of 1934, failed in every instance after one
or two years. Almost invariably, a small group of *ejido* members
gained control of the executive board and used the position to
withhold the best land for themselves. The rank and file soon
rebelled against collective farm practices, and some form of
provisional division of land ensued.

Another serious problem of the new *ejidos* was absenteeism.
A large number of the original recipients of land simply abandoned it during subsequent years. Figures obtained from a census
taken in the Ejido 'Taretan' by the Department of Agrarian Affairs
in 1940 illustrate the point:

Ejido members in possession of their parcel	108
Ejido members absent from the community	65
Names listed on the original petition, but un- known in the *ejido*	11
Ejido members dedicated to commerce	15
Dead without heirs	49
Dead with heirs	38
Repeated names	4
'Those who have not wanted to belong to the *ejido*'	60
Others	9
Total	359

Thus, of a total of 359 original *ejidatarios*, only 108 were still in possession of their parcel some five years after they had obtained land in Taretan.

A second kind of grass-roots organization appeared in Taretan during the late 1930s. Like the *ejido*, its foundation was determined by the passage of a national law. The Banco Nacional de Credito Ejidal established a regional office in Taretan in 1937, headed by one of the 'L' brothers. Guided by the provisions of the Agricultural Credit Law, the Bank encouraged the formation of credit societies in each of the new *ejidos*. The functioning of those societies did not differ significantly from present practice, to be described in some detail at a later point.

Both *ejidos* and credit societies were grouped into a Confederación Regional de Campesinos y Obreros de Taretan, the Regional Confederation of Peasants and Workers of Taretan, founded by the 'L' family as early as 1930. This was affiliated at the state level with the Confederación Revolucionaria Michoacana de Trabajo. It should be mentioned that, apart from its ostensible purpose of encouraging peasants in their struggle for land, the function of the latter organization was at the same time to build a basis of political support for Cárdenas and his followers. The purpose of the 'Ls' regional confederation was similarly dual: to help peasants *and* to give the 'Ls' a political base. Leaders of the regional confederation occupied high posts in the CRMT at the state level. One of the 'L' brothers was, in fact, the last Secretary of Organization of the CRMT (during the period 1936–38).

In 1939 Cárdenas himself (by that time President of the Republic) dissolved the old CRMT as part of his plan to reorganize all the peasants and workers of Mexico separately into two new organizations—the Confederación Nacional Campesina (CNC) and the Confederación de Trabajadores de Mexico (CTM) respectively. This separation of peasants from industrial workers was probably a deliberate step on the part of Cárdenas to prevent the formation of too powerful a mass organization. Within this new dual organizational structure the *peasant* sector of the CRMT simply became a state affiliate of the Confederación Nacional Campesina, while the industrial workers were affiliated with the CTM. In the process the name of the CRMT was changed to the Liga de Comunidades Agrarias y Sindicatos Campesinos de Michoacán. Thus the regional (Taretan) confederation of the 'Ls' was automatically linked to the CNC.

The statutes of the CNC provided for the processing of peasant demands through a hierarchy of organizations, beginning at the local or regional level with a 'regional peasant committee' (*comité regional campesino*), to be elected by the *comisariados* (executive board) of all *ejidos* within the region. In Taretan that *comité* was of course nothing more than the regional confederation of the 'L' brothers. Despite this reorganization, then, there was no real challenge to the leadership of the 'Ls' and no change in the functioning of local peasant organizations after the establishment of the CNC in 1939.

The second period of organization, 1947–55. A new period in the organization of peasants in Taretan began with the construction of a sugar mill there in 1946, owned by the Banco Nacional de Credito Ejidal (BNCE). Members of the 'L' group had asked as early as 1937 that the mill, which was formerly owned by a private individual, be moved to Taretan from another part of the state and placed under the control of the Ejido Bank in Taretan. They hoped in that way to provide an industry which could eventually be owned and operated by the peasants and mill workers of the region. Their request was partially granted in 1946, when the mill was moved to Taretan. But the Bank never agreed to turn the factory over completely to peasants and workers—though the 'Ls' were able to ensure that the local administrators of the enterprise, from the time of its founding until 1955, were members of their family or men sympathetic to their programme.

It was inevitable that the introduction of a relatively sophisticated new factory in the region would produce changes in the organizational life of Taretan. The establishment of the mill created a group of factory workers who could be unionized; it distributed much larger amounts of credit to cane growers than those previously available, and therefore required more extensive credit supervision; and it produced a continually increasing num-per of peasant cane growers, with more and more interests in common.

The establishment of the mill in the period after world war II coincided roughly with the decision of the 'Ls' to withdraw from the CNC and to join others in the founding of a new, more left-oriented, national organization of peasants and workers, the Unión General de Obreros y Campesinos de Mexico (UGOCM), the General Union of Workers and Peasants. UGOCM was thus set up to rival the CNC and the CTM. The 'Ls'' decision was based on a thorough distrust of the motives behind the creation of the new PRI, the Partido Revolucionario Institucional, the government-sponsored successor of the PNR. The PRI, of course, controlled the CNC and the CTM just as the PNR had done earlier. The distrust of the 'Ls' was shared by friends of theirs such as Jacinto López, later to become Secretary General of UGOCM, and they established a new left-oriented political party to complement the UGOCM: the Partido Popular, rival to the PRI. In 1949, therefore, the 'Ls' withdrew from the government-controlled CNC, refused to join the PRI and became a part of UGOCM and the Partido Popular. All organizational activity in the *municipio* from 1949 to 1955 took place under the banner of UGOCM and the Partido Popular (PP—later the PPS, the Partido Popular Socialista). The leaders of existing *ejidos* and credit societies apparently followed the 'Ls' out of the CNC without any opposition.

During the first year after the establishment of UGOCM the 'Ls' organized a union of sugar mill workers in Taretan, affiliated with UGOCM through the regional confederation of the 'Ls'. The union was apparently founded to strengthen the political base of its leaders and of the PPS in the *municipio*. Defence of the workers against the management of the mill could not have been the most important function of this union, since that management was already under the control of the 'L' brothers!

It was also in 1949 that a regional union of cane producers was created, under the direction of the 'Ls', to unite the credit societies then operating with credit from the Ejido Bank to supply the Bank's mill with cane. The reasons for the creation of this union were obviously quite similar to those underlying the establishment of the mill workers' union. Because the number of cane growers increased each year, and all were forced by law to be members of ejidal credit societies in order to receive credit, a regional association of those credit societies provided a strong basis of political support for the 'L' family.

UGOCM, at the national level, considered the possibility of organizing cane producers sufficiently promising to encourage them to establish, in January 1953, the Federación Nacional de Productores de Caña. Representatives of all nine of the Taretan credit societies attended the first general congress of the Federation, and 'S.R.' (long a protégé of the 'Ls') was elected its first Organizing Secretary.

Legislators in the capital of Michoacán apparently also realized the political advantages of encouraging the formation of peasant pressure groups. In 1954 they passed the State Cattle Law, which specifically required cattlemen to join organizations which might represent them before the government. The Unión Ganadera de Michoacán (Cattle-men's Union of the State of Michoacán) sent a letter to the municipal president of Taretan during the same year, asking him to call a convention of cattle-men and to form a regional association of cattle owners. Since the municipal president at the time was 'S.R.' the new interest group was immediately controlled by the PPS—a result probably not intended by the state (PRI-controlled) legislators who initiated the project!

3. The third period of organization (1955 to the present)

The latest period in the history of organizational efforts in Taretan began with the overthrow of the 'L' machine in 1955. It was entirely natural that an organization as strong as the regional confederation of the 'Ls', affiliated with the PPS, would cause concern in various quarters. At the national level, it seems likely that the PRI saw the necessity of capturing Taretan from the PPS. As early as 1949 the tax collector in the *municipio* began organizing a local branch of the PRI, and it is generally agreed that he received increasing support from above as time passed. Similarly, the directorate of the Banco Ejidal in Mexico City opposed the 'Ls'. Not only was the national directorate of the Bank composed of members of the PRI, but it was also reported to have been frightened by the 'Ls' plan to turn the mill over to the peasants and workers of Taretan. Therefore, although the local administrator of the mill remained loyal to the 'Ls' until their overthrow, the Bank apparently sent other representatives to the *municipio* to encourage defection by individual *ejidatarios*.

The immediate cause of the eventual defeat of the 'L' machine was the murder of 'E.L.', the most outstanding of the 'L' brothers, in 1950. Most of his followers ascribe his death to henchmen of the PRI. Others suggest that he was shot by a personal enemy, a *cacique* (boss) from a neighbouring *municipio*. Whoever might have been responsible for his death, the fact remains that without his leadership the regional confederation declined rapidly. His brother 'J.L.', who assumed control of the *municipio* after 'E.L.'s' death, had neither the latter's intelligence nor his personal charm. According to several informants, 'J.L.' relied far too heavily on force and the threat of force to carry out his orders; by 1955 he had succeeded in alienating most of the former supporters of the 'L' programme in Taretan. It should be noted that acts of violence—gun battles in the *plaza* or in bars or restaurants; peppering houses with shots at night—have been a matter of course in Taretan for a long time. In the case of many incidents there is doubt whether or not a political motive might also be involved.

The first organization to withdraw from the regional confederation was the mill workers' union. After several years of discussion behind the scenes a group of workers went to Mexico City in 1955 to ask that the Taretan union change its affiliation from UGOCM to the PRI-controlled CTM (Confederación de Trabajadores de Mexico). They charged that the union had not won any benefits for its members in years because its leaders were under the control of the manager of the mill, one of the 'L' brothers. At first, the executive committee of the National Union of Sugar Mill Workers of the CTM doubted that Taretan could be taken from the PPS and its union equivalent, the UGOCM. It finally consented, however, to call a general meeting of the Taretan workers. At that meeting, which was marked by brawls and demonstrations, members of the union overwhelmingly voted to withdraw from UGOCM and to join the CTM. The present section 11 of the National Union of Sugar Mill Workers was thereupon established.

The second, and critical, defection from the 'Ls'' regional confederation also occurred in 1955, when representatives of seven of the nine *ejidos* of Taretan wrote to the League of Agrarian Communities (the state level of the CNC) asking that their *ejidos* be affiliated with the CNC rather than UGOCM. As a result of

that letter, general meetings were held in each *ejido* during the
month of November in order to obtain petitions, signed by large
numbers of *ejidatarios*, asking that the CNC re-enter Taretan.
It will be recalled that all *ejidos* had belonged to the CNC in
the period 1939–49, before the 'L' brothers left it to help establish
UGOCM. Shortly thereafter the regional association of cane producers, a unit of UGOCM's National Federation of Cane Producers, was replaced by a so-called *circulo cañero* (sugar producers' group) which joined the CNC's National Union of Cane
Producers.

The power of the 'Ls' was broken. They tried for several years
after 1955 to regain control of the *municipio* but failed, and
finally the family found it necessary to leave Taretan. In 1961
their rights as members of the *ejido* in which they held land were
revoked. Although a few workers and peasants tried to remain
loyal to the family and to the PPS, at the time of our study in
1966 no one in Taretan could recall a single person who was
willing to acknowledge membership of the PPS after 1958.
Peasant organization is now firmly in the hands of the PRI.

Only two peasant organizations were founded after the defeat
of the 'Ls', and both are made up of small private landowners.
One is the Unión de Pequeños Propietarios de Caña de Azúcar
(Union of Smallholder Cane Producers), a credit society of small
private cane producers specifically established to work with the
Ejidal Bank through the mill. It was created in 1956. According
to the letter of the law, it had no right to exist, for article 5,
paragraph XII of the Agricultural Credit Law expressly prohibited
credit from the Ejidal Bank from being made available to private
landowners. But the local government was beneficial both to the
mill and to this group of private cane producers. The mill, owned
by the Bank, needed more cane than the *ejidos* could produce
in order to survive, while the small private land-owners needed
credit and a guaranteed market for their cane. Therefore, despite
the fact that the law prohibited the creation of smallholders'
credit societies under the Banco Ejidal, the latter seems to have
taken the initiative in the formation of the Smallholders' Union.

The most recent organization founded in Taretan is the Associa-
ción de Pequeños Propietarios (Smallholders' Association).
Much on the pattern of the Cattle-men's Association, the establishment of the local smallholders' interest group was encouraged
by a letter to the *municipio* president from the state federation
of small land-owners. The letter, dated November 1965, requested

that a general meeting be held to form an organization for the defence of private property.

It should be noted that small property owners in Taretan had been organized specifically to defend their interests against the *ejidos* during only one year before 1965, in 1940. At that time it seemed possible that the granting of the definitive title for the Ejido 'Taretan' might nullify the legality of previous sales of small plots by the owner of the old Hacienda 'Taretan'. The 'Ls', however, representing the Ejido 'Taretan', made a pact with the small land-owners assuring them that their property rights would be respected by *ejido* members. Thus reassured, the association of smallholders dissolved immediately. The programme of its successor, now less than a year old, will be discussed in the following sections.

In retrospect we can see that the establishment of organizations in which peasants cooperated with each other to pursue common goals owed much to the existence of *incentives*. Incentives for the establishment of peasant organizations were provided at all levels: national, state, and local. At the *national* level, the formation of peasant interest groups was encouraged by the passage of laws. *Ejidos*, credit societies, cattle-men's associations—all must be established, according to the law, before land is granted, credit extended and (in the case of cattle) before taxes are lowered on sales.

Incentives for the establishment of peasant organizations in Taretan also came from the *state* capital, where a federation of small private land-owners was created to meet the threat, whether real or imagined, emanating from *ejidatarios* who wanted to expand their land holdings at the expense of small land-owners. Also at the state level, a cattle-men's state association was established, again as the result of legal requirements before certain benefits could be obtained. A local unit of both groups was established in Taretan after invitations were received from Morelia, the state capital.

At the *local* level, initiative for the establishment of almost every organization in Taretan was provided by 'E.L.', a charismatic figure who had led the earlier agrarian movement. Since he was assassinated some fifteen years before this study was conducted, it is not easy for us to gauge accurately what his motives were. The impression we have is that both idealism—the eradication of injustice; helping the weak—and the desire for personal and familial power, prestige and wealth played a part. The

21—T.B.O.G.

motives of the 'L' family certainly included personal economic gain. It is a fairly widespread contention that the 'L' brothers monopolized pasture land in the Ejido 'Taretan'. Yet at the same time the 'Ls' made no attempt to appropriate the irrigated land of the community, taking their turn with other *ejidatarios* in the drawing of lots for plots of land. They thus seem to have made only limited use of their power for the promotion of private economic interests.

In any case, and whatever his motives, 'E.L.' worked hard to build a strong organizational basis for reform of the economic and social structure of the *municipio*. The peasants supported 'E.L.'s' programme while he lived; they did not support it when a less able man was forced to take his place.

An additional reason, an economic one, for the formation of interest groups in Taretan was the appearance of the mill in 1946. The introduction of a new enterprise created new groups to be organized, and it altered existing relationships among established entities. The practical needs of the mill also dictated the establishment of one society specifically prohibited by law, the Smallholders' Credit Union.

The question of the role of the peasants themselves in the reorganization of interest groups in Taretan after 'E.L.'s' death is an interesting one, because it suggests that perhaps they learned to direct their own affairs to some extent in the years following the original founding of peasant organizations by the 'Ls'. During the 1940s the peasants followed 'E.L.' from the CNC to the UGOCM without complaint. But the majority of them voted in the general meetings of 1955 to oppose the remainder of the 'L' machine and voted to re-enter the CNC. Were they only following new organizers, sent from the PRI, as they had followed 'E.L.' before? We believe not, for there is little evidence that the PRI made a massive effort to recapture Taretan. Was the prestige of the national government, combined with a vague fear of eventual reprisals, sufficient to force the change? These may well have played a part. Or did *campesino* leaders in Taretan in fact take the initiative in their own reorganization? There is no real way to measure the relative importance of each of those factors after the event. It is our belief, however, that the *campesinos* of Taretan in 1955 were simply a more independent group than their predecessors, and were no longer willing to follow a *cacique*.

Finally, to return to the national level (and for those who have some sympathy with a limited version of the 'great man' theory of history), it is clear that General Lázaro Cárdenas and his political philosophy provided a great deal of impetus for the founding of peasant organizations in Taretan. It was he who supported the programme of the Confederación Revolucionaria Michoacana de Trabajo, and consequently of the 'L' brothers, for the creation of strong unions of workers and peasants. It was also he who ultimately destroyed the CRMT and drew Taretan into the Confederación Nacional Campesina. Both institutional incentives and personal leadership at the local, state and national levels clearly played important parts in this story.

II. *Peasant organizations in a post-revolutionary setting*

1. *Bases for conflict and consensus*

Taretan is now a *municipio* predominantly of cane producers and mill workers, but one in which a growing number of landless peasants petition for the scarce remaining land and, to a lesser extent, for jobs in the mill. Those who cannot find such jobs and who have no land usually become day labourers in cane fields. Some rent the land of widows of *ejidatarios* or work it as share-croppers. Some rent land from private owners. Thus Taretan today has a very heterogeneous population in so far as its relation to the land is concerned: *ejidatarios*, smallholders, tenants, share-croppers, labourers, mill workers, various combinations of these (e.g. mill workers who also have an *ejido* plot *and* rent another), and their sons, daughters and widows.

Mill workers definitely enjoy the most economically privileged status of the groups listed above. They receive a long series of benefits under the nation-wide collective contract of the National Union of Sugar Mill Workers, the Sindicato Nacional de los Trabajadores en la Industria Azúcarera: a well enforced wage scale, which varies from roughly nineteen to sixty-six pesos ($US1·50 to $US5·25) a day; job security; payment for a seventh day per week if the previous six were worked without being absent, i.e. an attendance bonus; paid vacations and holidays; time and a half for night work and dangerous jobs; rent subsidies, etc. Their demands are continually pressed upon the administration of the mill by a strong local union, in contrast to the dissension-ridden cane growers' association.

On the whole, members of *ejidos* are better off—both economically and socially—than are most smallholders. Concerning prestige, table 5—based on the results of a small survey conducted in Taretan[13]—indicates vividly how highly regarded are the members of *ejidos*. Various groups of respondents thought that Mexicans as a whole placed *ejidatarios* either first or second in prestige as compared with other locally relevant groups. Their only rivals in prestige are the mill workers.

Table 5

Perceived national prestige of certain socio-economic groups

(Rank of the average rank given by each group of respondents to the four groups each respondent was asked to rank)

Question: 'Which groups are the most respected by everyone in Mexico?'

	Group ranked				
Respondents	(1) Ejidatarios	(2) Workers	(3) Small-holders	(4) Day labourers	(N)
Ejidal leaders	1	2	3	4	(28)
Ejidal followers	1	2	3	4	(36)
Members of smallholders' credit society	2	1	3	4	(12)
Non-members of smallholders' credit society	2	1	3	4	(6)
Day labourers	1	2	3	4	(20)
Mill workers	2	1	3	4	(21)

In so far as economic status is concerned, the same survey revealed that the average size of holding of the thirty-eight *ejidatarios* interviewed was in the neighbourhood of six hectares (fifteen acres) while that of fourteen out of sixteen private small-holders interviewed was only about 4·4 hectares (about eleven acres) although the two others reported owning ninety-five and fifty acres respectively. The extent of misinformation cannot, of

[13] The total number of peasants interviewed (approximately 130) is not large by modern survey standards. Only one sub-group, *ejido* members, was represented by more than thirty individuals, and non-members of the small-holders' credit society by as few as six. Nevertheless, within each group, individuals were selected substantially on a random basis, and the results appear to be sufficiently clear-cut to inspire some confidence. The Taretan survey was planned as a pilot study, and a much more substantial survey, involving approximately 400 respondents, was conducted by the two authors in the summer of 1967 with the help of the Agricultural Development Council as well as the various entities mentioned in the acknowledgement at the end of this chapter. The report of the larger study is available from the Interamerican Development Bank, Washington, D.C., under the title *Peasant Organizations in La Laguna, Mexico: history, structure, member participation and effectiveness*.

course, be measured, but these figures correspond roughly with our personal impression of the economic status of most private land-owners. We did, however, hear repeatedly that there were one or two large land-owners, whom our survey net clearly did not catch. There may also be a few relatively large cattle-men in the area, though cattle are declining as more and more land is devoted to sugar cane.[14] By and large, however, private small-holders are clearly worse off than *ejido* members—an interesting result of the Mexican revolution at the local level, at least in this area.

The outstanding characteristic of the peasant society outlined above is the diversity of individual interests within it. There are often no clear boundaries between members of *ejidos*, small land-owners, day labourers, tenant farmers and mill workers. Members of *ejidos* almost always work at times as day labourers; they may own a small private plot or rent one from a private owner; and they may very well work in the mill at the same time. This complex structure of economic interests inevitably influences the type of organization found in the *municipio*. Two other facts are of importance in understanding the interaction of peasant groups in Taretan. First, the possibility of forming separate interest groups of richer and poorer peasant factions is lessened by a Mexican government policy of forcing many different kinds of peasants into the same organization. The local cattle-men's association of Taretan is the perfect example of an organization which unites relatively well-to-do cattlemen with men on *ejidos* who own only one cow. It does so because federal and state laws require all cattle-men to join such an association or pay double taxes.

Finally, the fact that the Taretan sugar mill continually encourages the production of more sugar cane has created a group of cane cultivators which now includes some 75 per cent of the inhabitants of the region. *Ejido* members, small land-owners, *rentiers*, mill workers and the relatively wealthy cattle owners—all are likely to plant some cane. And in order to guarantee that the mill will accept it they must belong to a credit society, either ejidal or private. The existence of the mill has therefore placed many different kinds of people within the same organizations and has provided them with a broad range of interests in common.

[14] According to the records of the Unión Ganadera Regional de Michoacán, there were 6,500 head of cattle in the *municipio* of Taretan in 1945. There are now 3,500. No one interviewed in Taretan believes that any cattle-man now has more than 200 heads of cattle.

The interests of all cane growers, whatever their status, can be summarized briefly. Their most basic concern is, of course, to deliver as much cane as possible to the mill at the highest possible price. The mill has always needed more cane than it has received, and for that reason its needs coincide with the interests of growers on the question of increasing the amount of cane delivered to the mill. At the same time the growers have an interest in the efficient functioning of the mill itself because they—like the mill workers—hope to receive a share of the profits of the enterprise. For the past several years, however, the mill has recorded losses.

The cane growers are, of course, extremely interested in obtaining as much credit as possible from the Bank for the cultivation of cane, and ideally they would like to receive credit for other crops as well.[15] They also have an interest in reforming the system of selling sugar at the national level, As it now stands, all mills in the country—whether private or government-run—are regulated by the presidential decrees of 1943 and 1944. The first,[16] signed during a period of sugar shortages during the second world war, declares that in order to ensure a sufficient supply of cane to mills throughout the country the peasants in certain areas surrounding sugar mills will be required by law to devote themselves exclusively to the cultivation of cane. It is that decree on which the present policy of the Ejidal Bank is based: to provide credit in the Taretan area only for the production of cane. The same rationale (the encouragement of cane production) undoubtedly contributed to the fact that cane growers and their dependants are the only peasants in the *municipio* entitled to the services of the national health and welfare service (Seguro Social). Cane producers are thus in some ways the prisoners of the mill, and they would like to see a repeal of the decree.

The second presidential decree, issued in 1944,[17] is even more directly opposed to the interests of cane producers. It establishes the basis for the division of money received for raw sugar between the mill and the growers. As the system now functions, all sugar produced by sugar mills in Mexico must be delivered to the Unión Nacional de Productores de Azúcar, a powerful union formed by representatives of every sugar mill in the republic,

[15] The money received is, of course, often spent on many things aside from the cultivation of cane!
[16] 23 September 1943 (*Avila Camacho*).
[17] 20 April 1944 (*Avila Camacho*).

public and private. UNPASA has complete control over the sale and distribution of sugar, both at home and abroad, although it has no legal right to alter the price of sugar, which is set by the government. After selling the sugar furnished it, UNPASA divides the receipts among the mills which are members of the Unión. Each enterprise then keeps 50 per cent of that amount as payment for the milling of cane and divides the other 50 per cent among local cane producers, in a two-stage process. Cane growers receive a first payment (now about sixty pesos, or $US4·80, per ton) when their cane is first delivered to the mill. After UNPASA pays the mill, cane producers receive a second amount, which, with the earlier payment, equals 50 per cent of the amount given the mill by UNPASA.

Cane growers are unhappy with the arrangement on three counts: first, because they suspect that UNPASA is controlled by a few very wealthy men who cannot be trusted to manage the sale of their sugar; second, because they charge that they should receive more than half the money returned to the mill by UNPASA; third, because they do not like the system of deferred payment.

The specific interests outlined above are common to approximately 75 per cent of the peasants in the *municipio* of Taretan. In addition, cane growers have interests which unite them with those peasants who do not grow cane. All peasants in the *municipio* are extremely interested in obtaining services from the government: electricity, systems for drinking water, better schools, roads, irrigation systems and a more effective crop insurance programme (Seguro Agrícolo). Those who already receive assistance from Social Security want better service, and those who are not eligible as yet would like to be included in the programme.

Thus it is obvious that there is a very wide range of shared interests in the *municipio*. Nevertheless, certain bases for conflict among groups of peasants do exist and should be noted. The most basic is the combination of an almost universal desire for land with a very limited supply of remaining land for distribution. Sons of *ejido* members petition for *ampliaciones* (extension of the *ejido*); day labourers are engaged in an attempt to establish a new *ejido*; and most mill workers who are not already members of *ejidos* or smallholders are apparently extremely anxious to obtain land as well.[18] These competing interests seem to be more latent

[18] Statement based on survey results.

than open at the moment; frank recognition of the need to pre-empt available land before others do so is not evident. The problem will probably grow more serious, however, as time passes. A few smallholders have, in fact, already organized to protect themselves against *ampliacones* and against outright invasions of members of *ejidos*, which they claim to fear.

Other sources of conflict are not hard to discover in Taretan, even for an outsider. Cattle-men, for example, are being crowded off available pasture land by the extension of cane growing in the region. Most seem capable of adapting to the new situation by growing cane themselves, but some cattle-men are more disposed to fight the system than to join it. Another segment of the rural population, the day labourers, have interests which conflict with those of their employers, whether *ejido* members or small farmers. Day labourers receive low wages (about twelve pesos or $us0·96 per day outside the harvest season) and are not organized. Finally, certain interests of mill workers are in conflict with those of the cane growers: the former continually demand benefits from the mill—more jobs, higher wages, remodelling of their local headquarters—and their success in getting these demands met has contributed substantially to the current financial difficulties of the mill.

Despite these latent bases for conflict, the fact remains that the goals of different groups of peasants in Taretan are generally not seen with any degree of clarity by the peasants themselves as mutually incompatible. Some reasons for such 'blindness' have been discussed above: day labourers, members of *ejidos*, smallholders and mill workers may be one and the same. Nevertheless, another reason for relative unity among peasants should be noted: all possible goals seem at the moment to be pursued to a maximum, without consideration of the real need to concentrate on one or two to the detriment of others. The mill is expected at the same time to raise workers' wages and provide them with numerous fringe benefits, carry out social projects in surrounding *ejidos*, pay more money for cane—and still produce profits at the end of each harvest which can be divided among workers and growers.

Not only is conflict *among campesino* organizations surprisingly limited but differences within groups over goals and means are also minimal. Such divisions at the local level as exist are the result of struggles over leadership at the regional or national level of peasant associations and have no local roots. The characteristics of these struggles will become clearer in the following analysis of individual organizations and their relations to the national political system.

2. The organizational spectrum

Ejidos By far the largest number of peasants in Taretan belong to *ejidos*; 640 of them are divided among nine *ejidos* in the *municipio*. At the same time, most of these *ejido* members (some 474) are also members of a credit society. Two organizations thus exist within each *ejido*, as Fig. 10 illustrates. The result is often confusing for members and leaders of both organizations.

Each *ejido* elects an executive board (the *comisariado ejidal*) composed of six members: president, secretary, treasurer and three members who constitute a watchdog committee. The duties of the board are defined by law as the representation of *ejido* members before governmental authorities, the administration of ejidal property in accordance with the law, and the calling of general assemblies which are the ultimate authority of the *ejido*. All decisions of the *comisariado* may be revoked by a majority of the general assembly, and the decisions of both are subject to the approval of the Department of Agrarian Affairs. The *ejido*, in its totality, is thus best conceived of as both a land-owning and a (rural) local government unit.

In practice the functioning of *ejidos* varies considerably within the *municipio* of Taretan. Some, like 'Purisima', seem to operate with a minimum of discontent among members; others, like 'Tomendan', have serious internal splits. Although the causes of these differences are obscure, it can be noted that 'Purisima' is much smaller than 'Tomendan'; it includes many young men who attended the School of Agronomy in Antuñez for a year; and there is apparently much less inequality in size of ejidal parcels in 'Purisima' than in 'Tomendan', and much less open renting of plots.

Differences in the level of mutual trust within *ejidos* seem to be related to differences in their organizational efficiency. In 'Purisima', for example, general meetings are held once a month and attendance is fairly good. In all other *ejidos* sampled, only one or two general meetings had been held in the past year, although more were often scheduled and cancelled for lack of attendance. (In 'Taretan' eight were called, but a simple majority appeared at only one.) Matters discussed at general meetings were similar in all cases: the election of new members of the *comisariado*; the assignment of vacant lots to sons of members or long-time residents of the community; the necessity to obtain definitive titles to ejidal plots; the exploitation of pasture land and forests (if any were included in the *ejido*); and the state of the community's finances.

Important matters seem generally to be considered first by the executive board, which then seeks support through informal discussion with individual members of the *ejido*. The executive

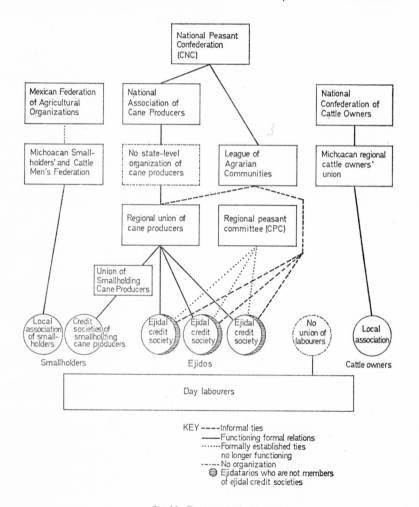

Fig. 10 The organizational spectrum

board of most *ejidos* met two or three times during the past year, although that of 'Tahuejo' met seven times. Topics of conversation were again similar in all *ejidos*: the resolution of boundary problems with other *ejidos*; the need for more irrigation water, or for the cleaning and repairing of the canals; the question of building more rooms for the school or obtaining a second teacher. These matters, unlike questions considered by the general assembly, have more to do with changing the environment of the *ejido* than with merely maintaining its internal organizational structure.

To deal with such problems, members of the *comisariado* generally go directly to Morelia, the state capital, two or three times a year, where they talk to representatives of the CNC at the state level (the Liga de Comunidades Agrarias); to the state delegate of the Department of Agrarian Affairs (on questions of possible *ampliaciones*, definitive title to land, or boundary problems); or to a representative of Fondo de Fomento Ejidal (the government agency which holds funds obtained from the exploitation of ejidal woods and pasture and which must be consulted before such funds can be spent by the *ejido* for such improvements as constructing school-rooms or dams).[19] At times *comisariados* also request assistance from the administration of the mill, which may lend machinery for building projects, make loans or even agree to match funds contributed by cane growers for a specific project (such as the installation of a system of drinking water). The assistance of the mill must, however be channelled through ejidal credit societies, and for that reason the role of *comisariados* in obtaining such aid is only marginal.

It is interesting that the CNC and the government's Department of Agrarian Affairs are extremely weak at the local level. Representatives of both perform few functions in the local problem-solving system. The Department's area officer, who lives in Uruapan, seems to appear in Taretan only when a change in the directorate of an *ejido* is required. For other assistance *comisariados* must go directly to Morelia. Similarly, the *comité regional campesino* (regional peasant committee) of the CNC is little more than a paper organization. At the time when we did our field work the secretary-general of the regional committee (elected in

---

[19] Three of the nine *ejidos* in Taretan have money deposited with the Fondo de Fomento Ejidal in Morelia: 'Tahuejo' (11,040 pesos or $us883); 'Taretan' (66,700 pesos or $us5,336); and 'Tomendan' (33,450 pesos or $us2,676). That money cannot, however, be spent on the expenses of official visits.

a meeting of all executive boards of the region) had been sick ever since his election and had done nothing. A more basic reason for the lack of strength of the regional committee, however, was the existence of a regional union of cane producers which included almost all the *ejido* members supposedly served by the *comité*.

To pay the expenses of two or three trips a year to Morelia (at a cost ranging from 300 to 600 pesos, or $us24 to $us48, per trip, according to the length of stay) most *comisariados* collect a small amount from each member of their *ejido*. If the community has voted to impose dues on its members, money for trips to Morelia may also come from that source. In 'Purisima', for example, each *ejido* member pays 5 per cent of the value of his crops to the ejidal treasury (aside from another 5 per cent paid in taxes) and five to ten pesos ($us0·40 to $us0·80) for each head of cattle sold. In 'Taretan', there is a yearly quota of forty pesos $us3·20) per members, but only ten members have paid it. Almost no money seems to be needed by *comisariados* for expenses aside from *comisiones* (official visits to other places).

The state level of the CNC, the Liga de Comunidades Agrarias (League of Agrarian Communities), in Morelia seems to be of genuine assistance to *ejido* members when they travel to the state capital to deal with the type of problem suggested above. The League obviously has several functions: the supervision of elections held in CNC affiliates at lower levels; the transmission of demands to the national headquarters in Mexico City (necessary in only about 5 per cent of the cases); and, most important, the guidance of ejidal delegates who want to talk to representatives of government agencies in Morelia. The offices of the organization are crowded with people from *ejidos* seeking advice on the proper office to visit in the Department of Agrarian Affairs, or the steps required by law before an *ampliación* can be requested. The staff of the League make strategic phone calls to government officials or write letters of introduction or inquiry for its constituents. As one board member put it, 'The League is important because it assures that our problem will be heard in government offices, even if it cannot assure that our problem will be resolved.' Thus *ejido* members seem to see the organization neither as an instrument of the dominant political party, imposing control from above, nor as their own instrument, gaining strength from below. Rather the League apparently stands in an intermediate position

in their eyes: it is something of a broker, an ally with good con-
nections.

Credit societies: ejidal. Four hundred and seventy-four of the
640 *ejidatarios* of Taretan plant cane and are therefore members
of a credit society which works with the Banco Ejidal through the
Taretan mill. They are thus integrated into the CNC through a
second hierarchy of organizations—in theory completely separated from those described above but in fact often thoroughly
confused with them. The credit society is basically concerned
with the annual problems of production; the *ejido* with a permanent capital asset, land.

Each of the nine credit societies of Taretan has two important
officers: the delegate (*socio delegado*) and the president of the
watchdog committee (not to be confused with the *ejido's* watchdog committee). We found that of these eighteen men, twelve
were also members of the executive boards of their *ejido*. Because
the leaders of both organizations are so often the same, it is
difficult at times to distinguish the functions of one from the
other. Nevertheless, it seems obvious that credit societies are
much more dynamic entities—and their leaders potentially (if
not always) more powerful figures—than *ejidos* alone could ever
be. The reasons are not hard to find.

The credit system of the BNCE demands quite a detailed programme of supervision. Cane growers are granted a standard
amount of credit per hectare (4,300 pesos, or $us344, per hectare
for new cane; and 1,485 pesos per hectare, or $us118, for older
cane), to be paid on a weekly basis according to the cultivation
schedule of the mill and the good faith of each grower in applying
his credit properly. Six inspectors are paid by the mill to ensure
a minimal misuse of credit in the region. (We use the impersonal
'the mill' instead of 'the manager' because in this as in other
instances the impression one has is of a large, impersonal system
whose real decision-makers are unknown. The local manager
certainly has little say about price, quantity of production, wages
and whether or not to have a system of field inspectors.) In any
case, the burden of the task of asking for credit falls on the
shoulders of the elected delegate of each credit society, who
must spend a good part of three days a week inspecting the
fields of his society, reporting to the mill, receiving the weekly
allowance of credit for all members of the group, and distributing
it each Saturday. For his services the delegate is paid a small
amount, averaging about seventy pesos, or $us5·60, each week

from a fund accumulated by deducting 1·5 pesos, $US0·12, for every ton of cane furnished to the mill during the previous harvest.[20]

The existence of that fund for each credit society gives the organization resources which the *ejido* as a whole generally does not have, unless it receives income from the extraction of resin in its forests. Therefore the credit society is often responsible for the launching of such projects as repairing the school building, as in 'Rancho Seco', or installing a system of drinking water, as in 'Purisima'. A second source of power of the credit society, as contrasted with the *ejido* as a whole, is simply that it is entitled to ask favours of the mill. The manager may lend machinery or money for some purposes.

The credit society delegate is given other important responsibilities because of his association with the cultivation of sugar cane. Since social security is available only for *ejidatarios* who are also cane growers or their dependants, the delegate of the credit society deals with all complaints or requests related to health and welfare benefits. And because the school plots of *ejidos* are now planted with cane financed with credit from the BNCE, the credit society delegate has assumed increasing responsibility for the management of that plot.

The establishment of the mill and the creation of credit societies have encouraged a mild form of cooperativism among cane growers, and the credit society delegate must also direct those cooperative efforts. For instance, all growers participate in a yearly cleaning of the canals which supply water for the irrigation of the cane fields. The harvesting of cane is also done in common. Day labourers, paid by the credit society delegate from funds discounted by the mill, move through the cane fields of the *ejido* in an order determined by a meeting of all members of the society in consultation with representatives of the mill. Finally, the credit society is entitled by law to take over and administer the plot of any member who seems in danger of losing his investment in cane. All growers in the *ejido* theoretically have an interest in preventing such a failure, because the group is ultimately liable for any debts remaining at the end of the year. In fact, the societies of the region now have a cumulative debt with the mill of some three million *pesos* ($US240,000) which the Bank appar-

---

[20] The fund of the credit society of the Ejido 'Rancho Seco' contains 4,000 pesos ($US320); that of 'San Joaquin' contains roughly 2,000 pesos ($US160).

ently makes no strenuous effort to collect. Such permissiveness may constitute a serious disincentive to the rational use of credit by *ejido* members.

Credit societies: private landowners' One credit society out of the ten in the *municipio* of Taretan is not composed of *ejidatarios*. It is made up of smallholders and *rentiers*. Combined with a second smallholders' credit society for the neighbouring *municipio* of Nuevo Urecho, the two form the Unión de Pequeños Propietarios de Caña de Azúcar (Union of Small Cane Producers). The Unión is the only organization of its kind (i.e. of private landowners) working with the Banco Ejidal in the whole republic, since the Bank is supposed to serve *ejidatarios* only. It contains some eighty members in all, and through it a large part of the private smallholders of Taretan are affiliated with the CNC. Figure 10 illustrates the position of the Union of Small Cane Producers in the entire organizational structure.

An examination of the composition of this *Unión* discloses some interesting facts. Ten to twenty of its members are wives or sons of *ejido* members who now own a small plot of land in addition to their ejidal parcel. Since credit received through ejidal societies can be used only for cane planted within the *ejido*, and since no person may at the same time be a member of both an ejidal and a private credit society, *ejido* members who want to obtain credit to plant cane on private land must register sons or wives as the 'managers' of the private parcels.

Another thirty members of the smallholders' union are not really property owners at all; rather, they rent private property in order to grow cane on it. Both the current president of all cane growers in the region and the acting secretary-general of the regional committee of the CNC fall within that category. At the same time the group includes other important political figures in Taretan who are 'large' land-owners (thirty to forty hectares constitutes a large holding by Taretan standards). And, finally, smallholders who have only one or two hectares of land are members of the organization.

The varied membership of the group means that—as is indeed the case at the moment—it is entirely possible for a very small land-owner (who may be simultaneously a day labourer) to lead an organization containing the most powerful men in the *municipio*. Simultaneously the strange composition of the group suggests that some important political figures of Taretan join if not to receive credit (which in some cases they do not need) but rather to qualify as cane growers in the political realm. That hypothesis will be discussed more thoroughly at a later point.

Given the conflicting interests represented within the Union of Small Cane Producers, as well as geographical handicaps to uniting its members, it is not surprising that it functions badly. The organization has few of the cooperative aspects of its ejidal counterparts. It does not supervise the collective cutting of cane, nor the cleaning of canals. The Unión serves only to secure credit for members and to supervise the supply of their cane to the mill. The secretary acts as credit society delegate, inspecting members' fields and distributing their weekly credit allowance. During the harvest all members meet with a representative of the mill-management who tells them which fields are ready to be cut first and how much cane the entire group may supply daily to the mill. The president of the society must be sure that the specified amount is delivered on time—apparently quite a difficult task.

Apart from the yearly meeting to decide on harvesting procedures, there are no general meetings of this organization. Revenue is supposed to be provided by dues of ten centavos ($US0·008) per ton of cane furnished to the mill by each member, but only half the members of the group have paid those dues. There is no fund such as that discounted by the mill for ejidal societies.

Regional Union of Cane Producers Unlike members of the executive boards of *ejidos*, the representatives of neither private nor ejidal credit societies find it necessary to travel frequently to Morelia. For their demands are transmitted upward through the Unión Regional de Productores de Caña (Regional Union of Cane Producers), with headquarters in Taretan. For many reasons the Unión is the most powerful organization of peasants in the region —despite its relative weakness when compared with the local mill workers' union.

The Unión, as can be seen from Fig. 10, is composed of the twenty-one ejidal *and* the two private credit societies which supply cane to the Taretan mill. Nine of the twenty-one ejidal societies and one of the private groups are from the *municipio* of Taretan itself. The rest include organizations in the *municipios* of Nuevo Urecho and Ziracuaretiro, and part of Uruapan. Each society, represented by its credit society delegate, casts one vote in decisions of the Unión—although general meetings are always attended also by numerous members (i.e. cane growers) who hold no office in the directorate of their local organization.

The total membership of the Unión is 1,386 members, approximately 200 of whom are small land-owners and the remainder members of *ejidos*. The number includes about 75 per cent of the population of the region, and almost 100 per cent of its elite. That is the case for two reasons: not only is it difficult not to respond to governmental and community pressure to plant cane in the area, but also it is politically unwise not to be a grower. The Agrarian Code, for example, stipulates that, among other things, no member of an *ejido* can be a member of an executive board unless he first joins any credit society which may exist within the *ejido* (i.e. in Taretan, unless he plants cane). Therefore all board members are members of the Regional Union of Cane Producers. At the same time, private land-owners with political aspirations must be cane growers in order to be able to claim that they 'understand' the most obvious and difficult problems of their future constituents. The president of the Regional Union of Cane Producers therefore heads a group of the most influential men in Taretan, Ziracuaretiro, Nuevo Urecho and Uruapan.

The weakness of the regional peasant committee of the CNC (portrayed in Fig. 10 by dotted lines), which should represent the interests of all *ejidatarios*, cane growers or not, gives the Union of Cane Producers additional power. Its specific functions as the representative of the growers are to carry out collective bargaining with the administration of the mill, to deal with government agencies offering assistance to cane growers, and to serve as a link with the National Association of Cane Producers in Mexico City. In fact, however, the directorate of the Unión is now serving as the representative of all members of *ejidos*: introducing members of ejidal executive boards to members of the Liga de Comunidades Agrarias in Morelia; requesting electricity, drinking water and roads from state agencies, etc. A tentative tie between the Regional Cane Producers' Union and the League of Agrarian Communities in Morelia has thus been established (see Fig. 10).

Aside from using the services of the League to obtain water or electricity, the Regional Cane Growers' Union deals with the latter for other reasons. At the present time no state federation of cane producers exists, as we indicate in Fig. 10. Therefore the resolution of the current bitter struggle between leadership factions within the Unión is sought through the good offices of the

League, which has recently supervised several general meetings of cane producers in Taretan called in order to discuss the situation. That duty normally falls to a state association of cane growers.

The most basic task of the Regional Union of Cane Producers—the negotiation of a collective contract with the mill management and the supervision of compliance with its clauses—is carried out on two levels, the local and the national. A glance at the history of the contract signed in November 1965 will illustrate how the process works. The growers' demands were the following: (1) the provision of 4,300 pesos per hectare (about $us341) in credit for the cultivation of new cane, and 1,485 pesos per hectare ($us118) for older cane; (2) the supply of fertilizer at half price; (3) the payment to growers of two pesos ($us0·16) per ton of crushed cane stalks used as fuel by the mill; (4) a lower price for refined sugar sold by the mill to cane growers; (5) ample long-term credit for development projects; (6) ten scholarships a year, to be provided by the mill for sons of growers; (7) a commission of five cane producers, named by the Unión but paid by the mill management, to guard the warehouses and scales of the mill; (8) payment of crop insurance benefits by the mill management itself rather than by the government agency concerned.

The mill management eventually agreed to points 1, 4, 5, and 7 and compromised on points 3 and 6 (offering the growers two scholarships instead of ten and 50 per cent of the profits realized from industrialized cane stalks). Before the settlement was reached, however, members of the Regional Union were forced to threaten that they would not deliver cane to the mill during the coming harvest season. The Unión's board of directors also found it necessary to seek the support of the National Association of Cane Producers in Mexico City and talk personally with the director of the Ejidal Bank. The relative importance of each of these three stages in the negotiation (local threat of strike, support of the national association, and personal contact with the head of the Banco Ejidal) is impossible to determine. Nevertheless, the importance of negotiation on the local level seems to be considerable. The organization has won other concessions from the mill management, such as payment of transport costs in excess of thirteen pesos ($us1) per ton of cane, change in the location of offices where social security benefits are paid—all without the assistance of organizations at the higher level.

The Taretan contract of 1965 was at the time generally recognized as the most advanced agreement of its kind in Mexico. The success of the Regional Union in negotiating it seems definitely related to the fact that the Taretan mill is one of three in Mexico now managed by the Banco Ejidal. The administration of the enterprise insists that its purpose is not to make money but to serve as a means for the development of the region; and on the whole, *ejido* members seem to accept that interpretation. Nevertheless, it is obvious that the management of the mill must consider its financial viability and that its concession on all the points listed above does indicate strength on the part of the growers' organization.

The effectiveness of the Unión Regional is seriously handicapped, however, by internal division—encouraged by manoeuvres at both the national and the local level. Within the local organization itself, two factions are engaged in a struggle for control of the board of directors. One is led by a former president of the Unión, who was removed from office with the intervention of the state delegate of the Ministry of Agriculture. Although the reason for his removal was officially stated to have been that of bringing the structure of the Unión in line with existing laws on agricultural organizations, it is fairly obvious that he was, in fact, replaced because peasant organizers at the state level lost confidence in him. Reports were current that he had embezzled a large amount of money—a charge also levelled against most of his allies. The most interesting characteristic of his group is that its members—a mixture of *ejidatarios*, smallholders and tenant farmers—are the 'old guard' of Taretan. They have long held the municipal presidency (in the period after the departure of the 'L' family) as well as important posts in numerous associations (the Cattle-men's Association, the *comité regional campesino*, the smallholders' credit society), from which they were reported to have extracted substantial amounts of money.

The second faction of the Unión Regional is led by its current president, a relatively young man of apparently high ideals but little education, who was formerly president of the smallholders' credit society. His allies—who again include smallholders as well as *ejido* members and tenant farmers—form a large majority of the Unión. Nevertheless, he must constantly defend himself against his rivals' charges that he has been 'bought' by the mill management. Such insinuations are especially damaging because many growers do not understand the admittedly complicated national system for selling sugar and reimbursing mills and cane producers. They are therefore willing to believe that delays in payment for their cane, or a low price for it, are the fault of their leaders rather than of the system itself.

In order to protect himself from the manoeuvres of the 'old guard' the president of the Unión Regional spends an inordinate amount of time and money travelling to Morelia and Mexico City. In Morelia, as previously noted, he talks with the executive committee of the League of Agrarian Communities; in Mexico City he sees the secretary-general of the National Association of Cane Producers. In both offices he asks that representatives be sent to explain the sugar marketing system to members of the Unión, and that they supervise general meetings in which votes of confidence in the president will be taken. A second purpose of such trips to Morelia or Mexico City seems frankly to be the establishment of good relations with state and national officials of the CNC, who could, if they chose to do so, have the current president replaced.[21]

The expenses of more than twelve trips a year to Mexico City and six to Morelia are large, Last year, in fact, almost the entire fund of the Unión was spent on such trips. This amounted to about 14,000 pesos ($us1,120), discounted by the mill management at the rate of twenty centavos ($us0·16) per ton of cane per member. The cost in terms of time lost by the president from more useful pursuits is, of course, also disturbing, as are the implications for the fate of the organization—to be discussed at a later point.

The disunity of cane producers on a national scale reinforces the difficulties caused for the Unión Regional in Taretan by its own internal disputes. There are now no fewer than ten national organizations of cane growers in Mexico. Only two of those are really nation-wide confederations; the rest are splinter groups of defeated national leaders, or entities with bases in only one region or state.

The oldest of the two large cane growers' groups is the National Union of Cane Producers. It was founded in 1942 in Vera Cruz; although it signed a 'pact of mutual assistance' with the CNC in 1952, it remained formally outside the national peasant union organization until 1963. The union was for many years the largest representative of cane producers in Mexico. During the late

---

[21] In talks at the headquarters of the CNC in Mexico City officials drew attention to the fact that it is possible to replace any board of directors which functions badly.

1950s, however, the president of the organization apparently accepted large amounts of money from the managers of private sugar mills. The corruption of the leadership of the National Union eventually persuaded Francisco Hernandez y Hernandez, then secretary-general of the CNC and later president of the Ejidal Bank, to found a rival organization; the Asociación Nacional de Productores de Caña therefore appeared in 1961.

A period of struggle ensued, during which the new Association succeeded in capturing a large number of regional organizations once affiliated with the National Union. In Taretan, for example, cane growers agreed in a general assembly to change their affiliation. The president of the Taretan union at the time was, however, a friend of the Union's corrupt president. The former had to be offered a position on the executive committee of the new Association before he finally agreed to make the change.

The National Union's corrupt president has since been removed from his post, and the organization is trying to stage a come-back. The battle between the Union and the Association seems at present to be joined purely on the basis of which organization can be most effective in dealing with representatives of the mill management. Both groups have the same programme: the modification of the presidential decrees of 1943 and 1944 described earlier. Both organizations even occupy offices on the same floor of the new CNC building in Mexico City! The leaders of both seem roughly similar, and although one is a private cane producer and the other a former owner of a now bankrupt mill, the latter is even more vehemently opposed to the millers' association, UNPASA, than the former. Finally, both claim to control between 65 and 85 per cent of the cane producers of Mexico, of which 80–90 per cent, both contend, belong to *ejidos*.

This totally confusing situation at the national level makes divisions among growers at the local level almost inevitable. In Taretan, for example, leaders of the 'old guard' apparently sought the support of the Union in their attempt to displace the current president, who is supported by the Association. Open support by the Union for the 'old guard' was, in fact, obtained, perhaps because of the local group's rather tarnished reputation. Nevertheless, the 'old guard' could always hope for support from another national entity—and, even more likely, it can pretend that such support is forthcoming in order to encourage defection from the present board of directors.

The smallholders and the cattle-men Two *campesino* interest groups in Taretan remain outside the hierarchy of organizations ultimately affiliated with the CNC. One, the local cattle-men's association, can be passed over rather briefly. Its most interesting attribute is its heterogeneous membership. Given the relative wealth (especially in the past) of the few large cattle-men in the *municipio*, the association might have been an interest group dedicated to the maintenance of their power. The executive committee of the association has been, indeed, dominated by the larger cattle-men (who, by the way, are often *ejido* members). But the organization has not been used to strengthen the position of those men for the simple reason that the overwhelming majority of its members are the owners of a few heads of cattle who were forced by law to join the association or pay double taxes.

In fact the organization seems to have little programme of any kind aside from the supervision of the sale of cattle, for which it receives ten pesos ($US0·80) per sale. Members also supposedly pay dues of five pesos ($US0·40) per year, and there has been some discussion of using the 6,000 pesos ($US480) now in the treasury to establish a veterinary dispensary or work towards the construction of a factory to make cattle food from the molasses and crushed stalks of the Taretan mill. The group is so loosely organized, however, that any real plan of action seems unlikely.

Contact between the local cattle-men's association and its state counterpart is minimal. Delegates from Taretan go to Morelia only to attend an annual general assembly, in which they hear of any changes in tax laws or discuss methods of guarding against the theft of cattle. The lack of contact between officials at the local and state level is interesting because the state federation seems to be dominated by small land-owners of a rather conservative bent. Even if leaders of the Taretan association agree with the point of view of state officials, however, the composition of their constituents makes the carrying out of any conservative programme impossible.

The second organization in Taretan which is not affiliated with the CNC is even more disorganized than that of the cattle-men. The Smallholders' Association (Asociación de Pequeños Propietarios) was founded in late 1965 and at the time of our study in 1966 had yet to hold a general meeting. Most peasants in the *municipio*, including the president of the smallholders' credit society, do not even know that the Association exists. Its thirty members joined for only one reason—to protect themselves against the possibility of invasion of their land by *ejido* members. They hope to receive counselling on the legal steps necessary to safeguard their property as well as representation before governmental agencies in Morelia if such an invasion occurs.

The function of the local organization seems to be simply that of serving as a channel of communication with Morelia, the state capital, where aid can be obtained from the Federación de Pequeños Propietarios Agrícolas y Ganaderos de Michoacán. To date, there has been only one incident involving an attempt by a group of landless petitioners to obtain part of the holdings of one member. The petition was dismissed when it was proved that the land-owner had only thirty-seven hectares. Nevertheless, the significance of the founding of the local Smallholders' Association is less in the real threat which may exist to its members than in the reflection of their heightened fear of invasion by landless peasants or members of *ejidos*.

The state organization of smallholders is not affiliated with a national confederation, although one exists. This body, the Confederación Nacional de la Pequeña Propiedad Agrícola, with offices in Mexico City, does maintain several representatives in Michoacán. But they are, in fact, completely unknown in the offices of the state federation: quite possibly this organization serves only as a front for large land-owners posing as 'smallholders'. The state federation of smallholders is tentatively affiliated with another national organization known as FEDEMOA (Federación Mexicana de Organizaciones Agrícolas) but it receives no aid of any kind from that group.

3. *Tactics employed by peasant organizations in Taretan*
Keeping both the setting and structure of peasant organizations in mind, we can now go on to analyse the tactics used by peasant groups to promote their interests in the post-revolutionary period. Some of these have been suggested in the preceding section; we shall refer to others below. It should be noted at the beginning that one possible course of action—the threat or use of group violence—is no longer considered as a valid tactic by peasant organizations in Taretan. Nor do they seem to find it necessary or desirable to engage in any other form of activity—such as public demonstrations—outside the established channels of communication between the Mexican government and peasant pressure groups. Such a fact could, of course, be explained by fear of government retaliation, and such fear can never be entirely dis-

counted. In Taretan, however, the non-use of violence seems more accurately explained by a reasonably high expectation on the part of peasant leaders that working through legitimate channels will eventually get the desired result.

In the post-revolutionary period the most serious kind of threat posed by peasants in Taretan in order to obtain their goals has been the plan of the Regional Union of Cane Producers to refuse to plant cane if certain parts of the proposed collective contract of 1965 were not accepted by the administration of the sugar mill. The tactics of the growers were explained in some detail above: consultation with representatives of their national organization, with the director of the Banco Ejidal and with the mill management at the local level. The majority of their demands were ultimately accepted by the Bank, and the most advanced collective contract between cane growers and sugar mills in the country was signed in November 1965.

During the negotiation of the collective contract the mill workers supported the demands of the growers.[22] Their support does not seem to have played a significant part in the victory of the growers' organization, but it is nonetheless important because it represents a new trend in the alliance system of groups in Taretan. Until the fall of the 'L' brothers in 1955 both workers and peasants were, as we have seen, members of one single regional confederation, controlled by the same groups which also controlled the management of the mill itself. Therefore there were no open conflicts between the mill and either workers or cane growers. After 1955, however, peasant leaders and representatives of the sugar mill workers were no longer united in one single regional confederation, and each group pressed its demands against the mill management with little support from the other. There was, in fact, considerable antagonism between the executive board of the cane producers and that of the mill workers' union, based not upon perceived conflict of interest but rather upon personal feuds.

The recent period of renewed cooperation between mill workers and cane growers is closely related to a change in the composition of the peasant leadership group. When the directorate of the Regional Union of Cane Producers was reorganized in late 1964 a young man who was then and continues to be a mill worker replaced an older man whose interests were more those of a

---

[22] Information provided in an interview with a leader of the cane growers.

cattle-man than of either a cane grower or a mill worker. At the same time the secretary-general of Section 11 (the mill workers' union) was another young man who not only worked in the mill but also grew cane and had held offices in the Ejido 'Taretan'. Communication between the directorates of the two organizations was therefore not difficult to reinstitute.

Despite renewed friendship between the leaders of the growers and the workers, however, it must be stressed that cooperation between the two groups is not substantial. Each has supported the other in threats to strike against the mill, and the president of the growers confers with the union executive committee from time to time about the efficient functioning of the mill itself. Nevertheless, a large area of cooperation between workers and cane growers has never been explored by either group.

On one important question, that of the unionization of day labourers in the cane fields, representatives of the mill workers and cane growers have acted together—against the interests of day labourers. In 1963 the directorate of the National Union of Sugar Mill Workers in Mexico City decided to encourage the organization of day labourers associated with the sugar industry. It hoped to increase the membership of the national union and to bring day labourers under the protection of the new social security law covering employees in the sugar industry. The national directorate therefore asked representatives of the Taretan union to organize day labourers in their region into a sub-unit of Section 11. Despite the promise of the union directorate that the purpose of such organizational activity was not to raise the wages of day labourers, cane growers in Taretan (the great majority of whom are members of *ejidos*) strenuously objected to the plan. Using the argument that the costs of benefits to unionized day labourers would ultimately have to be paid by the mill, and that such additional costs might in fact force the mill to close, cane growers urged representatives of the mill workers' union not to continue with their project to organize day labourers. The Taretan union ultimately abandoned the project, convinced by that argument, as well as by other considerations, that the scheme was unworkable. Other reasons for their decision were the fact that many mill workers are also cane growers, that many day labourers are at the same time growers, and that the day labourers who do not belong to *ejidos* or who are not small farmers in Taretan often appear there only during the harvest and migrate afterwards to other areas. The difficulties of organization in such a setting are obvious.

Aside from the threat of strikes, and alliances with other groups, a third means is employed by peasants in Taretan to further their goals. People from *ejidos* sometimes go direct to government agencies to ask for help, without processing their demands every time through peasant organizations at higher levels. That is particularly true of matters which have nothing to do with cane and therefore do not fall under the control of the Regional Union of Cane Producers. On matters of boundary disputes with other *ejidos*, or of requests for definitive titles to land, for example, official representatives of the *ejidos* may go directly to the Department of Agrarian Affairs in Morelia or in Mexico City. The offices of the department in both cities are always full of people from *ejidos* waiting to see a government official. The fact that peasants do not process some complaints through the various levels of the CNC, but engage instead in direct communication with the Department of Agrarian Affairs, can easily be explained. Demands for such services as the granting of definitive titles to ejidal plots are of such long standing that the resources of the Liga de Comunidades Agrarias were probably exhausted some years ago. Once an ejidal representative has been introduced to the proper people in government offices and his rights have been explained, there is really little more which the state or national offices of the CNC seem to be able to do for him. The granting of the title is a matter between him and the Department of Agrarian Affairs—and his chances of success in that particular endeavour are definitely not good.

Representatives of *ejidos* may also deal directly with the Banco Ejidal without first processing their demands through regional, state or national peasant organizations. Officials of credit societies can obtain benefits—such as assistance in the building of drinking water systems or the construction of sheds for milk cows— from the BNCE, through the Taretan mill, without reference to either the Regional Union of Cane Producers or higher entities of the CNC. In fact, although the directorate of the regional cane grower's group may be brought into planning at a later stage, there is evidence that the mill management would prefer to dispense the favours of the Bank by dealing with local ejidal leaders directly—not through the Unión Regional. The reason for the attitude of the administration is not difficult to find. They have been given two roles: first, to run a sugar mill in difficult financial straits; second, to carry out a limited development programme with the funds of the Banco Ejidal. In carrying out their first task the directorate of the mill must engage in collective bargaining with the Regional Union of Cane Producers; the weaker that organization is the less able it is to enforce demands which will worsen the financial situation of the sugar mill itself. Therefore the management would prefer not to strengthen its opponent in the collective bargaining process by channelling money through it for development projects in the region.

Despite these examples of a large area of direct contact between government agencies and peasant representatives without the intervention of peasant organizations above the local level, the majority of the problems dealt with in the system seem to be processed through regional, state or national interest groups. This is especially true of matters concerning the production and processing of sugar cane, and the protection of private property from invasion or legal claim. It was explained earlier, for example, that the sole function of the local association of smallholders seems to be that of linking its members with the state organization, whose legal aid is available. The Regional Union of Cane Producers, also, counts upon the support of the National Association of Cane Producers to maintain its strength against the mill management. And the Regional Union of Cane Producers at the same time has begun to replace the *comité regional campesino* of the CNC as the channel of complaints from ejidal committees to the Liga de Comunidades Agrarias of the CNC (at the state level).

Reference upwards by local peasant groups may involve an element of politics: that is, a local group may appeal for assistance to a rival of its own parent organization. That was the case when the 'old guard' of the Unión Regional de Productores de Caña sought support from the National Union rather than the National Association of Cane Producers. However, two characteristics of such 'politicking' and playing of two organizations against each other should be noted. First, the rival group consulted was still a member of the Confederación Nacional Campesina. There has been no threat in Taretan (since the fall of the 'L' brothers in 1955) that peasant groups would join a national confederation not sanctioned by the government, such as the left-oriented Central Campesino Independiente (CCI), a breakaway from the original UGOCM. Second, when political manoeuvres do occur they are motivated not by a desire to solve outstanding problems of the region nor by changes in policy orientations, but are related to struggles for leadership at a local, regional or national level.

4. Peasant leadership in Taretan

The quality of leadership in the peasant organizations seems to be surprisingly high at the local level, but unfortunately that quality does not seem to increase as one goes up to the state and federal levels at a pace equal to the increase in the complexity of the problems to be solved at these higher levels. In Taretan notable progress in the formation of peasant leaders seems to have been made in the past thirty years. The agrarian movement of 1930–37 necessarily had to be led by the relatively well educated young sons of wealthy land-owners, with little initial help from the fearful and uneducated day labourers on the *hacienda*. But now the ranks of ejidal executive committees and credit society delegates include a large number of peasant leaders of peasant origin who make a serious attempt to understand the problems of their communities and who seem to represent their constituents rather well before the Banco Ejidal and the Department of Agrarian Affairs.

Several characteristics of peasant leadership groups at the local level, as indicated by our survey, are worth noting. First, most of the members of ejidal executive boards and credit society directorates are in the prime age range between thirty and fifty years (68 per cent as against 38 per cent of *ejido* members). Whether they are sons of peasants who fought for land in Taretan or are more recent immigrants into the region from outside, they do not remember the agrarian struggle, or remember it only vaguely, nor have they ever lived in a position of servitude. These new leaders are proud of belonging to *ejidos* and they are rather cautiously optimistic about the future.

The educational level of executive board members and of credit society delegates in Taretan is low in absolute terms, even though the Agrarian Code stipulates that all must at least be able to read and write. Their lack of education undoubtedly limits their effectiveness when dealing with government officials. The limiting effect of too little schooling is partly offset in some cases, however, by experience at work in the mill and by regular travel to Morelia and occasional visits to Mexico City. But in any case, their education is better than that of the rank and file: only 22 per cent did not attend school, as compared with 47 per cent of the members. In addition, many of the current ejidal leaders have held offices in their community or society before, and they understand its problems.[23]

There are cases of ineptitude and corruption among ejidal leaders in the *municipio*. In the Ejido 'Ex-hacienda de Taretan', for example, the treasurer could not account for several hundred pesos; the past president of the Ejido 'Taretan' tried to redistribute land among his friends; the then president of the executive board of 'Tomendan' has many enemies. Nevertheless, the extent of democratic control over leaders exercised in most *ejidos* in the region is remarkable. The belief that leaders cannot act without the approval of the majority of their constituents is widespread, among both leaders and followers, and seems quite often to be put into practice.[24] After the death of the 'L' brothers, peasant leadership at the regional level was dominated for several years by a small group of men who, in the preceding sections of this paper, have been called the 'old guard'. Some belonged to *ejidos*, some were small land-owners or cattle-men, and some were tenant farmers. Politically some belonged to the PRI and others to PAN, a Catholic-oriented party generally regarded as conservative. Their distinguishing characteristic, however, was not the political or economic group from which they came, but rather their desire to gain as much personal benefit as possible from various posts in peasant organizations and local government.

The 'old guard' has been successfully challenged in many peasant organizations during the past few years. It has certainly not disappeared, however, and its leader occupied one of the key posts in the municipal government of Taretan at the time of our study. The challengers are younger men, united under the president of the Regional Union of Cane Producers, who now hold the presidency of the smallholders' credit society and the regional peasant committee of the CNC, as well as control of the growers' regional union. They also enjoy the support of the mill workers' union.

It is highly encouraging that new elements have been introduced into the regional leadership of Taretan. The development

[23] In some *ejidos* there seems to be a tendency toward the monopoly of leadership by a few men; but, in general, offices seem to rotate among a fairly wide number of people. Thirty-three per cent of the *ejido* leaders, but 69 per cent of the members, had held no organizational positions other than the one they were currently holding.

[24] That belief was continually voiced in unstructured interviews with leaders, as well as during the administration of the individual questionnaires.

of a parasitic oligarchy has thereby been made more difficult. Nevertheless, the circumstances which condition the retention of power at the regional level are not so encouraging. It is quite obvious that government representatives at the state and national level have both the authority and the resources to determine who will lead the Regional Union of Cane Producers at any given moment. The 'old guard' was removed from the leadership of the organization with the assistance of a representative of the Ministry of Agriculture in Morelia; the new group will remain in power only so long as it has strong friends in the appropriate state and national organizations. For that reason the president of the Unión Regional will probably always be forced to spend an inordinate amount of time making friends in Morelia and Mexico City. Leaders at lower levels, *comisariados ejidales* and credit society delegates, do not seem to have that crippling handicap.

Little time was spent with leaders of state and national organizations; no real evaluation of their quality is therefore possible. Two generalizations can, however, be made. The members of the directorates of the Liga de Comunidades Agrarias (the CNC at the state level), the Asociación Nacional de Productores de Caña, the rival Unión Nacional, and the CNC itself are not peasants. Nevertheless, many of the leaders of these organizations displayed an impressive understanding of the problems of the people whom they represented.

III. *Summary and conclusions*

The most significant finding of this study is that, under certain conditions, peasants may be capable of directing their own organizations to a significant degree within as brief a period as twenty to thirty years from the founding of such organizations.

We hope that this finding will not be considered banal, on the one hand, or condescending on the other. For it specifies, or attempts to specify, the length of time necessary to overcome the handicap of the kind of extreme cultural and psychological deprivation to which the Mexican peasantry has been subject for centuries, as has that of Peru, Ecuador and many other countries in Latin America and elsewhere. The term 'deprivation' is used here in a partly rather ethnocentric sense. By 'cultural deprivation' we mean exclusion from the possibility of acquiring the knowledge and of learning the subtle skills necessary to manage the kinds of complex political and economic organization which seem to be an inevitable concomitant of the Western-style modernization in which Mexico is increasingly engaged. By 'psychological deprivation' we mean, in this context, exclusion from the possibility of acquiring feelings of self-confidence and some degree of activism, initiative and optimism—attitudes and characteristics considered by many as necessary to function successfully in a modernized world of complex, impersonal organizations.[25]

The fact that these organizational and managerial skills, and the necessary psychological attitudes, can be acquired in a generation—given certain conditions—needs to be judged against the fact that the political and economic organizations of, for example, small farmers in France in the twentieth century and of the United States in the nineteenth century and after involved a 'peasantry' which over many centuries had had at least some experience with self government. In England, for example, even under the feudal system, villagers had some autonomy[26] and the same was true of Germany and Russia, not to mention the United States of America. But in other countries—particularly where relations of conqueror to conquered were compounded by cultural cleavages between these two, and then served to reinforce cleavages based on property—under these circumstances the peasantry was often so oppressed that it had no opportunity to acquire organizational skills even in embryonic form.

Taretan seems to have been such an area of extreme peasant oppression and hence apathy. The question—best put in quantitative terms—is, then: how much time is required for a deprived group to make substantial headway in overcoming its handicap? Does it happen overnight, because the ability is there in all of us and is merely superficially suppressed by circumstances? Is it a matter of one or two years (the rate at which one learns to read and write, perhaps)? Is it five or ten years? A generation? Several generations? Never (if incapacities are innate)? This study would lead one to believe that the time lapse until a substantial proportion of a certain population is capable of managing its affairs is about one generation, or twenty to twenty-five years, if the previous period has been one of severe deprivation. And we regard the time lapse of one generation as short.

In our opinion, therefore, the peasant organizations studied in

[25] Reference here is, of course, to the writings of Alex Inkeles, Joseph A. Kahl, Gabriel Almond and his collaborators, etc.

[26] George C. Homans, *English villagers of the thirteenth century*, Russel & Russel, New York, 1941, pp. 102–6, 309–38.

Taretan work remarkably well, considering the problems they have been forced to overcome and the relatively short time which has passed since their founding. It is, of course, easy to point out their numerous weaknesses and, indeed, the problems besetting them have been analysed in this report and will be listed again below. Nevertheless, the deficiencies of peasant organizations are too often over-emphasized and their notable accomplishments, at least in relative terms, ignored.

Mexican experience thus lends support to the lesson of the Vicos project, carried out in Peru by the late Allan R. Holmberg from the late 1940s onward. Holmberg's experimental project indicates, as does our study, that the length of time necessary to produce functioning peasant groups in a rural society with initially few or none of the apparent prerequisites for successful organization may, in fact, be relatively short.[27]

Four conditions seem to be essential, however, for the initial establishment (generally not the work of peasants themselves) of peasant interest groups: (1) the existence of national laws which encourage the founding of such groups; (2) the provision of concrete assistance at the local level to implement those laws, by national institutions such as the Department of Agrarian Affairs and the Banco Nacional de Credito Ejidal; (3) the creation of both direct and indirect incentives to organize (credit, taxes, etc.); (4) the utilization of human resources such as idealism, energy and organizing ability. Be it noted that in Mexico these conditions were met only after rapid and very substantial changes in the general socio-political system of the nation.

All four prerequisites seem to be essential for the organization of viable peasant groups. For that reason the emphasis throughout this report on the importance of national legal support, on the existence of functioning governmental institutions at both national and local level, and on idealism and energy at the national as well as the local level, is not a banal assertion. It implies that leadership training programmes to encourage the growth of peasant organization at the grass-roots level may be insufficient if concrete assistance (legal, institutional, human, and the offer-

[27] See Allan R. Holmberg, 'Changing community attitudes and values in Peru: a case study in guided change', in Richard N. Adams *et al.*, *Social Change in Latin America Today*, chapter 2, pp. 63–107, Vintage Books, New York, 1960. Holmberg was writing a mere ten years after his organizational experiment began, but there is reason to believe that his Indian communities had enjoyed more autonomy than the peasants of Taretan.

ings of incentives) from the national government is not also present.

Laws In Taretan the first attacks on the *hacienda* system were responses to the passage of agrarian legislation at the national level. Not until the power of the estate had been considerably weakened by fear of eventual expropriation were peasant groups organized. In addition, it was national legislation which determined the form taken by peasant organizations in the region. *Ejidos*, credit societies, cattle-men's association—all were prescribed or encouraged by law.

Institutions at the national and local levels Legal incentives to organizations would not have been effective if the national government had not created institutions capable of offering direct assistance at the local level to the newly created peasant entities. The Department of Agrarian Affairs supervised elections of executive boards and mediated disputes among *ejidos*. The Banco Nacional de Credito Ejidal provided credit in Taretan as early as 1937; in 1946 it established a sugar mill in the *municipio* which encouraged the cooperation of credit societies and the creation of similar interests among many groups within the peasant population. Finally, the national government supplied administrative personnel at the level of the *municipio* to make tax incentives (such as those encouraging the organization of cattle-men) effective.

Incentives Direct incentives to *campesino* (peasant) organizations in Taretan have been furnished by the government, in large part through a sugar mill operated by the Banco Ejidal. Credit is extended only through credit societies associated with the Bank through the sugar mill; and social security is available only to members of the mill workers' union, members of credit societies, their dependants and permanent employees. Another direct incentive is the law which stipulates that all cattle-men who are not members of a local cattle-men's association must pay a double tax on every unit sold.

A more indirect kind of incentive to peasant organization on a local level is the encouragement of new federations at the state level which, in order to obtain recognition, must engage in a campaign to establish affiliated organizations in each municipal area. Both the cattle-men's and the smallholders' associations in

23—T.B.O.G.

Taretan were founded in general assemblies requested by new state federations, established as a response to legal requirements (in the case of the cattle-men) or to perceived threats from the ejidos (in the smallholders' case).

Human resources The most basic condition for the successful organization of peasants is the presence of such human resources as idealism, energy and organizing ability. These are also the most difficult to find, particularly since, like institutions, they must be present at both the national and the local levels. A national leader cannot carry out a successful organizational drive without the support of effective local leaders, nor vice versa. In Taretan both the necessary elements were present. General Cárdenas, first as state governor, later as President of the Republic, provided effective leadership at the state and national level. And in the *municipio* itself a charismatic leader of the agrarian movement established almost all the peasant organizations now found there.

The idealism of Cárdenas and of local organizers in Taretan is no doubt shared by many potential leaders in Latin America today and constitutes an important resource in the effort to organize rural populations. Nevertheless, idealism must be combined with energy, persistence and organizing ability before effective peasant groups can be created. The latter are the scarcest resources in the process of peasant organization. Hopefully, they will become less so as their importance is increasingly recognized.

Strengths of the present system in Taretan

Multiple membership Because of the existence of numerous pressure groups in Taretan, many peasants find themselves members of more than one organization. Such a situation provides the kind of overlapping interest-group structure which encourages moderation in the pursuit of goals and increases the possibility that no small group of leaders can control all the sources of political power in the *municipio* for an indefinite period of time.

Heterogeneous membership Organizations such as the cattle-men's association and the smallholders' credit society have been forced, by law and economic necessity, to include within their ranks many different kinds of cattle-man or smallholder, from the poorest to the most powerful. Therefore the present system is strengthened not only by a blurring of divisions among interest groups, but also by the lessening of conflict between the substrata within the same occupational categories.

Rotation of leadership Although a tendency towards monopolization of power seems visible in several organizations in Taretan, the majority of the local groups have for the past ten years been led by executive committees whose membership has continually changed. At the regional level the period following the departure of the original agrarian leaders has been characterized by a struggle between two groups. At the time of our study the younger, and apparently more responsible, of the groups was in control of the majority of the key posts in the local government structure.

Responsibility of leadership On the whole, leaders of local peasant organizations in Taretan are aware of the responsibilities of their offices. The belief that leaders cannot act without the approval of the majority of their followers is widespread, and is often reflected in concrete actions. Consensus is sought in informal consultation and at times in general assemblies.

Good communication There is little feeling among peasants in Tareton that complaints cannot be taken to any one of a number of government agencies, or that such complaints will not be heard. In fact, communication between peasants and government agencies is remarkably easy.

Feeling of efficacy The absence of any resort to the threat or the actual use of violence by peasants as a group in Taretan since the end of the agrarian struggle is closely related to their relatively high expectation that their representatives can obtain benefits by operating through existing channels of communication.

Dynamism of the system The history of peasant organization in Taretan, and at higher levels, is marked by the growing strength of some entities and the atrophy of others. Such a process is the result of adaptation to changing needs and should not be alarming. At the regional level, for instance, the increase in the number of cane growers and in their awareness of their interests has strengthened the Regional Union of Cane Producers. That organization is now far more important than the *comité regional campesino* of the CNC, the regional organization of all members of *ejidos*. Most of these are now cane growers and channel their demands through the Union of Cane Producers.

At the national level the Confederación Nacional Campesina seems to be following the path of numerous trade union movements throughout the world. Like the British TUC, for example, the CNC seems to be leaving more and more of its administrative and bargaining functions to specialized affiliates, and to be devoting an increasing amount of energy to political lobbying activities and public relations programmes. This is particularly evident in the case of the National Association of Cane Growers, an affiliated confederation of the CNC which bargains quite effectively with sugar mill representatives.

Weakness of the System

Lack of clarity of function Perhaps in part owing to the dynamism of peasant organizations described as advantageous above, there is a notable lack of division of labour among peasant interest groups in Taretan. Confusion among both leaders and followers over the specific function of each organization is illustrated by the use of ejidal funds to pay the expenses of trips made by delegates of credit societies; by voting at meetings of credit society delegates for officers of a purely ejidal organization, the *comité regional campesino*; and by the increasing use of the Regional Union of Cane Producers as the channel for making demands (e.g. for electricity or drinking water systems) which have little to do with the production of cane. Overwork of a few key leaders seems to be the result.

Dissension Confusion over the specific function of each organization also encourages dissension among its members. Men who hope to gain control of the Regional Union of Cane Producers, for example, try to discredit its directorate by telling members that the executive committee is not obtaining certain benefits which in fact are outside the range of benefits that any leader of the organization could possibly obtain.

Dissension is also evident at the national level, where no fewer than ten groups compete for control of cane producers throughout the country. Such division makes it difficult for directorates of organizations at lower levels to avoid involvement in power struggles. The fear is often expressed that this multiplicity of competing organizations is encouraged by official groups who do not want any sector (such as cane growers) to become too powerful.

Absence of long-term goals It has been noted above that communication between peasant groups and government agencies is remarkably good. Difficulties in the problem-solving system arise, however, because specific demands do not seem to be aggregated into a coherent proposal for long-term action. The Liga de Comunidades Agrarias (the CNC at the state level), for example, directs individual complaints of peasants to government officials for resolution. That is an important service. But the League does not unite all members of *ejidos* behind any general, long-term plan to improve their lot.

Paternalism of the Banco Ejidal Some of the policies of the Banco Ejidal, carried out through the Taretan sugar mill, appear to be based in part at least on the assumption that *ejidos* never perform well and therefore should not be held responsible for their mistakes. The Bank does not, for example, insist on the repayment of debts by *ejido* members. The same mentality is visible in the Department of Agrarian Affairs, where frequently no attempt is made to straighten out financial irregularities brought to light in general meetings of *ejidos*.

Such an attitude could be the result of a more general policy of paternalism towards the *ejidos*—a phenomenon noted by many students. Or it could be based on a desire for political peace. Whatever its causes, government agencies' low expectation of performance by members of *ejidos* encourages irresponsibility on the part of the latter. The fact that during the last harvest a large amount of damaged cane and weeds was supplied to the sugar mill is an example of that point.

It is clear, then, that these peasants as a class, and the organizations which represent their interests, have arrived at a critical point. To a very considerable extent they are autonomous, at least in the sense that they no longer depend on other social strata to provide leadership and make policies. Yet the organizational environment in which the new peasant organizations have to survive and on which they depend—the Banco Ejidal, whose credit is vital; the National Association of Sugar Millers, which buys their sugar; the Department of Agrarian Affairs—these and other agencies in effect can make or break the existing peasant organizations. It is in the immediate self-interest of some of these agencies not to strengthen the peasantry or their associations. But it may well be to the long-term advantage of Mexico as a whole to nurture a relatively content and strong group of peasants, intensively cultivating small and medium sized plots, and directing their own interest groups. The last thirty years have shown that progress towards such a goal is possible. Less outside help is needed now than once it was. But it is definitely still needed. Will it be given?

Acknowledgements

This study was financed in part by the Interamerican Committee for Agrarian Development (CIDA) and in part by Cornell University's School of Industrial and Labor Relations and its Latin American Program. We are very grateful to these institutions, but they are not, of course, responsible for the views we express. Our study was part of a much larger one sponsored by CIDA in cooperation with the Mexican Centre for Agrarian Studies. To the director of the latter, Dr Sergio Reyes O.; to the then representative of CIDA in Mexico, Dr Rodolfo Stavenhagen; to Sr Sergio Alcantara F. of the Centre; and to Dr Thomas F. Carroll of the Interamerican Development Bank, we also wish to express our deepest thanks, while absolving them from all responsibility.

John S. Saul Marketing cooperatives in a developing country: the Tanzanian case

There is no country in tropical Africa where marketing coopera- tives have come to play a more central role in economic life than Tanzania. Moreover, while the movement there has achieved considerable successes, it has also met with its share of difficulties and setbacks. Tanzania, therefore, provides a useful case study of the effect of a particular social structure upon the functioning of cooperative institutions, a case study which is also valuable in contributing to any more general effort to identify the range of 'social prerequisites' for successful agricultural cooperation. In writing this paper I have chosen to focus, in the first instance, upon those cooperatives which deal with the marketing of agri- cultural produce, both because of their tremendous economic importance and because they have, until very recently, been the major focus of Tanzania's efforts to make use of the instrument of cooperation in realizing her development goals. And I have chosen a macro-sociological focus (in this case a national one) because it will enable me to make certain points which are of crucial importance for the topic under discussion and which in a microscopic analysis are all too readily consigned to the category of 'external variables' (and, regrettably, left unanalysed). It is clear that my own approach can lead to over-simplification, and I shall have to paint with fairly broad strokes, but perhaps, at the very least, some of the questions of most relevance can be further clarified by a small dose of 'intentional naivete'.

This must not be done at the expense of fairness. The Tanza- nian government has been remarkably willing in recent years to publicize the shortcomings of the country's institutions in order that they might be the more easily and quickly reformed. In con- centrating, as I do, on the *problems* of Tanzania's cooperative movement and attempting to view them temperately in socio- logical perspective I have therefore taken my cue from the gov- ernment itself. It would be unfortunate, however, if this emphasis were to obscure the substantial achievements of the movement or the dedicated service of many who have been connected with it. Only on the basis of further detailed research will we eventually be able to strike a more judicious balance in our general assessment of Tanzania's cooperatives.

1. The setting

It would be impossible in a brief essay to identify all the aspects of Tanzania's social structure which are relevant to the functioning of her cooperative movement, but several aspects of particular importance may be introduced here. In general, these elements take their meaning from the fact that contemporary Tanzania is a 'backward' society which has been introduced into the world market system (though not completely transformed) by the mechanism of Western imperialism and that the historically specific legacy of her colonial past remains the most important factor defining her current situation. Thus the pattern of *racial stratification* has continued to be a fundamental variable through an extended period, for, as Balandier has noted, this is a key feature of the 'colonial situation'.[1] Racial consciousness mingled with nascent 'nationalist' sentiment to power the drive for independence, a drive which was directed as much (or more) against the Asian community, who had come to occupy a particularly strategic position in the middle levels of the trading sector (and thereby were in more immediate contact with the Africans), as against the European colonial hierarchy. There can also be little doubt that in many areas of the country exploitation by these 'foreign' middlemen was a grievance of major importance, providing a 'spontaneous' element in the beginnings of the cooperative movement, for example, in the East Lake cotton growing area, where much the most important cooperative constellation in the country arose with startling rapidity during the early 'fifties.[2] It began with a movement of independent African weighers at various cotton buying stations, and expanded rapidly, initially without significant external stimulus and support, to become the complicated organization of the Victoria Federation

---

[1] See Georges Balandier, 'The colonial situation' in *Africa: social problems of change and conflict*, ed. P. van den Berghe, San Francisco, 1965.

[2] It is also clear that the Asian community vigorously resisted the rise of the cooperative movement during the colonial period, though the political weapons at its disposal were very limited.

of Cooperative Unions (now Nyanza Cooperative Union), the largest cooperative on the continent. Economic exploitation which had an identifiable racial colouring thus became a spur to peasant consciousness.

This dimension is of continuing national importance, so much so that President Nyerere, eager to blaze a socialist path towards development, has on several occasions reiterated the theme that 'socialism is not racialism'[3] and that a drive directed merely towards extensive Africanization of the economy may degenerate into a rather spurious form of 'radicalism'. We would emphasize, too, that consciousness of exploitation in colonial and post-colonial Africa is the more likely to become an active force where that exploitation parallels a racial cleavage. In addition, the importance of racial stratification to the colonial situation helps us to understand the origins of the cooperatives in Tanzania, the emergence of their leadership, and gives us a clue to the current character of the movement.

An understanding of these processes, however, requires a much deeper analysis of the character of *intra-African stratification* than has as yet marked much of the discussion concerning the social prerequisites for agricultural cooperation. All too often such discussion has been exclusively preoccupied with the relevance of features of 'traditional' society for the success or failure of modern cooperative–collective organizations.[4] In its extreme form this can become primarily an exercise in forcing data into the Procrustean dichotomies of Weberian and Parsonian sociology (the traditional–modern dichotomy and the attendant 'pattern variables') and an evasion of much more nuanced historical processes.

The likely utility of the concept of 'traditional society' for serious investigations of Tanzanian reality must be carefully weighed, for any definition which emphasizes too one-sidedly the

---

[3] 'Socialism is not racialism', article in the *Nationalist* (Dar es Salaam) of 14 February 1967, reprinted in J. K. Nyerere, *Freedom and socialism*, Oxford University Press, Nairobi and London, 1968; also the President's speech of 9 December 1968, reported in the *Standard* (Dar es Salaam) under the headline 'No room for racialism'.

[4] Cf. Percy S. Cohen, 'Traditional societies and modern cooperatives' (a mimeographed paper prepared for the Sixth World Congress of Sociology); R. Dore, 'Traditional communities and modern cooperatives' (see chapter 1). These essays were circulated as background papers for the conference on 'Social prerequisites of agricultural cooperation', for which the original version of this paper was prepared.

centrality of 'traditional legitimation' and the 'self-perpetuating' character of Tanzania's social sub-systems will not take us far in arriving at an understanding of post-colonial Tanzania,[5] to expect it to do so would be to ignore the character of the colonial impact on Tanzanian society. Kilson has said that the key to the colonial situation is the growth of what he terms the 'cash nexus' within the framework of the imperial market system. In much the same vein, Balandier has called for a mode of analysis which can 'grasp the twofold effect of foreign economic forces on traditional societies: destructive effects leading to destructuration, and positive ones leading to new structures and new forms of integration'.[6]

Though Tanzania is *comparatively* untransformed economically, socio-economic differentiations of a 'modern' order have long begun to make themselves felt, especially in those areas where cooperatives have come to play their most central socioeconomic role. In emphasizing the inegalitarian character of certain traditional communities, Dore has argued that economic transition in Europe from 'feudal village communalism, through private property individualism to modern quasi-collectivism' required an '*individualizing* phase': 'Without the equalizing trend—and the gradual evolution of democratic constitutional forms which enable groups of equals to secure for themselves effective and respected leadership—modern forms of cooperation would be impossible.'[7] But surely in Europe such a legalistic focus is too narrow; the new forms of socio-economic differentiation which emerged from the process of 'bourgeois revolution' brought into being not only new formal equalities but also novel inequalities. Similar, related, processes of differentiation are already at work in Africa, even in various kinds of 'traditional milieux', and set restricting limits upon 'modern forms of cooperation'.

In Tanzania there has certainly been a move away from traditionally legitimated modes of authority (already undermined to some degree by the 'indirect rule' system of colonial administration), but whether such developments were unequivocally egalitarian is more questionable. John Iliffe, writing of Tanganyika in the 'twenties and 'thirties, notes, first, that 'growers' associations became the natural centres of opposition to chiefly privilege'. 'This

---

[5] These phrases figure prominently in Cohen's analysis, ibid.

[6] Martin Kilson, 'African political change and the modernisation process', *Journal of Modern African Studies*, I, 4 (1963); G. Balandier, 'Traditional social structures and economic changes' in Van den Berghe, op. cit., p. 386.

[7] Dore, op. cit., 4.

conflict', he then observes, 'was most bitter in the two most developed parts of the country, Kilimanjaro and Buhaya. It was not a conflict between rich and poor but a conflict between wealthy groups, one with official status and the other without it.'[8] In Kilimanjaro, where the first major cooperatives in the country emerged—the Kilimanjaro Native Coffee Union (KNCU)—the cooperative movement was a particularly important arena for much of this struggle. And in the third important area where cooperatives became a major force, Maguire remarks that 'to the Sukuma [the dominant tribe in East Lake, centre of the powerful VFCU–NCU mentioned above], whose fondness for their chiefs had never been excessive ... the cooperatives must also have seemed attractive because chiefs, headmen and other traditional status figure were not permitted to assume prerogatives beyond those of simple membership, unless specifically asked to do so. Egalitarian pressures within Sukuma society have been remarked by both administrators and anthropologists.'[9] But here too 'egalitarianism' had its limits.

Maguire's account of the origins of the VFCU is particularly revealing on this matter, for he traces the manner in which the organization grew out of a group of African traders in Mwanza town organized into the Mwanza African Traders' Cooperative Society. This group was hard-pressed by the stiff competition of the Asian traders, and a number of their commercial ventures failed. After Paul Bomani had taken over active leadership in 1949, however, 'within three years the traders extended their concern to the marketing of native produce. Ultimately Bomani concentrated his attention on problems of cotton marketing, where, it was felt, African producers were most flagrantly exploited by Asian middlemen.'[10] The district officer, writing to his superior in Mwanza, argued that 'it is extremely suspect that erstwhile members of an active traders' cooperative should suddenly ... [be] promoters of a producers' cooperative ...' and noted that ' "the three promoters in Bukumbi of the collection are African traders, not cultivators". He questioned the suitability of the Mwanza African Traders' Cooperative Society for the task

[8] J. Iliffe, 'The age of improvement and differentiation, 1907–45' in I. N. Kimambo and A. J. Temu, A history of Tanzania (in press).

[9] Andrew Maguire, 'Towards uhuru in Sukumaland, 1945–60', unpublished Ph.D. dissertation for the Department of Government, Harvard University, 1966, p. 160.

[10] Ibid., p. 122.

of organizing producers, [and] whether money raised from the farmers for the cooperative should be deposited in the Traders' account.'[11] As we have suggested, there was tinder a-plenty in the form of popular grievances waiting only for such a spark to set them alight. But it would be a mistake to miss the extent to which the new leadership found in the cooperative movement, itself supported by government, new opportunities for self-advancement in a social situation where entrepreneurial business opportunities were blocked because of racial stratification. Thus Maguire further observes that, in spreading the movement, 'Bomani worked with native authorities, *more often with traders and ambitious cotton farmers*, and sometimes, too, with traditional village leaders' and he describes one of the areas which most firmly resisted the spread of the VFCU as being 'suspicious of what seemed to them a Bomani-led, Mwanza-based economic imperialism'.[12] Migot's characterization of the three dominant figures in the cooperative movement in Maswa over a fifteen-year period, all of whom had had an extended and growing range of entrepreneurial involvements in various economic spheres, is equally revealing.[13] The cooperative movement thus provided opportunities for upward mobility which affected the character of the cooperative's operations. It should thus be clear that we cannot describe the process of cooperative development simply as an outcome of the 'solidarity' of the 'traditional society'.

Yet equally obviously Tanzania has not entered a full-blown capitalist phase; its pattern remains a distinctively transitional one. As Balandier points out in a similar connection, 'the whole difficulty of the analysis and the impossibility of resorting exclusively to concepts of economic individualism and social class in order to interpret the new situation, comes from the fact that the two systems . . . (or, rather, some of their elements) coexist and closely interpenetrate one another'.[14] The degree to which rural Tanzanians are involved in, aware of, or dependent upon the external economic sphere and the 'modern' organizations which touch their lives . . . indeed varies widely from person to person

[11] Ibid., p. 136.

[12] Ibid., p. 159 (emphasis added).

[13] S. E. Migot-Adhola, 'The politics of a growers' cooperative society', unpublished undergraduate dissertation paper, Department of Political Science, University College, Dar es Salaam. A revised version of this dissertation will appear in *Marketing cooperatives in Tanzania* (tentative title, forthcoming), ed. S. E. Migot-Adhola and John S. Saul.

[14] Balandier, op. cit., p. 389.

even within the same locality. For some, at the one extreme, subsistence agricultural activities and familial ties are of the essence; cash-cropping is an altogether more marginal phenomenon and a retreat to mere subsistence remains some sort of live option, an apathetic withdrawal from active institutional participation an ever-present possibility. That such options are possible is in part explained by the absence of genuine population pressures in many areas of a country like Tanzania which might serve to force more people to relinquish their hold upon the minimal allotment of the means of production necessary for subsistence.

At the other end of the spectrum lie those who are full-fledged 'activists' in the money economy; for them 'possessive individualism' has become the *modus operandi*. I have referred to this kind of differentiation elsewhere as a process of differential enlargement of the scales of operation of the people involved,[15] and it is a sociological phenomenon of central importance to contemporary Tanzania. For it is out of this gap between the commercial 'activists' and their less 'liberated' peasant colleagues that rural exploitation emerges, and it manifests itself not only in private entrepreneurial activity but also within the framework of the cooperative movement. In contemporary Tanzania such a 'class division' is at present probably more important for the rural sector than any division between capitalist farmer and rural proletariat, though this pattern too is emerging.[16]

Balandier's 'interpenetration' may effect *both* 'activists' and 'parochials' in another sense, since even for the activists certain traditional ties may continue to carry some weight. In Tanzania, as in most of Africa, the ties of kinship are of particular importance.[17] Under certain conditions, advantage to one member of

[15] John S. Saul, 'Towards a critique of modernization theory', in Giovanni Arrighi and John S. Saul, *Ideology and development: essays on the political economy of Africa*, East African Publishing House, Nairobi (forthcoming).

[16] This contrasts with the emphasis of President Nyerere himself, who has indeed argued that 'the present trend is away from the extended family production and social unity, and towards the development of a class system in the rural areas', but is particularly concerned with the development of a 'rural proletariat'. See his *Socialism and rural development*, Government Printer, Dar es Salaam, 1967.

[17] Peter Lloyd in the introduction to *The new elites of tropical Africa*, Oxford University Press, London, 1966, emphasizes that this remains true for the educated elite which has emerged into dominant positions of power at the national level; though he probably over-states his case with reference to the elite, the point is important and would obviously have even more validity with reference to the sort of local 'activists' which we are discussing here.

a clan or narrow locality can still be interpreted as a gain for all, even though the particular individual may have begun to succeed in cutting himself off from too many claims upon the fruits of his success. The exact boundaries of the group which delimits the universe of *relevant morality* for people operating within, say, the cooperative structure will remain affected by traditional patterns, and carries with it certain predictable results in the form of such phenomena as nepotism. Unfortunately, there are insufficient data to assess precisely the extent to which kinship ties in different areas may have been converted into patron–client relationships, or to enable us to determine the mix in the motivations of 'activists' within the cooperative movement between deference to traditional solidarities and the attempt merely to build constituencies for furthering personal aggrandizement. But in transitional Tanzania it is apparent that there *is* a mixed pattern with the *differential adoption* of patterns of individualism being a fundamental dimension whose implications need to be much more carefully studied.

Other salient aspects of Tanzania's social structure which affect cooperative development must also be dealt with. The low level of general development which characterizes Tanzania's condition of 'historical backwardness' results in a very low educational level. This affects the availability of skills and trained manpower and therefore the quality of work in an organization like the cooperative. But it also means that the mass of the peasant population lacks those basic tools of literacy which might well prove a necessary concomitant to genuine control of a 'modern' organization from below. Thus the realities of education reinforce the pattern of inequality created by the process of differential 'enlargement of scale', this combination serving to block any precise awareness on the part of the bulk of the rural population of the social forces which actually affect their lives. In the past racial consciousness has sometimes been strong enough to permit a breaking through such barriers, and, as we have noted, has therefore been a prerequisite to generating effective resistance to exploitation. But in the post-colonial period race becomes a less clear-cut index of exploitation. The result is that a population which has not been sufficiently aroused from parochial concerns either by the pressures of social change or, politically, by the self-conscious use of ideology and organization finds it difficult to attain a level of consciousness adequate to an understanding of their situation. Further resistance to exploitation, which might revitalize the cooperatives, therefore comes slowly.

A final factor of some importance is the 'uneven development' *between* various areas of Tanzania. The economic, social and political impact of the colonial system was indeed variable, and some areas experienced more destructuration than others, Kilimanjaro, Bukoba and East Lake, which we have already mentioned, were among such areas. They were also the places in which cooperatives arose earliest and with a greater degree of spontaneity. In other, less transformed parts of the country it was only when the new government formed under the Tanganyikan African National Union (TANU) took a strong initiative after independence that cooperatives were begun, often on very shaky foundations indeed: 'the political pressures [after 1961] were considerable. Societies were organized from "on top" without genuine local demand, or even understanding, but in their enthusiasm in the first flush of freedom, people went along'.[18] In such areas the social patterns of differentiation which we have discussed will be less pronounced, though generally by no means absent; it was, for example, in relatively undeveloped Ulanga District that a cooperative inspector explained the demise of the cooperative there (and the necessity for a government take-over of the local movement) to me by saying that 'It was like a gold rush, Bwana'. But the character of the various cooperatives will of necessity differ widely in this range of settings, as will many other institutions. Indeed, these differences mean that national decision-makers will have to formulate flexible policies which will take into account the differing needs of each area. But such subtleties in the policy-making process will not always be easy to achieve. More important, uneven development tends to reinforce local and regional consciousness, which often has an important tribal dimension as well. This too presents a challenge to national decision-makers, for an ideal allocation of resources, manpower and the like may be all the more difficult to arrive at if such 'regional' interests became articulate. Thus the sociological factor of uneven development will also have implications for the success or failure of policy-making in the cooperative sector.

[18] *Report of the Presidential Special Committee of Enquiry into Cooperative Movement and Marketing Boards*, Government Printer, Dar es Salaam, 1966, p. 5. For a brief commentary on this report see John S. Saul, 'An introduction to the cooperative report', *Mbioni*, 3, 7 (Dar es Salaam, December 1966), pp. 2–8.

2. *The aspiration*

We have been moving towards a discussion of policy, and this is no accident, for it is clear that the government of Tanzania has taken a great interest in the cooperative movement; moreover, it increasingly expects the movement to play a wide variety of roles. This must be constantly borne in mind, since the sociological variables which we have been discussing will have different implications for the success or failure of the cooperatives depending upon *the exact range of roles* which the movement is called upon to play. Too wide a range of functions, for example, may strain the capacity of the movement, given the technical qualifications of the management cadres upon which it can draw; moreover, the extension of the range of functions the cooperatives are called upon to undertake may expand the variety of situations which engender new temptations to corruption—already an ever-present danger. Certain policies may also—at least in the short run—entail the provision of increased government supervision which it might not be easy to meet, or could have the negative effect of prematurely strangling dawning initiatives emanating from the rank-and-file membership. In addition, policies pursued in *other sectors* of the society are of great potential significance for the cooperatives, even if the links are not always made explicit. Thus general educational policy and strategies for political and ideological mobilization might perhaps help to produce the social prerequisites for effective cooperation—in the form of necessary skills and attitudes, for example—otherwise lacking at present.

Obviously, however, the major function which marketing cooperatives have been expected to carry out is still that of marketing agricultural produce. The motives behind this are clearly expressed in the *Report of the Presidential Commission on the Establishment of a Democratic One-party State*, where the contribution of the cooperatives is said to have been 'decisive because the steady expansion of cooperative enterprise has enabled Africans to participate in and obtain control of certain sectors of the economy which would otherwise have remained in the hands of immigrants or foreign companies'.[19] This avoids a precise definition of *which* Africans' interests were to be most effectively served, of course, though we do know that, even in areas of more spontaneous genesis of cooperatives prior to independence, a

[19] Dar es Salaam, 1965, p. 27.

combination both of 'activist' interest and mass grievance was
involved. Nonetheless, from the beginnings of the movement in
the colonial period one of the government's aspirations was to
guarantee internal democratic control, though there was a concomitant pressure towards external controls, via a wide variety
of mechanisms introduced under the Cooperative Ordinance
(notably a network of government cooperative officers and inspectors). Such checks were primarily designed to ensure the
efficiency and *honesty* of the marketing operations of these institutions. The control function became more of a challenge when,
after independence, as noted, 'it was decided to embark on a
crash programme for the organization of cooperatives in vast
sections of the country which until then were largely untouched
by the movement'.[20] Thus the number of societies increased from
857 in 1961 to 1,533 in April 1966, and the volume of produce
handled from 145,000 tons in 1960 to 496,000 tons in 1965. In
addition, more and more crops were put under compulsory
marketing orders which enforced single-channel marketing
through the cooperatives, thereby ensuring the latter's dominant
position. The pace of expansion, the variety of different social
settings, and the diversity of crop patterns involved placed a
heavy, if necessary, burden upon the emerging movement. Such
burdens are heaviest where 'vertical integration' and 'greater participation by growers in the processing of their products'[21] are
furthest developed (e.g. extensive take-over of ginneries), and
where the government encourages the cooperatives to take on
additional retailing functions, as has been the recent trend in
Tanzania.

The post-independence government has, quite naturally, been
more eager than the colonial regime to force the pace of development in Tanzania, with the result that a second set of expectations
concerning the cooperative movement has emerged since 1961.
The government has felt that the cooperative should be playing
a far more active developmental role for two reasons. First,
certain cooperatives, through their levies, have accumulated large
surpluses in the past and continue to do so. Since the amount of
surplus generated in all sectors of the economy for use as productive investment will be limited in a poor country, the government
is almost inevitably bound to take an interest in the use to which

[20] *Report of the Presidential Special Committee . . .*, op. cit., p. 5.
[21] *Annual Report of the Ministry of Commerce and Cooperatives*, 1964,
p. 12.

the cooperatives will put their funds. In addition, the cooperative movement presents the government with a potential ready-made instrument for development. There are few other instruments available which touch the peasantry so directly, and the cooperatives, too, have a special capacity in the field of credit, which can be geared to the underwriting of new agricultural inputs and whose repayment can be tied, through the cooperative, to deductions from growers' returns for their marketable produce at season's end (the promise of these returns thus replacing existing smallholder assets in guaranteeing the loan).

There is no other type of organization which is so suited to the problems and concept of rural development . . . It would be impossible for the government's administrative machinery to deal with the numerous individuals requiring government assistance and services, including credit for raising production and productivity. Without the use of cooperatives the number of people wanting government help will make dissemination of government services and assistance financially very expensive and administratively almost impossible.[22]

The government—with an interest in introducing new inputs (mechanization, fertilizers and insecticides and the like)—finds itself in the position of jockeying with the quasi-autonomous cooperatives over the exact contributions they can be expected to make in terms of the *financing* of development and of the *initiatives* to be undertaken. This is the key to much of the recent politics of Sukumaland, for example, and the government has had some success in defining the course which the cooperatives are to follow. But it is in this context that our earlier queries as to the likely load which can be effectively assumed by these institutions, the implications of increasing the range of 'temptations', and the costs and benefits of increased government supervision, become particularly relevant.

Underlying certain of the calculations about policy in the cooperative sector has been the aspiration to construct a socialist society which has arisen in Tanzania. Part of the drive behind the spread of cooperatives 'does stem', in the President's own words, 'from the socialist principle of avoiding the exploitation of man by man'. Thus 'marketing by farmers, without the intervention of middlemen who are endeavouring to pay as little as possible to the farmer and receive as much as possible from

[22] *Government Paper No. 4—1967*, Government Printer, Dar es Salaam, p. 15.

the consumer, can be of benefit to both the farmers and the rest of the community'. But even on this front the government, as it has come to adopt a more aggressive socialist policy, has begun to have misgivings about the impact of the cooperatives, and these misgivings may introduce a third set of general policy expectations of potential significance for the movement's functioning. The President himself goes on to argue that '. . . although marketing cooperatives are socialist in the sense that they represent the joint activities of producers, they could be socialist institutions serving capitalism if the basic organization of agricultural production is capitalist . . . For a farmers' cooperative marketing society is an institution serving the farmers; if they are capitalist farmers, then the existence of a cooperative marketing society will mean that one group—the farmers—are safeguarding their own interests, as against another group—the middlemen'. He concludes that 'it is only if the agricultural production itself is organized on a socialist pattern that cooperative marketing societies are serving socialism'.

The President's ideas about class formation in Tanzania may be insufficiently broad. His major concern has been with the emerging differentiation which he has perceived between capitalist farmers and a 'rural proletariat'. The sorts of crypto-class distinction which are rooted in the differential rates of movement out of traditionalism and the subsistence economy have not similarly engaged his attention. When he discusses the actual working of the cooperatives themselves he can thus argue that they have tended 'merely to replace the exploitation of man by man by the exploitation of inefficiency and bureaucratic dishonesty' and that such 'practical' problems can be dealt with by 'better and more skilled management and commercial machinery'.[23] I argue, on the contrary, that these problems reflect not merely some institutional deficiency but also the fundamental sociological fact which has already been discussed in section 1, and the full implications of which shall be further clarified in the following section—*the emergence of novel forms of inequality in Tanzanian society.* What is important to note at this stage, however, is that the cooperatives are now to be assessed by government from a more consistently socialist standpoint. This appraisal will affect the range of new demands which are likely in future to be made upon them; it is already apparent that some such questions have

[23] Nyerere, op. cit.

become an aspect of the current drafting of the new five-year plan, for example.

3. The problems

Enough has been said to suggest that two of the major problems which stand in the way of realizing a fully effective cooperative movement are *inefficiency* and *corruption*. Even at the height of the period of rapid expansion of the movement, these problems were by no means overlooked by the government; the then Minister for Commerce and Cooperatives, J. S. Kasambala, observed in the National Assembly in June 1964 that 'rapid as has been the expansion of our cooperative movement since independence, it is only fair to inform the House that less than half of the secretaries of our primary societies have received any cooperative training whatever, and quite a number of these have either seen a jail sentence or are still there cooling their castle-building ambitions'.[24] The situation had not changed markedly by the time a Presidential Committee of Enquiry into Cooperative Movement and Marketing Boards reported in 1966 that a 'second basic defect is the shortage of the appropriate manpower to staff the cooperatives... There are two aspects of the shortage of appropriate manpower, although they are inter-related: dishonest employees, and inadequately trained employees'.[25] Both inefficiency and corruption were thus prices which had to be paid for historical backwardness, and presumably efforts both to raise the general educational level of the populace and to provide skills to specialized cadres will eventually affect the measure of efficiency achieved. In the short run government controls will continue to be looked to as a major guarantee of efficiency. But here, too, manpower is stretched thin. Ideally, one investigating commission commented, 'the maximum rate of expansion is governed by the rate at which the division can expand its accounting control and supervision', but it seems evident, from observation and on the basis of what one can learn about the as yet confidential findings of another recent investigation into the movement, that the government's Cooperative Division has not had at its disposal all the tools necessary to its task.

It is, of course, always difficult to separate mere inefficiency

[24] The Hon. J. S. Kasambala, M.P., 'Policy statement to the Budget session of the National Assembly', Government Printer, Dar es Salaam, 1964.

[25] *Report of the Presidential Special Committee...*, op. cit., p. 9.

from actual corruption. Inefficiency (e.g. the unsatisfactory keeping of accounts) provides more openings in which corrupt practices can safely breed. But corruption can also promote what may appear to be inefficiency; in Sukumaland it seems evident that some of the bad book-keeping that dogged a tractor programme organized through the cooperative movement was intentional, allowing those who could gain privileged access to the tractors to escape individual repayment. The result was that losses were spread over the entire membership of the cooperative society, and were repaid through a general levy! Corruption of various sorts has been so widely observed within the cooperatives and reported upon that it cannot be viewed as anything other than a major dimension of the Tanzanian cooperative movement and one of its biggest problems. It is a problem that finds its expression both in the work of the cooperative employees who are the bureaucrats with managerial responsibilities in the various organizations, and in that of the committeemen, who are, in formal terms, the elected representatives of the growers on cooperative 'boards of directors'.

Indeed, as the 1966 Special Committee of Enquiry observed: 'With regret we must report that, in a great many cases, society secretaries engage in petty thievery, often in collaboration with a corrupt committeeman and sometimes not so petty'.[26] In 1958 in an annual report of the cooperative officer from Mwanza (home of the VFCU, which—it will be recalled—was a cooperative with rather more grass-roots support than most in its early days) it was argued that

a more ominous symptom of the corruption of cooperative principles by wealth is apparent in the tendency of committeemen of the Unions and Federation to consider themselves entitled to a sort of privilege enjoyed by co-directors. The substantial increases in allowances and honoraria voted to committeemen in excess of actual out-of-pocket expenses, are beginning to constitute an office of profit and a lucrative career.[27]

Though they are by the very nature of the case difficult to check, striking tales of profiteering abound. They are sufficiently common currency in discussion in all quarters that they must be taken seriously. One student researcher reports, for example, that one Cooperative Union president who started from a low income base had acquired in a few years 'one Toyota car, two tractors, a

[26] Ibid.
[27] Annual report of the Cooperative Officer, Lake Province, 1958.

house and a bar, wife's house, one Isuzu lorry, canoes (two) and fish-nets', the lowest possible total value of which was estimated at 86,000 shillings[28]; it was widely believed in the area, undoubtedly with some justification, that manipulation of the cooperative underlay part of this rags-to-riches story.

Evidence of another kind is provided by various reports on specific cooperative unions and societies prepared by the government's Audit and Supervision Section. Thus, the report of the Audit and Supervision Section, Mwanza, on the affairs of one East Lake union, covering the period running from 1 December 1965 to 30 September 1967 mentions, under 'motor vehicle running expenses', strikingly large purchases of petrol on Sundays and holidays, much hiring of private vehicles from the union manager, secretary and others, and of lorries from committeemen, and comments that 'it is interesting to note that the Union buys fuel from the ... Esso station ... in which the union manager, secretary and other officials are partners'. 'Unauthorized cash advances', 'staff posho [subsistence] and travelling allowances' and 'committee posho and travelling allowances' reveal similar patterns. In one six-month period the president of the union had claimed daily posho allowances for more days than the working days in the month, ranging from twenty-seven days to forty-three![29] In another union ten union committee members claimed and received 2,000 shillings each in expense money for a 'study-tour of East Africa' (!), though at least two of them appear not even to have gone on the trip. In yet another union, in connection with a private business venture, 'the manager ... used the union car in collaboration with the president of the Union, treasurer and secretary to send fish to Malya, Ngudu and Shinyanga in April–June'.[30] Similarly, a student researcher's report that 'it had recently been discovered that estimates for Shs. 60,000/- had been given for a guest house where only 30,000/- were actually needed, the rest going to benefit the Union Committee' is of a piece with many similar fiddles, rumoured and proven, in the contracting side of cooperative activities.[31] As noted in the introduction, we must

[28] Student research report, September 1968, to be incorporated into a general report by John S. Saul on the reorganization of the VFCU to be published in S. E. Migot-Adhola and John S. Saul, op. cit.

[29] From a report by the Audit and Supervision Section of the Ministry of Agriculture, Food and Cooperatives based in Mwanza.

[30] Student report, December 1968 (see note 28).

[31] Student report, September 1968 (see note 28).

guard against mistaking this for the whole picture of Tanzanian, or even East Lake, cooperatives. But it is clear that too little advance has been made beyond the situation described by the reports of two government teams of enquiry into the affairs of the two most valued cooperatives in the country, the KNCU and the VFCU, in 1963 and 1962 respectively.[32] And these make depressing reading, ringing the changes, as they do, on the various abuses we have already discussed.

When new 'developmental' functions are added to the unions' and societies' list it may, as we have noted earlier, merely expand the range of temptations. Indeed, one of the union investigations mentioned above observed (under the heading 'tractor ploughing services') that 'union officials are using the tractors for ploughing their own fields without paying hire charges', and this tendency has been regularly paralleled elsewhere. Migot, in a useful recent study of the Sukumaland tractor scheme in one small area, mentions, among other things, that 'cooperative inspectors and union officials hinted at the practice whereby the driver and the committeeman divided the money for which no receipt was issued but no specific case was mentioned. But talk about this practice was so rife that it must have been an open secret in Sukumaland.' 'Indeed', he continues, 'many of the farmers expressed the view that they would themselves have struggled to get into the committee but now that the tractor project was being discontinued by the government it was no longer profitable to be a committeeman'![33] Migot does observe that traditional ties and parochialism played their part; tractors were often assigned as much to the general neighbourhood of powerful committeemen as to their own farms.

But since tractors, like other new inputs, are a scarce resource, it is not surprising that the 'activists' were quick to turn them primarily to their own benefit. Under such circumstances, activists

[32] 'Report on the Kilimanjaro Native Cooperative Union Ltd', 25 February 1963; 'Report on the Victoria Federation of Cooperative Unions', 28 September 1962. A confidential report on the VFCU prepared at the same time as the *Report of the Presidential Special Committee of Enquiry . . .*, by the same committee, apparently made the same case five years later as was made in 1962, though in much stronger terms. It is interesting to note that another of the larger and older unions, the Bukoba Cooperative Union, seems to have been much freer from the sorts of problems discussed here. The reasons for its record of efficient management would be well worth analysing.

[33] Migot-Adhola, op. cit.

can also make quite sophisticated calculations in order to secure more indirect benefits; this probably influenced successive annual general meetings of the VFCU, numbering among its delegates primarily local 'activists' from the union level, consistently to approve the granting of a subsidized rate per acre for tractor rental. Even when they had to pay, activists could in any event expect to have privileged access to the tractors and so would benefit—the difference between what they paid and the actual cost to the cooperative of supplying the service being met out of general revenues.

Perhaps enough evidence has been adduced by now to suggest that an analytical model which focuses upon the implications of the interpenetration and simultaneous operation of both capitalist and pre-capitalist modes of production (with the balance of each peasant's involvements being tilted in the direction of one 'world' or the other) helps us to tie together a wide variety of data concerning inefficiency and corruption. Furthermore, it permits us to see the patterns which emerge as a coherent system of exploitation (however muted) which is rooted in Tanzania's social structure.

Moreover, such a model helps to explain another aspect of this general process, one which innumerable observers have commented upon: the lack of *generalized mass peasant involvement* in what should, ostensibly, be their own cooperatives. The report of an economic advisory mission to Tanzania in 1965 spoke of the growth of power of union and federations and found 'cause for alarm' in 'the divorce of this power and the way it is exercised from the interests of the individual societies and their members'. It was just such realities which prompted the author of the Lake Province cooperative report of 1958 cited above, after recounting the various abuses he had observed, to call upon the Cooperative Department 'to build up public opinion of the ordinary member at the primary level against tolerance of excessive allowances, unnecessary capital works and extravagance and to instil a habit of democratic action within the constitution against such malpractices'.[34] And the Special Committee's report of 1966 concluded that

there are a great many societies whose members are uninformed about the nature of the cooperatives, how they are supposed to function, the duties of the committee of the society and the powers and responsi-

[34] Annual report, op. cit.

bilities of the members assembled in the general meeting ... The whole structure thus rests, in many places, on a weak foundation; without an informed membership cooperatives cannot function soundly.[35]

Under such circumstances, pressures from below tend to be lacking or at best fragmented and ineffective; thus one government team had 'collected abundant evidence of the lack of efficiency of the unions and of discontent among a number of farmers. It must, however, be borne in mind that criticisms come mainly from the younger, more educated and more voluble minority of the community. The more conservative majority would not consider it necessary to give evidence unless they were members of the committee'. In such a statement one sees one of the main sources of current difficulties (though possibly also the seeds of a future transformation of the situation).

The results at local level are predictable:

... discussions on the budget during general meetings are rather technical and tedious affairs with which only the more enlightened members can be expected to be familiar. Such gifts could thus be very easily passed by default through the general meetings [of the primary society]. It was not possible to obtain figures for these bonuses, but there is reason to believe that they have been quite substantial in recent years.[36]

Even at the union level, a government's investigating team in one dramatic instance had occasion to excoriate 'the tactics of the economic adviser, the general manager and other senior staff in hoodwinking members of the committee and a general meeting'. Thus not only has a push against the 'activists' from the mass below been lacking for the reasons we have suggested, but we also find some evidence of actual manipulation from the top, often of a most flagrant kind. Once again various reports on the activities of the nation's most important cooperatives provide particularly graphic instances. After initial incredulity, the team investigating an important union felt compelled to give considerable credence to allegations that there were pressures from the top in the election process, including bribes, that particular care was taken to ease the passage of any man 'who had a large amount of land and was influential' and so on. The team concluded that tougher measures were necessary 'to ensure that undue influence

[35] *Report* ... , p. 9.
[36] Migot-Adhola, op. cit.

by union staff is not exercised'. Most graphic of all, and blandly reported in an isolated paragraph of a governmental team's report on another large cooperative organization in the early 'sixties, is the flat assertion that 'thirty growers from a cooperative society ... were invited to give their views to the team by the Cooperative Officer of [the] District, but he later informed the team that they had been prevented from attending because of pressures exerted by the general manager ...'

The existence of grass-roots discontent with the state of the cooperative movement must not be overlooked; it found expression in Parliament after the influx of new, more competitively elected MPs in the wake of the 1965 election, and led to the establishment of the President's Special Committee of Enquiry. But much of this criticism has been vague and does not adequately discriminate deterioration of prices due to world market conditions from losses of income caused by exploitation. Nor has such criticism really been channelled into the cooperative structure itself, where it might become focused so as to be an effective instrument for internal transformation. In any event, all too often a dawning awareness of corruption has resulted in apathy and withdrawal rather than in outrage; the 'institutionalized suspicion' which Dore and others have seen as necessary to cooperative success requires both the involvement of the constituency concerned and the sense that action to redress grievances can be efficacious.

The alternative mode of control has been ever more active government intervention—control from the top. The report of the President's Special Committee emphasized the importance of an expanded education programme for growers and cooperative servants alike, but it also made the proposal, which echoed an earlier idea of the Cooperative Department, to create a 'Unified Cooperative Service'. This was to be a centrally directed body with the power to impose standards upon cooperative personnel and to move them from place to place in line with national policy decisions. One main object of this proposal seems to have been to inculcate a spirit of 'profession' and thereby create, in effect, a new universe of relevant morality for the people involved while protecting them against the worst pressures of local committeemen. Though the proposal has now been enacted, at least in part, it is too early to comment upon its likely effect. But the legacy of uneven development and local chauvinism is still very much in evidence. Parochialism and jealousies between areas and, in some instances, between tribal groups remain, and are the sentiments most easily aroused and manipulated by local 'activists' anxious to safeguard their positions from the rationalizing impact of national policies. It remains uncertain whether the planned movement of personnel can be effective under such circumstances. But the case is revealing, for it indicates the manner in which central initiatives to safeguard the mass of the peasantry against the depredations of their local 'activists' tend to be misinterpreted and condemned by the mass of the population, which remains unconscious of the full significance of such efforts.

Frustrated by the inability of the populace to run their 'own' organizations and safeguard their interests, government has sponsored ever more direct intervention. Thus in 1966 sixteen cooperative unions, including hundreds of societies in the most backward areas of the country where cooperatives had been post-independence innovations, were peremptorily taken over. Committees were dismissed and government personnel placed in managerial positions. Somewhat later the government moved to reorganize the giant VFCU completely, acting even more radically than had been the case in a similar intervention (in the affairs of the KNCU) a few years previously. In the case of the backward areas the organizations were to be held in trust until put on an even keel; in East Lake popular participation in much of the transformation was encouraged right from the start. But again, in both instances, the results reveal the limitations upon government activity. To begin with, as we have seen, the government, wearing other hats, pursues more than efficiency and honesty alone; it is also interested in taxation and in having a say in how surpluses are to be used. Even were the membership to be successfully involved and the cooperative activities streamlined, there might remain problems of squaring national and local 'needs'. But more important in the current situation is the fact that, for reasons which we have discussed, such government intervention 'on the growers' behalf' is subject to misinterpretation. Since a likely response of the mass of the peasantry is a reinforced parochialism, rather than effective challenge to the activists, government intervention to 'set things right' may simply 'backfire'; the growers could become even further alienated from the movement. Only in these terms can we explain the paradoxical accumulated findings of a number of student reports on the East Lake reorganization of the last few years: they show general dissatisfaction with the old VFCU, relatively little pressure for change from within, *and* a certain measure of resentment against government moves to improve the structure from without, this resentment being only in part something which had to be stirred up by the 'activists' (who are nonetheless quick to use parochialism and tribalism to bolster their own positions).[37]

4. The future

We have already discussed a number of points of relevance in any evaluation of the likely future trajectory of the Tanzanian cooperative movement. Perhaps in the short run even more government intervention will be felt to be necessary. Though this may well bring certain benefits it will also probably entail real costs that are more difficult to quantify. The rise of the educational level of the population, both in the skilled categories and more generally, will also begin to have effects. It is with the sorts of problem we have discussed in mind that planners in Tanzania have recently decided, in the next five-year plan period, to begin a process of bringing the date for universal primary education much nearer (possibly to 1989), a programme which will constitute a significant change from the strategy of the first plan. On the other hand it seems evident that the cooperatives will be called upon to shoulder an even wider range of responsibilities than at present, and the movement will thus continue to walk a delicate tightrope between its capacities and its activities.

Mass education will make some difference, but 'education' may not automatically provide the answer. What is perhaps more pressingly needed is the generalized spread of critical consciousness, which can only develop as the result of *a certain kind of educational experience*. It is no accident that President Nyerere has laid great emphasis in his speeches over the past two years upon telling the peasants to increase their suspicions of their leaders! It is not inconceivable that the ten-house 'cell' system (designed to create, below the Party branch level, much smaller units for face-to-face political participation by the populace which would then serve as centres for political education and political mobilization) could act at some point as a cell within the cooperative to constitute an organized prod upon the movement. Operating within the framework of a socialist ideology antagonistic to exploitation in all its various forms, it might make

[37] On this subject see the forthcoming report mentioned in note 28 above.

an essential contribution to arousing the peasant population to seize control of its own destinies.

This stress upon the possible contribution of politically created 'social prerequisites' may serve to remind us of the fact that Tanzania is in fact a society with genuine socialist aspirations. She is, increasingly, not content to risk reliance merely upon the free play of the market mechanism, with its promise, real or imagined, to ensure development over the long haul through the conversion of all who remain on the soil into 'activist' capitalist farmers *or* rural proletarians (thereby eliminating the marginal, cash-cropping parochial and replacing his indirect exploitation by a more clear-cut form). On the contrary, in the President's pamphlet *Socialism and Rural Development*, some move towards the establishment of a socialist mode of production is suggested, though this trend is still very much in embryo. Initial emphasis was upon the creation of new 'Ujamaa villages' in unsettled areas but as socialist aspirations have become stronger, attention is increasingly turned towards the existing cooperative structures and ideas as to how to give them a new basis rooted in a novel mode of production have begun to circulate. Such ideas were in fact to be found as early as 1965 in a paper prepared by the then Minister of Commerce and Cooperatives entitled *Proposals for Reorganization of the Cooperative Movement in Tanzania*, but have been emphasized more vigorously since the introduction of the Arusha declaration in 1967 and the more tangible socialist commitment which it heralded. In Government Paper No. 4 of 1967, for example, a quite explicit call is made for the 'creation of multi-purpose [cooperative] societies in which each farming family should be a member of the society', with the corollary that 'changes in attitudes so essential for bringing about required structural changes are likely to take much longer than if cooperatives are effectively organized, emphasizing production'.[38] In effect such a policy, if it should emerge, would be founded upon the tacit premise that in contemporary Tanzania the *transitional society* which one finds, with its novel pattern of inequalities, cannot fully sustain 'modern forms of cooperation' in the marketing sphere. The average peasant must therefore be mobilized, 'deparochialized' and related to his institutions in a new, more vital and egalitarian way, Rather than cooperation being necessary for socialism, socialism may be necessary for cooperation!

[38] *Government Paper No. 4—1967*, p. 16.

Such, at any rate, would seem to be the position towards which Tanzania is moving on the basis of its experience. That experience, analysed in this paper, does therefore serve to underscore a concluding argument of relevance to any further discussion of the social prerequisites for agricultural cooperation: that the 'destructuration' introduced by the international market system has gone much too far in most of contemporary Tanzania for any great reliance to be placed upon traditional communalism as a guarantee of effective cooperation. If cooperation is to be a goal the major emphasis must be placed upon the *conscious creation* of the 'social prerequisites' for such cooperation via educational, political and organizational mechanisms, which, quite literally, help the majority of the peasants to help themselves. To think otherwise is to ignore the realities of how cooperatives actually function in a transitional society where they readily fall under the sway of 'economic activists'—be they bureaucrats or elected officials—and can be seized upon by these groups for their own aggrandizement and manipulated against the interests of their more parochialized kinsmen. To think otherwise would be to fall back upon the over-simplified and romantic faith in a vital traditionalism, a 'natural' *Gemeinschaft*, characteristic of a 'populist' perspective on the world.[39] To think otherwise would be to misconstrue the precise dimensions of the task of building a cooperative and a socialist society in contemporary Africa.

Acknowledgement

An earlier version of this paper was presented to the conference on 'Social prerequisites of agricultural cooperation' held at the University of Sussex, 31 March–3 April 1969. In revising it I have profited from the editorial comments of Professor Peter Worsley.

[39] Cf. Peter Worsley, *The Third World*, Weidenfeld & Nicolson, London, 1964, pp. 164–7.

Bibliography and index

Ingallil Montanari **Bibliography of works (in Western European languages) dealing with features of the social structure or culture of traditional agrarian societies which facilitate or hinder the development of various forms of cooperation**

AISC: *Archives Internationales de sociologie de la coopération*

General

'Agricultural programming' in UN Food and Agriculture Organization report *The state of food and agriculture*. FAO, Rome, 1960.

Ardant, G., *Le Monde en friche*. Presses Universitaires de France, Paris, 1963.

Barberis, C., *Sociologia rurale*. Edizioni Agricole, Bologna, 1965.

Bassaignet, P., *Coopération et capitalisme d'Etat: l'expérience suédoise de coopération agricole*. Presses Universitaires de France, Paris, 1953.

Bermann, T., 'Factors influencing optimum size and decision-making in cooperative farms'. Paper prepared for the second World Congress of Rural Sociology, Enschede, 1968.

Belshaw, C. S., *see* FAO.

Bolomey, M., 'Coopération et expansion économique dans les pays en voie de développement'. *AISC*, vol. 6, No. 11.

Bureau International du Travail, *see* ILO

CIRCOM, *Democratic management and economic efficiency in rural cooperative communities*. Second World Congress of Rural Sociology, Enschede, 1968.

— *Modern cooperatives and traditional rural societies*. Tel-Aviv, 1968.

Clauson, Sir G., *see* FAO

Cohen, P. S., 'Traditional societies and modern cooperatives'. Paper prepared for the sixth World Congress of Sociology, Evian, 1966.

Comarmond, P. de, 'Structures sociales traditionelles et coopération agricole moderne'. *AISC*, No. 23, 1968.

Constandse, A. K., and Hofstee, E. W., *see* FAO.

Desroche, H. (ed.), '*Coopération agricole et développement rurale. Actes du Colloque international de Tel-Aviv, Israël, mars 1965*. Mouton, Paris and the Hague, 1966.

— 'Coopération et développement: mouvements coopératifs et stratégie du développement'. *Collection Tiers Monde: problèmes des pays sous-développés*. Presses Universitaires de France, Paris, 1964.

— (ed), 'Planification et volontariat dans les développements coopératifs'. Mouton, Paris and the Hague, 1963.

Digby, M., *see* FAO.

Dobyns, H. F., 'Sociological and anthropological approaches to engineering successful economic organizations'. Paper presented at an Agricultural Development Council seminar at the University of Kentucky, 1967.

Dumont, R., *African agricultural development: reflections on the major lines of advance and the barriers to progress*. Reports of the UN Economic Commission for Africa, No. 6. United Nations Organization, New York, 1966.

— 'Des Développements coopératifs classiques à la conjoncture coopérative dans les pays en voie de développement'. *AISC*, vol. 6, No. 11.

— *Lands alive* (especially chapter VIII). Merlin Press, London, 1964. (First published in French in 1961.)

— 'Les Obstacles au développement agricole'. *Cahiers de la République*, mai–juin 1960.

— *Types of rural economy*. Methuen, London, 1957. (First published in French in 1954.)

Erasmus, C., 'Community development and the *encogido* syndrome'. *Human Organization*, vol. 27, No. 1, 1968.

Food and Agriculture Organization:
   Agricultural Development Papers
      No. 61, *Cooperatives and land use* by M. Digby. Rome, 1957.
      No. 79, *Rural sociology in action* prepared by A. K. Constandse with E. W. Hofstee. Rome, 1964.
   Agricultural Studies
      No. 17, *Communal land tenure* by Sir G. Clauson. Rome, 1953.
      No. 46, *Agricultural credit in economically under-developed countries* by C. S. Belshaw. Rome, 1959.
      No. 68, *Agricultural credit through cooperatives and other institutions*. Rome, 1965.
   Report on land tenure and land use problems in the Trust territories of Tanganyika and Ruanda–Urandi by A. Gaitskell. Rome, 1959.

Foster, G. M., 'Inter-personal relations in peasant society'. *Human Organization*, vol. 19, No. 4, 1960–61, with comments by O. Lewis and J. Pitt-Rivers and rejoinder by G. M. Foster.

— 'Peasant society and the image of limited good'. *American Anthropologist*, vol. 67, 1965.

Gaitskell, A., *see* FAO

Geertz, C., 'The rotating credit association: a middle rung in development'. *Economic Development and Cultural Change*, vol. x, No. 3, 1962.

Goodenough, W. H., *Cooperation in change: an anthropological approach to community development*. Russell Sage Foundation, New York, 1964.

Granger, R., 'Problèmes généraux du mouvement coopératif dans les pays en voie de développement'. *Annales Malgaches,* vol. ɪ, No. 1.

Holmberg, A. R., and Dobyn, H. F., 'The process of accelerating community change'. *Human Organization,* vol. 21, No. 2, 1962.

Huizer, G., 'The role of peasant organizations in the process of agrarian reform in Mexico'. Comité Interamericano de Desarrollo Agrícola, 1968.

International Labour Organization, *The role of cooperatives in the economic and social development of developing countries.* ILO, Geneva, 1964.

Joy, J. L., 'Problems of agricultural administration and extension services'. Paper presented to the thirteenth International Conference of Agricultural Economists, Sydney, 1967. Institute of Development Studies, Brighton, 1968.

Lamming, G. N., 'Possibilities and limitations of cooperation in underdeveloped countries'. *AISC,* No. 5, 1959.

— 'The projection of cooperative enterprise'. *AISC,* vol. 5, Nos. 9 and 10.

Mead, M. (ed.), *Cultural patterns and technical change,* a manual prepared for the World Federation of Mental Health. UNESCO, Paris, 1953.

Meister, A., 'Participation organisée et participation spontanée'. *L'Année sociologique,* Presses Universitaires de France, Paris, 1961.

Moore, B., Jr., *Social origins of dictatorship and democracy: lord and peasant in the making of the modern world.* Beacon Press, Boston, Mass., 1966.

Nordy, M., 'Socio-economic report on the following cooperatives. . .'. Report on seven cooperatives prepared for the US Peace Corps, Lima, 1966.

Schiller, O., 'Gemeinschaftsformen im landwirtschaftlichen Produktionsbereich'. *Zeitschrift für ausländische Landwirtschaft,* No. 5 DLG Verlag, Frankfürt a. M., 1966.

Scott, J. T., and Fletcher, L. B., 'Potential and feasibility of cooperatives as instruments of market reform in under-developed areas: the economist's view'. Paper presented at an Agricultural Development Council seminar at the University of Kentucky, 1967.

Shanin, T., *Peasants and peasant societies.* Penguin Sociology series. Penguin Books, Harmondsworth, 1971.

Sicard, E., 'Autour des persistances ou "traces" communautaires'. *AISC,* vol. 2, No. 4, 1958.

Stavenhagen, R., 'Changing functions of the community in underdeveloped countries'. *Sociologia ruralis,* vol. ɪv, 1963.

Thorner, D. (ed.), *Peasant economy as a category in economic history.* Proceedings of the International Economic History Association, Aix en Provence, 1962, vol. 2. Mouton, Paris and the Hague, 1965.

— *et al* (ed.), *Chayanov on the theory of peasant economy.* Irwin, Homewood, Ill., 1966.

United Nations Organization, *Land reform: defects in agrarian structure as obstacles to economic development*. UN document E2003. UNO, 1951.

Van Dam, F., *Collective farming in densely populated under-developed areas*. 1961.

Warriner, D., *Land reform in principle and practice*. Clarendon Press, Oxford, 1969.

Weintraub, D., 'The concepts "traditional" and "modern" in comparative social research: and empirical evaluation'. *Sociologia ruralis*, vol. ix, No. 1, 1969.

Wolf, E., 'Aspects of group relations in a complex society: Mexico'. *American Anthropologist*, vol. 58, 1956. Reprinted in *Contemporary cultures and societies of Latin America* ed. D. B. Heath and R. N. Adams, Random House, New York, 1965.

— *Peasants*. Foundations of Modern Anthropology series. Prentice-Hall, Engelwood Cliffs, N. J., 1966.

Worsley, P. M., *The Third World*. Weidenfeld & Nicolson, London, 1967.

Africa

Apthorpe, R. J. (ed.), *Land settlement and rural development in Eastern Africa*. Nkanga Editions No. 3. Transition Books, Kampala, 1968.

— 'Planned social change and land settlement' in *Land settlement and rural development in Eastern Africa*.

— and MacArthur, J., 'Land settlement policies in Kenya' in *Land settlement and rural development in Eastern Africa*.

— *Peasants and planistrators*. Oxford University Press, Nairobi; forthcoming.

Arrighi, A., and Saul, J. S., *Ideology and development*. Nairobi, 1969.

Balandier, G., 'Traditional social structures and economic change' in *Africa: social problems of change and conflict* ed. P. L. van den Berghe. Chandler, San Francisco, 1965.

Belloncle, G., 'Le Développement des collectivités rurales par la formation d'animateurs'. *AISC*, vol. 5, No. 10, 1961.

— *Une Expérience d'animation coopérative au Niger*. BECC–CRC, Paris, 1966.

— 'Pédagogie de l'implantation du mouvement coopératif au Niger'. *AISC*, No. 23, 1968.

'Problèmes du crédit coopératif à l'agriculture africaine traditionelle'. *AISC*, No. 19, 1966.

Belshaw, D. G. R., 'An outline of resettlement policy in Uganda, 1945–63' in *Land settlement and rural development in Eastern Africa* ed. R. J. Apthorpe (*q.v.*).

Bodard, C., 'Aperçu sur la situation du mouvement coopératif au Niger' in the Archives of the Collège Coopératif, Paris, 1963.

Bohannan, P., *Tiv farm and settlement*. London, 1954.

Brett, E. A. (ed.), *Rural development and public policy in East Africa*. Nairobi, 1969.

Chambers, R., *Settlement schemes in tropical Africa*. Routledge, London, 1969.

Charsley, S., 'The group farm scheme in Uganda' in *Land settlement and rural development in Eastern Africa* ed. R. J. Apthorpe (*q.v.*).

Coshow, J. E., 'A high-density scheme' in *Land settlement and rural development in Eastern Africa* ed. R. J. Apthorpe (*q.v.*).

Desroche, H., 'Coopératismes africains: jalons inductifs d'une recherche comparée', *AISC*, No. 16, 1964.

Dumont, R., *African agricultural development: reflections on the major lines of advance and the barriers to progress*. Reports of the UN Economic Commission for Africa. FAO, New York, 1966.

— *False start in Africa*. Deutsch, London, 1966.

El Tom, A., 'Land reform and associated rural institutions in the Republic of the Sudan'. Khartoum, 1961.

Feldman, D., 'The economics of ideology' in *Politics and change in developing countries: studies in the theory and practice of development* ed. C. Leys. Cambridge University Press, London, 1969.

Feldman, R., 'Social factors in peasant farming'. Unpublished dissertation, Department of Sociology and Social Anthropology, Manchester University, 1968.

Hirschfeld, A., 'Les problèmes agraires en Afrique Noire'. *Revue des Etudes coopératives*, vol. 43, No. 138, 1964.

— Sur quelques expériences coopératives ou pré-coopératives en Afrique Noire'. *Revue des Etudes coopératives*, vol. 44, No. 139, 1965.

Hutton, C., 'Making modern farmers' in *Land settlement and rural development in Eastern Africa* ed. R. J. Apthorpe (*q.v.*).

Jones, A. D., *Bulimi: a study of social and economic development among the Plateau Tonga farmers of Zambia*. Institute for African Studies, Lusaka; forthcoming.

Kapferer, B., *Cooperation, leadership and village structure: a preliminary economic and political study of ten Bisa villages in the Northern Province of Zambia*. Zambian Papers, No. 1. Manchester University Press for the Institute for Social Research, University of Zambia, 1967.

Kates, R. W., McKay, J., and Berry, J., 'Twelve new settlements: a comparative study of success'. Paper prepared for the USSC conference, Kampala, 1969.

Kilson, M., 'African political change and the modernization process'. *Journal of Modern African Studies*, vol. i, No. 4, 1963.

Laville, P., 'Des institutions administratives aux avant-veilles de l'indépendance: le cas du coopératisme sénégalais'. *AISC*, No. 16, 1964.

— 'Quelques Aléas de l'implantation coopérative au Sénégal'. *AISC*, No. 22, 1967.

Mann, H. S., 'Pilot field study in systems of land tenure: landlord–
tenant relations in Chore Mikitil Woreda'. Khartoum, 1964.

Meister, A., 'Ambitions et aléas d'un socialisme coopératif au Tanganyika en Afrique de l'Est'. AISC, No. 16, 1964.

— Développements coopératifs et développement en Afrique de l'Est:
Ouganda, Kenya, Tanganyika. Ministère de la Coopération, Paris,
1964.

— 'Le Développement économique de l'Afrique orientale'. Etudes
Tiers Monde. Presses Universitaires de France, Paris, 1966.

Morris, J., 'The evaluation of settlement schemes' performance: a
sociological appraisal' in Land settlement and rural development in
Eastern Africa ed. R. J. Apthorpe (q.v.).

Migot-Adholla, S. E., 'The politics of a growers' cooperative society'.
Unpublished dissertation, Department of Political Science, University College, Dar es Salaam.

Nyerere, J., Socialism and rural development. Dar es Salaam, 1967.

Oluwasanmi, H. A., 'L'Adaptation de structures coopératives modernes
au développement de l'agriculture nigérienne'. AISC, vol. 9, No. 18,
1965.

Raoely-James, R., 'Adaptation des institutions traditionelles des pays
sous-développés aux conditions actuelles: problème d'implantation
coopérative sur la base du Fokonolona à Madagascar'. Mémoire de
l'Institute de Développement, Paris, 1961.

Saul, J. S., 'Agricultural politics in Tanzania: an introduction and an
approach' in Rural development and public policy in East Africa
ed. E. A. Brett. Nairobi, 1969.

Schmandt., L., 'Coopératives de crédit appliqués à l'agriculture en
Afrique'. AISC, vol. 6, No. 11.

Tamou Dodo, J. L., 'La Crédit agricole au Dahomey face aux structures socio-économiques traditionelles'. Diplôme EPHE, Paris, 1965.

Yeld, R., 'Land hunger in Kigezi, south-west Uganda' in Land settlement and rural development in Eastern Africa ed. R. J. Apthorpe
(q.v.).

— 'The resettlement of refugees' in Land settlement and rural development in Eastern Africa ed. R. J. Apthorpe (q.v.).

Latin America

Aguilar, A., 'Réforme agraire et coopération rurale au Mexique'.
AISC, vol. 9, No. 18, 1965.

Andrade, C. O., 'Problèmes agraires dans le nord-est du Brésil et
possibilités de développement coopératif (Etat de Pernambouc)'.
AISC, vol. 9, No. 18, 1965.

Arroyo, A. L., 'Développement rurale et organisation coopérative
au Mexique'. AISC, vol. 9, No. 18, 1965.

Arroyo, R. (ed.), 'Investigación sobre Conducta de Productores Rurales
como Miembros de Cooperativas Agropecuarias del Partido de
Pergamino'. INTA, Pergamino (Argentina), 1961.

Belshaw, M., *A village economy—land and people of Huecorico*. Columbia University Press, New York and London, 1967.

Björnberg, A., *Las poblaciones indigenas y el cooperativismo: observaciones y experiencias del desarrollo del programa Andino en Bolivia*. Biblioteca e Instituto de Estudios Iberoamericanos de la Escuela de Ciencias Economicas, Estocolino, 1959.

Chaves, F., *The agricultural cooperative movement in Latin America*. Washington, D.C., 1962.

Centre National de la Recherche Scientifique, *Les Problèmes agraires des Amériques Latines*. Editions du CRNS, Paris, 1967.

Desroche, H., 'Aléas d'un secteur coopératif sud-américain: étude d'un cas (Etat de Pernambouc, Brésil), mars 1904'. *AISC*, vol. 8, No. 15, 1964.

Donida, D. A., 'Sondage sur quelques coopératives au nord-est du Brésil'. *AISC*, No. 23, 1968.

Dumont, R., *Cuba: socialisme et développement*. Editions du Seuil, Paris, 1964.

Eckstein, S., *El ejido colectivo en México*. Fondo de Cultura Económica, Mexico, D.F., 1966.

Ferraqut, C., *Informe al Gobierno de Bolivia sobre reforma agraria*. EPTA report No. 1856. Rome, 1964.

Foster, G. M., *Tzintzuntzan: Mexican peasants in a changing world*. Boston, Mass., 1967.

Foytick, J., and Faris, J. E., 'Agricultural cooperatives in Latin America: the Chilean case'. Paper presented at an Agricultural Development Council seminar, University of Kentucky, 1967.

Garcia, A., 'Cooperativas y financiamiento agricola en Aconcaqua.' ICIRA, Departamento de Cooperativas y Crédito, Santiago, 1968.

— 'Las cooperativas pesqueras del Valle de Elqui'. ICIRA, Departamento de Cooperativas y Crédito, Santiago, 1968.

Gutelman, M., *L'Agriculture socialisée à Cuba: enseignements et perspectives*. Maspero, Paris, 1967.

— *Les ejidos et la réforme agraire au Mexique, 1910–60*. Maspero, Paris, 1971.

Henley, L., 'Alpaca: a *campesino* organization in the Peruvian Sierra'. Paper prepared for a seminar on 'Land policy problems in Latin America', Washington, D.C., 1969.

Hennessy, C. A. M., 'Shifting forces in the Bolivian revolution'. *The World Today*, May 1964.

Holmberg, A., 'Changing community attitudes and values in Peru: a case study in guided change' in *Social change in Latin America today* ed. R. N. Adams *et al.* Harper, New York, 1960.

Huizer, G., *Report on the study of the role of peasant organizations in the process of agrarian reform in Latin America*. ILO, Geneva, 1969.

Kirschbaum, A., Navarro Ochoa, P. A., and Ali Pino, O., 'El coopera-
    tivismo en el sector rural: análisis en el estado Aragua'. Officina
    Central de Coordinación y Planificación de la Presidencia de la
    República, Caracas, 1967.
Ritter, U. P., *Dorfgemeinschaften und Genossenschaften in Peru*.
    Göttinger wirtschafts- und sozialwissenschaftliche Studien, vol. 4.
    Schwarz, Göttingen, 1966. Abridged version published in Spanish
    as *Comunidades indígenas y cooperativismo en el Perú: estudios
    sobre la economía iberoamericana* by Ediciones Deusto, Bilbao,
    1965.
Ruiz, R., and Vega, A., 'Cooperativa de Producción Agrícola Indus-
    trial Victoria R.L. de Costa Rica' in *Las cooperativas como método de
    desarrollo de regiones y comunidades*, Estudios y Monografías XIV.
    Union Panamericana, Washington D.C., 1964.
Schiller, O., 'Kollective Landbewirtschaftung in Mexiko'. *Zeitschrift
    für ausländische Landwirtschaft*, vol. 2, No. 2.
Vasquez, M. C., and Dobyns, H. F., 'The transformation of manors into
    producers' cooperatives: comparative studies of cultural change'.
    Department of Anthropology, Cornell University, Ithaca N.Y., 1964.

The Mediterranean

Are, D., Cassu, A., and Meister, A., *Autonomia e solidarietà nel
    Montiferru*. Centro Europeo della Cultura, Montiferru, 1959.
Barberis, C., *Nurra: una società rurale alla vigilia della irrigazione*.
    Cassa per il Mezzogiorno, Alghero, 1960.
Chombart de Lauwe, J., and Poitevin, J., *Problèmes relatifs à la
    coopération agricole: étude de cas en Grèce*. OECD, Paris, 1964.
Kiray, M. B., 'Esodo agricolo e ristrutturazione fondiaria in Turchia'.
    Rivista di economia agraria, vol. xxiii, No. 3. Istituto Nazionale di
    Economia Agraria, Naples, 1968.
Meister, A., *Associations Coopératives et groupes de loisirs en milieu
    rural*. Editions de Minuit, Paris, 1967.
— and Segre, B., *La cooperativa di Montalenghe: un esperimento do
    conduzione agricola collettiva nel Canavese*. Centro di Sociologia
    della Cooperazione, Milan, 1958.
Rochefort, R., 'Les Coopératives en Sicile'. *AISC*, vol. 6, No. 11.
Segre, B., 'Un esperimento di collettivismo agricolo in Italia: studio
    monografico sulla cooperative di piccoli proprietari di Montalenghe
    (Piemonte)'. *AISC*, vol. 1, No. 1, 1957.
Thomas, H., 'Anarchist agrarian collectives in the Spanish civil war' in
    A century of conflict ed. M. Gilbert. Hamish Hamilton, London,
    1966.
Trintignac, A., 'Réforme agraire et implantations coopératives dans
    le Mezzogiorno'. *AISC*, vol. 6, No. 11.
Tsouderos, J. E., *Greek agricultural cooperatives*. Cooperative League
    of the USA, Chicago, 1961.

Eastern Europe

Baric, L., 'New economic opportunities in rural Yugoslavia' in *Themes in economic anthropology* ed. R. Firth. Tavistock, London, 1967.

Bouvier, C., 'La Collectivisation de l'agriculture: URSS—Chine—Démocraties populaires'. Cahiers de la Fondation Nationale des Sciences Politiques, No. 91. Colin, Paris, 1958.

Chombart de Lauwe, J., *Les Paysans soviétiques*. Editions du Seuil, Paris, 1961.

Clark, R. A., 'Soviet agricultural reforms since Khrushchev'. *Soviet Studies*, vol. xx, No. 2, 1969.

Desroche, H., 'Coopération et socialisme: éléments sociographiques du secteur coopératif polonais'. *AISC*, vol. 4, No. 8, 1960.

Ferretjans, J.-P., 'Récents Développements de la coopération agricole en Yougoslavie'. *AISC*, vol. 6, No. 11, 1962.

Galeski, B., *Basic concepts of rural sociology*. Manchester University Press, 1971.

Grigoroff, G., 'Réforme agraire et collectivisation de l'agriculture en Bulgarie'. Cahiers de la Fondation Nationale des Sciences Politiques, No. 2, Colin, Paris, 1956.

Jasny, N., *The socialized agriculture of the USSR*. Stanford University Press, 1949.

Karcz, J. F., *Soviet and East European agriculture*. California University Press, Berkeley and Los Angeles, 1967.

Legradic, R., 'The reorganization of the peasant production cooperatives in Yugoslavia'. *AISC*, vol. 1, No. 2, 1957.

Lewin, M., *La Paysannerie et le pouvoir soviétique, 1928–30*. Mouton, Paris and the Hague, 1966. Published in English as *Russian peasants and Soviet power* by Allen & Unwin, London, 1968.

Meister, A., *Socialisme et autogestion: l'expérience yougoslave*. Editions du Seuil, Paris, 1964.

Mitrany, D., *The Land and the peasant in Rumania: the war and agrarian reform, 1917–21*. Oxford University Press, London, 1930.

Nacou, D., *Du Kolkhoze an sovkhoze commune: artel, toze, kolkhoze, MTS, sovkhoze*. Editions de Minuit, Paris, 1958.

Nyers, R., *The cooperative movement in Hungary*. Pannonia Press, Budapest, 1963.

Pietzak-Panlowski, K., 'La Coopération rurale en Pologne populaire'. *AISC*, vol. 6, No. 12, 1962.

Preobrazkenskii, E., *The new economics*. Oxford University Press, London, 1965.

Robinson, T., *Rural Russia under the old regime*. New York, 1969.

Sicard, E., 'De la communauté domestique dite de *Zadruga* à la coopérative kolkhozienne'. *Revue d'Economie politique*. Sirey, Paris, 1953.

— 'Le passage du village-hameau de l'histoire au village-kolkhoze de l'actualité'. *Actes du XIVe congrès de l'IIS*, vol. III. Società Italiana di Sociologia, Rome, 1951.

Voutchkovitch, M., 'Coopérative agricole et autogestion en Yougo-slavie'. *AISC*, vol. 6, No. 11, 1962.

East Asia

Chen Chi-Yi, *La Réforme agraire en Chine populaire*. Mouton, Paris and the Hague, 1964.
Dore, R. P., *Land Reform in Japan*. Oxford University Press, London, 1959.
Dumont, R., *Révolution dans les campagnes chinoises*. Editions du Seuil, Paris, 1957.
Fitzgerald,, C. P., *Flood tide in China*. Cresset Press, London, 1958.
Freedman, M., *Lineage organization in south-eastern China*. LSE Monographs on Social Anthropology No. 18. Athlone Press, London, 1958.
Gamble, S. D., *North China villages*. California University Press, Berkeley and Los Angeles, 1963.
Hinton, W., *Fanshen: a documentary of revolution in a Chinese village*. Monthly Review Press, New York and London, 1966.
Hoynden, Y., *The cooperative movement in Japan*, vol. 3: *Agricultural and fishery cooperation in Japan*. Azuma Shobo, Tokyo, 1964.
Lebra, W. P., and Maretzki, T. W., 'The community cooperative in northern Okinawa'. *Economic Development and Cultural Change*, vol. XI, No. 3, part 1, 1963.
Lewis, J. W., *Leadership in communist China*. Cornell University Press, Ithaca, N.Y., 1963.
Marchisio, H., 'La Contradiction moteur de développement dans une commune populaire chinoise'. *AISC*, No. 23, 1968.
Myrdal, J., *Report from a chinese village*. Heinemann, London, 1965.
Schurmann, H. F., *Ideology and organization in communist China*. California University Press, Berkeley and Los Angeles, 1966.
Tawney, R. H., *Land and labour in China*. Allen & Unwin, London, 1932.
Tung Ta-Lin, *Agricultural cooperation in China*. China Knowledge series. Foreign Language Press, Peking, 1959.
Walker, K. R., *Planning in Chinese agriculture: socialization and the private sector, 1956–62*. Frank Cass, London, 1965.
Yang, C. K., *A Chinese village in early communist transition*. MIT Press, Cambridge, Mass., 1959.
— *Chinese communist society: the family and the village*, vol. I. MIT Press, Cambridge, Mass., 1966.

South and south-east Asia

Bailey, F. G., *Caste and the economic frontier: a village in highland Orissa*. Manchester University Press, 1957.
Baviskar, B. S., 'Cooperatives and politics'. *Economic and Political Weekly*, vol. III, 1968.

Belshaw, C. S., *Under the ivi tree*. Routledge & Kegan Paul, London, 1964.

Crocombe, R. G., 'Communal cash cropping among the Orokaiva'. *New Guinea Research Bulletin*, No. 4, 1964, Canberra.

— *Land tenure in the Cook Islands*. Oxford University Press for the Australian National University, Melbourne, 1964.

— *Land tenure in the Pacific islands*. Oxford University Press for the Australian National University, Melbourne, 1970.

— 'The M'buke cooperative plantation'. *New Guinea Research Bulletin*, No. 7, 1965, Canberra.

— and Hogbin, G. R., 'The Erap mechanical farming project'. *New Guinea Research Bulletin*, No. 1, 1963, Canberra.

Dakeyne, R. B., 'Cooperatives at Yega'. *New Guinea Research Bulletin*, No. 13, 1966, Canberra.

Epstein, T. S., *Economic development and social change in south India*. Manchester University Press, 1962.

Fairchild, H. W., and Hussain, M. Z., *A new rural cooperative system for Comilla, Thana*. Second annual report of rural cooperative pilot experiment. Pakistan Academy for Village Development, Comilla (East Pakistan), 1962.

Finney, B. R., 'A successful French Polynesian cooperative'. *Journal of Pacific History*, No. 3, 1968.

— *Polynesian peasants and proletarians*. Polynesian Society reprint series, No. 29, Wellington, 1965.

Guiart, J., 'Développement Communautaire et coopération dans le Pacific Sud'. *AISC*, vol. 3, No. 5, 1959.

— 'Observations Récentes sur le mouvement coopératif en Nouvelle Guinée orientale'. *AISC*, vol. 5, No. 9, 1961.

Khan, A.H., and Hussain, M. Z., *A new rural cooperative system for Comilla, Thana*. Third annual report of rural cooperative pilot experiment. Pakistan Academy for Village Development, Comilla (East Pakistan), 1963.

Khusro, A. M., and Agarwal, A. N., *The problem of cooperative farming in India*. Asia Publishing House, New York, 1961.

— 'L'Alliance Coopérative Internationale et les pays sous-développés: la conférence de Kuala-Lumpur'. *Coopération*, May 1958 and June 1959.

Laxminarayan, H., and Kanungo, K., *Glimpses of cooperative farming in India*. Agricultural Economics Research Centre, University of Delhi. Asia Publishing House, London, 1967.

Mann, H. S., 'Cooperative joint farming and peasant family farming in the Punjab: a comparative study'. *AISC*, No. 5, 1959.

Mohsen, A. K. M., *The Comilla rural administration experiment: history and annual report, 1962–63*. Pakistan Academy for Rural Development, Comilla (East Pakistan), 1963.

Myrdal, G., *Asian drama: an enquiry into the poverty of nations.* 1968. See especially part v. 'Problems of labor utilization', chapter 22, 'Labor utilization in traditional agriculture', and chapter 26, 'Agricultural policy'.

Nanavati, Sir M., *Cooperation in Kodinar.* Bombay, 1951.

Nand, S., 'Cooperative land-holding experiments in Fiji'. Paper presented to the third Waigani seminar, Port Moresby (Boroko), 1969.

— 'Land settlement cooperatives in the Fiji islands'. *Spectrum,* 1964–1965.

Ngata, Sir A., *Native land development.* Wellington, 1946.

Oppenfeld, H. von and J. von, Iglesia, J. C. Sta, and Sandoral, P. R., *Farm management, land use and tenancy in the Philippines.* College of Agriculture and Central Experiment Station, Manila, 1957.

Panoff, M., *Les Structures agraires en Polynésie française.* ORSTOM, Paris, 1964.

Philipp, P. F., 'Requirements for success of village cooperatives in developing countries of Asia'. *Annals of Public and Cooperative Economy,* No. 4, 1966.

Singh, B., *Next step in rural India: a study of land reforms and group dynamics.* Asia Publishing House, New York, 1961.

Smith, N., *Maori land corporations.* Wellington, 1962.

Srivastava, D., 'Agriculture coopérative et animation rurale en Inde'. *AISC,* vol. 9, No. 18, 1965.

Stibbe, T., 'Quelques Aspects du fonctionnement des *community development projects* et des coopératives en Inde'. *AISC,* vol. 5, No. 9, 1961.

Swarts, T., 'The cooperatives: Ol i-bagarapum Mani'. *New Guinea,* vol. 1, No. 8, 1966–67.

Thorner, D., *Agricultural cooperatives in India: a field report.* Asia Publishing House, London, 1964.

Van Dam, H., 'Cooperation and social structure in the village of Chibodas' in *Selected studies on Indonesia,* vol. vi: *Indonesian economics.* Van Hoeve, the Hague, 1961.

Van Wengen, G. O., *Social aspects of the cooperative movement in Ceylon and southern India,* Dico, Amsterdam, 1958.

Yasin, M. G., *A comparative study of villages with and without cooperative farming societies.* Publication No. 131. Board of Economic Inquiry, West Pakistan, 1965.

Yogua, N. A. A. K., *Cooperation and Indian agriculture.* Bangalore, 1957.

West Asia

Ben-David, J. (ed.), *Agricultural planning and village community in Israel.* UNESCO, Paris, 1964.

Cohen, P. S., 'Yemeni communities in Israel'. Unpublished PhD thesis, London University, 1961.

Daniel, A., 'La Coopération de production et de services en Israël'. Unpublished doctoral thesis, Faculté de Droit, Paris, 1963.

Datin-Drabkin, H., *The other society*. Gollancz, London, 1962.

Gabovitch, B., 'Les Origines communautaires dans l'Israël d'aujourd'hui'. *AISC*, vol. 5, No. 9, 1961.

Klatzmann, J., 'Les Enseignements de l'expérience israëlienne', *Collection Tiers Monde*, Presses Universitaires de France, Paris, 1963.

Meister, A., 'Principes et tendances de la planification rurale en Israël: problèmes posés par l'absorption de l'immigration de masse dans les villages coopératifs (*moshave olim*)'. *AISC*, vol. 5, Nos. 9 and 10. Also published by Mouton, Paris and the Hague, 1962.

Weingrod, A., *Reluctant pioneers: village development in Israel*. Cornell University Press, Ithaca, N.Y., 1966.

Weintraub, D., *Immigration and social change*, Manchester University Press and Israel Universities Press, 1971.

— and Bernstein, F., 'Social structure and modernization: a comparative study of two villages'. *American Journal of Sociology*, vol. LXXI, No. 5, 1966.

— Lissak, M., and Atzmon, Y,, *Mosava—kibbutz—moshav: Jewish rural settlement and development in Palestine*. Cornell University Press, Ithaca, N.Y., 1969.

— and Parness, T., 'Rural life, orientation to change and modernization: a pilot study of farm youths in Israel'. *Rural Sociology*, vol. 33, No. 3, 1968.

— and Shapiro, M., 'The traditional family in Israel in the process of change: crisis and continuity'. *British Journal of Sociology*, 1968.

Index